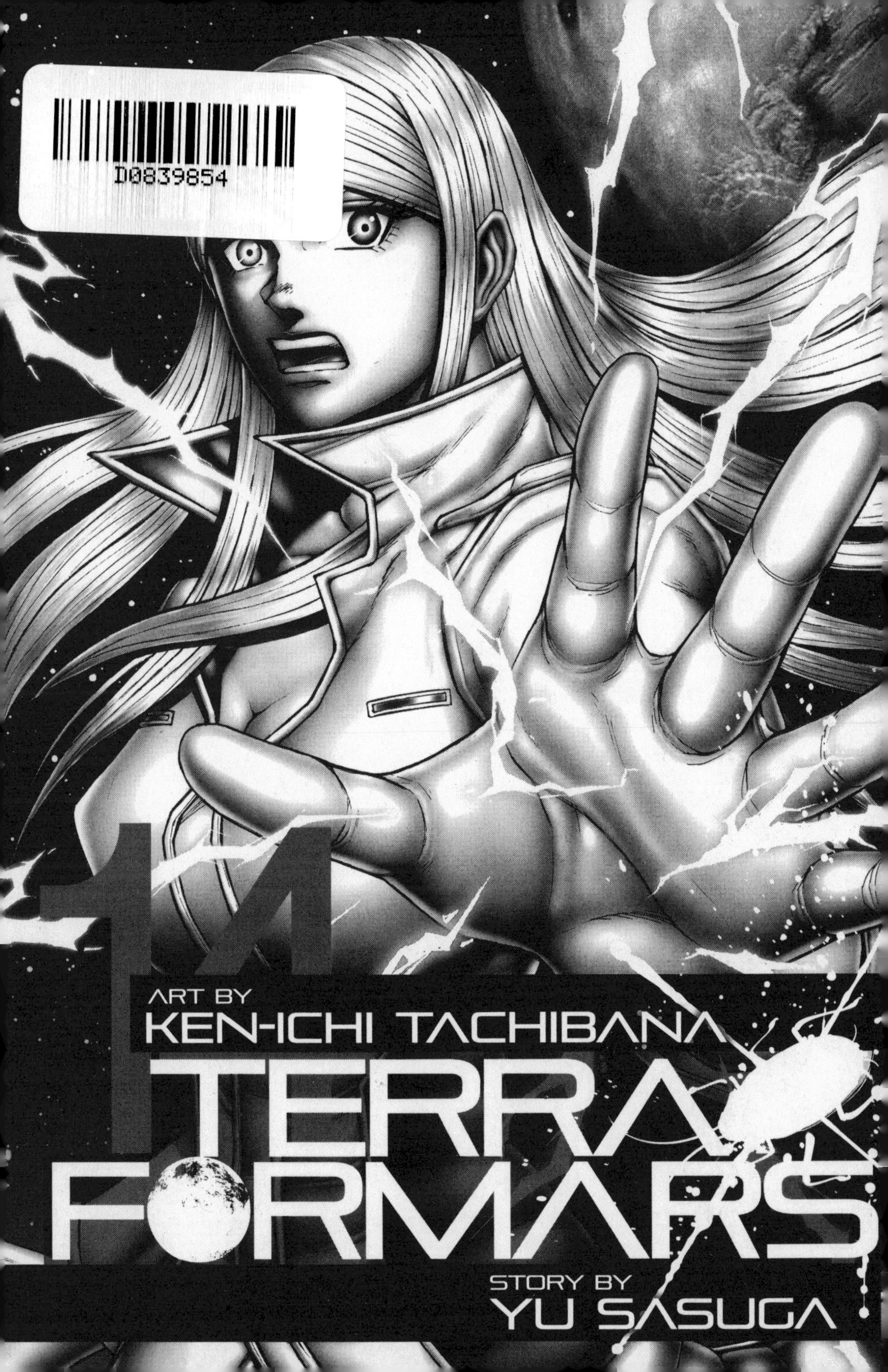

14

ART BY
KEN-ICHI TACHIBANA

TERRA FORMARS

STORY BY
YU SASUGA

TERRA FORMARS 14

CONTENTS

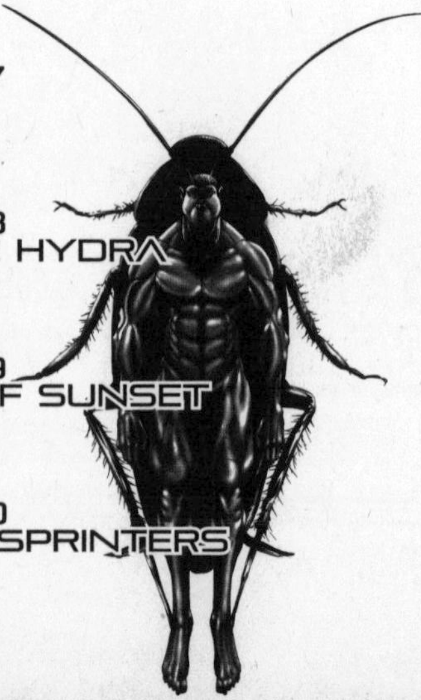

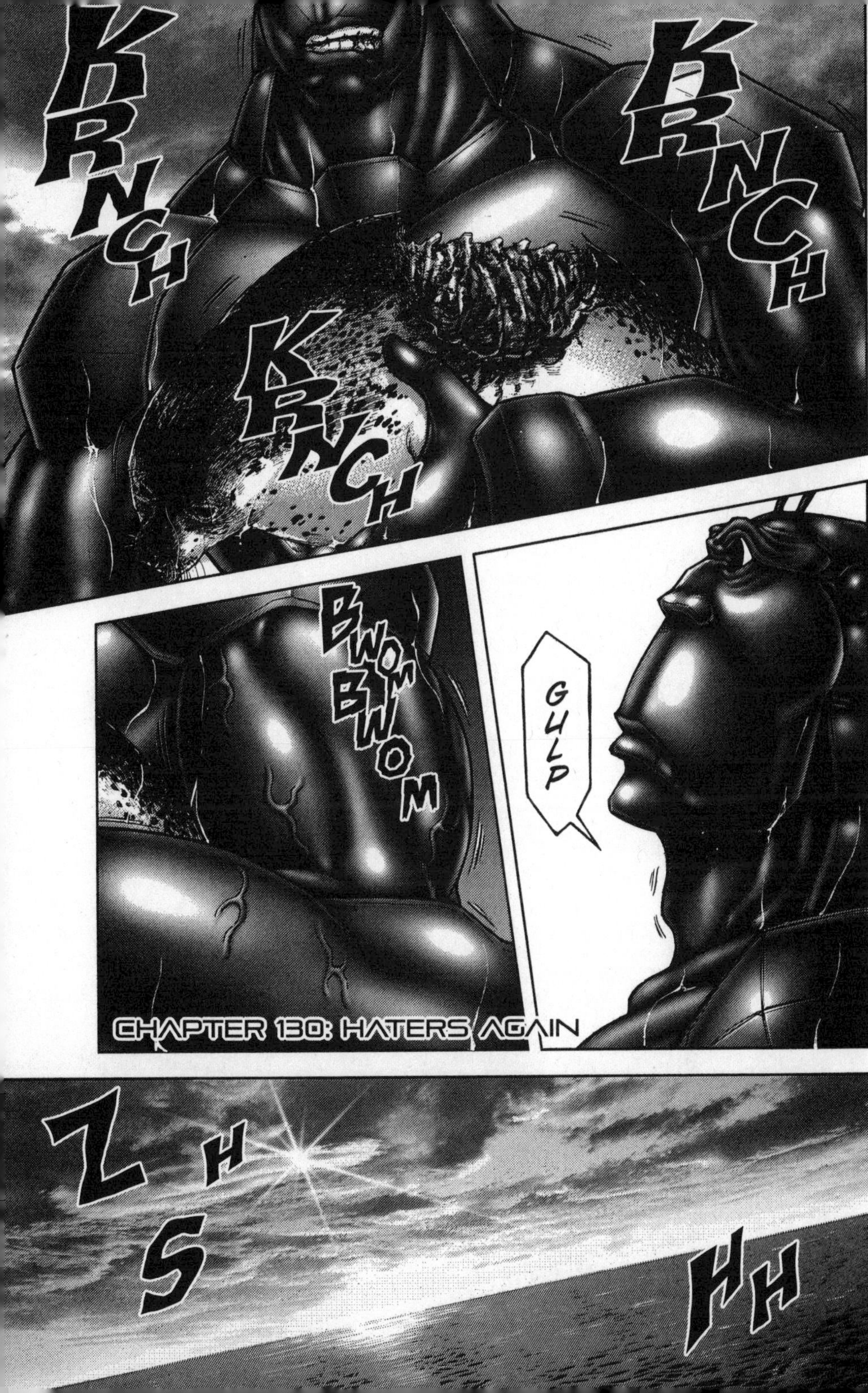
KRNCH
KRNCH
KRNCH
GULP
BWOM
BWOM
CHAPTER 130: HATERS AGAIN
ZHSHH

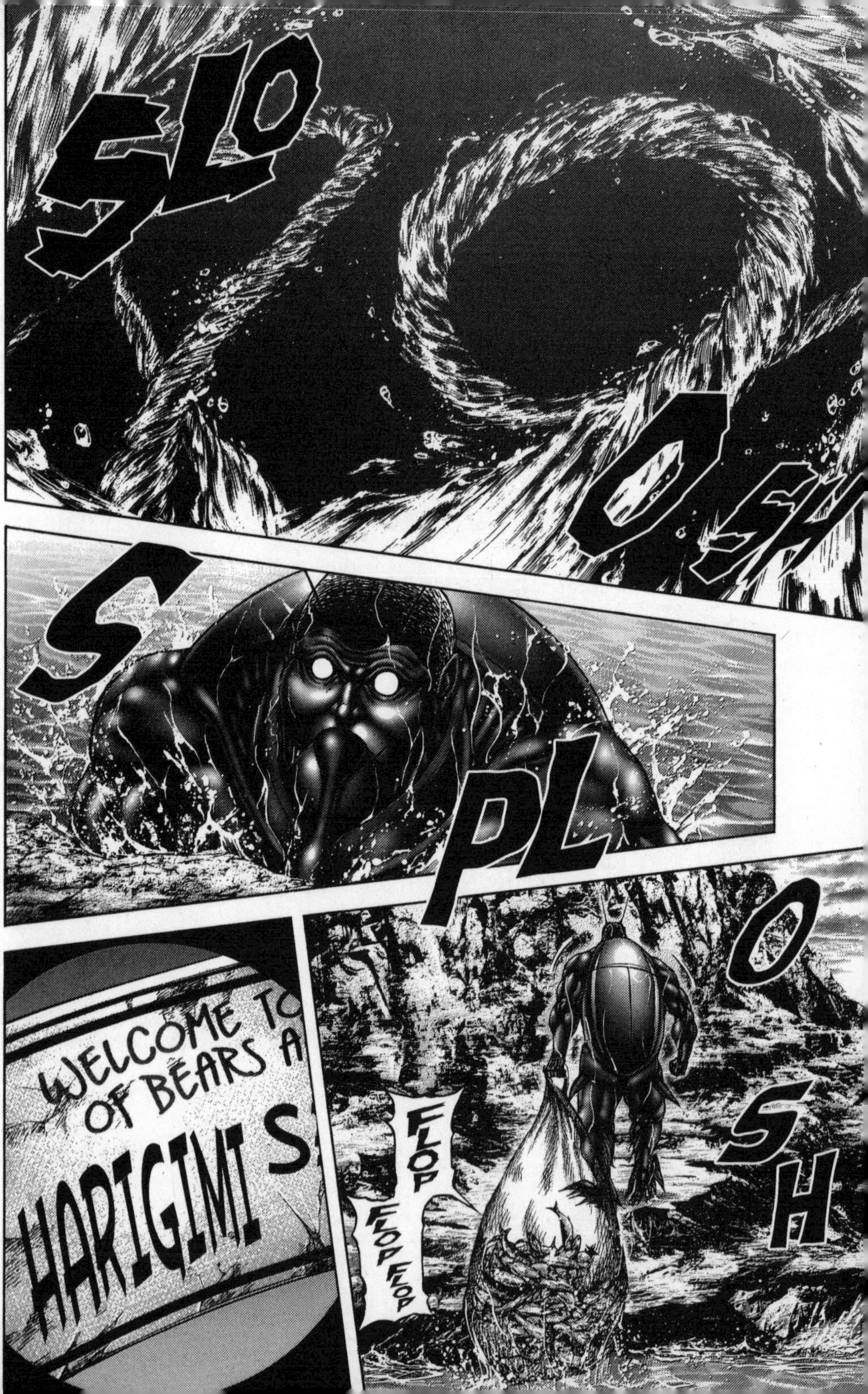
SLOOSH
SPLOSH
FLOP FLOP FLOP
WELCOME TO
OF BEARS A
HARIGIMI S

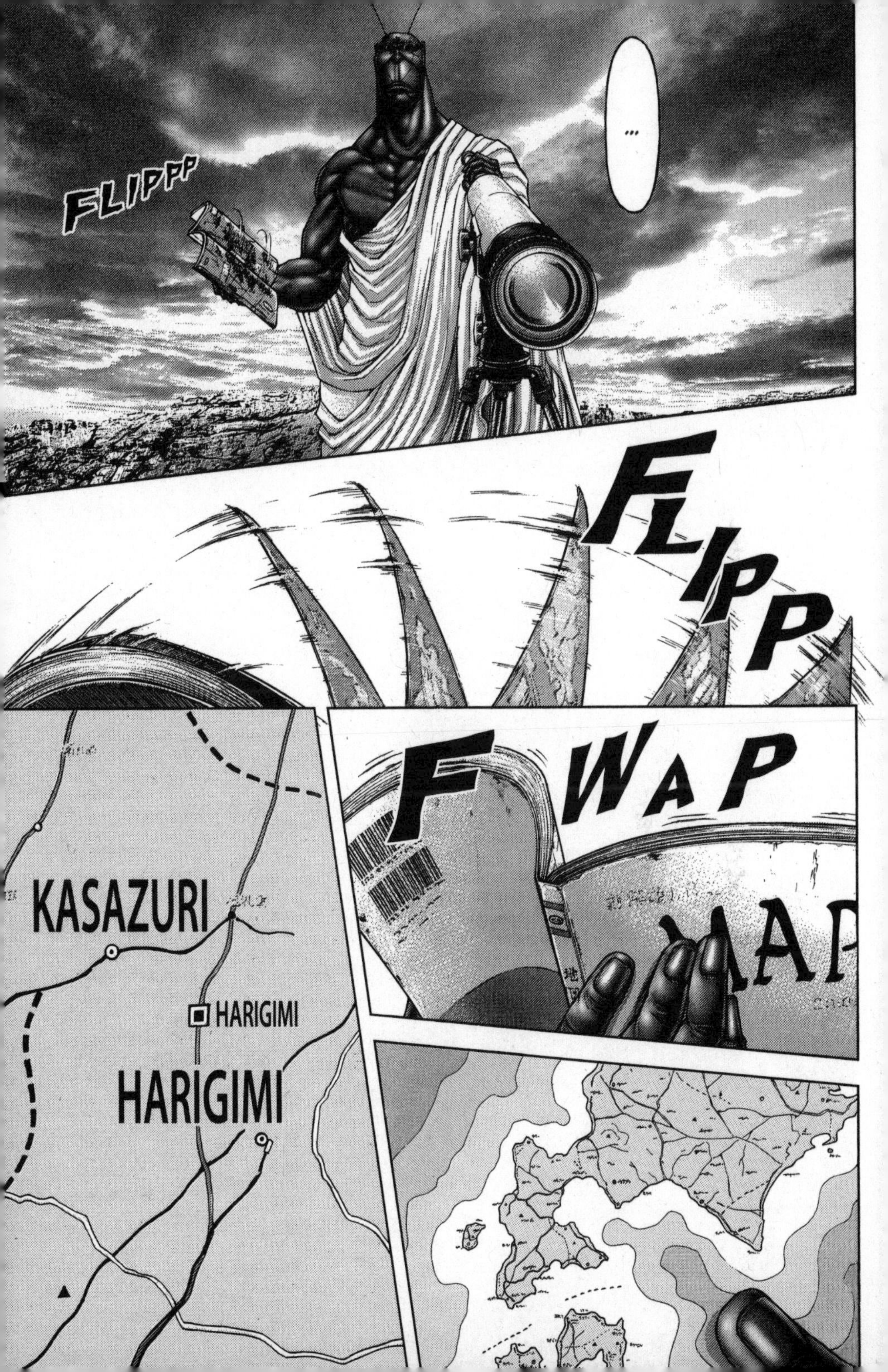
...
FLIPPP
FLIPP
FWAP
KASAZURI
HARIGIMI
HARIGIMI

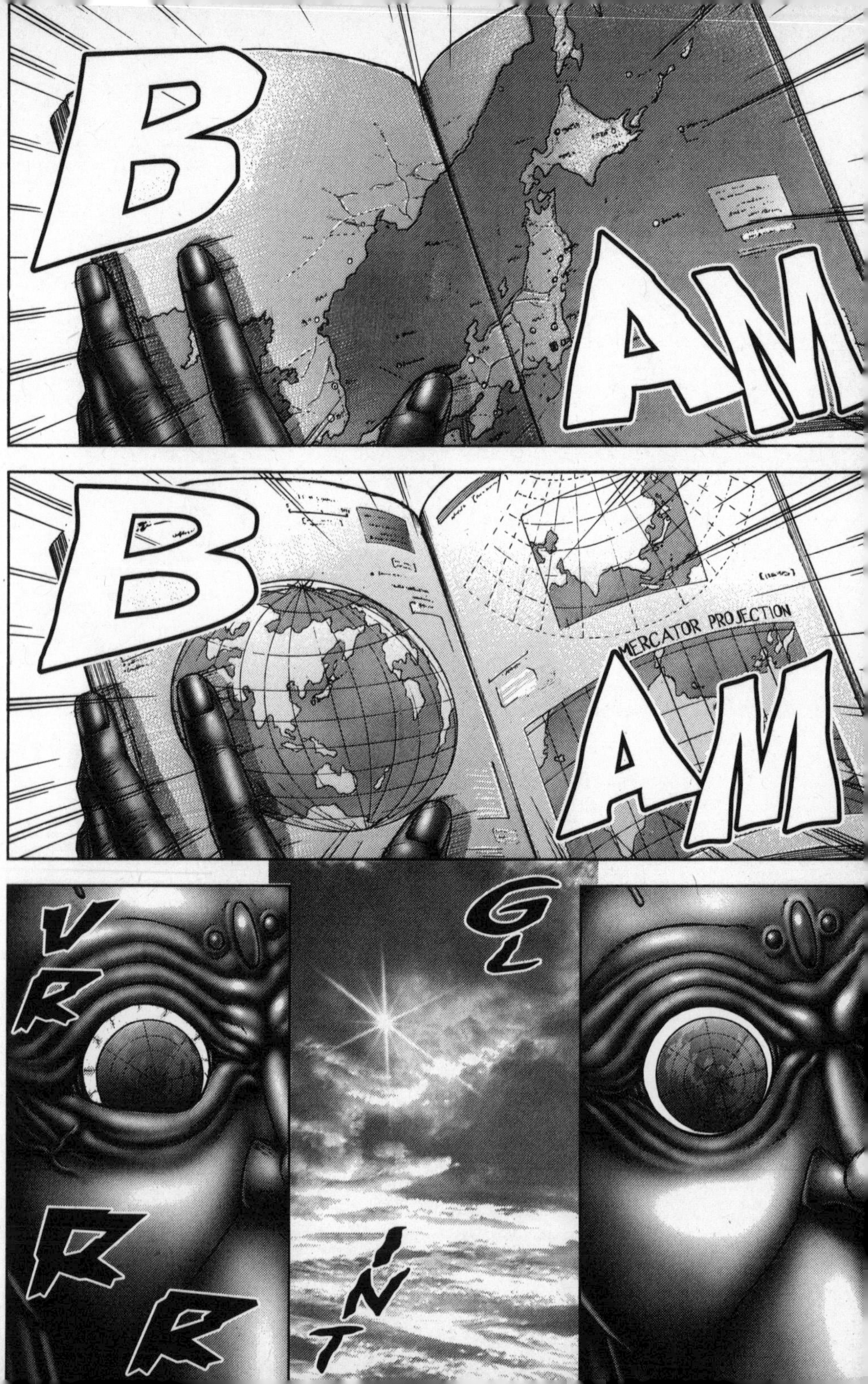
BAM
MERCATOR PROJECTION
BAM
GLINT
VRRR

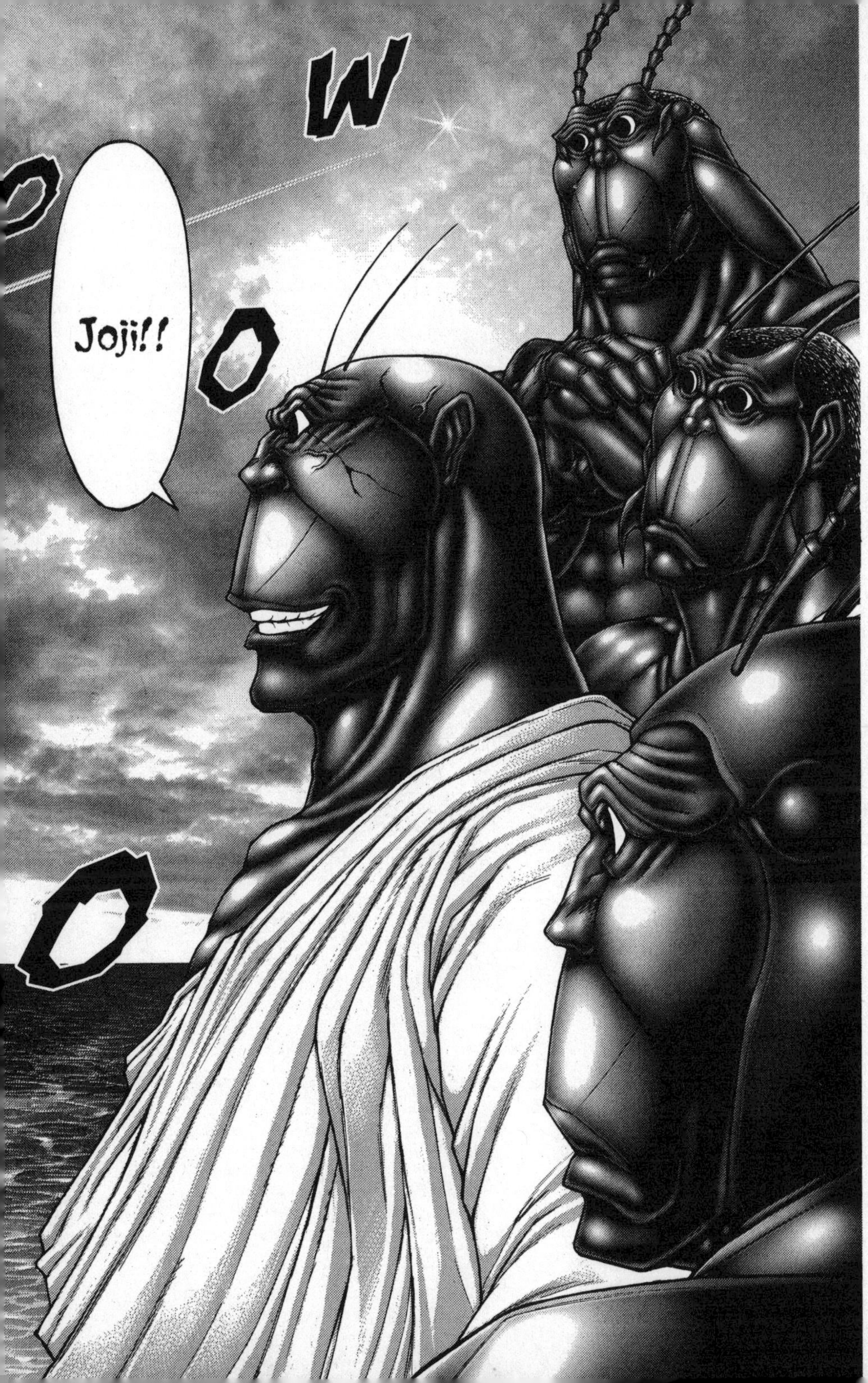
Joji!!

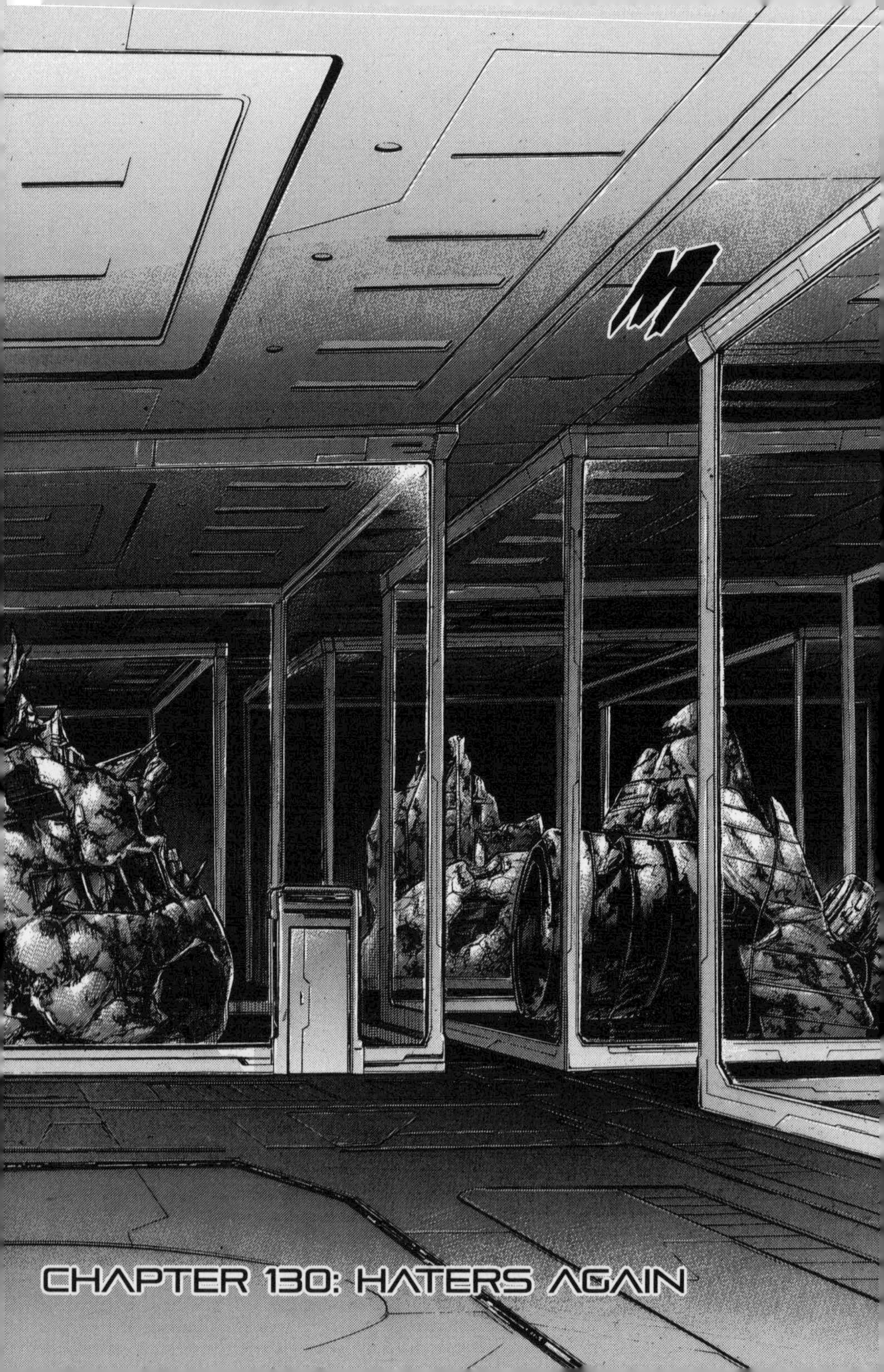
M
CHAPTER 130: HATERS AGAIN

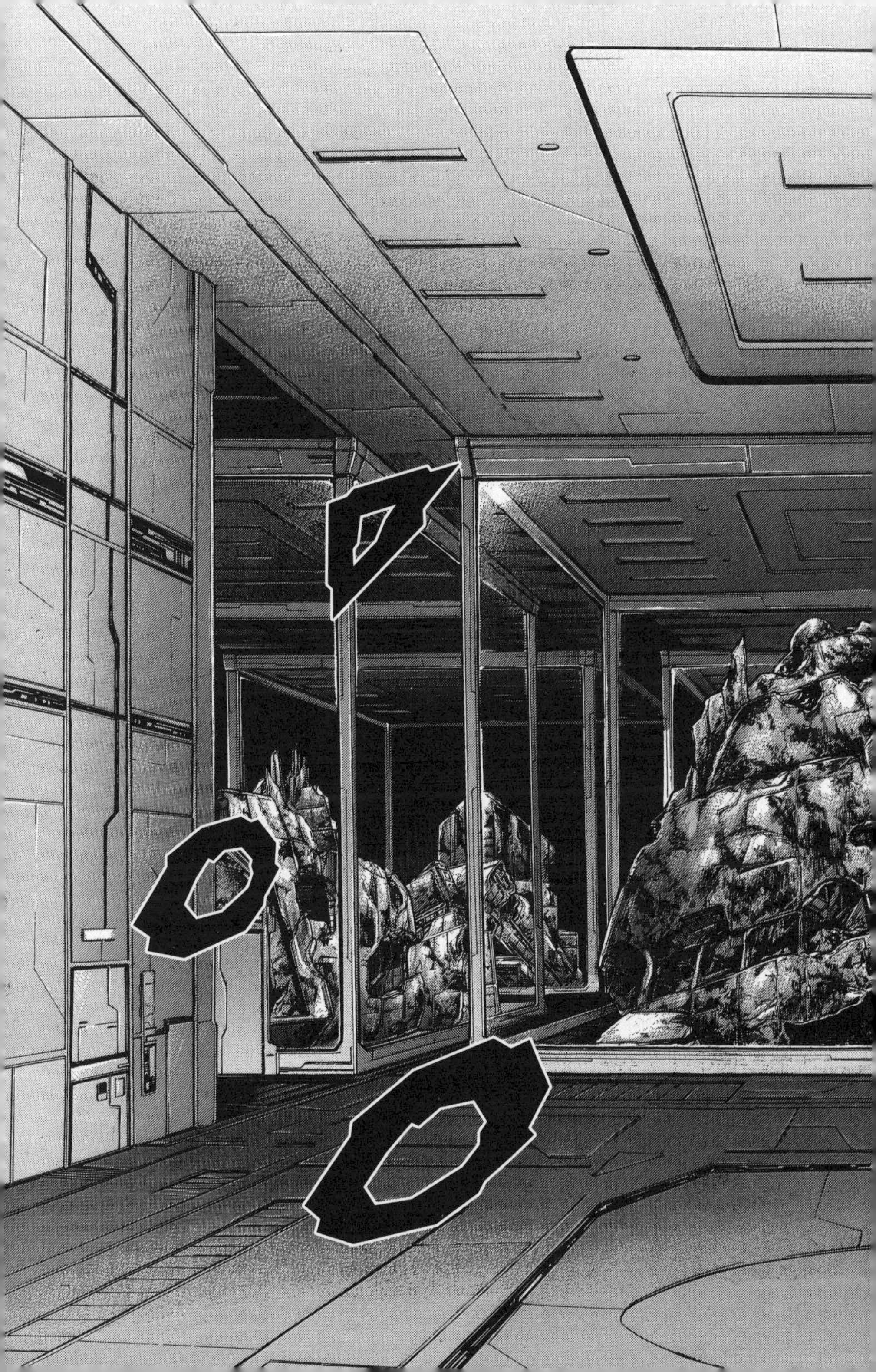

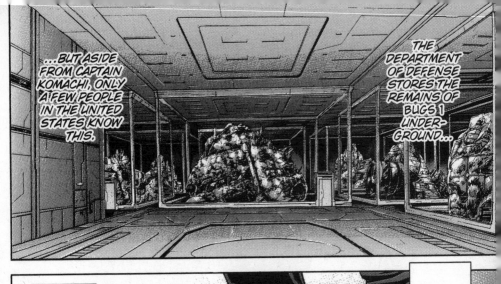

THE DEPARTMENT OF DEFENSE STORES THE REMAINS OF BUGS 1 UNDERGROUND...

...BUT ASIDE FROM CAPTAIN KOMACHI, ONLY A FEW PEOPLE IN THE UNITED STATES KNOW THIS.

HOW MANY YEARS AGO WAS IT?

YES, IT WAS TEN YEARS AGO...

...BEFORE WE EVEN KNEW ABOUT THE DANGER OF THE A.E. VIRUS.

I HAD NEVER EVEN HEARD OF ICHIRO...

...AND I WASN'T THE PRESIDENT, I WAS SECRETARY OF DEFENSE.

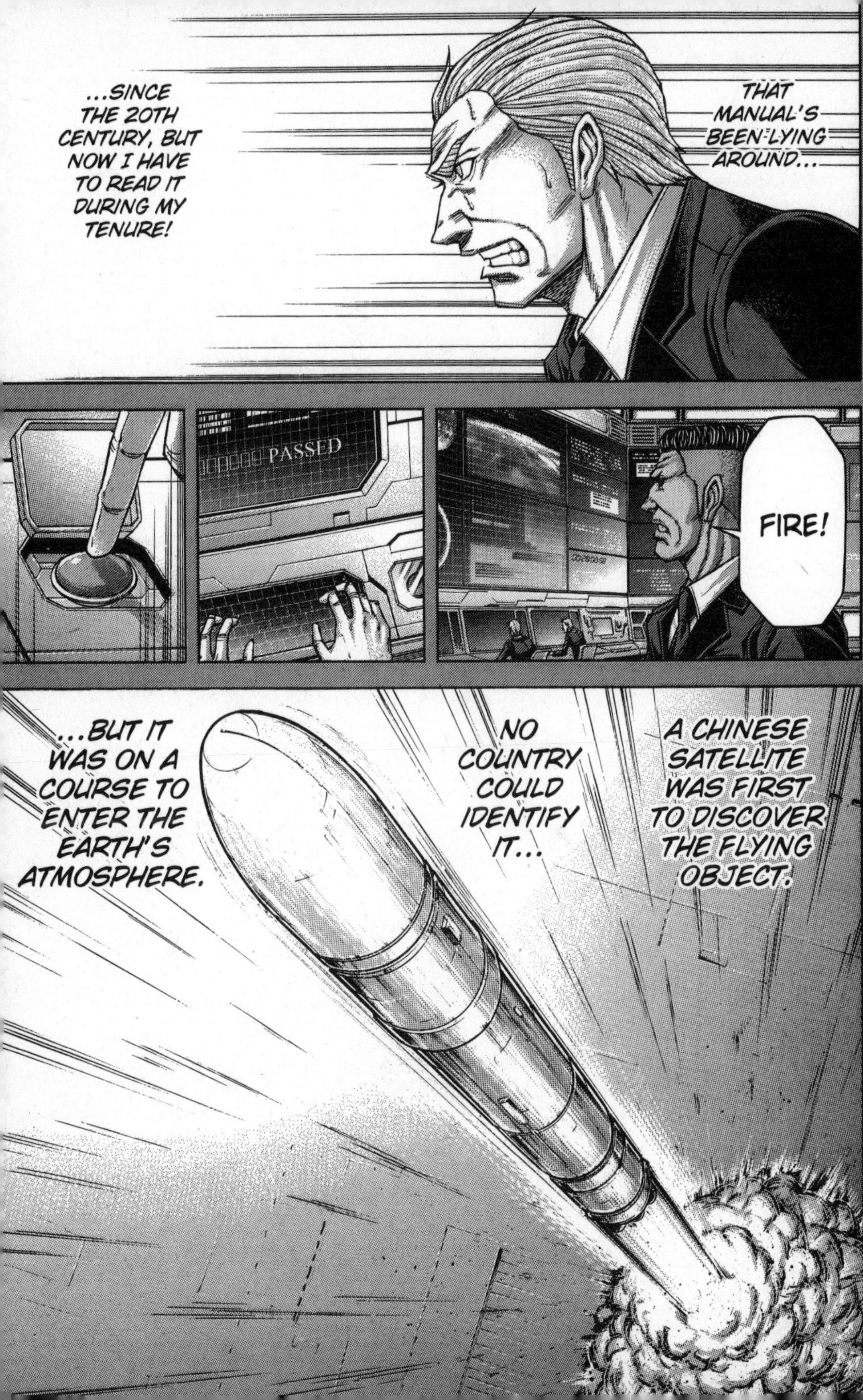
THAT MANUAL'S BEEN LYING AROUND...
...SINCE THE 20TH CENTURY, BUT NOW I HAVE TO READ IT DURING MY TENURE!
FIRE!
PASSED
A CHINESE SATELLITE WAS FIRST TO DISCOVER THE FLYING OBJECT.
NO COUNTRY COULD IDENTIFY IT...
...BUT IT WAS ON A COURSE TO ENTER THE EARTH'S ATMOSPHERE.

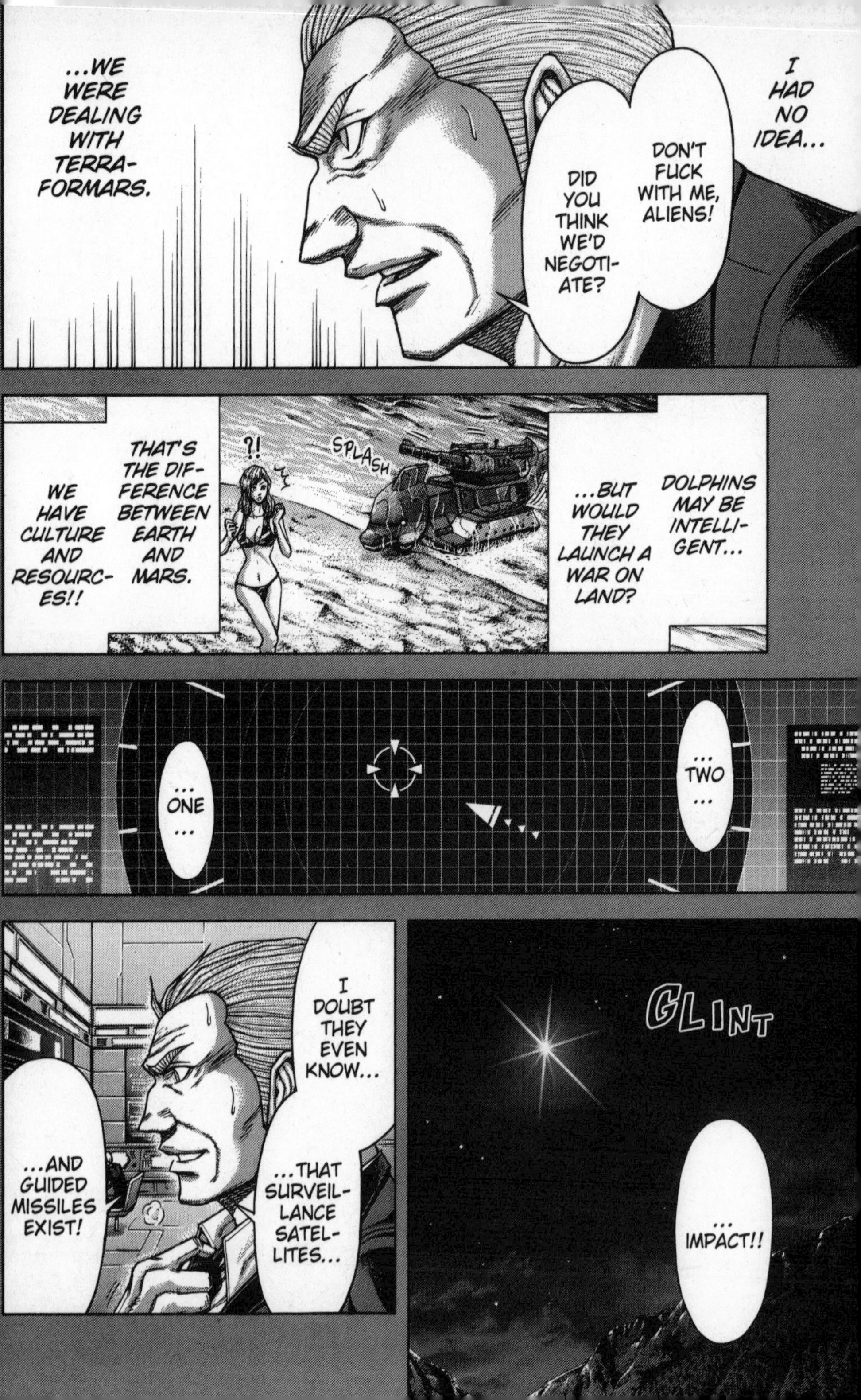
I HAD NO IDEA...
DON'T FUCK WITH ME, ALIENS!
DID YOU THINK WE'D NEGOTIATE?
...WE WERE DEALING WITH TERRA-FORMARS.
DOLPHINS MAY BE INTELLIGENT...
...BUT WOULD THEY LAUNCH A WAR ON LAND?
SPLASH
?!
THAT'S THE DIFFERENCE BETWEEN EARTH AND MARS.
WE HAVE CULTURE AND RESOURCES!!
...TWO...
...ONE...
GLINT
...IMPACT!!
I DOUBT THEY EVEN KNOW...
...THAT SURVEILLANCE SATELLITES...
...AND GUIDED MISSILES EXIST!

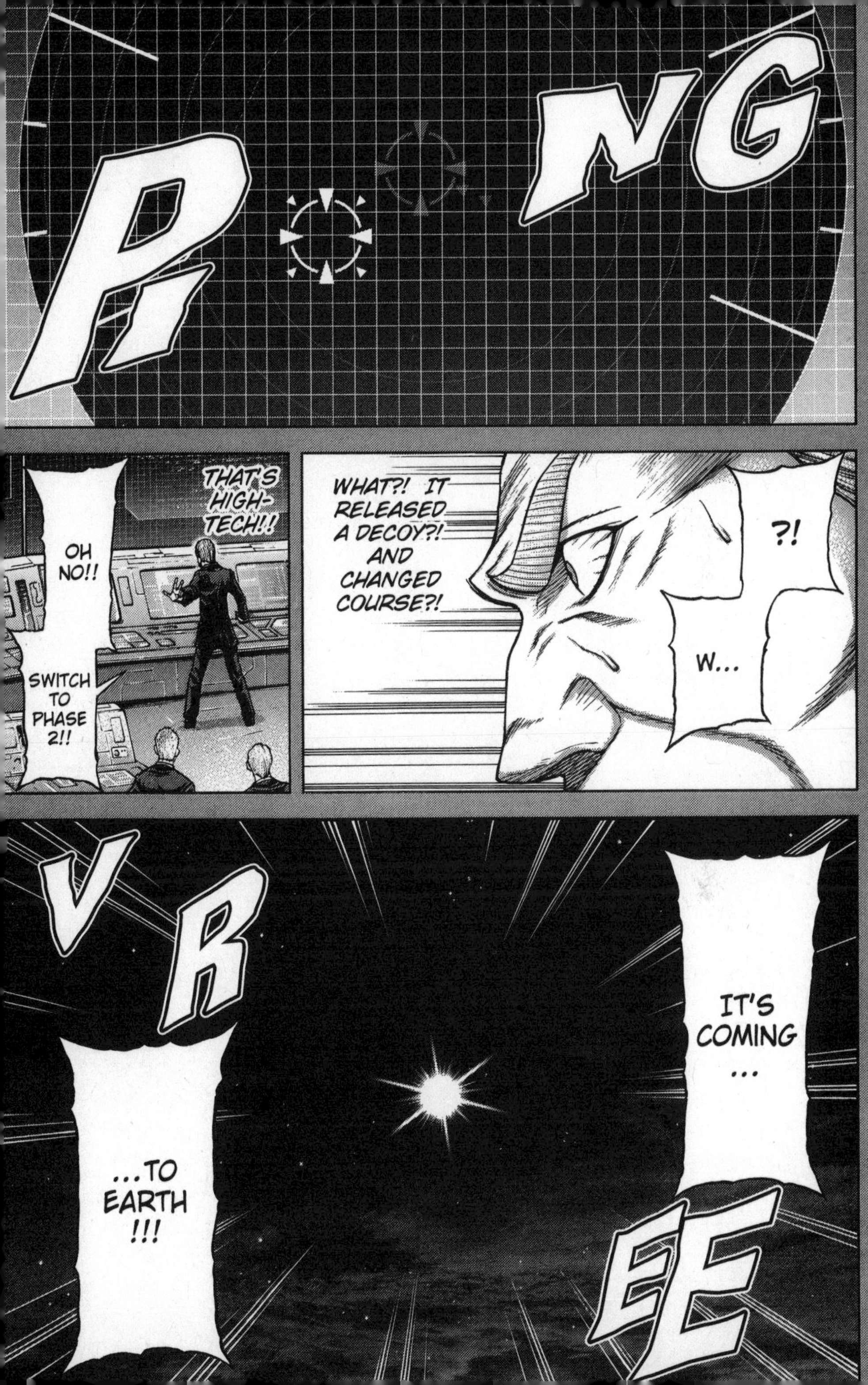
PI
NG
?!
W...
WHAT?! IT RELEASED A DECOY?! AND CHANGED COURSE?!
THAT'S HIGH-TECH!!
OH NO!!
SWITCH TO PHASE 2!!
VR
IT'S COMING...
...TO EARTH!!!
EE

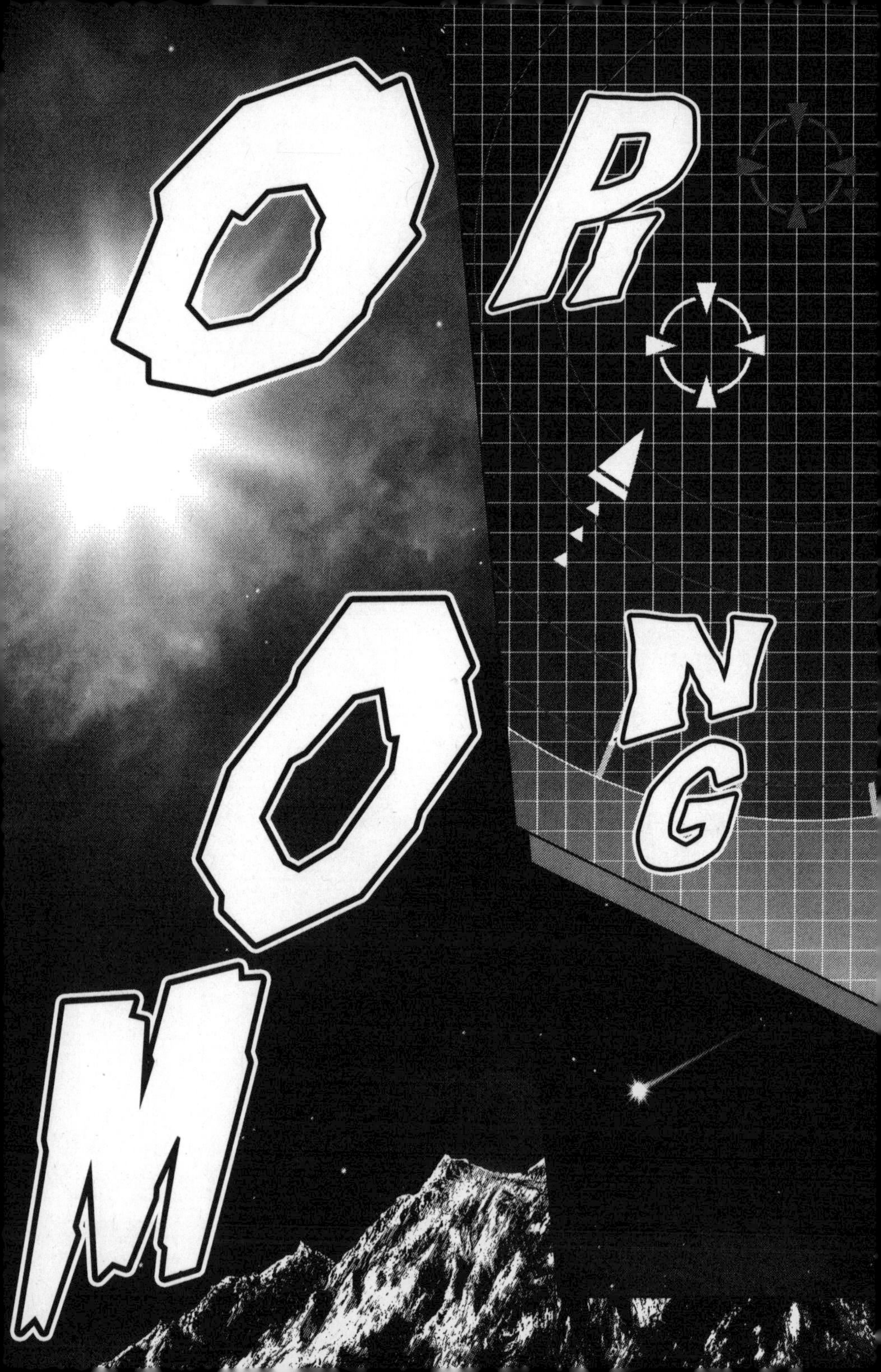
PING
DOM

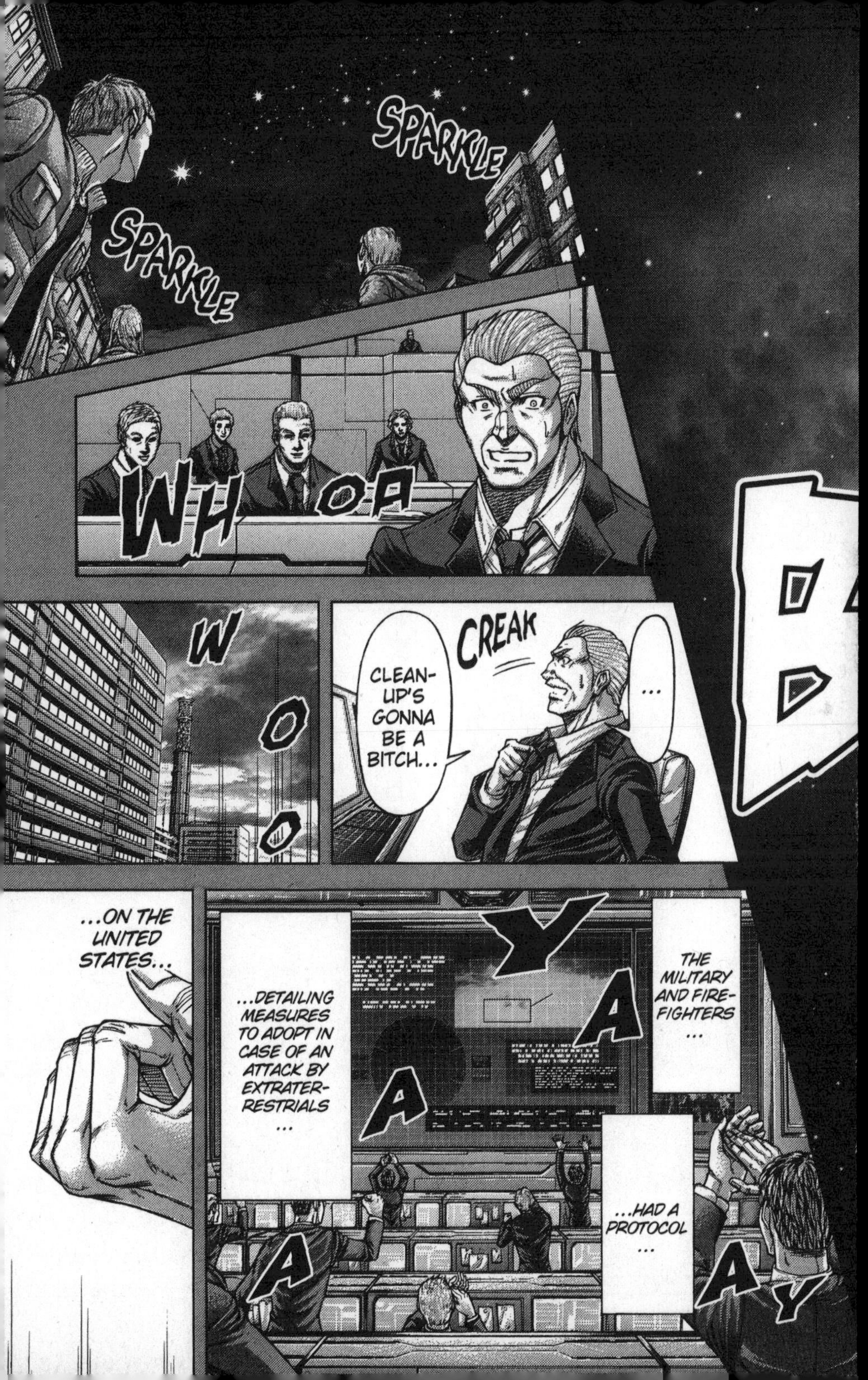
SPARKLE
SPARKLE
WHOA
CREAK
...
CLEAN-UP'S GONNA BE A BITCH...
WOOO
THE MILITARY AND FIRE-FIGHTERS...
...HAD A PROTOCOL...
YAAAAY
...DETAILING MEASURES TO ADOPT IN CASE OF AN ATTACK BY EXTRATER-RESTRIALS...
...ON THE UNITED STATES...

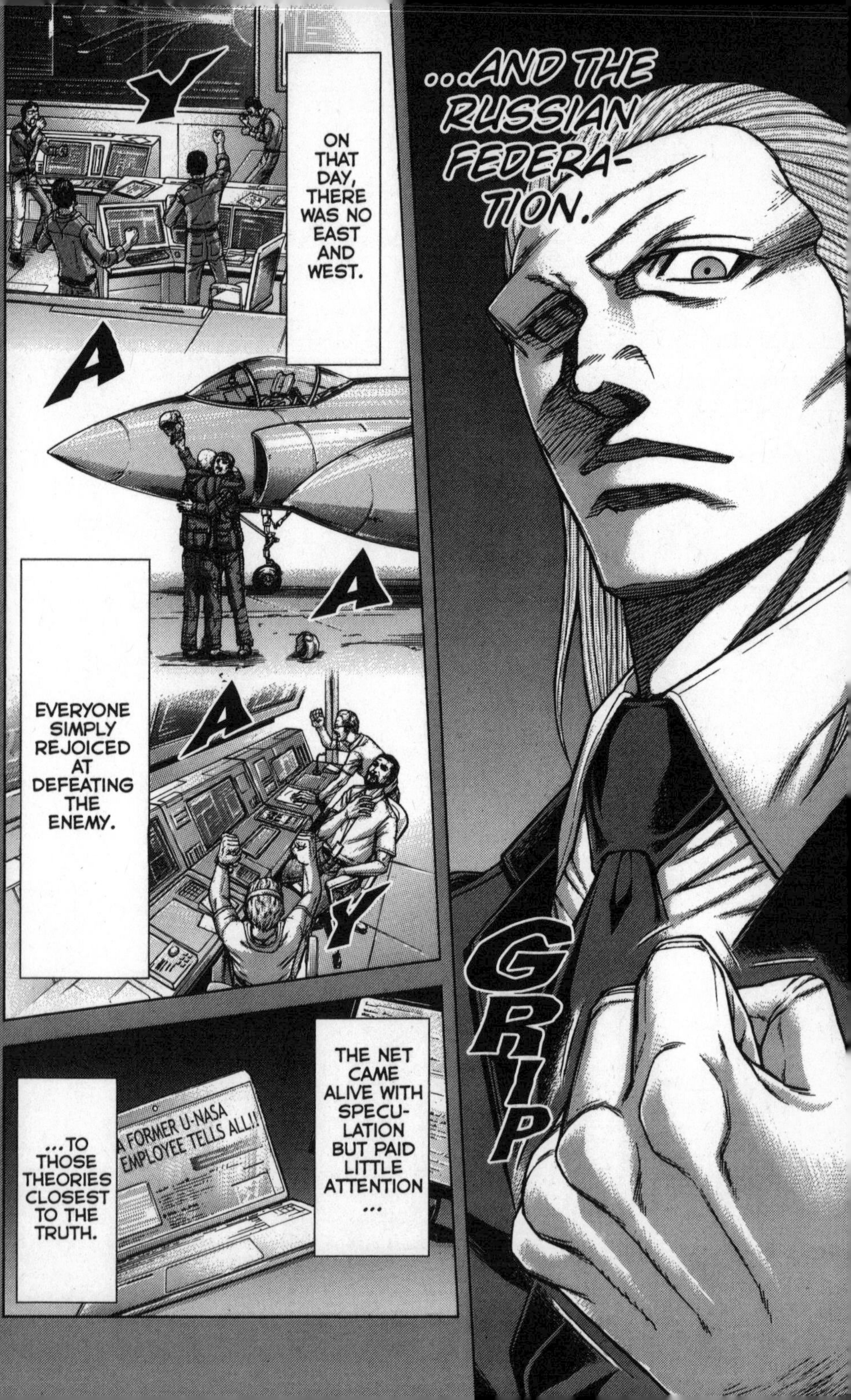
...AND THE RUSSIAN FEDERA-TION.
GRIP
Y
ON THAT DAY, THERE WAS NO EAST AND WEST.
A
A
A
EVERYONE SIMPLY REJOICED AT DEFEATING THE ENEMY.
Y
THE NET CAME ALIVE WITH SPECU-LATION BUT PAID LITTLE ATTENTION ...
A FORMER U-NASA EMPLOYEE TELLS ALL!!
...TO THOSE THEORIES CLOSEST TO THE TRUTH.

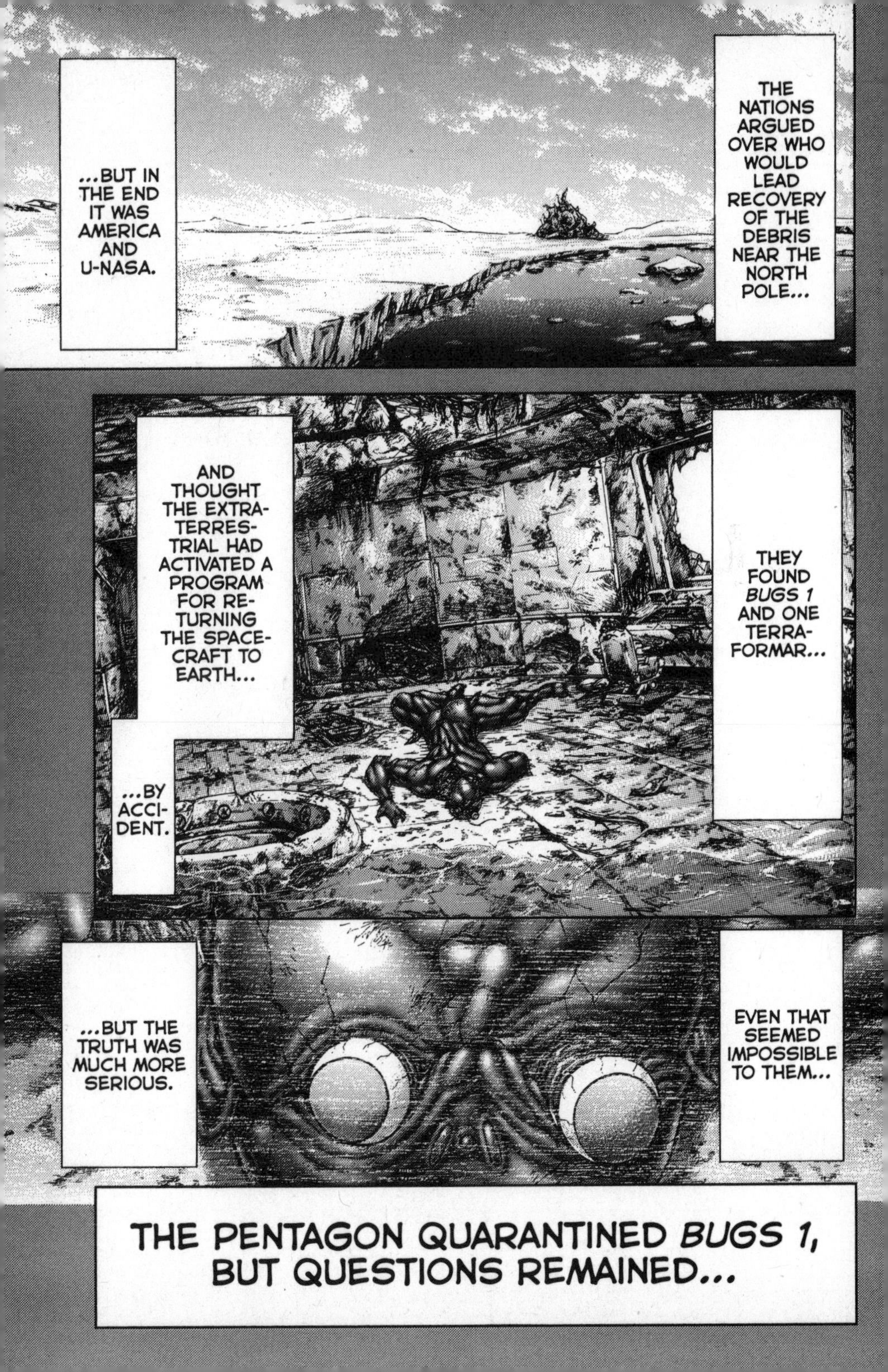
THE NATIONS ARGUED OVER WHO WOULD LEAD RECOVERY OF THE DEBRIS NEAR THE NORTH POLE...
...BUT IN THE END IT WAS AMERICA AND U-NASA.
THEY FOUND *BUGS 1* AND ONE TERRA-FORMAR...
AND THOUGHT THE EXTRA-TERRES-TRIAL HAD ACTIVATED A PROGRAM FOR RE-TURNING THE SPACE-CRAFT TO EARTH...
...BY ACCI-DENT.
EVEN THAT SEEMED IMPOSSIBLE TO THEM...
...BUT THE TRUTH WAS MUCH MORE SERIOUS.
THE PENTAGON QUARANTINED *BUGS 1*, BUT QUESTIONS REMAINED...

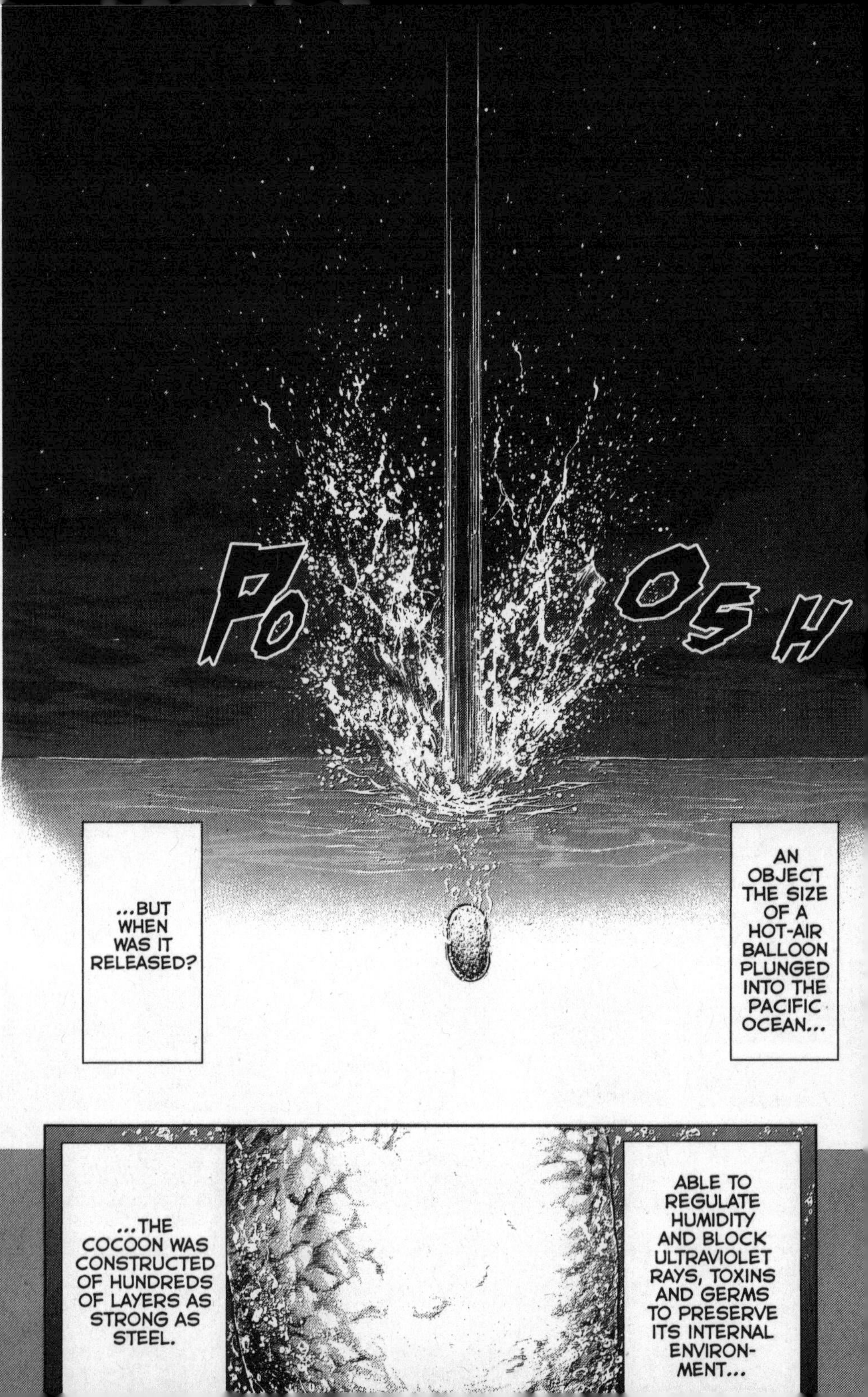
POOSH
AN OBJECT THE SIZE OF A HOT-AIR BALLOON PLUNGED INTO THE PACIFIC OCEAN...
...BUT WHEN WAS IT RELEASED?
ABLE TO REGULATE HUMIDITY AND BLOCK ULTRAVIOLET RAYS, TOXINS AND GERMS TO PRESERVE ITS INTERNAL ENVIRON-MENT...
...THE COCOON WAS CONSTRUCTED OF HUNDREDS OF LAYERS AS STRONG AS STEEL.

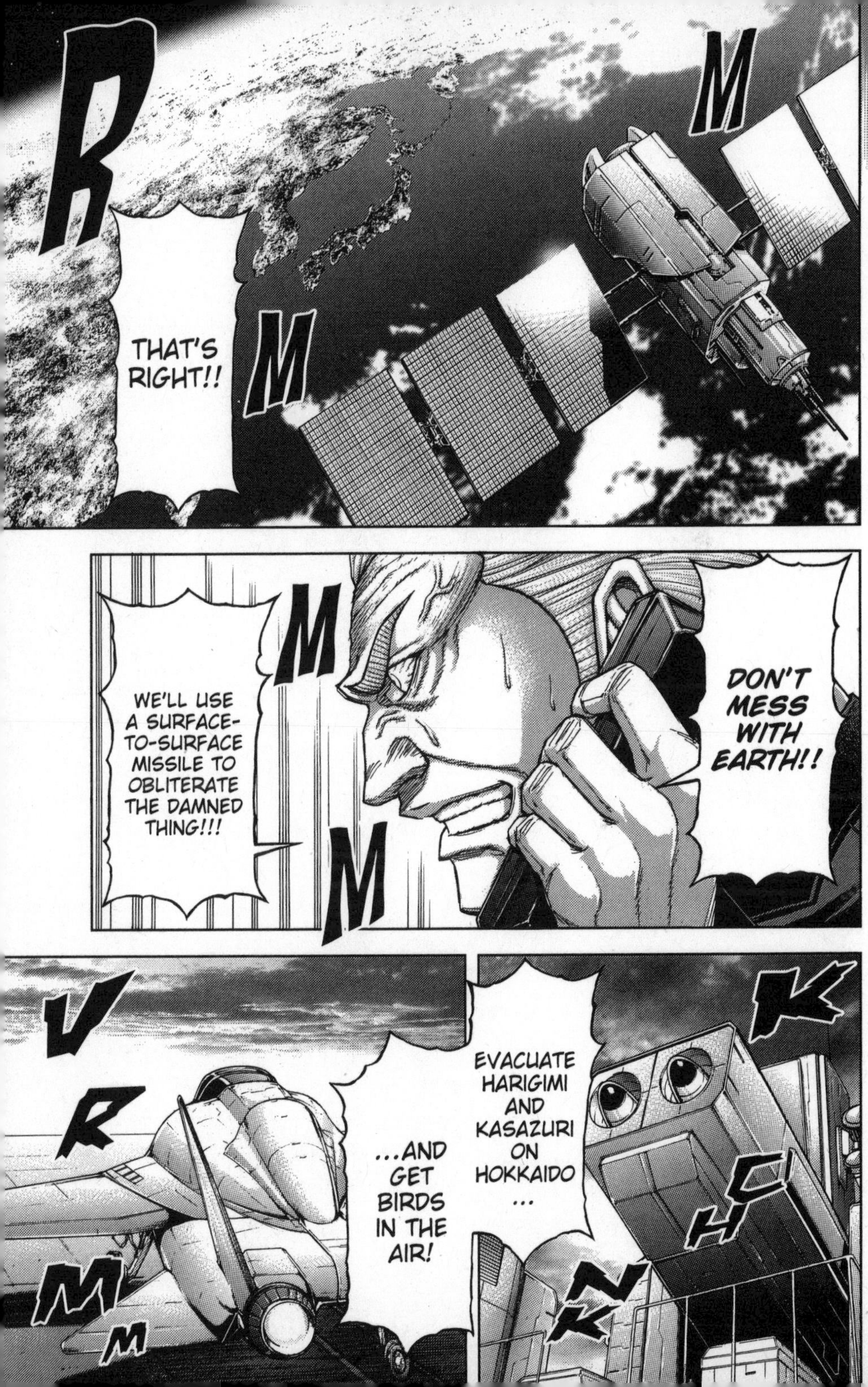
M
M
R
THAT'S RIGHT!!
DON'T MESS WITH EARTH!!
M
M
WE'LL USE A SURFACE-TO-SURFACE MISSILE TO OBLITERATE THE DAMNED THING!!!
K
C
H
N
K
EVACUATE HARIGIMI AND KASAZURI ON HOKKAIDO...
...AND GET BIRDS IN THE AIR!
V
R
M
M

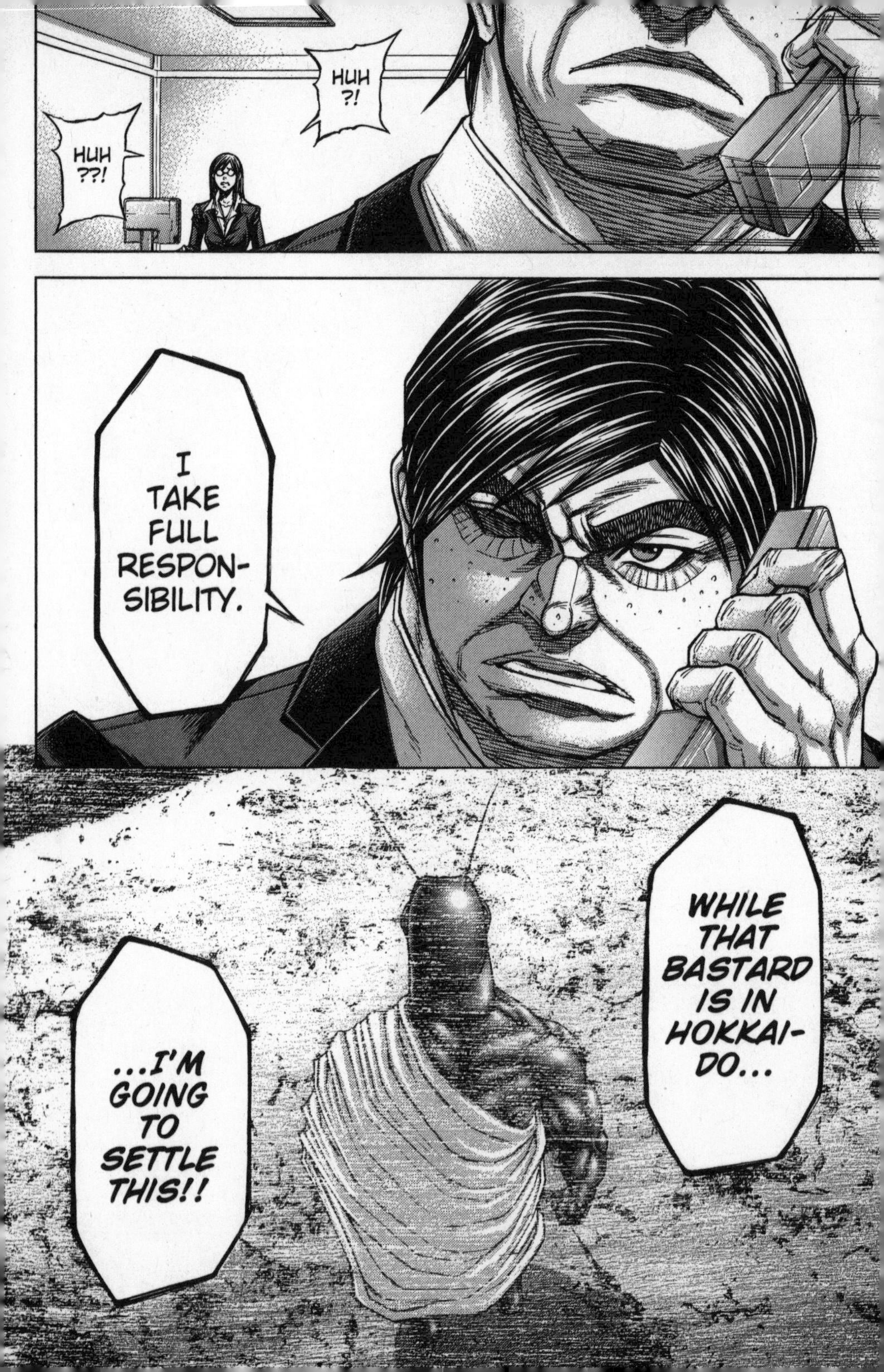
HUH ?!
HUH ??!
I TAKE FULL RESPON-SIBILITY.
WHILE THAT BASTARD IS IN HOKKAI-DO...
...I'M GOING TO SETTLE THIS!!

CHAPTER 131: HELL YEAH!

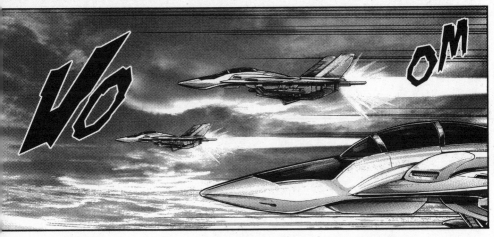

...AT PHASE 1.

IN THAT CASE...

IT'S BEST IF WE CAN HANDLE THIS...

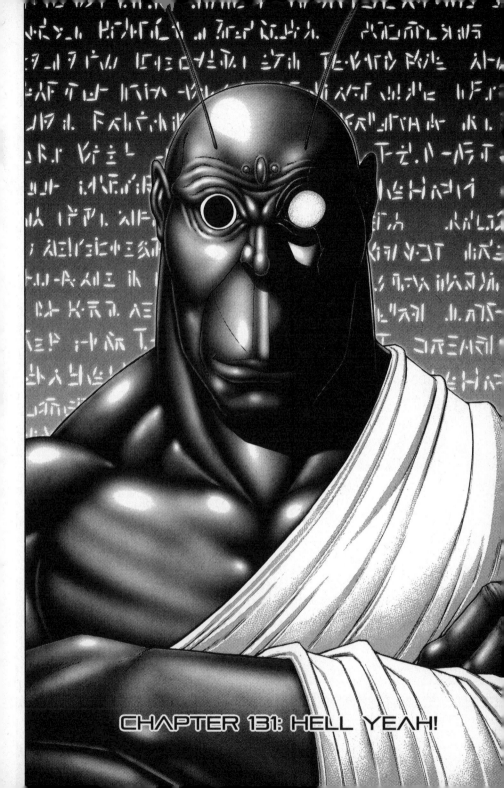

CHAPTER 131: HELL YEAH!

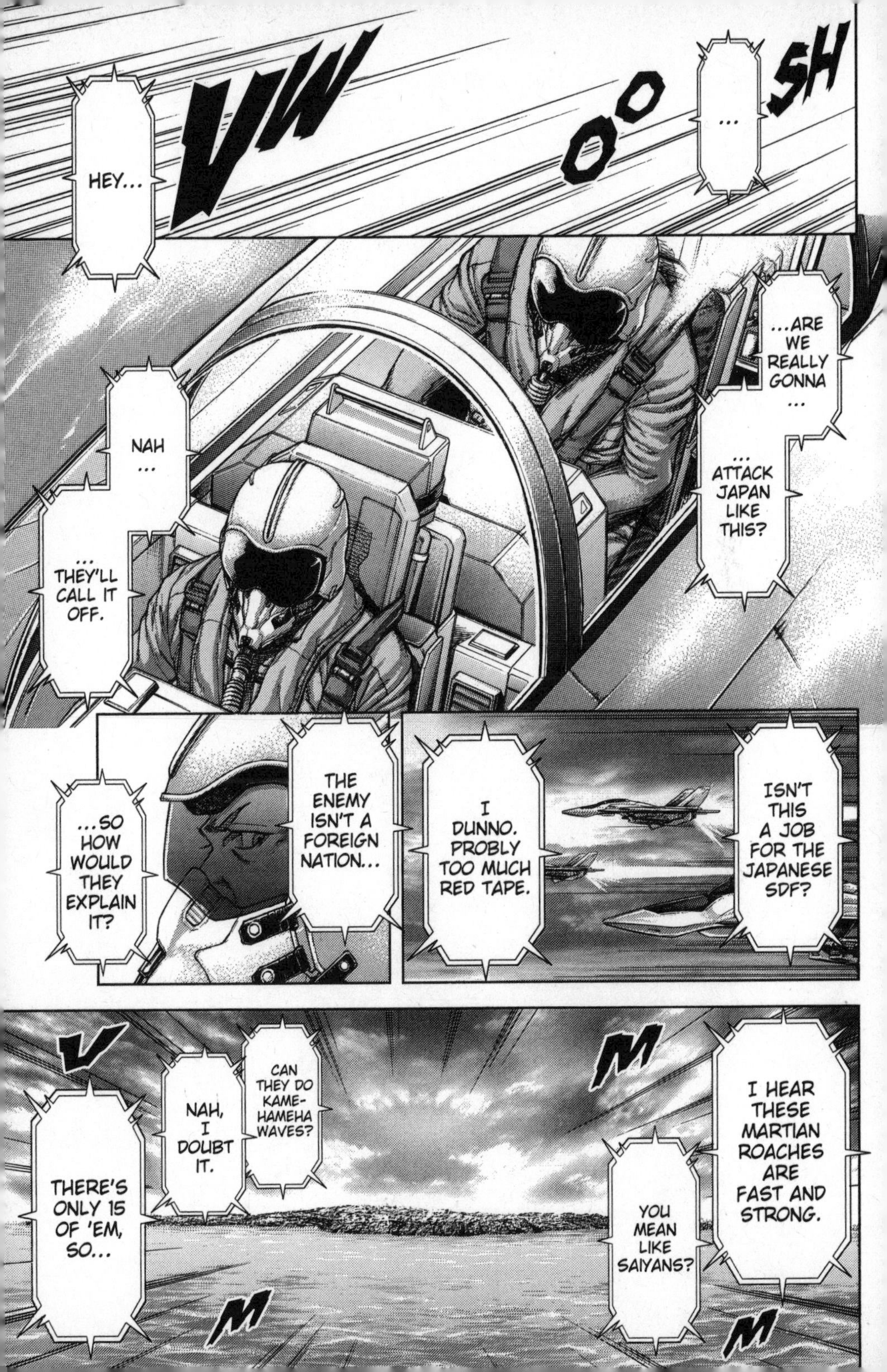
...
VWOOOSH
HEY...
...ARE WE REALLY GONNA ...
... ATTACK JAPAN LIKE THIS?
NAH ...
... THEY'LL CALL IT OFF.
ISN'T THIS A JOB FOR THE JAPANESE SDF?
I DUNNO. PROBLY TOO MUCH RED TAPE.
THE ENEMY ISN'T A FOREIGN NATION...
...SO HOW WOULD THEY EXPLAIN IT?
VMMM
I HEAR THESE MARTIAN ROACHES ARE FAST AND STRONG.
YOU MEAN LIKE SAIYANS?
CAN THEY DO KAME-HAMEHA WAVES?
NAH, I DOUBT IT.
THERE'S ONLY 15 OF 'EM, SO...

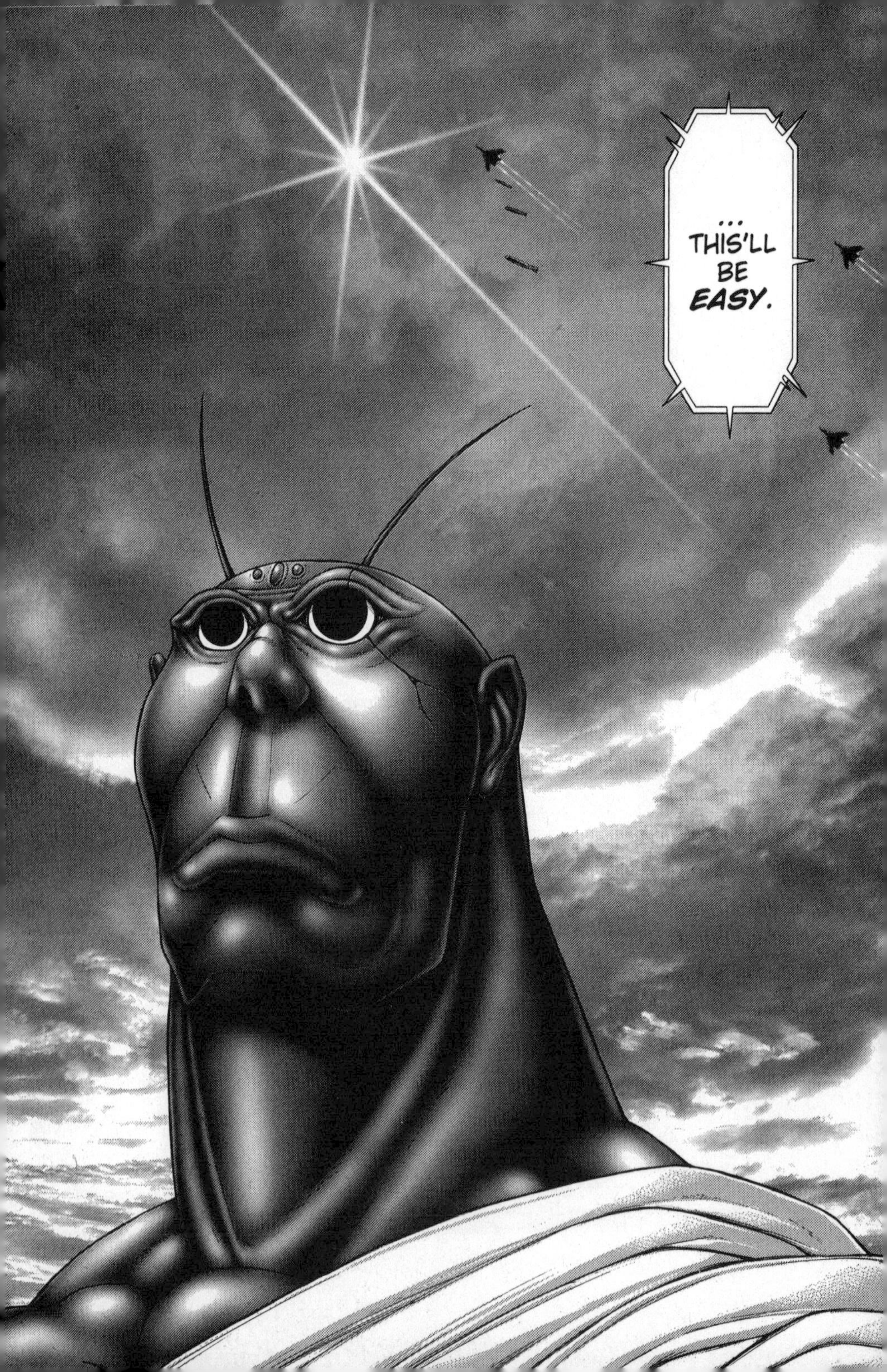
...THIS'LL BE EASY.

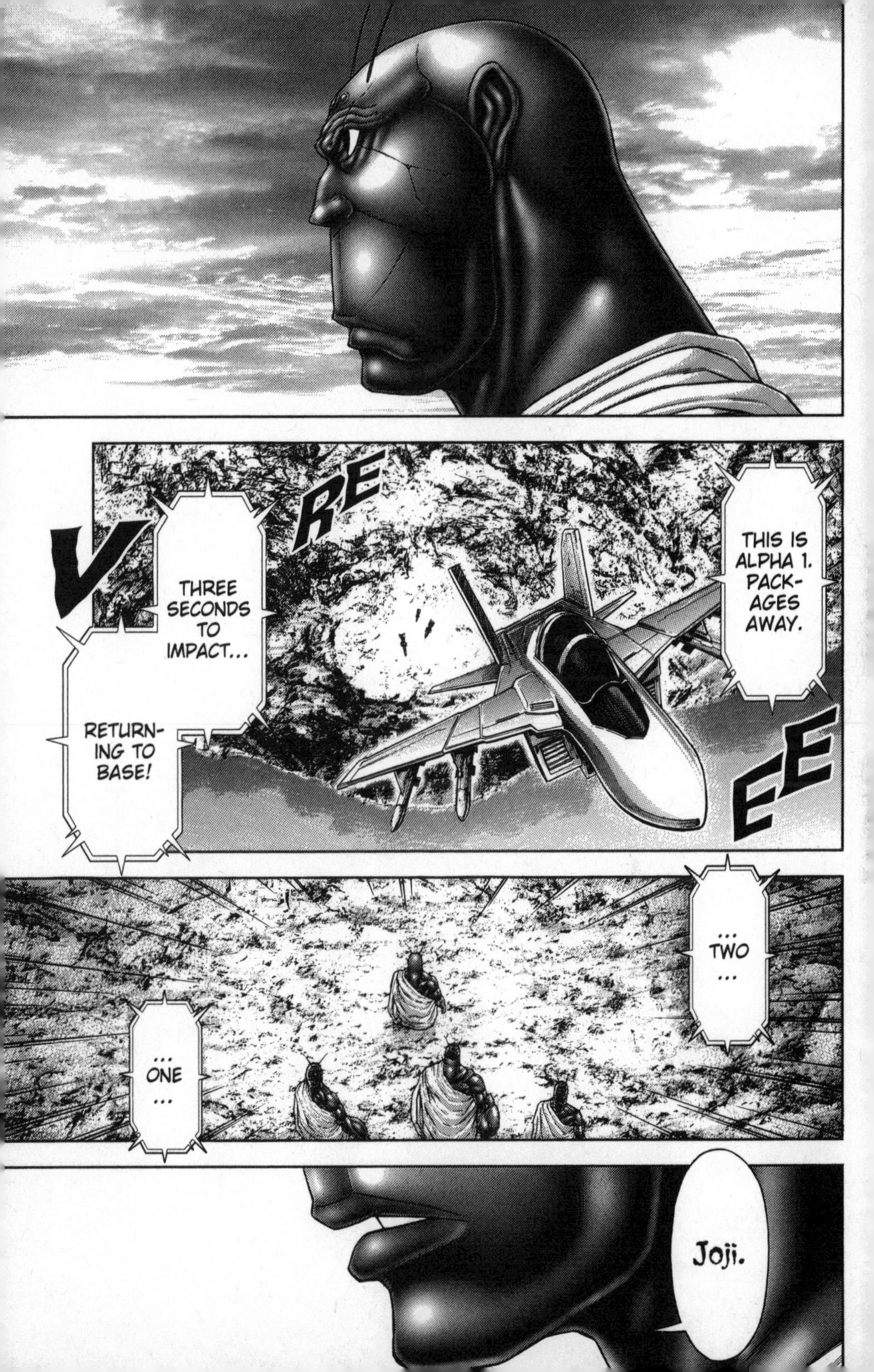
THIS IS ALPHA 1. PACKAGES AWAY.
VREEE
THREE SECONDS TO IMPACT...
RETURNING TO BASE!
... TWO ...
... ONE ...
Joji.

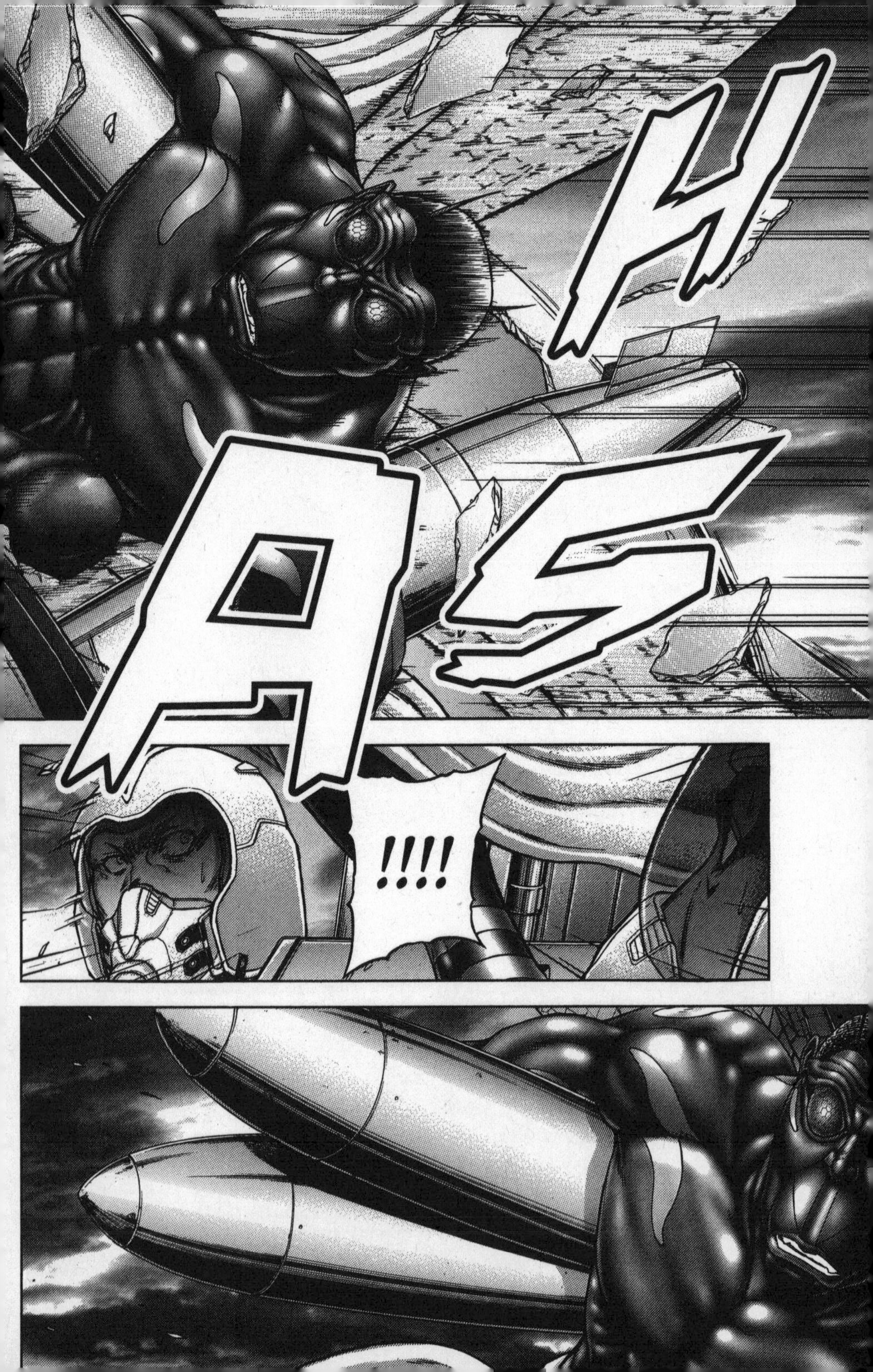
HAS
!!!!

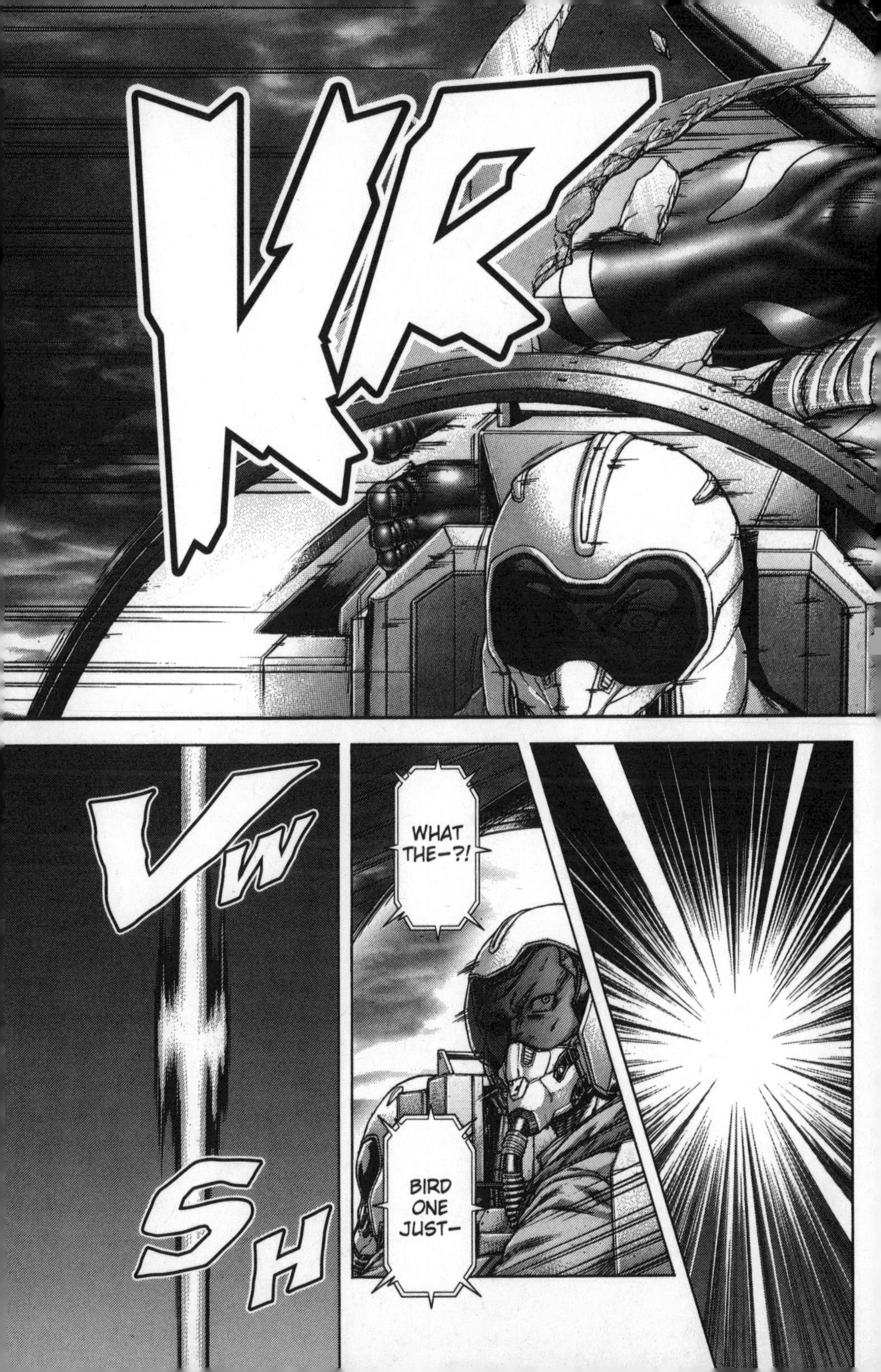
KR
WHAT THE-?!
BIRD ONE JUST-
VW
SH

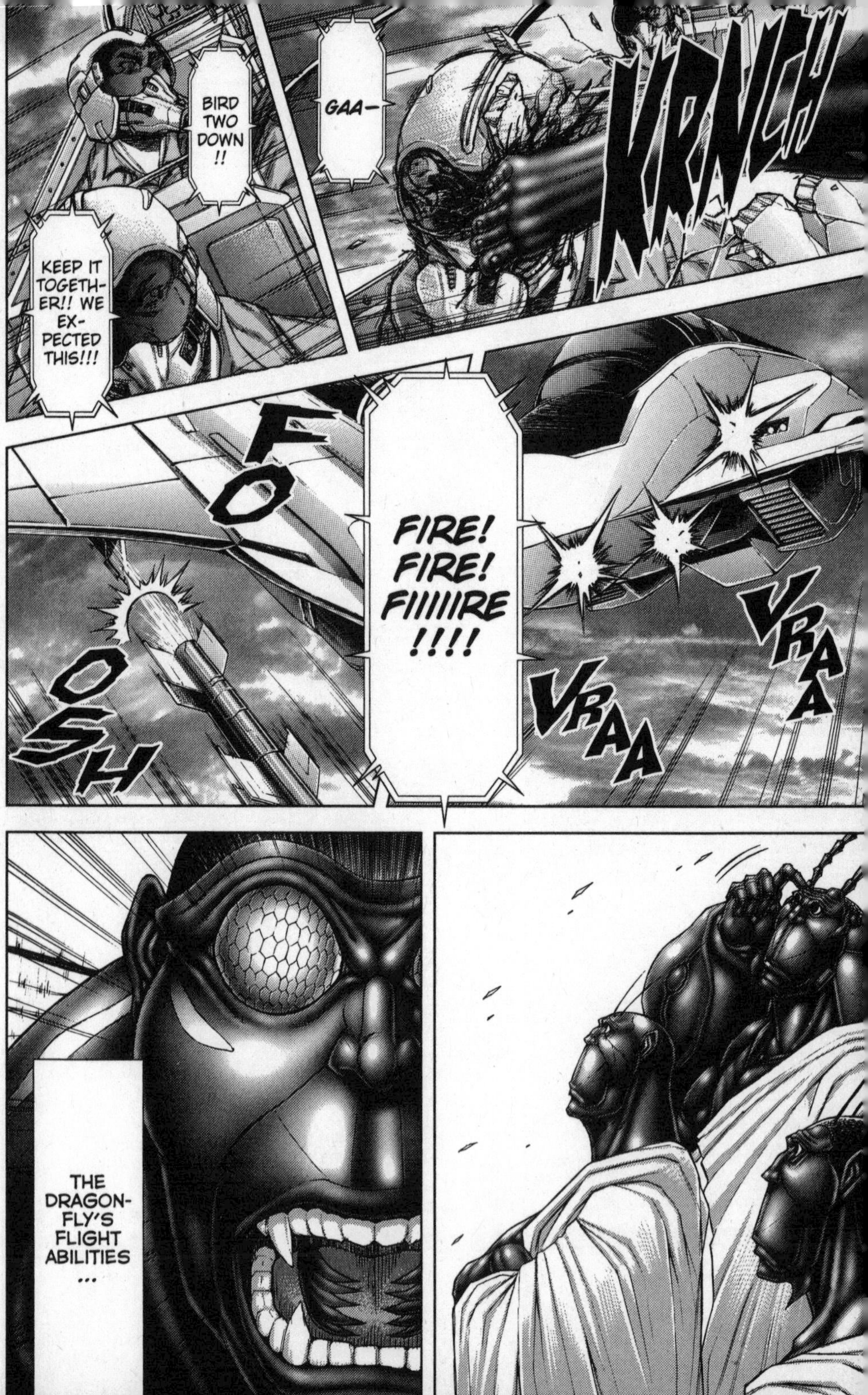
KRNCH
GAA—
BIRD TWO DOWN!!
KEEP IT TOGETHER!! WE EXPECTED THIS!!!
VRAA
VRAA
FIRE! FIRE! FIIIIIRE!!!!
FO
OSH
THE DRAGON-FLY'S FLIGHT ABILITIES...

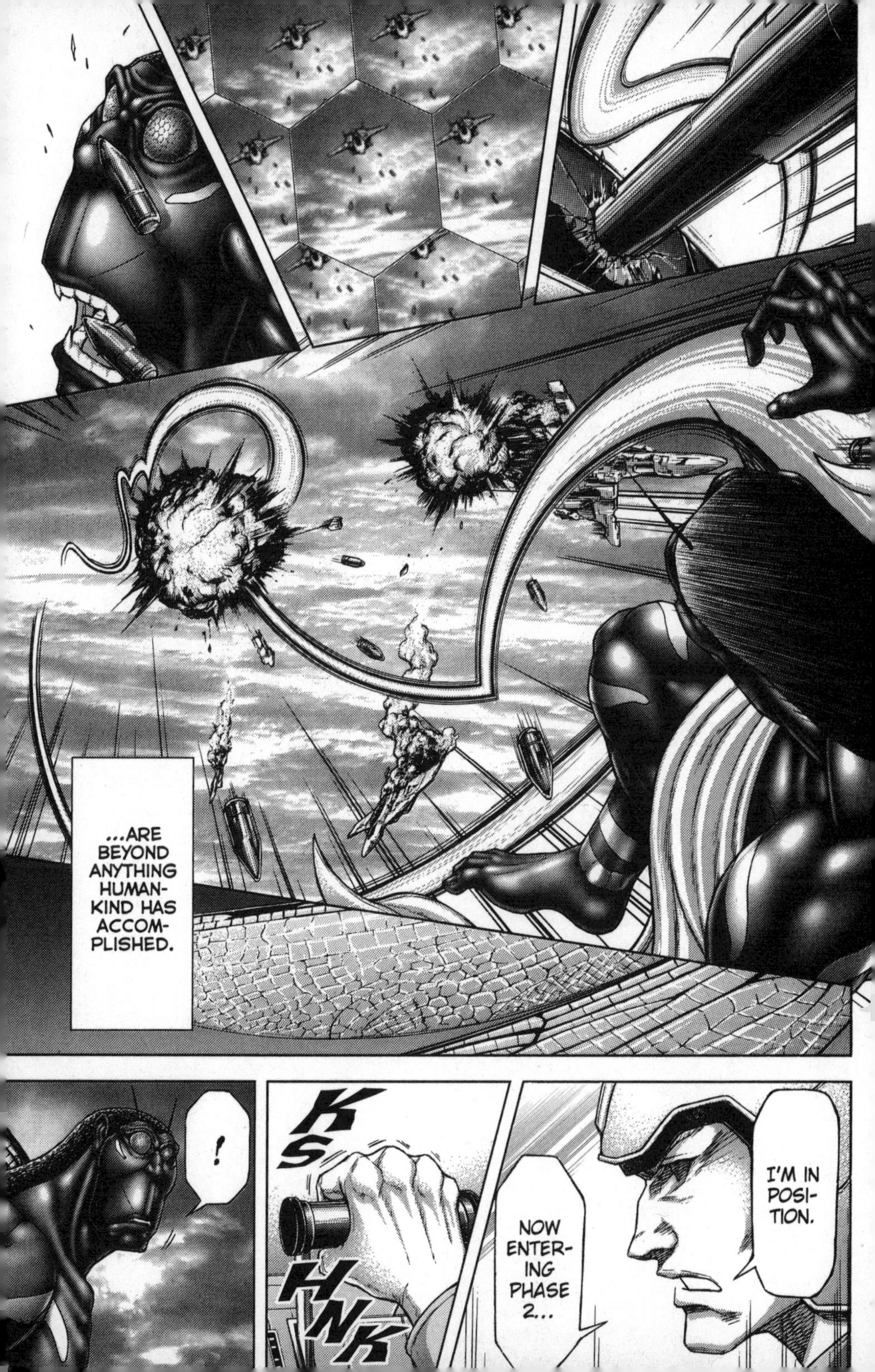
...ARE BEYOND ANYTHING HUMANKIND HAS ACCOMPLISHED.
I'M IN POSITION.
NOW ENTERING PHASE 2...
KS
HNK
!

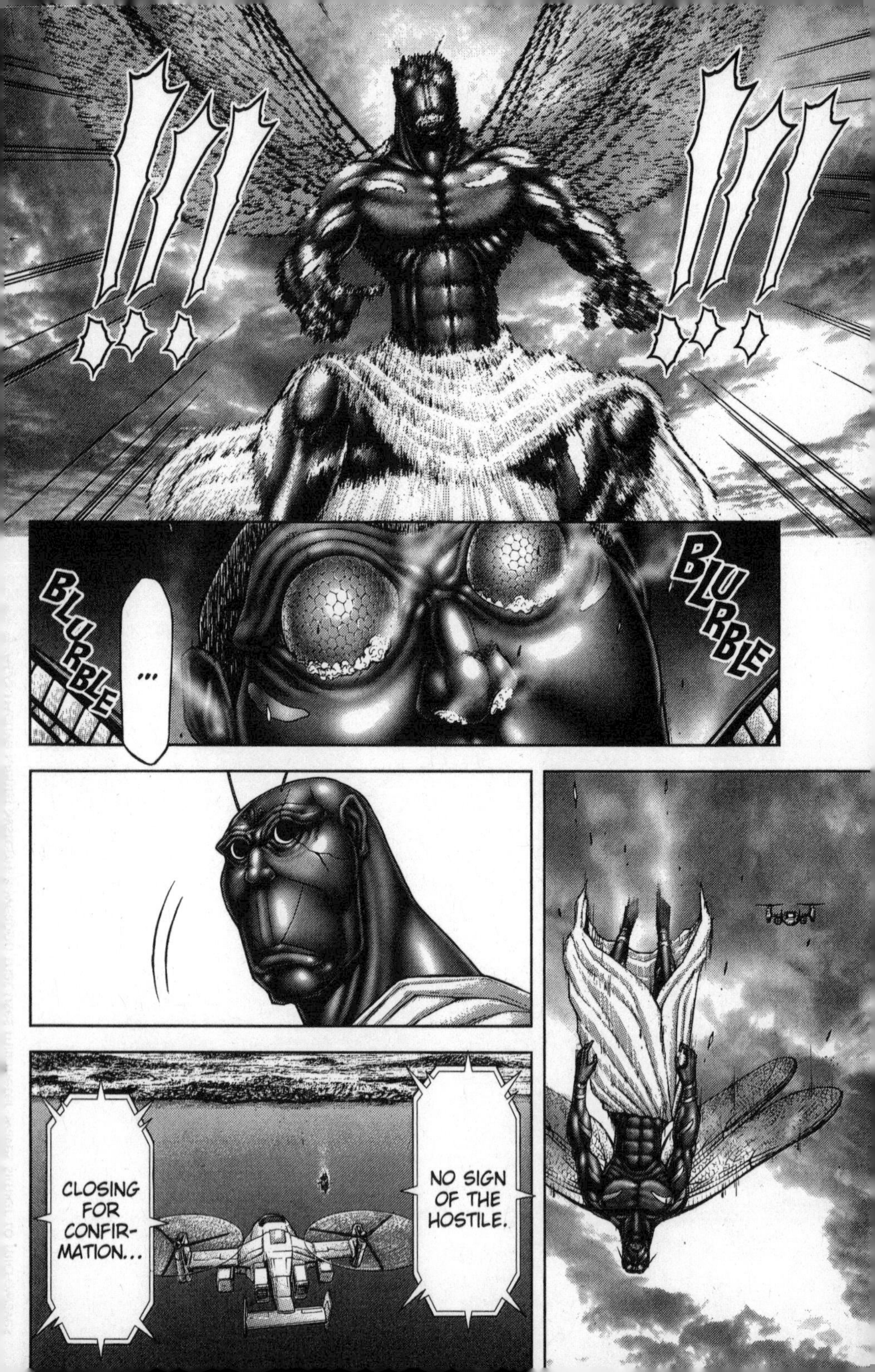
!!!
!!!
BLURBLE
...
BLURBLE
NO SIGN OF THE HOSTILE.
CLOSING FOR CONFIR-MATION...

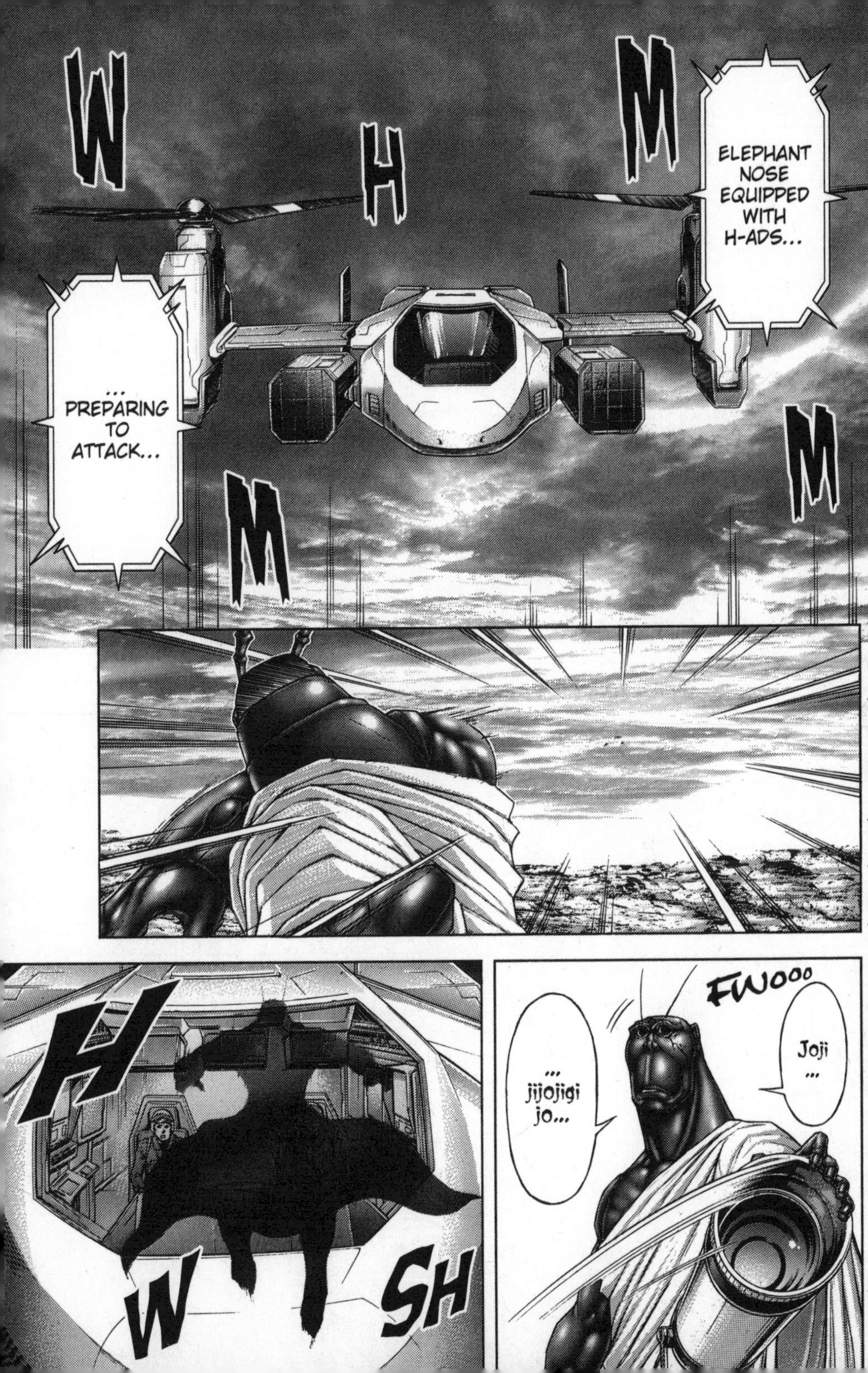
ELEPHANT NOSE EQUIPPED WITH H-ADS...
... PREPARING TO ATTACK...
WHMMMM
FWOOO
Joji ...
... jijojigi jo...
HWSH

ADS (Active Denial System): a weapon that uses millimeter waves similar to microwaves.

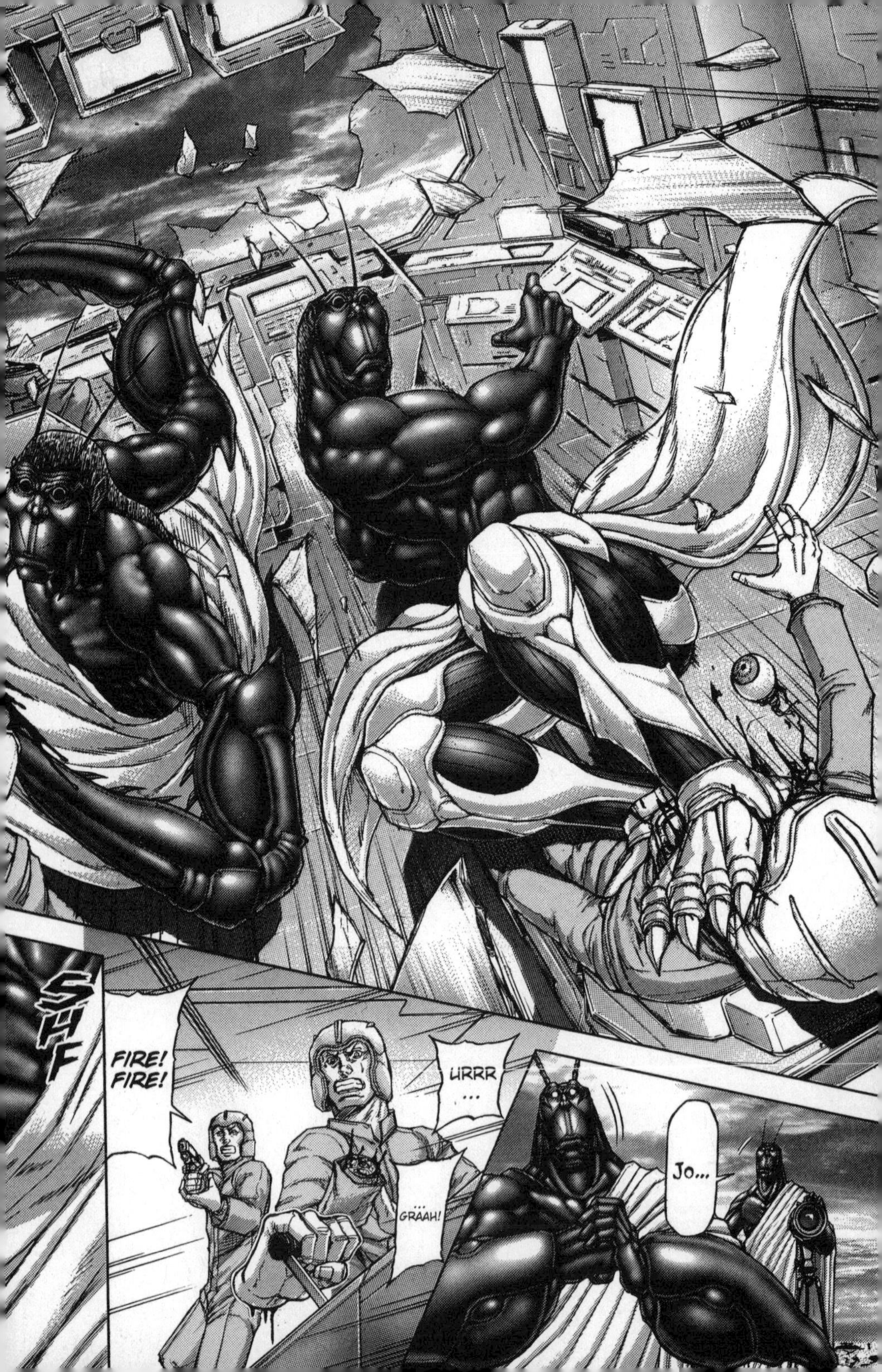

JO...
URRR ...
FIRE! FIRE!
... GRAAH!
SHF

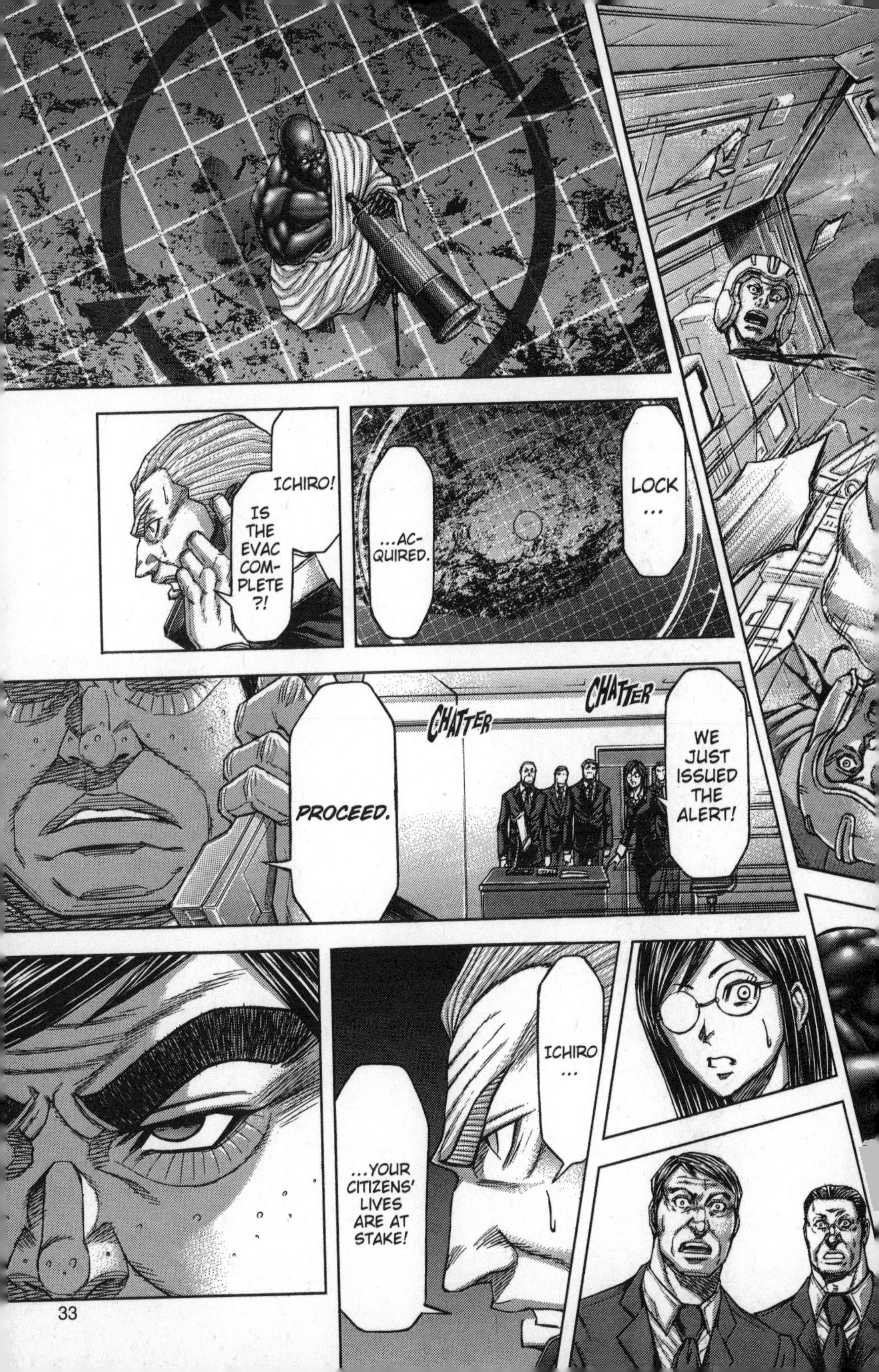
LOCK ...
...ACQUIRED.
ICHIRO! IS THE EVAC COMPLETE?!
WE JUST ISSUED THE ALERT!
CHATTER
CHATTER
PROCEED.
ICHIRO ...
...YOUR CITIZENS' LIVES ARE AT STAKE!

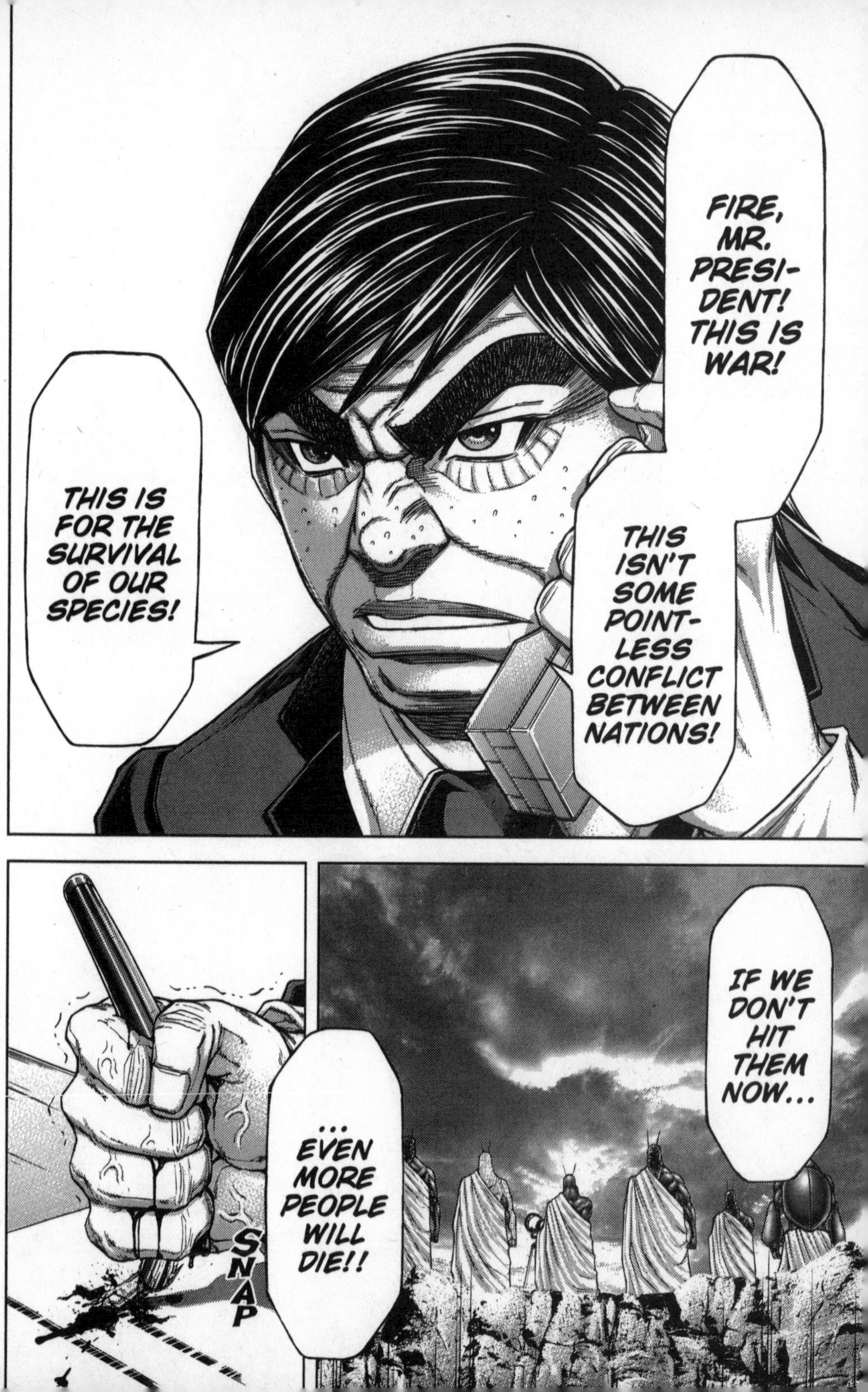
FIRE, MR. PRESIDENT! THIS IS WAR!
THIS ISN'T SOME POINTLESS CONFLICT BETWEEN NATIONS!
THIS IS FOR THE SURVIVAL OF OUR SPECIES!
IF WE DON'T HIT THEM NOW...
...EVEN MORE PEOPLE WILL DIE!!
SNAP

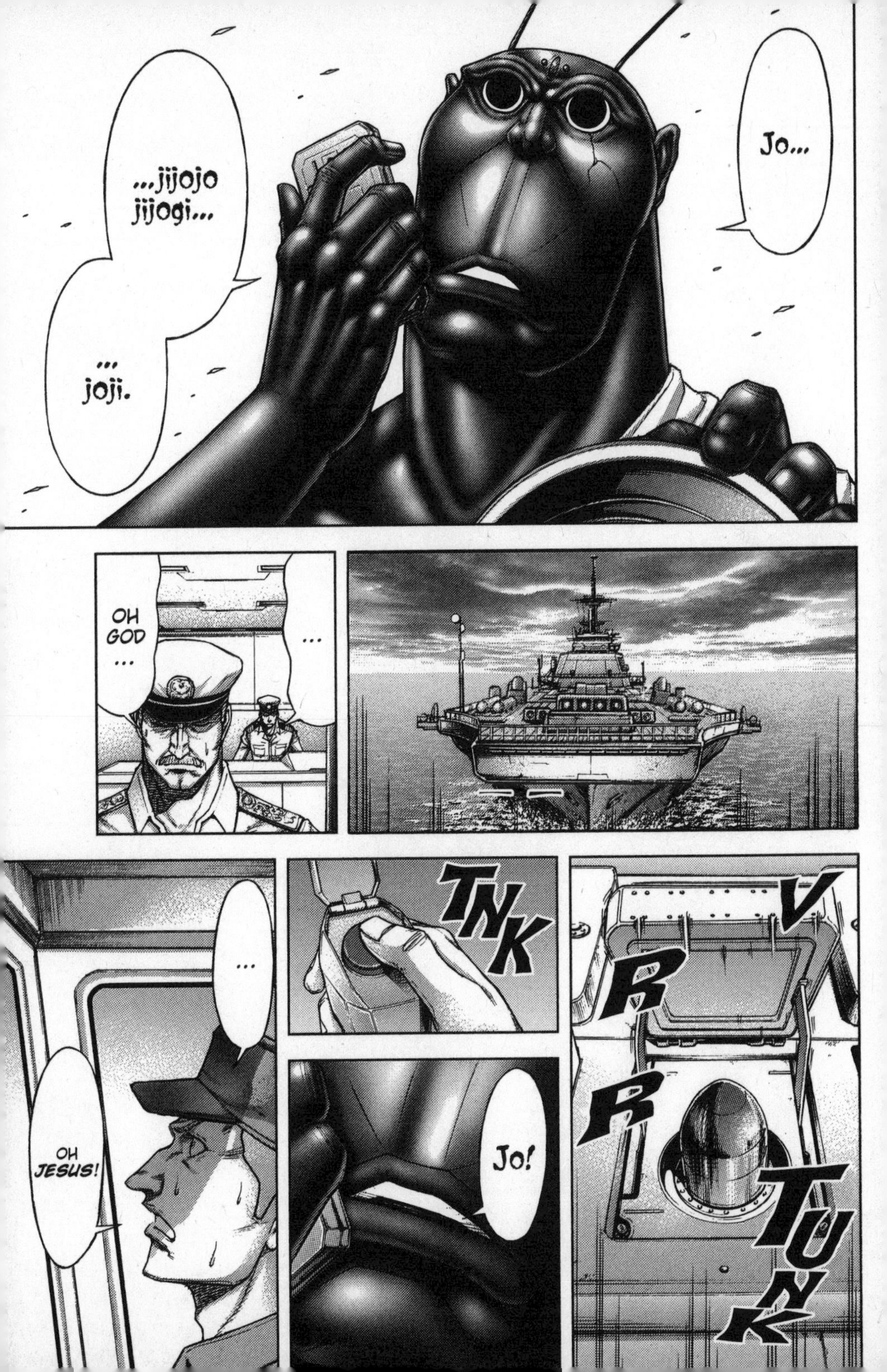
Jo...
...jijojo jijogi...
... joji.
...
OH GOD ...
VRRR
TUNK
TNK
Jo!
...
OH JESUS!

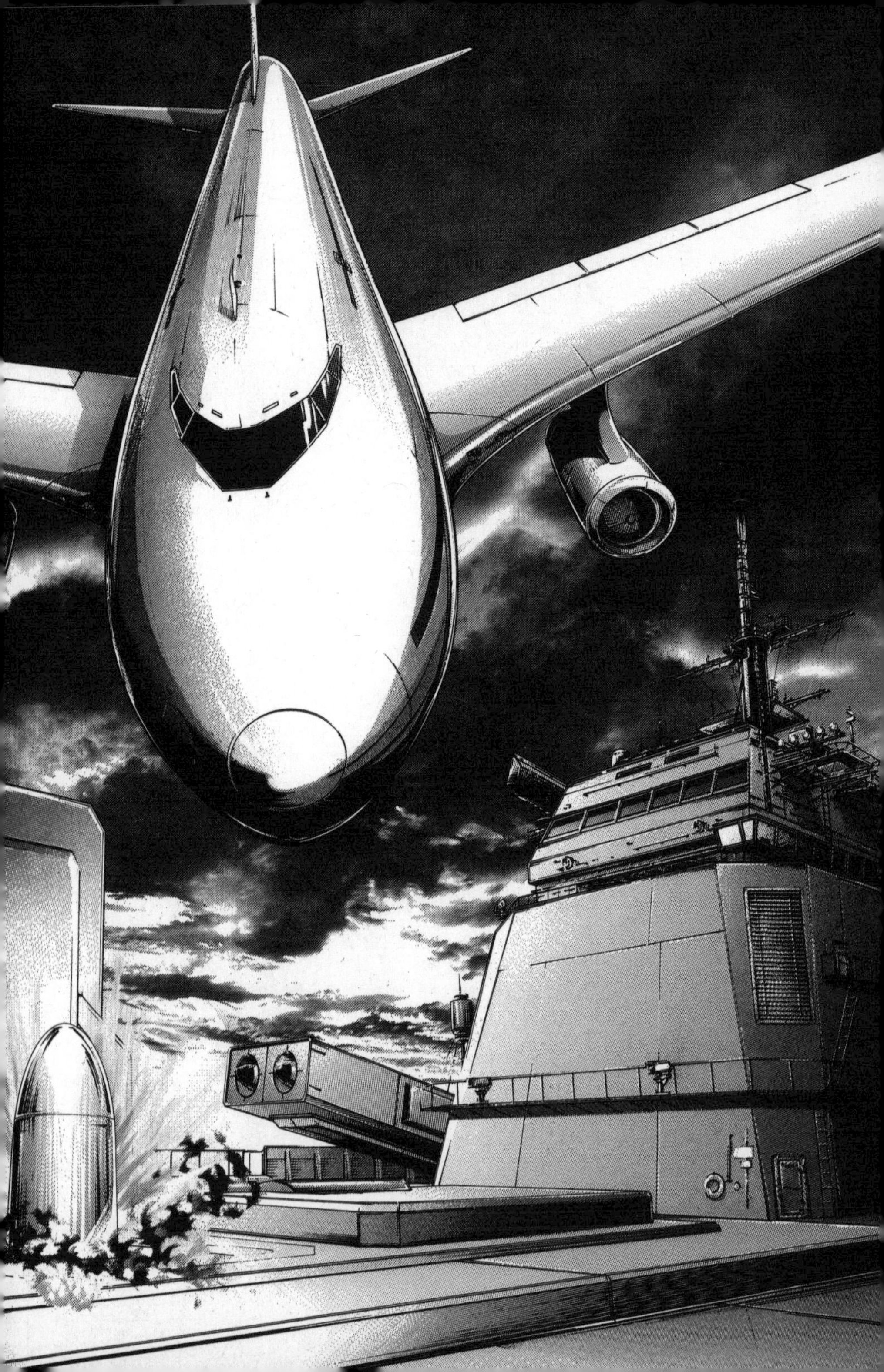

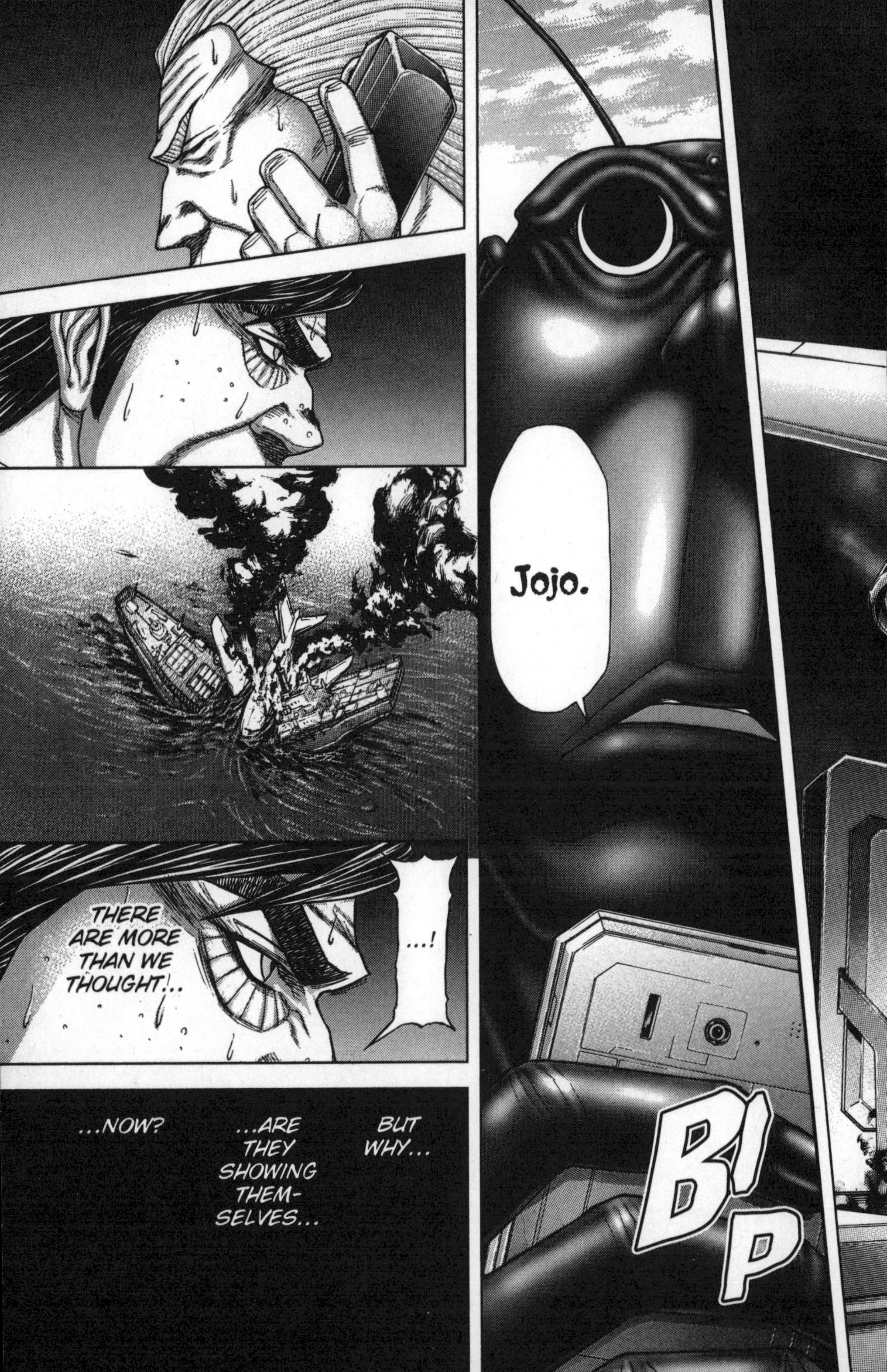
Jojo.
BIP
...!
THERE ARE MORE THAN WE THOUGHT!...
BUT WHY...
...ARE THEY SHOWING THEM-SELVES...
...NOW?

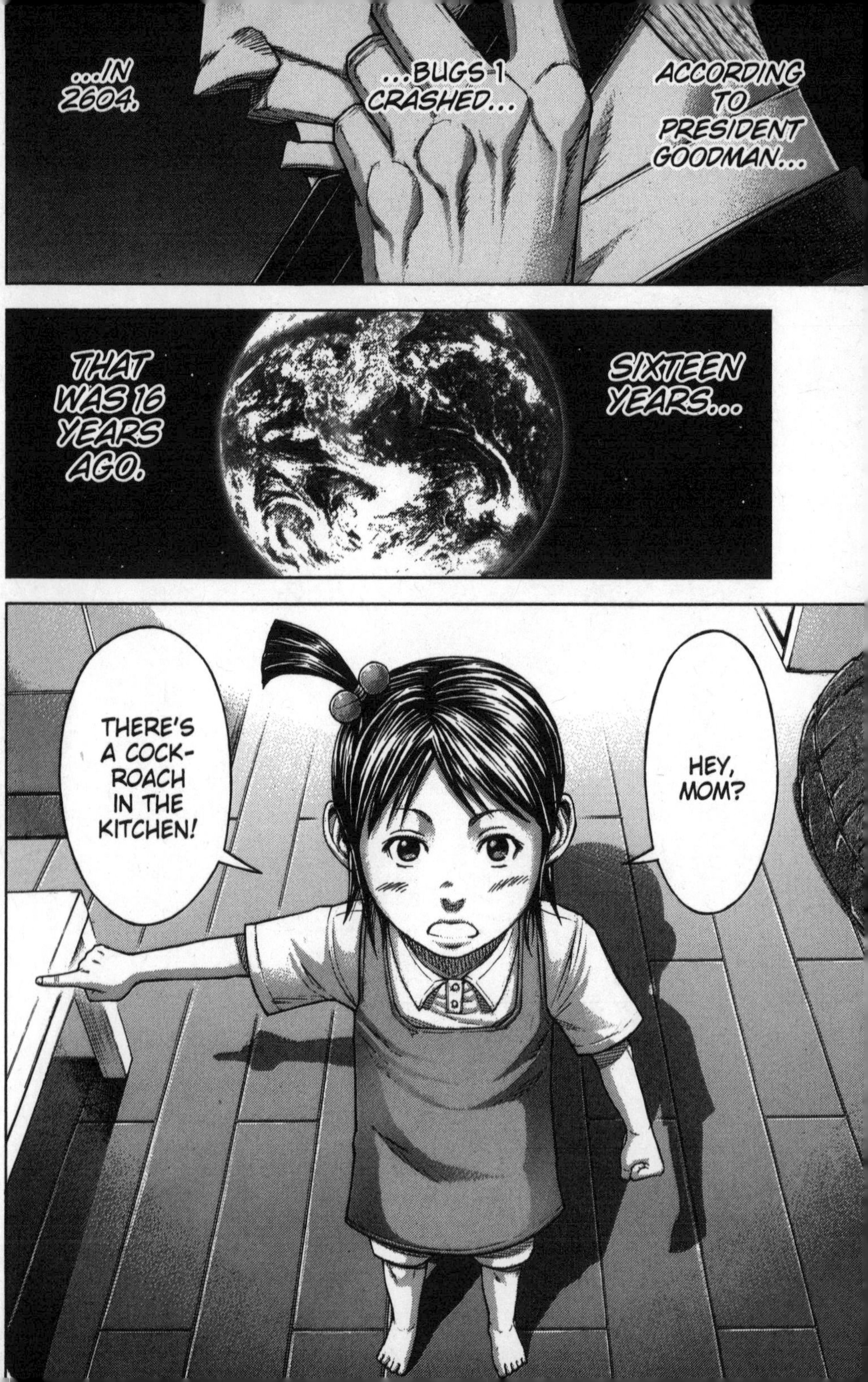
ACCORDING TO PRESIDENT GOODMAN...
...BUGS 1 CRASHED...
...IN 2604.
SIXTEEN YEARS...
THAT WAS 16 YEARS AGO.
HEY, MOM?
THERE'S A COCK-ROACH IN THE KITCHEN!

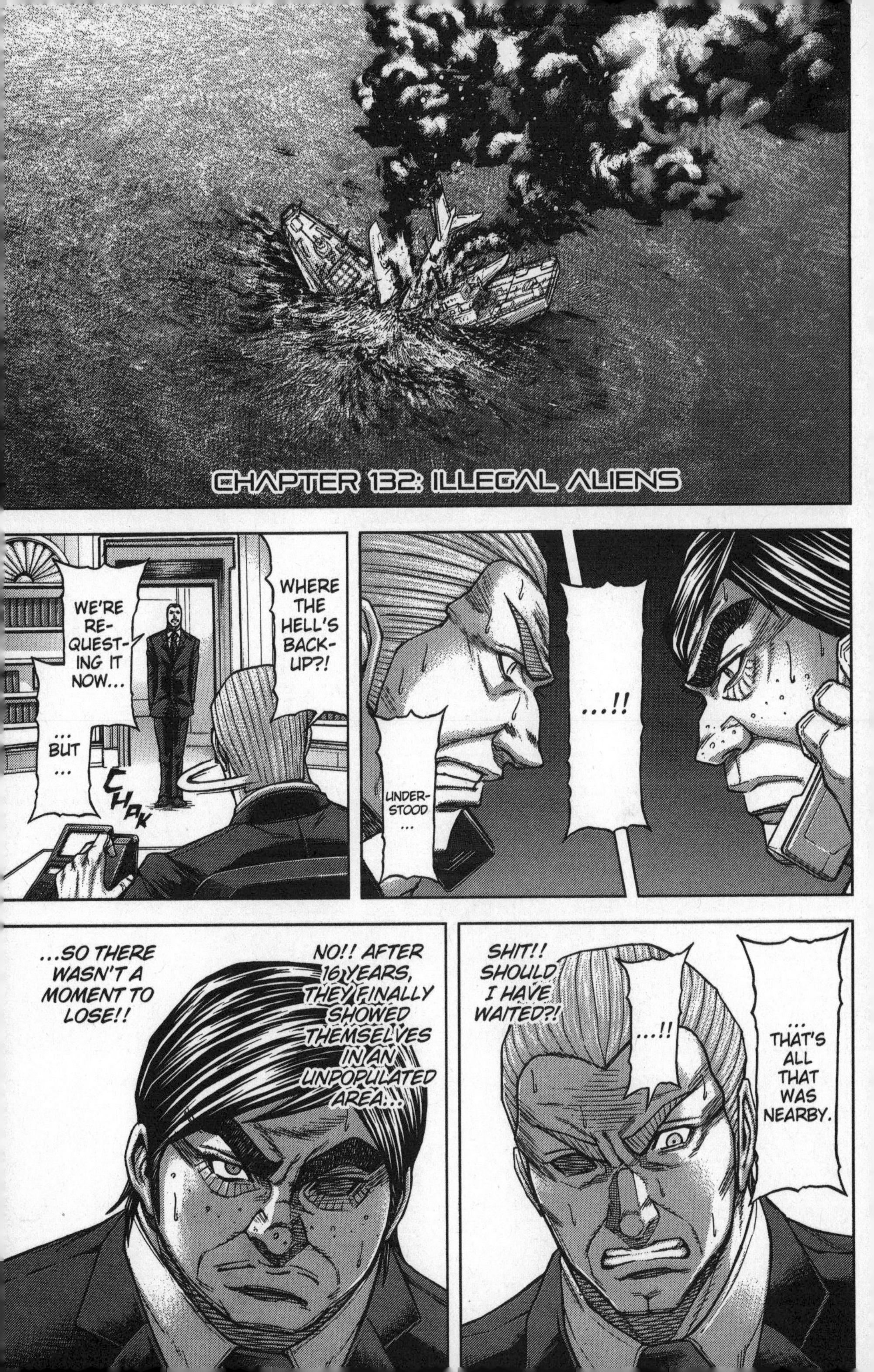
CHAPTER 132: ILLEGAL ALIENS
...!!
UNDERSTOOD...
WHERE THE HELL'S BACK-UP?!
WE'RE RE-QUEST-ING IT NOW...
...BUT...
CHAK
...THAT'S ALL THAT WAS NEARBY.
...!!
SHIT!! SHOULD I HAVE WAITED?!
NO!! AFTER 16 YEARS, THEY FINALLY SHOWED THEMSELVES IN AN UNPOPULATED AREA...
...SO THERE WASN'T A MOMENT TO LOSE!!

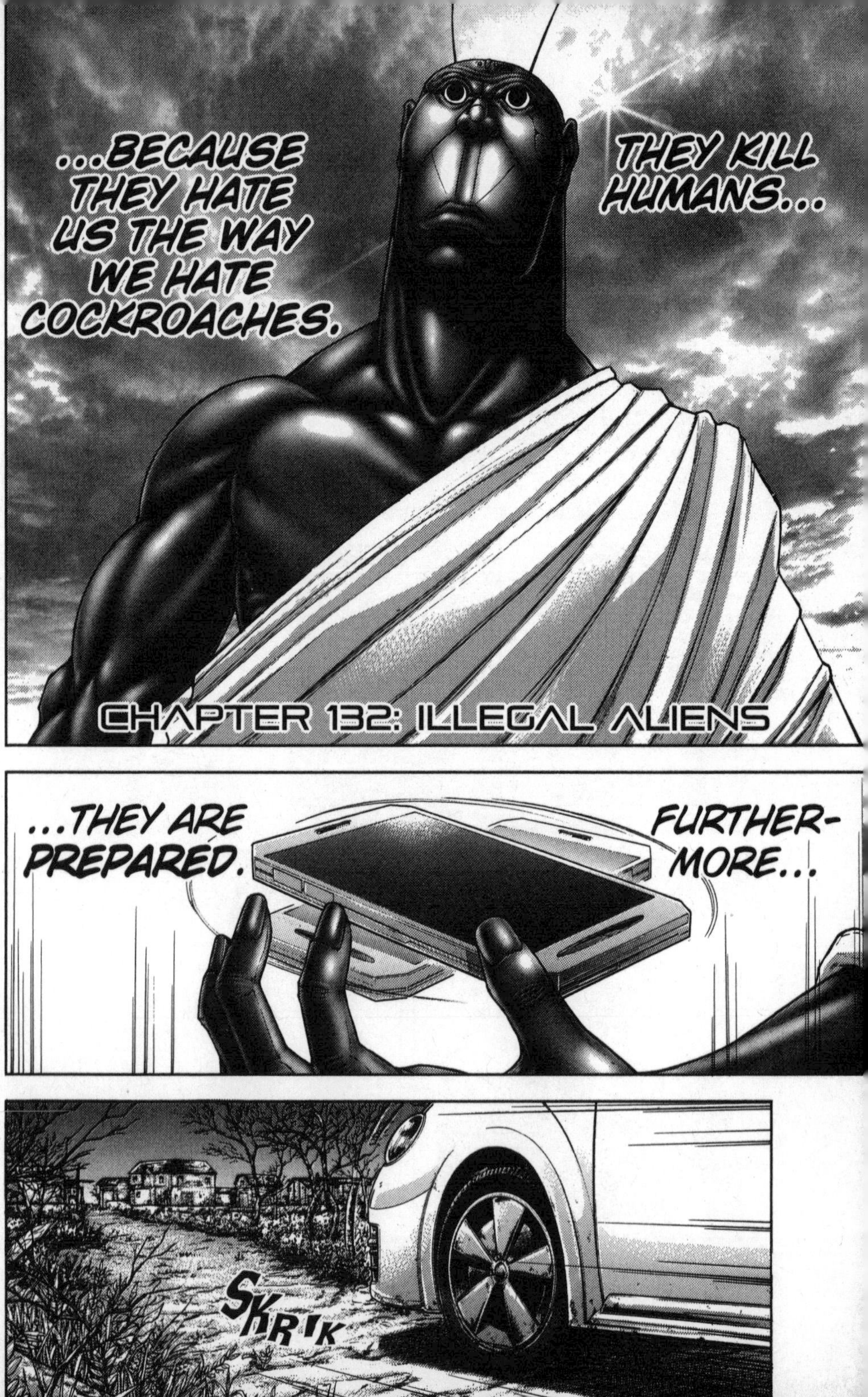
THEY KILL HUMANS...
...BECAUSE THEY HATE US THE WAY WE HATE COCKROACHES.
CHAPTER 132: ILLEGAL ALIENS
FURTHER-MORE...
...THEY ARE PREPARED.
SKRIK

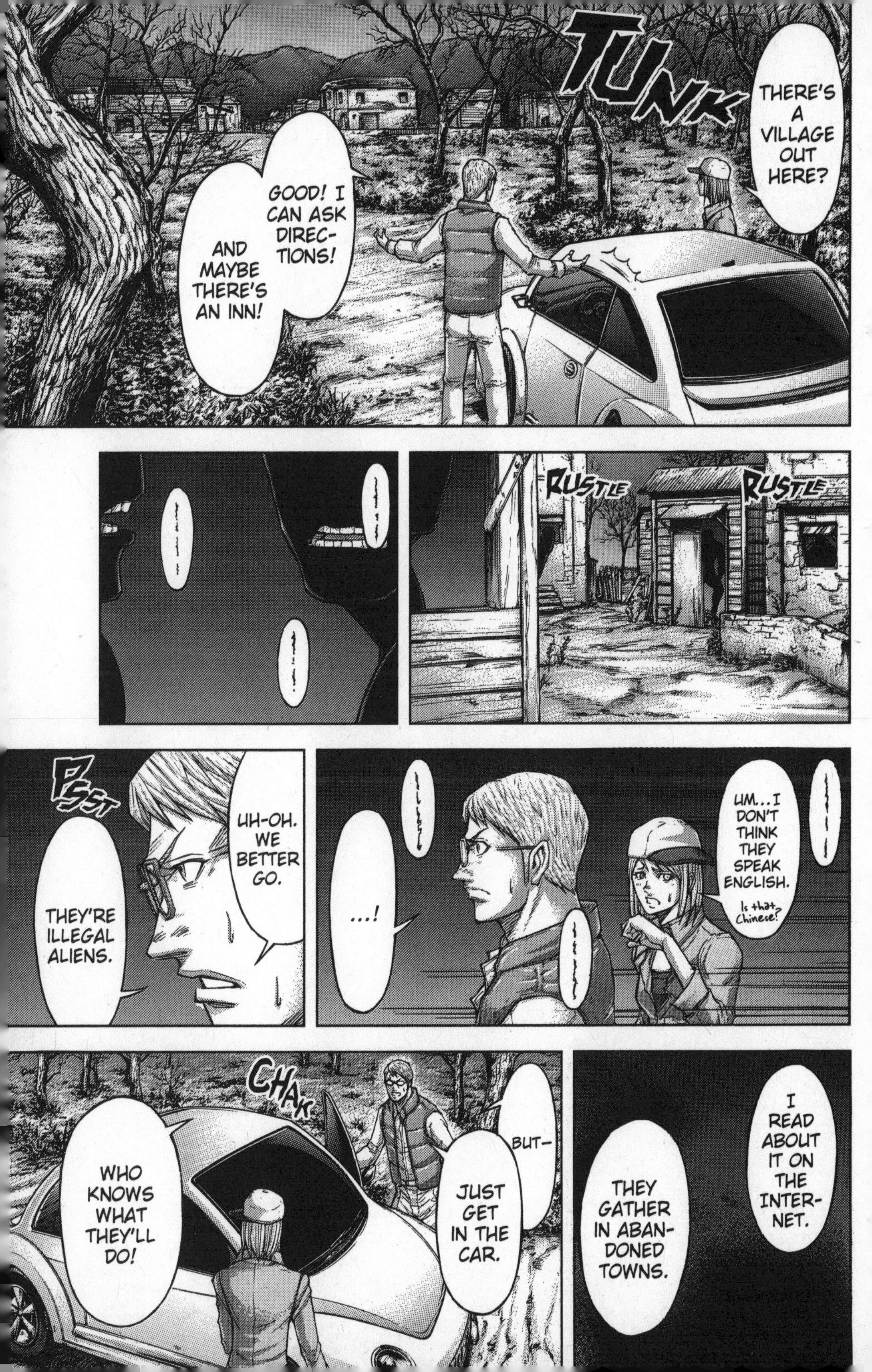
TUNK
THERE'S A VILLAGE OUT HERE?
GOOD! I CAN ASK DIRECTIONS!
AND MAYBE THERE'S AN INN!
RUSTLE
RUSTLE
UM... I DON'T THINK THEY SPEAK ENGLISH.
Is that Chinese?
...!
PSST
UH-OH. WE BETTER GO.
THEY'RE ILLEGAL ALIENS.
I READ ABOUT IT ON THE INTERNET.
THEY GATHER IN ABANDONED TOWNS.
BUT—
JUST GET IN THE CAR.
CHAK
WHO KNOWS WHAT THEY'LL DO!

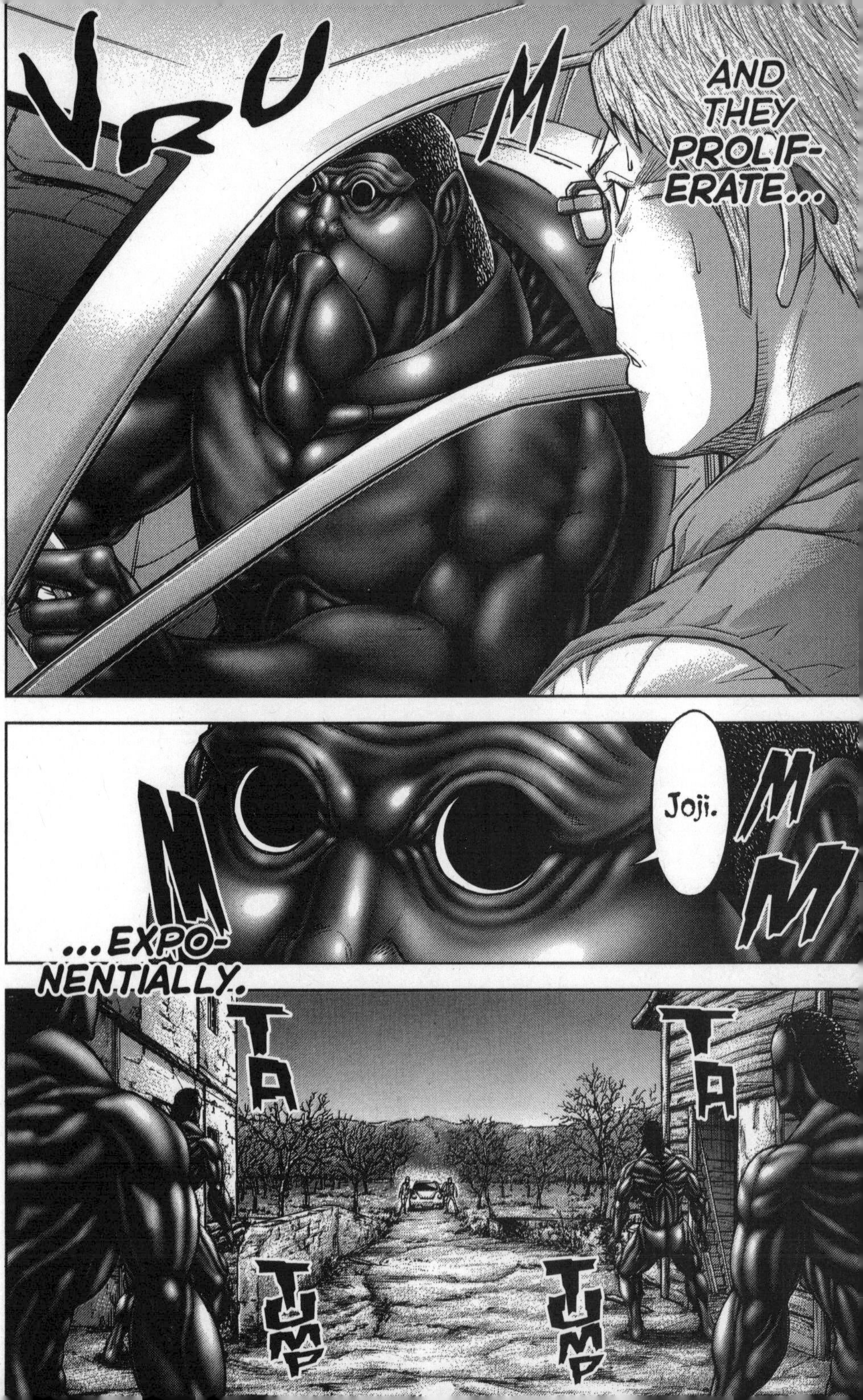
AND THEY PROLIF-ERATE...
VRUM
Joji.
...EXPO-NENTIALLY.
TA
TA
TUMP
TUMP

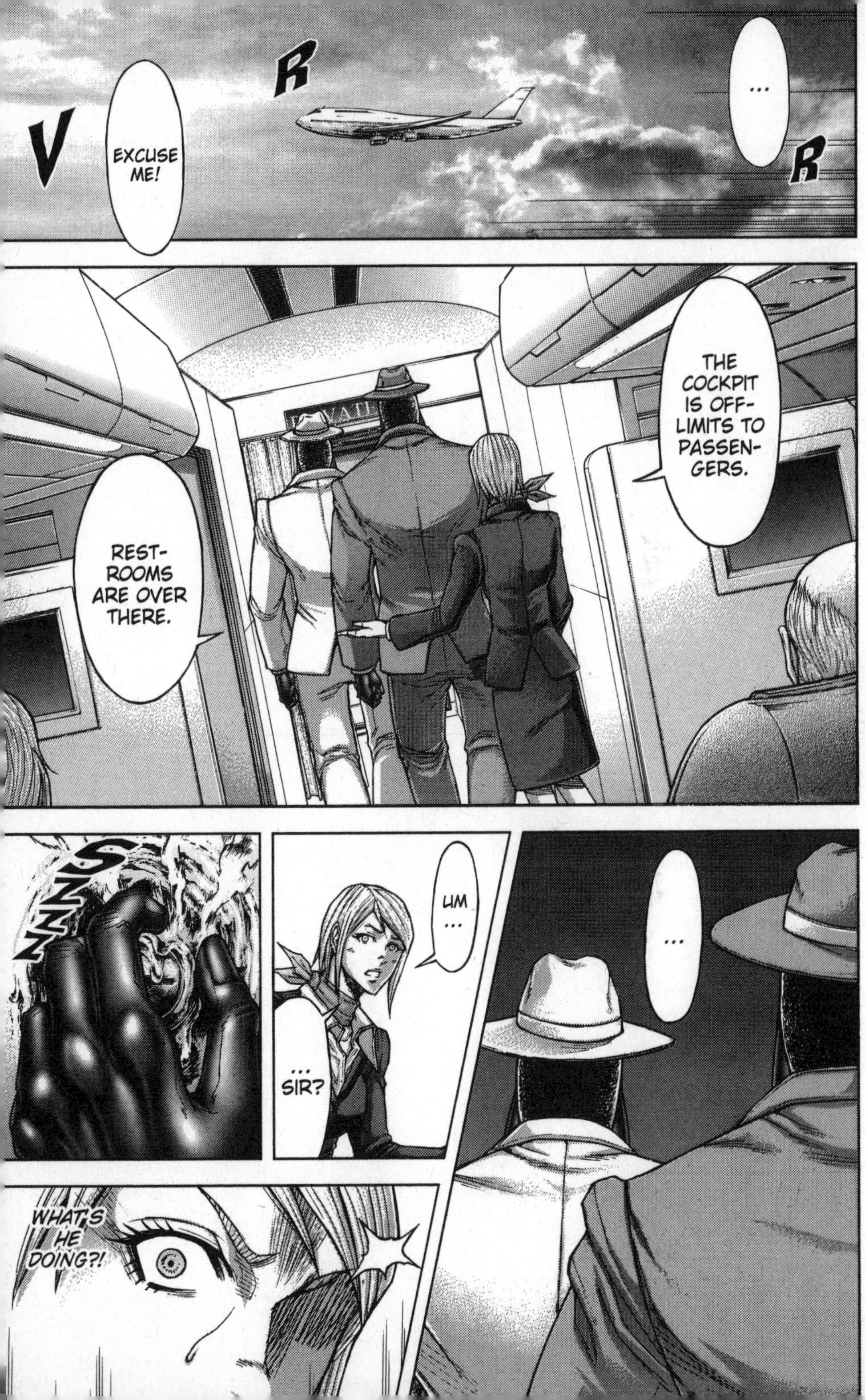
...
R
EXCUSE ME!
R
V
THE COCKPIT IS OFF-LIMITS TO PASSENGERS.
RESTROOMS ARE OVER THERE.
...
UM ...
... SIR?
SNNNN
WHAT'S HE DOING?!

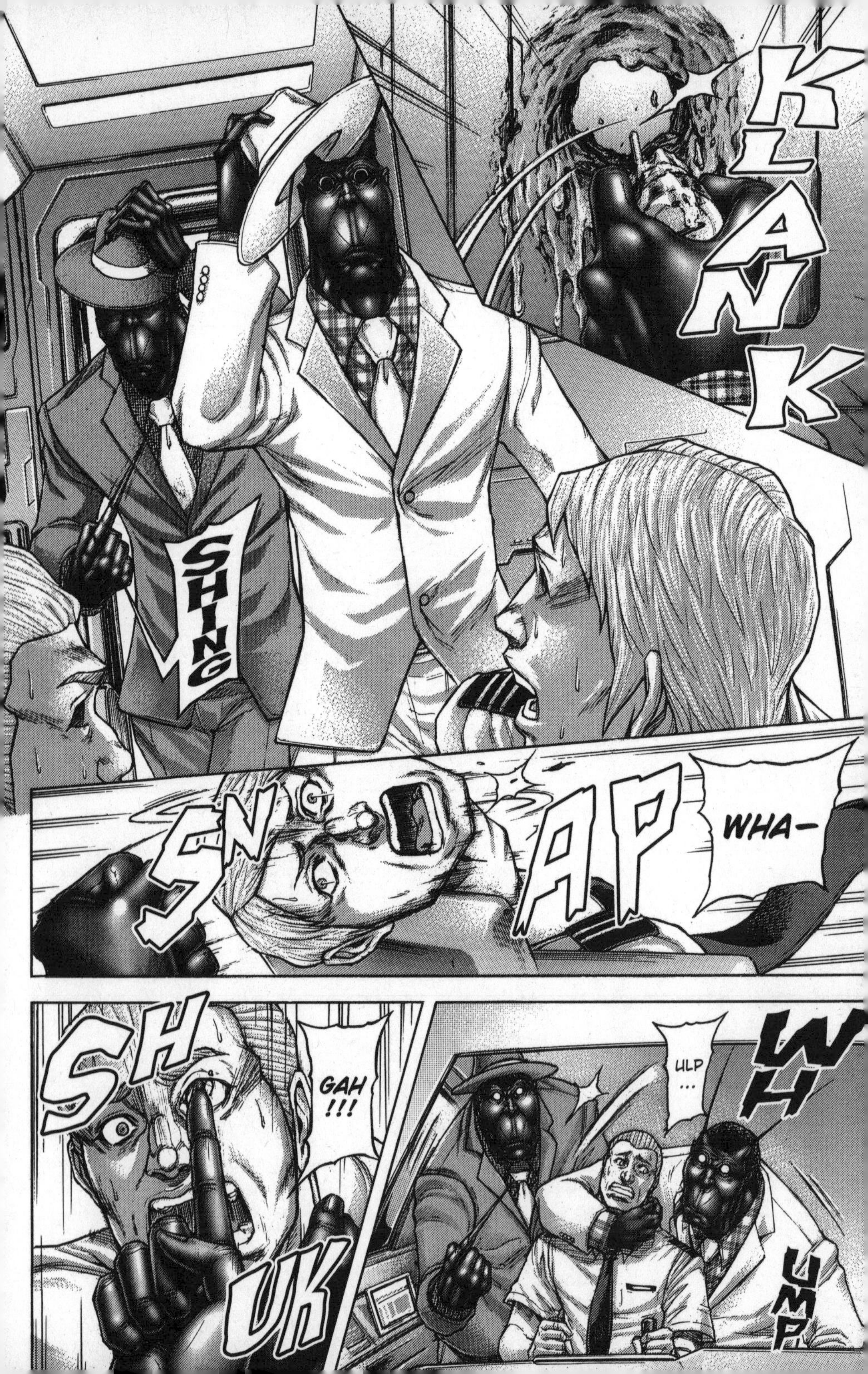
KLANK
SHING
WHA-
SNAP
WHUMP
ULP ...
GAH !!!
SHUK

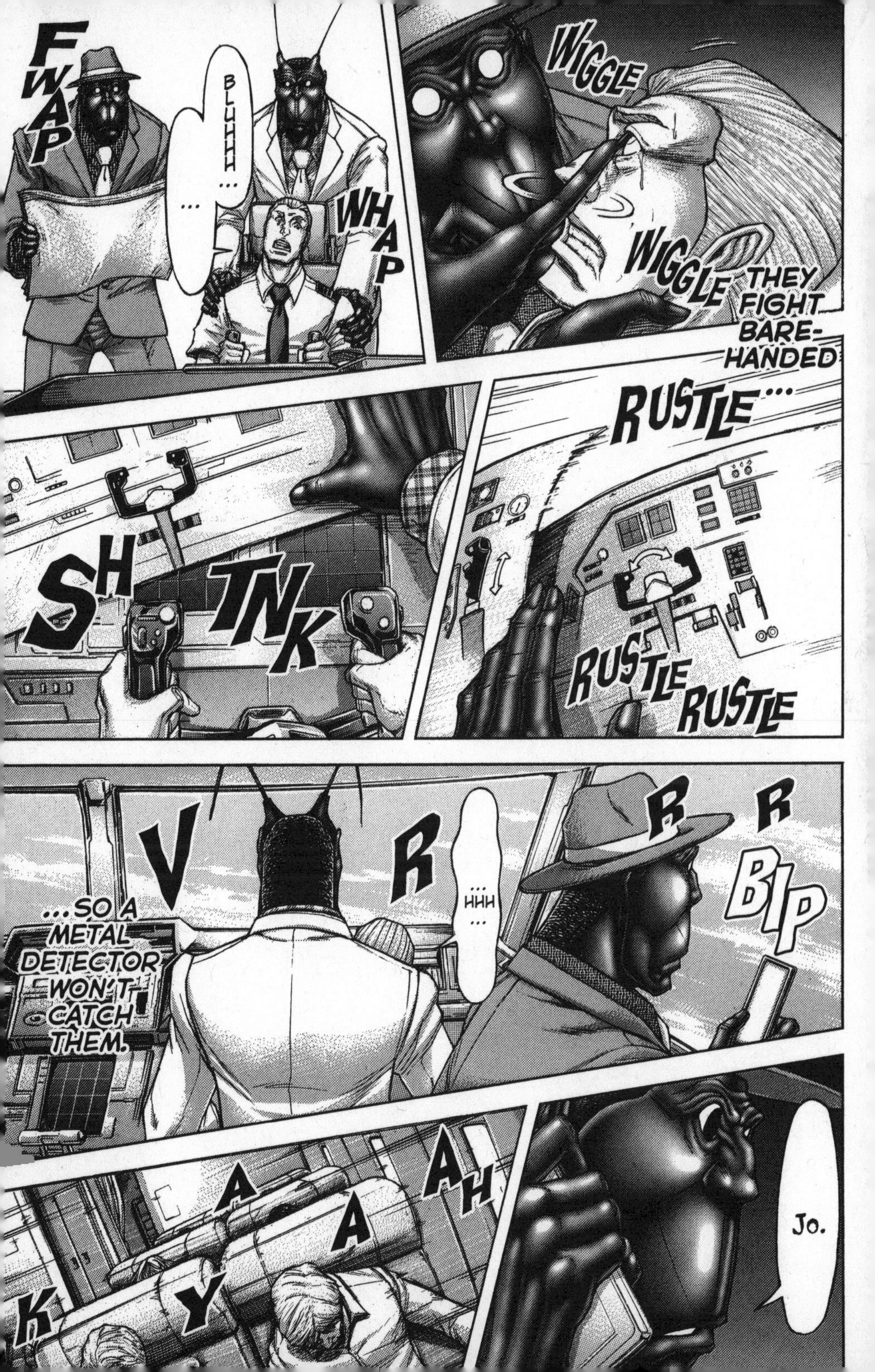
WIGGLE
WIGGLE
THEY FIGHT BARE-HANDED
FWAP
BLUHHH... ...
WHAP
RUSTLE...
RUSTLE RUSTLE
SH
TNK
RR
BIP
...HHH...
VR
...SO A METAL DETECTOR WON'T CATCH THEM.
Jo.
KYAAAH

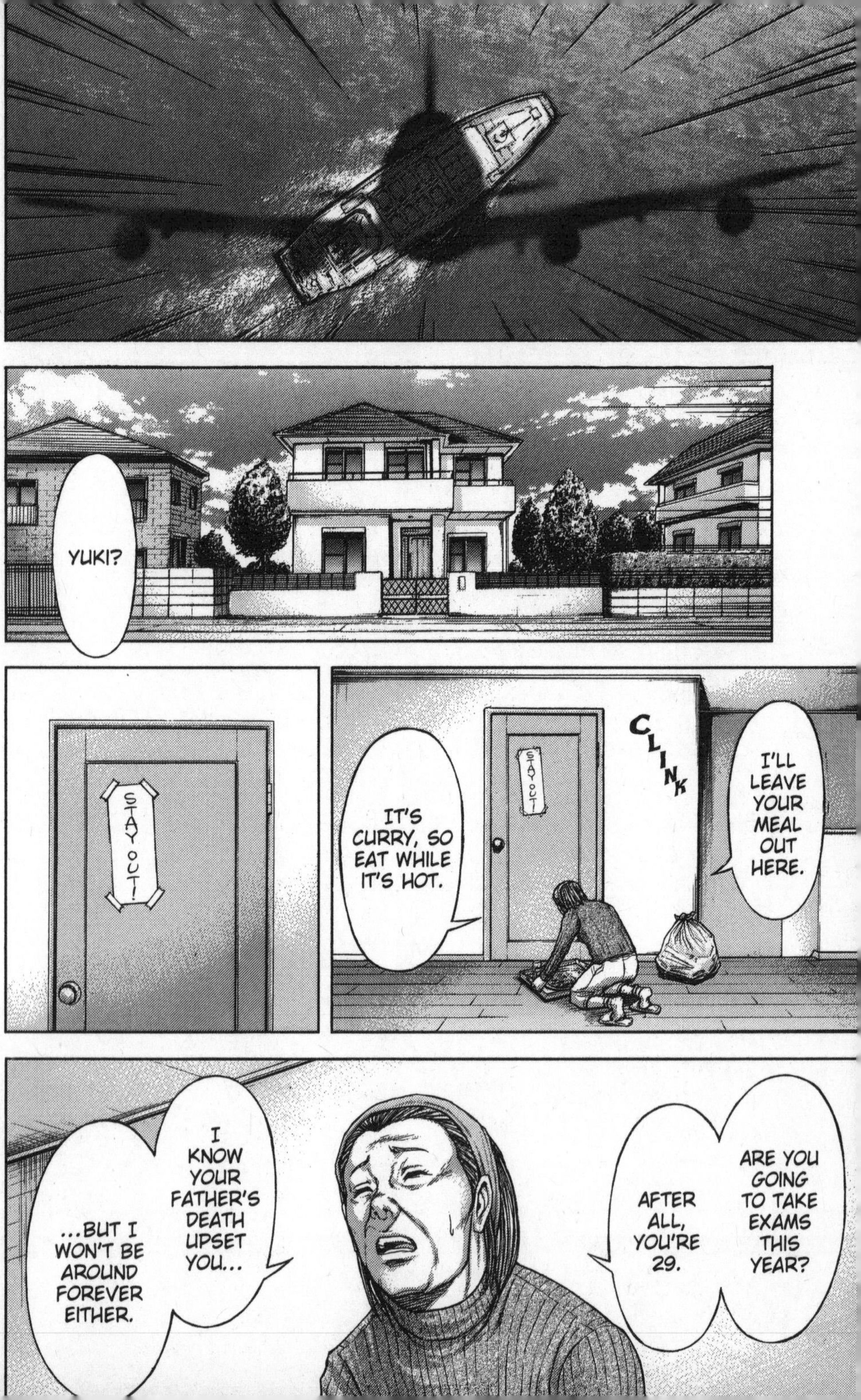
YUKI?
I'LL LEAVE YOUR MEAL OUT HERE.
CLINK
STAY OUT!
IT'S CURRY, SO EAT WHILE IT'S HOT.
STAY OUT!
ARE YOU GOING TO TAKE EXAMS THIS YEAR?
AFTER ALL, YOU'RE 29.
I KNOW YOUR FATHER'S DEATH UPSET YOU...
...BUT I WON'T BE AROUND FOREVER EITHER.

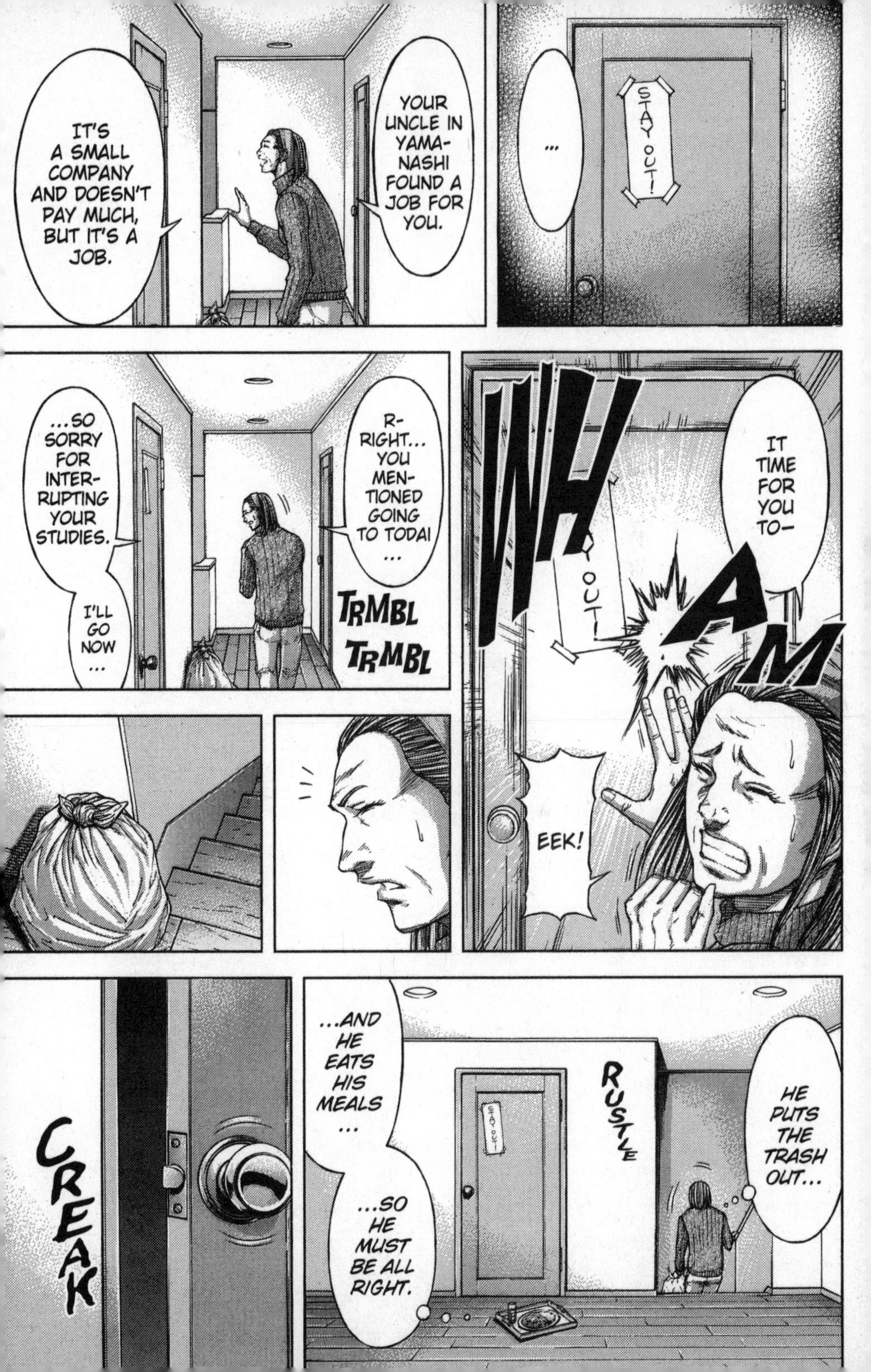

...
STAY OUT!
YOUR UNCLE IN YAMANASHI FOUND A JOB FOR YOU.
IT'S A SMALL COMPANY AND DOESN'T PAY MUCH, BUT IT'S A JOB.
IT TIME FOR YOU TO—
WHAM
OUT!
EEK!
R-RIGHT... YOU MENTIONED GOING TO TODAI...
TRMBL TRMBL
...SO SORRY FOR INTERRUPTING YOUR STUDIES.
I'LL GO NOW...
HE PUTS THE TRASH OUT...
RUSTLE
STAY OUT
...AND HE EATS HIS MEALS...
...SO HE MUST BE ALL RIGHT.
CREAK

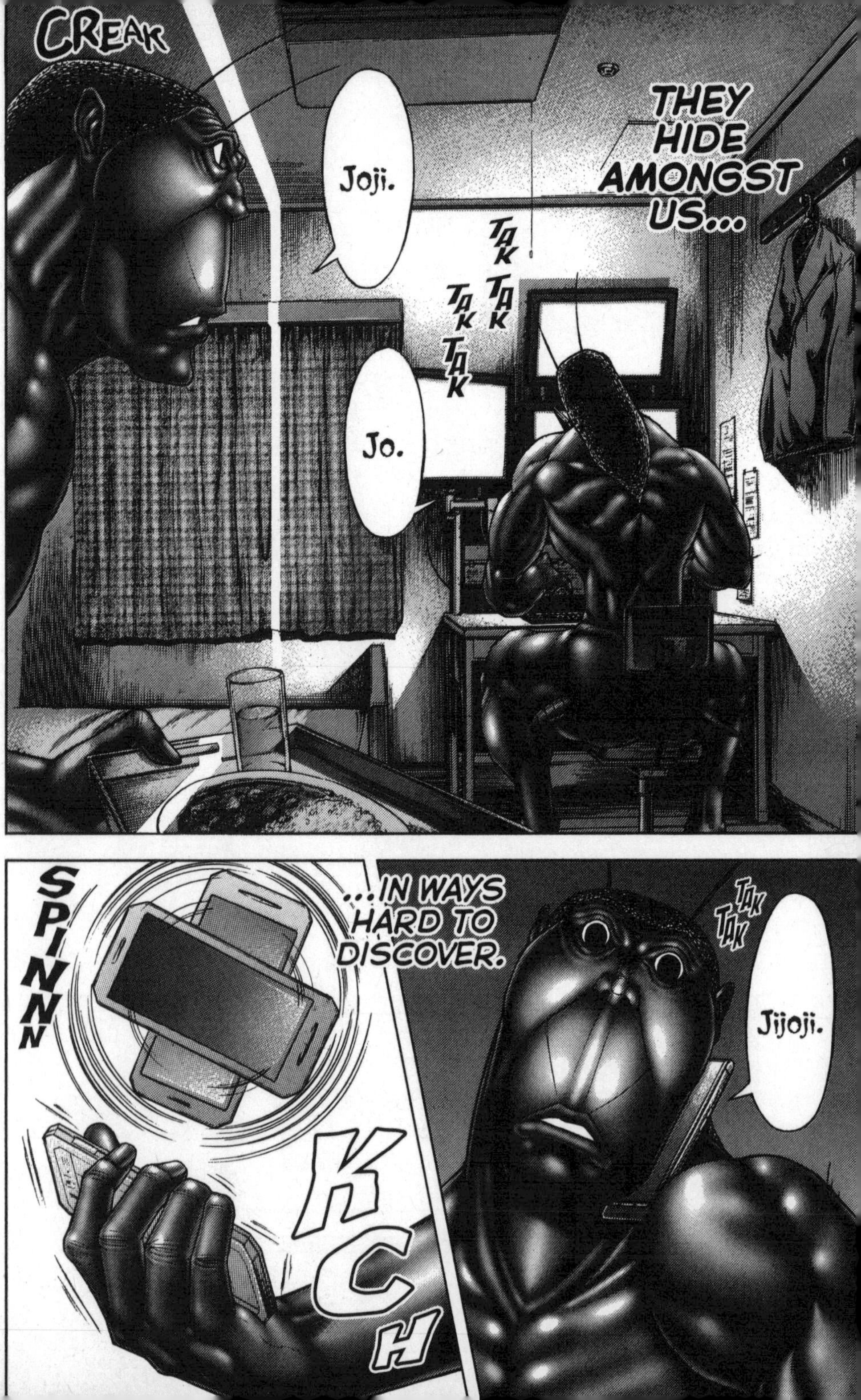
THEY HIDE AMONGST US...
TAK TAK
TAK TAK
Joji.
CREAK
Jo.
TAK TAK
Jijoji.
...IN WAYS HARD TO DISCOVER.
SPINNN
KCH

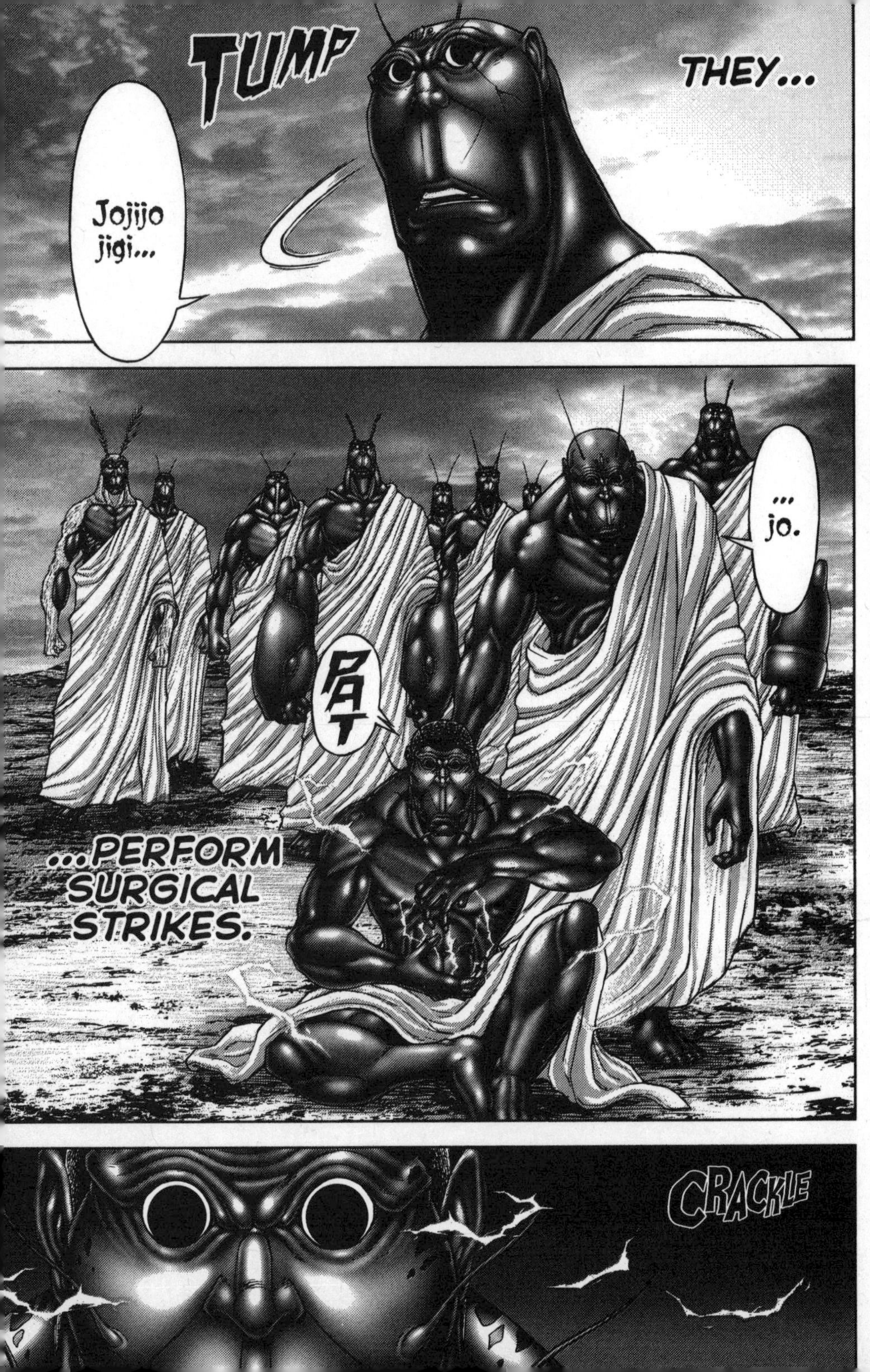
THEY...
TUMP
Jojijo jigi...
...jo.
PAT
...PERFORM SURGICAL STRIKES.
CRACKLE

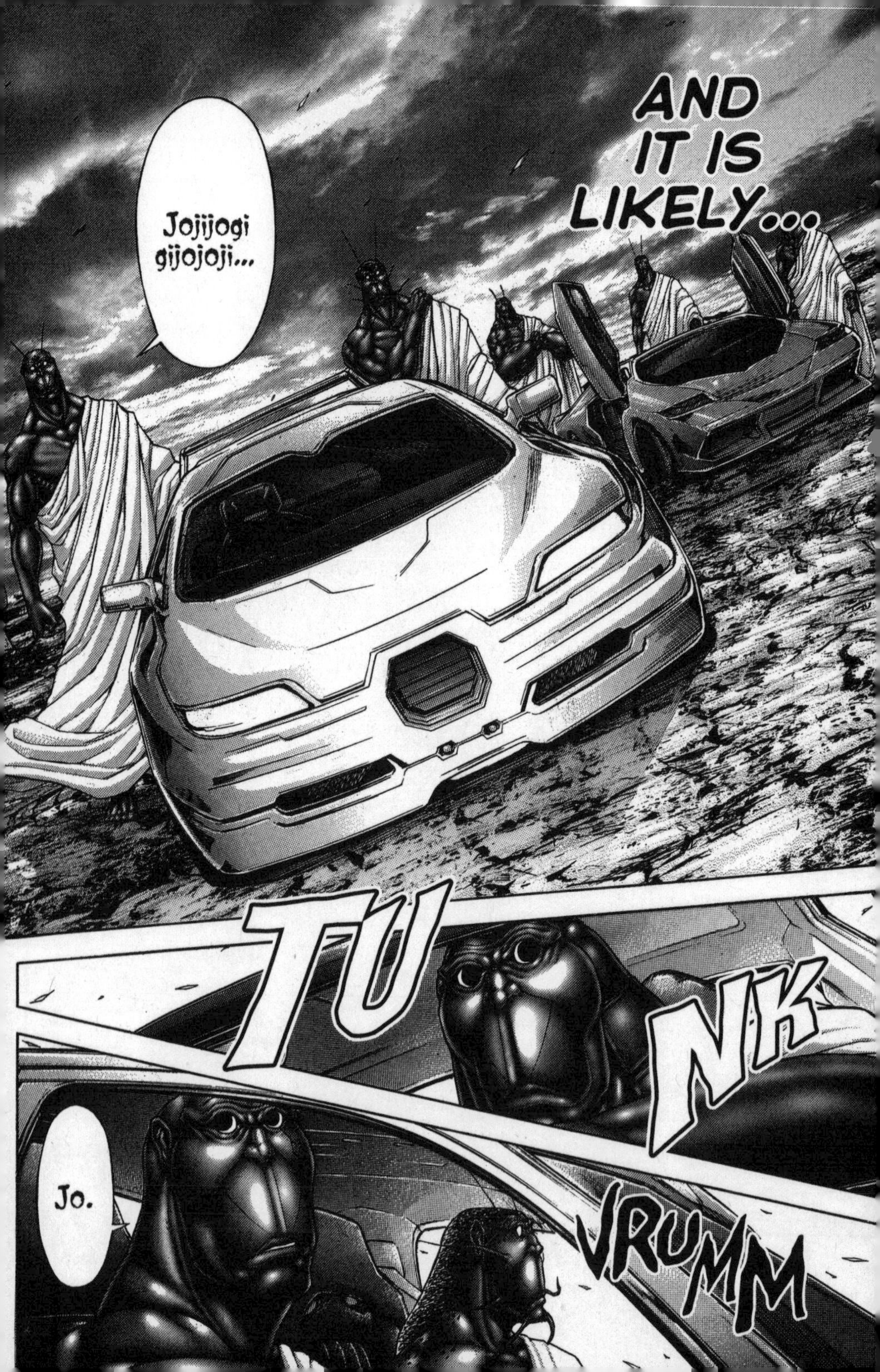
AND IT IS LIKELY...
Jojijogi gijojoji...
TUNK
Jo.
VRUMM

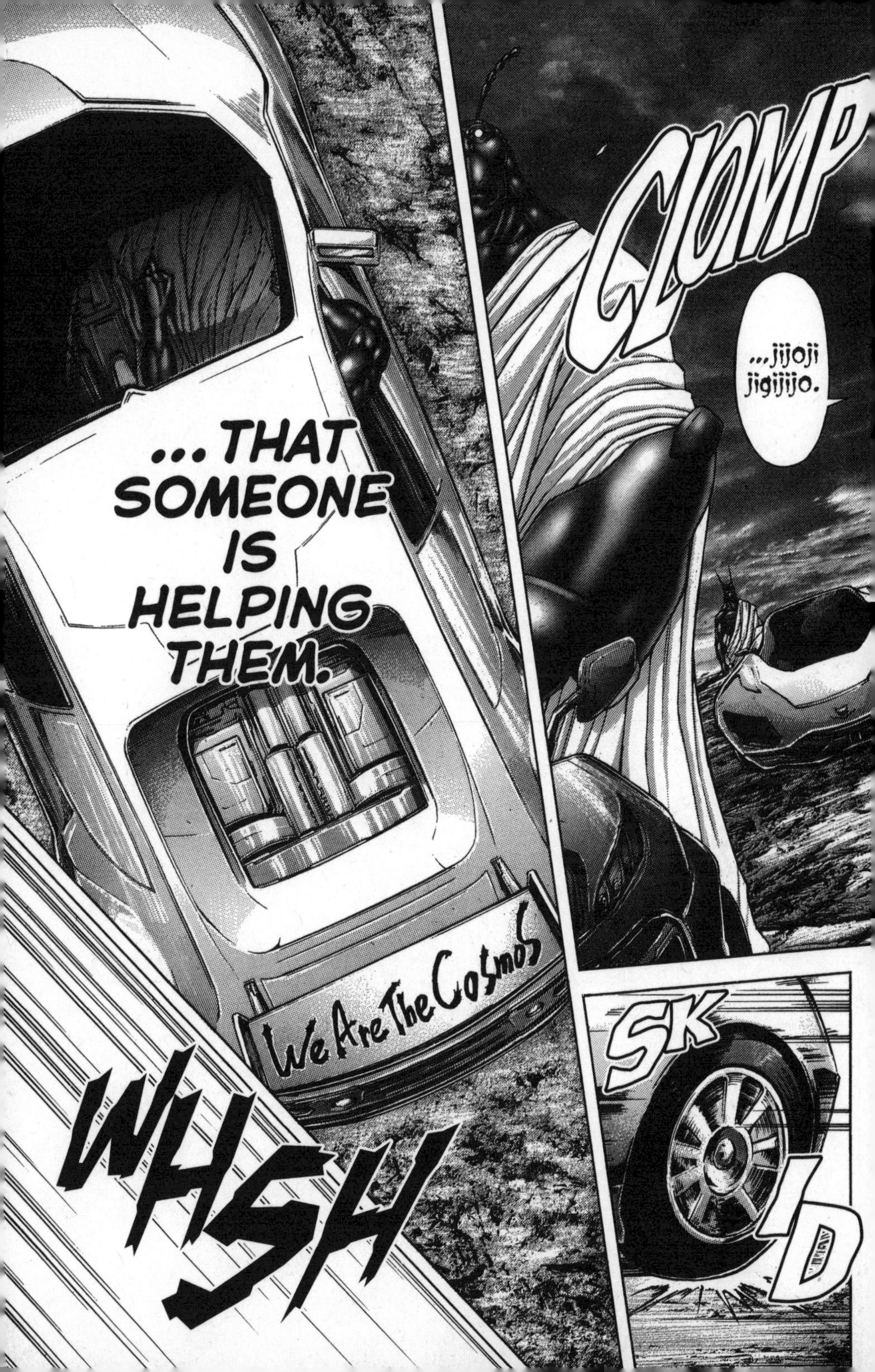
CLOMP
...jijoji jigijijo.
SKLD
...THAT SOMEONE IS HELPING THEM.
We Are The Cosmos
WHSH

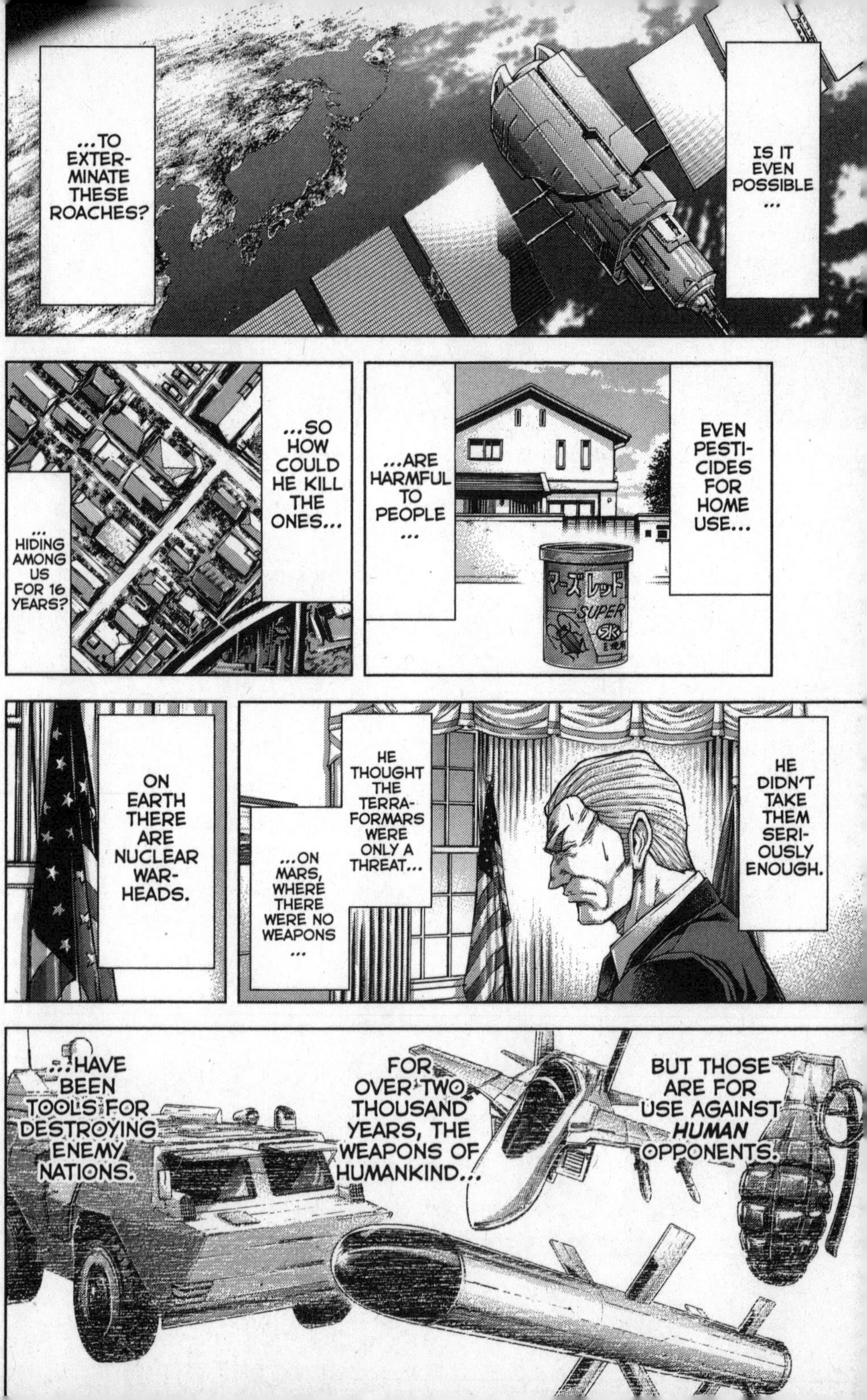
IS IT EVEN POSSIBLE...
...TO EXTERMINATE THESE ROACHES?
EVEN PESTICIDES FOR HOME USE...
...ARE HARMFUL TO PEOPLE...
マーズレッド
SUPER
...SO HOW COULD HE KILL THE ONES...
...HIDING AMONG US FOR 16 YEARS?
HE DIDN'T TAKE THEM SERIOUSLY ENOUGH.
HE THOUGHT THE TERRAFORMARS WERE ONLY A THREAT...
...ON MARS, WHERE THERE WERE NO WEAPONS...
ON EARTH THERE ARE NUCLEAR WARHEADS.
BUT THOSE ARE FOR USE AGAINST *HUMAN* OPPONENTS.
FOR OVER TWO THOUSAND YEARS, THE WEAPONS OF HUMANKIND...
...HAVE BEEN TOOLS FOR DESTROYING ENEMY NATIONS.

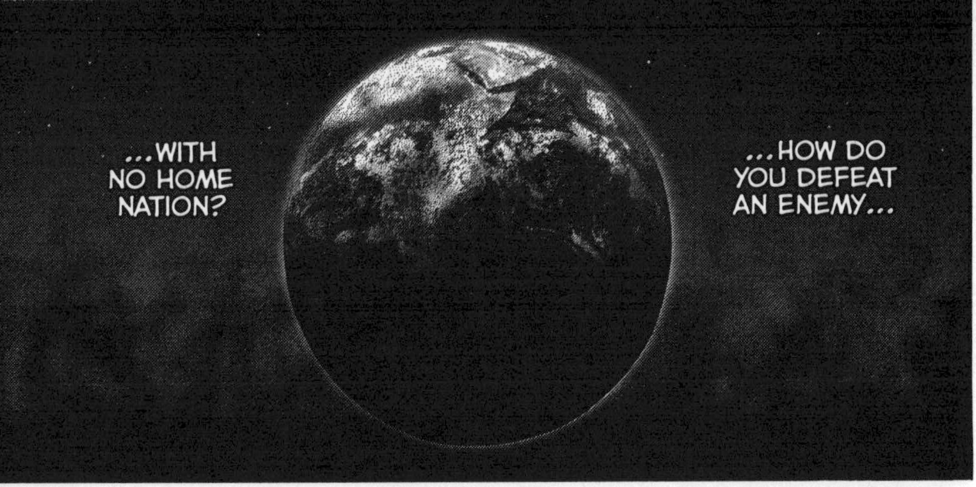
...HOW DO YOU DEFEAT AN ENEMY...
...WITH NO HOME NATION?

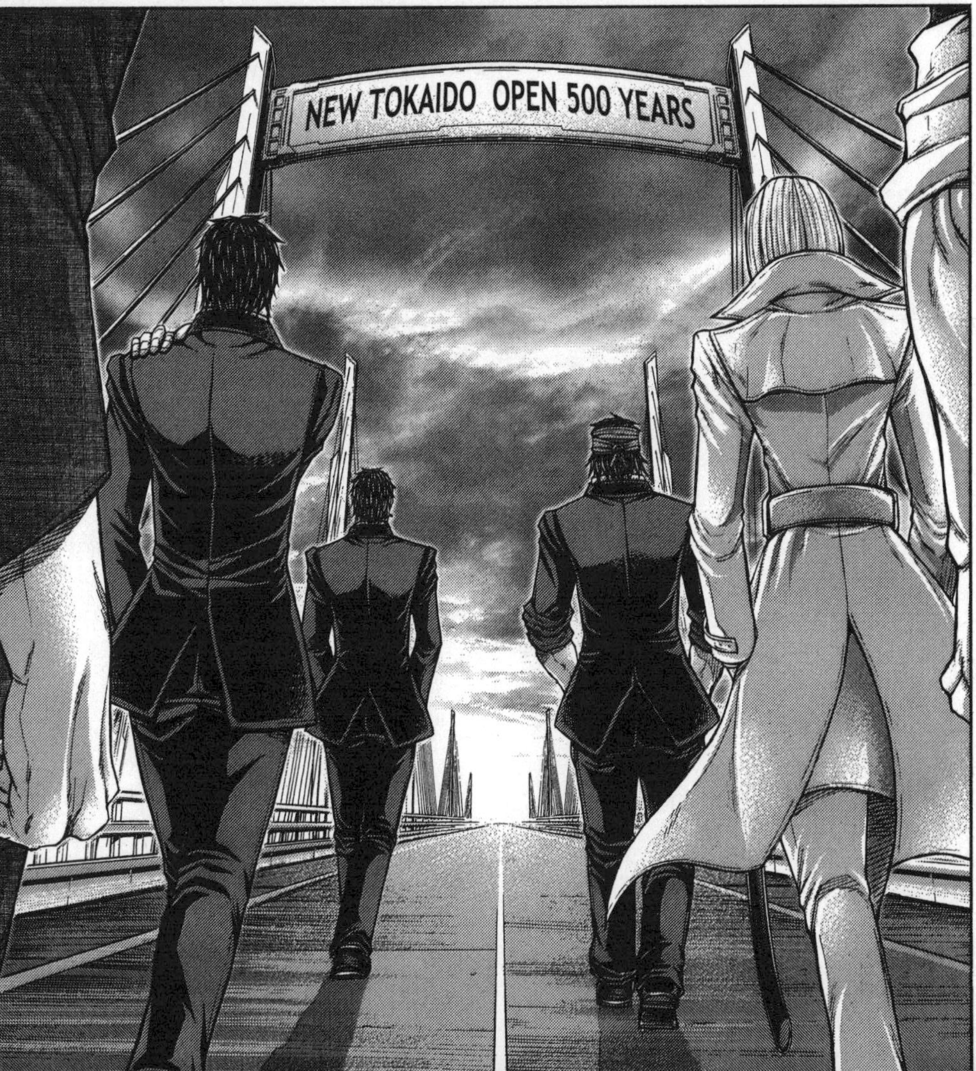
NEW TOKAIDO OPEN 500 YEARS

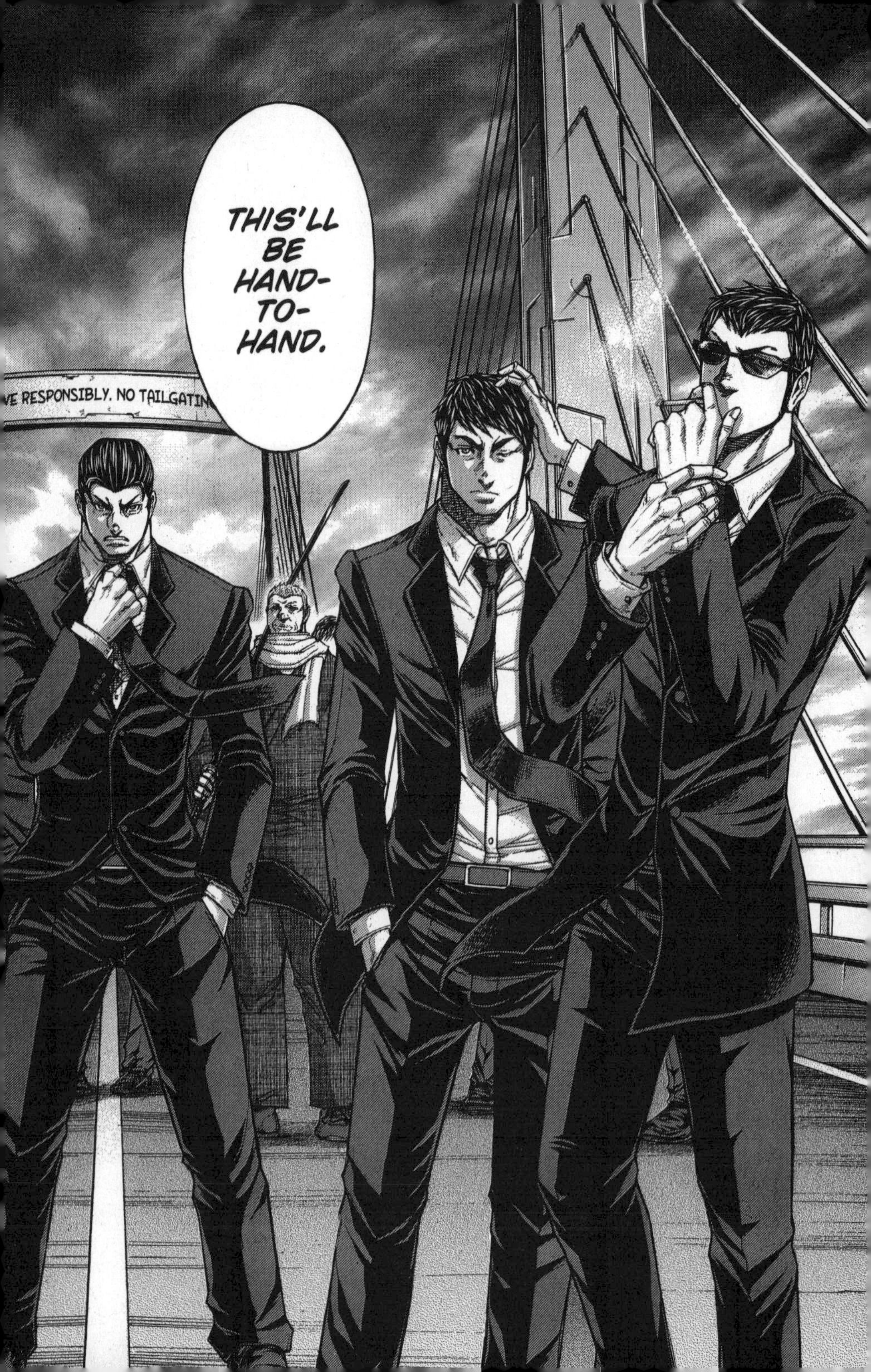
THIS'LL BE HAND-TO-HAND.
VE RESPONSIBLY. NO TAILGATIN

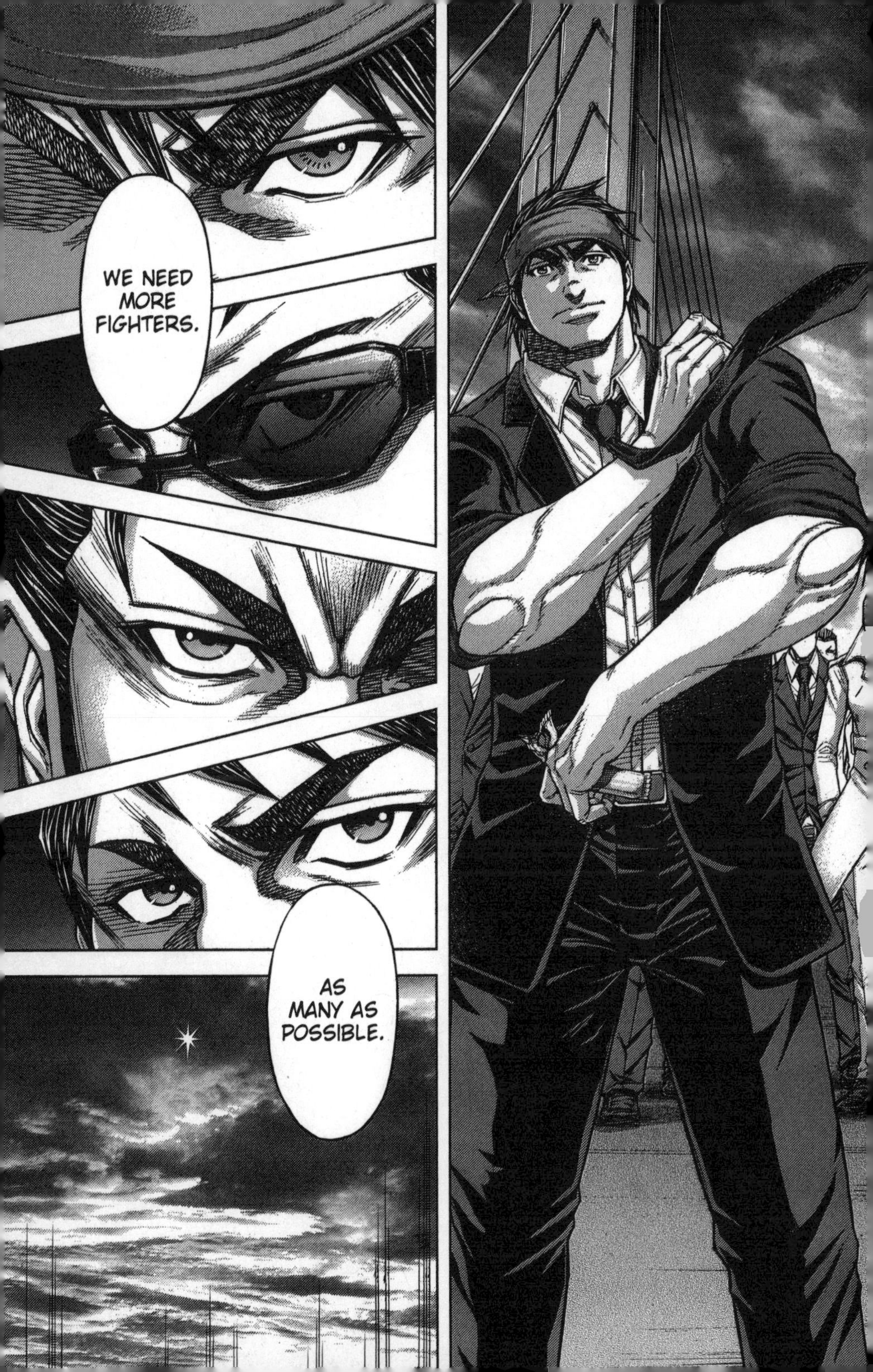
WE NEED MORE FIGHTERS.
AS MANY AS POSSIBLE.

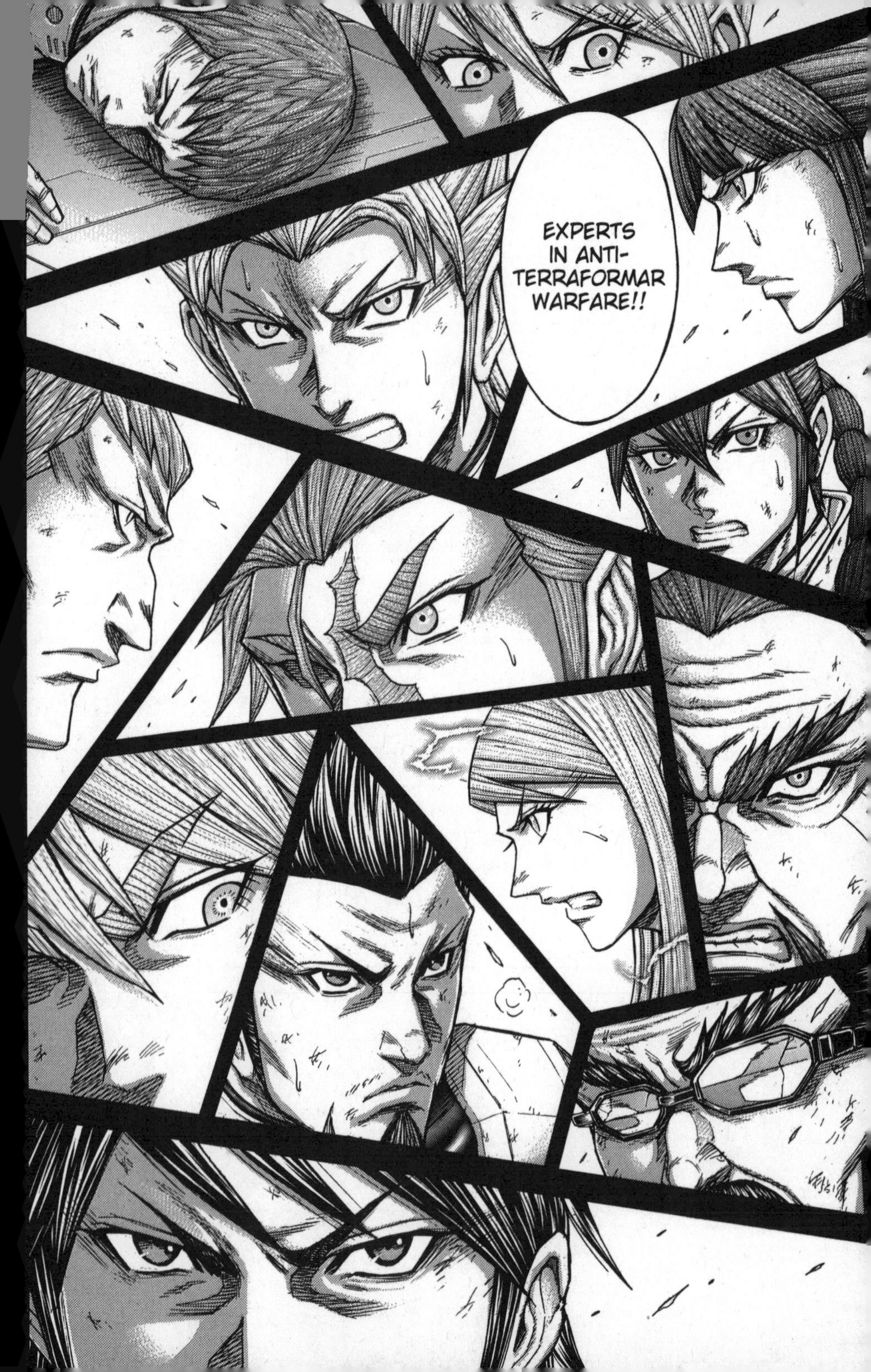
EXPERTS IN ANTI-TERRAFORMAR WARFARE!!

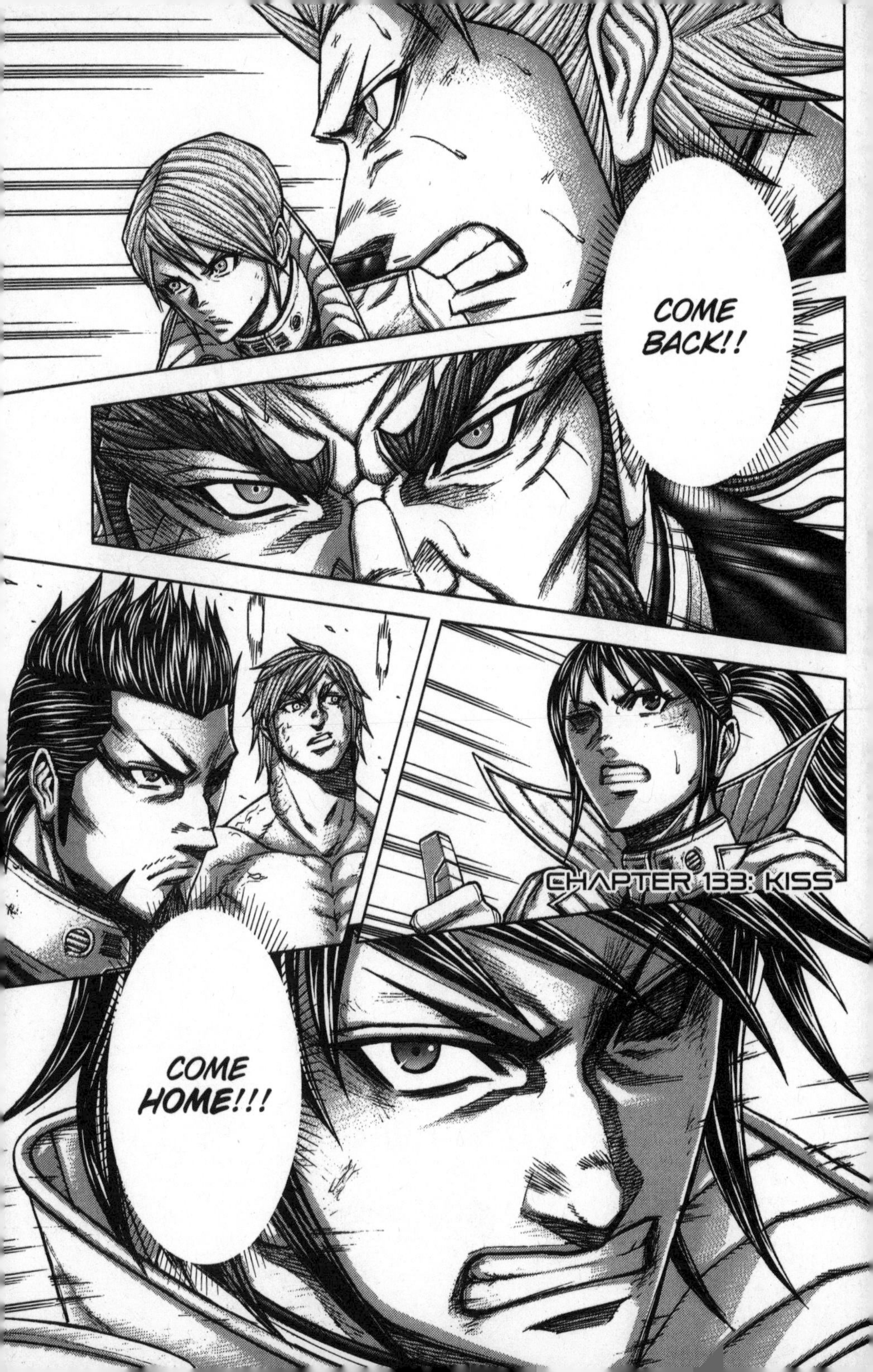
COME BACK!!
CHAPTER 133: KISS
COME HOME!!!

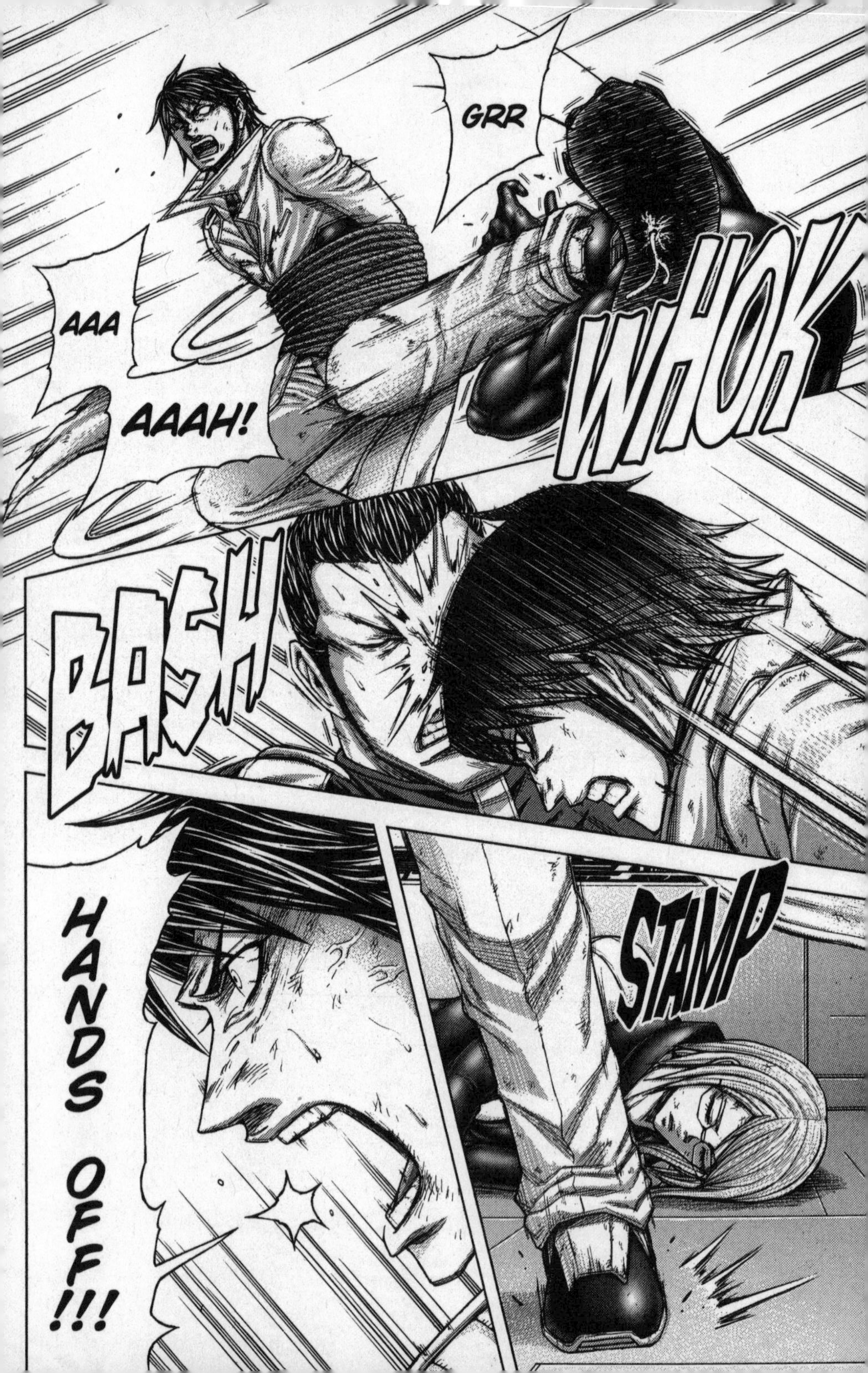
GRR
WHOK
AAA
AAAH!
BASH
STAMP
HANDS OFF!!!

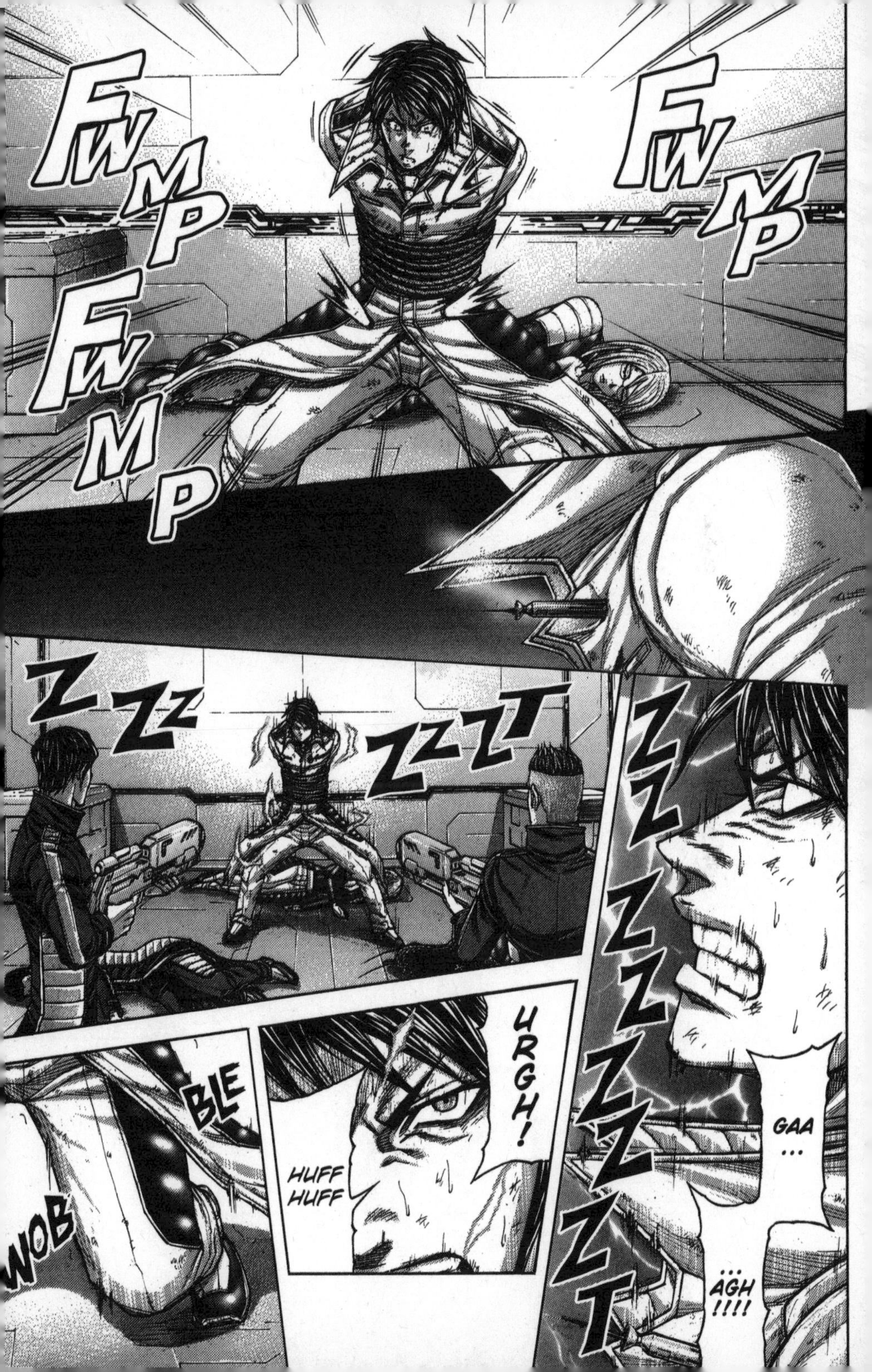
FWMP
FWMP FWMP
ZZZZT
ZZZ
ZZZZZZZT
GAA...
ÄGH!!!!
URGH!
HUFF HUFF
WOBBLE

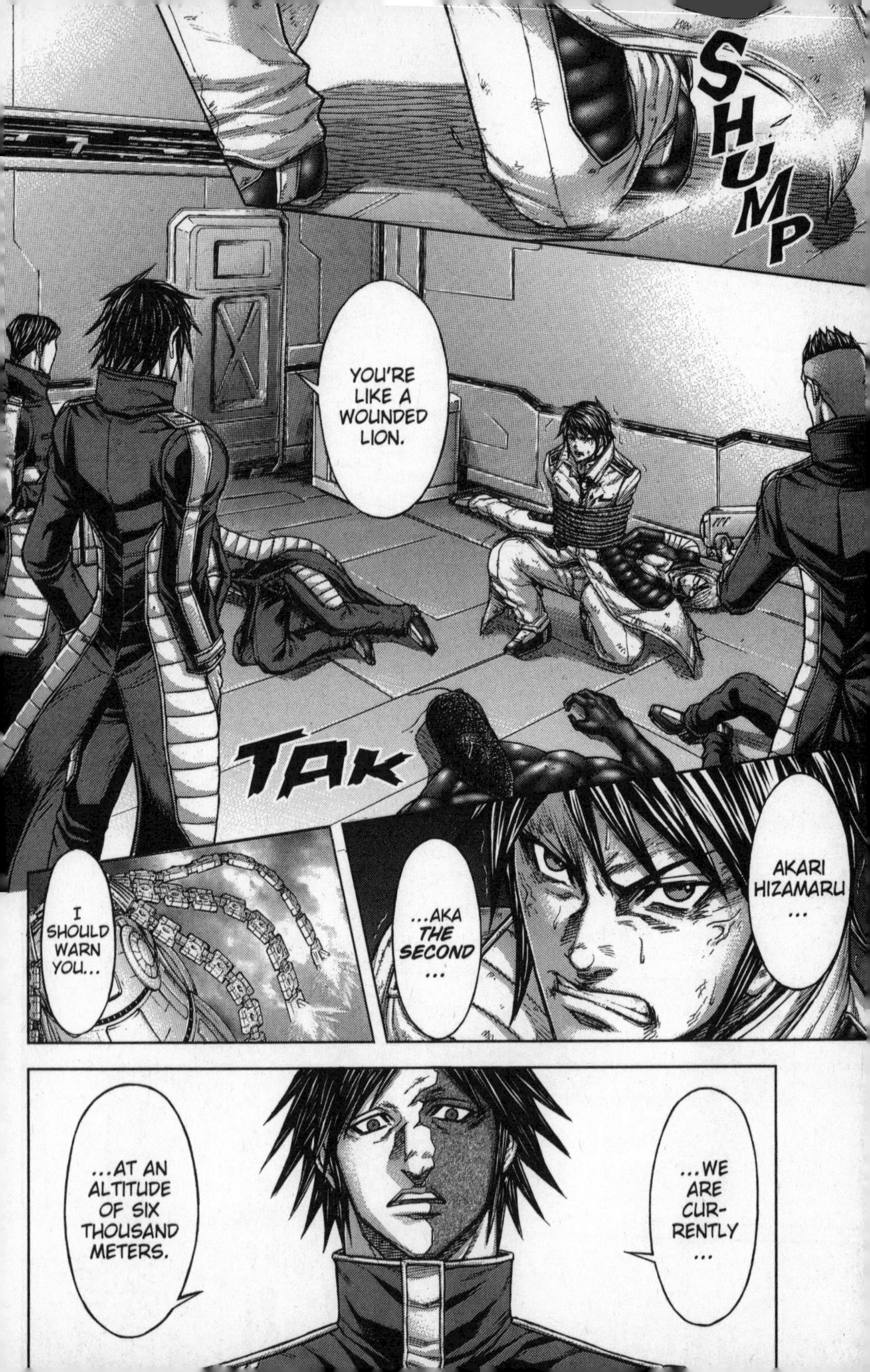
SHUMP
YOU'RE LIKE A WOUNDED LION.
TAK
AKARI HIZAMARU...
...AKA THE SECOND...
I SHOULD WARN YOU...
...WE ARE CUR-RENTLY...
...AT AN ALTITUDE OF SIX THOUSAND METERS.

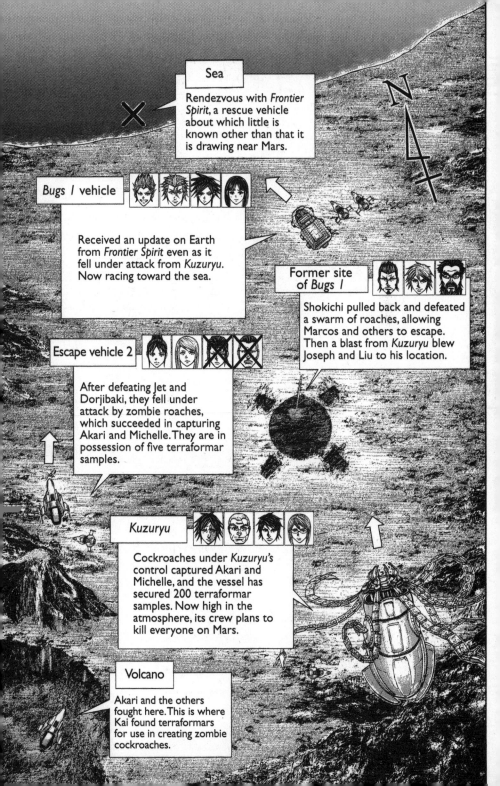

Sea

Rendezvous with *Frontier Spirit*, a rescue vehicle about which little is known other than that it is drawing near Mars.

Bugs 1 vehicle

Received an update on Earth from *Frontier Spirit* even as it fell under attack from *Kuzuryu*. Now racing toward the sea.

Former site of Bugs 1

Shokichi pulled back and defeated a swarm of roaches, allowing Marcos and others to escape. Then a blast from *Kuzuryu* blew Joseph and Liu to his location.

Escape vehicle 2

After defeating Jet and Dorjibaki, they fell under attack by zombie roaches, which succeeded in capturing Akari and Michelle. They are in possession of five terraformar samples.

Kuzuryu

Cockroaches under *Kuzuryu's* control captured Akari and Michelle, and the vessel has secured 200 terraformar samples. Now high in the atmosphere, its crew plans to kill everyone on Mars.

Volcano

Akari and the others fought here. This is where Kai found terraformars for use in creating zombie cockroaches.

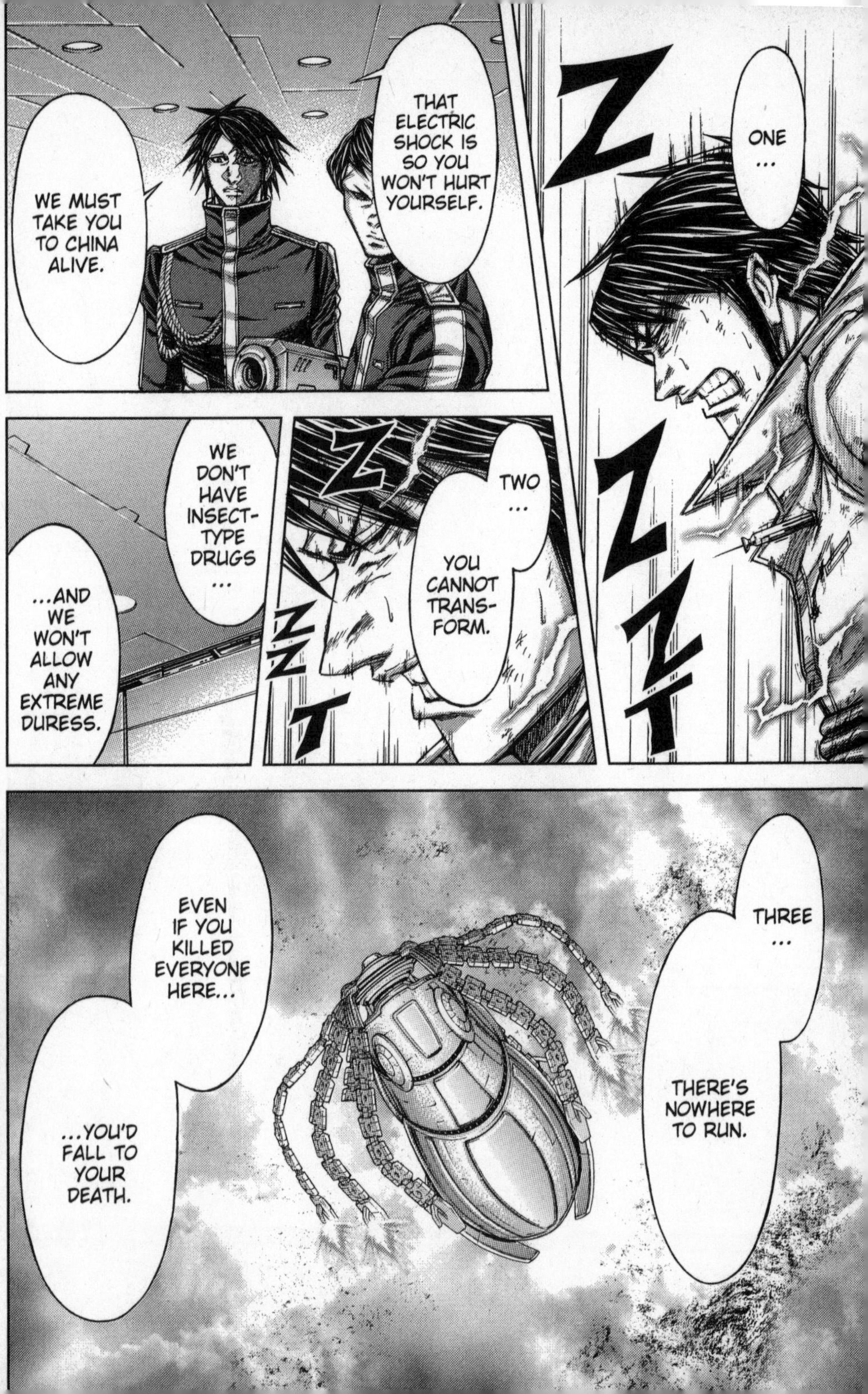
ZZZT
ONE...
THAT ELECTRIC SHOCK IS SO YOU WON'T HURT YOURSELF.
WE MUST TAKE YOU TO CHINA ALIVE.
ZZZT
TWO...
YOU CANNOT TRANSFORM.
WE DON'T HAVE INSECT-TYPE DRUGS...
...AND WE WON'T ALLOW ANY EXTREME DURESS.
THREE...
THERE'S NOWHERE TO RUN.
EVEN IF YOU KILLED EVERYONE HERE...
...YOU'D FALL TO YOUR DEATH.

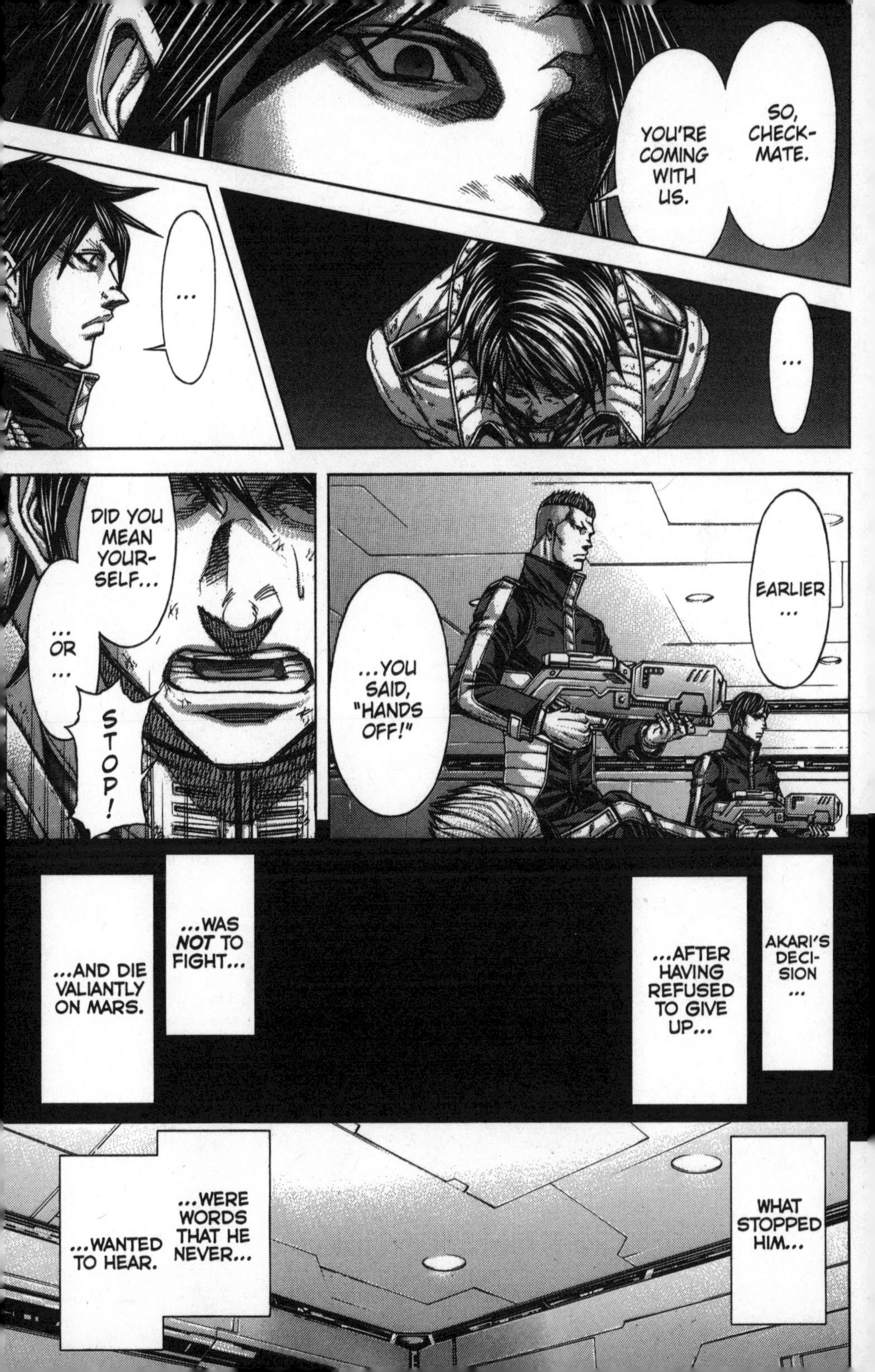
SO, CHECK-MATE.
YOU'RE COMING WITH US.
...
...
EARLIER...
...YOU SAID, "HANDS OFF!"
DID YOU MEAN YOUR-SELF...
... OR ...
STOP!
AKARI'S DECI-SION...
...AFTER HAVING REFUSED TO GIVE UP...
...WAS NOT TO FIGHT...
...AND DIE VALIANTLY ON MARS.
WHAT STOPPED HIM...
...WERE WORDS THAT HE NEVER...
...WANTED TO HEAR.

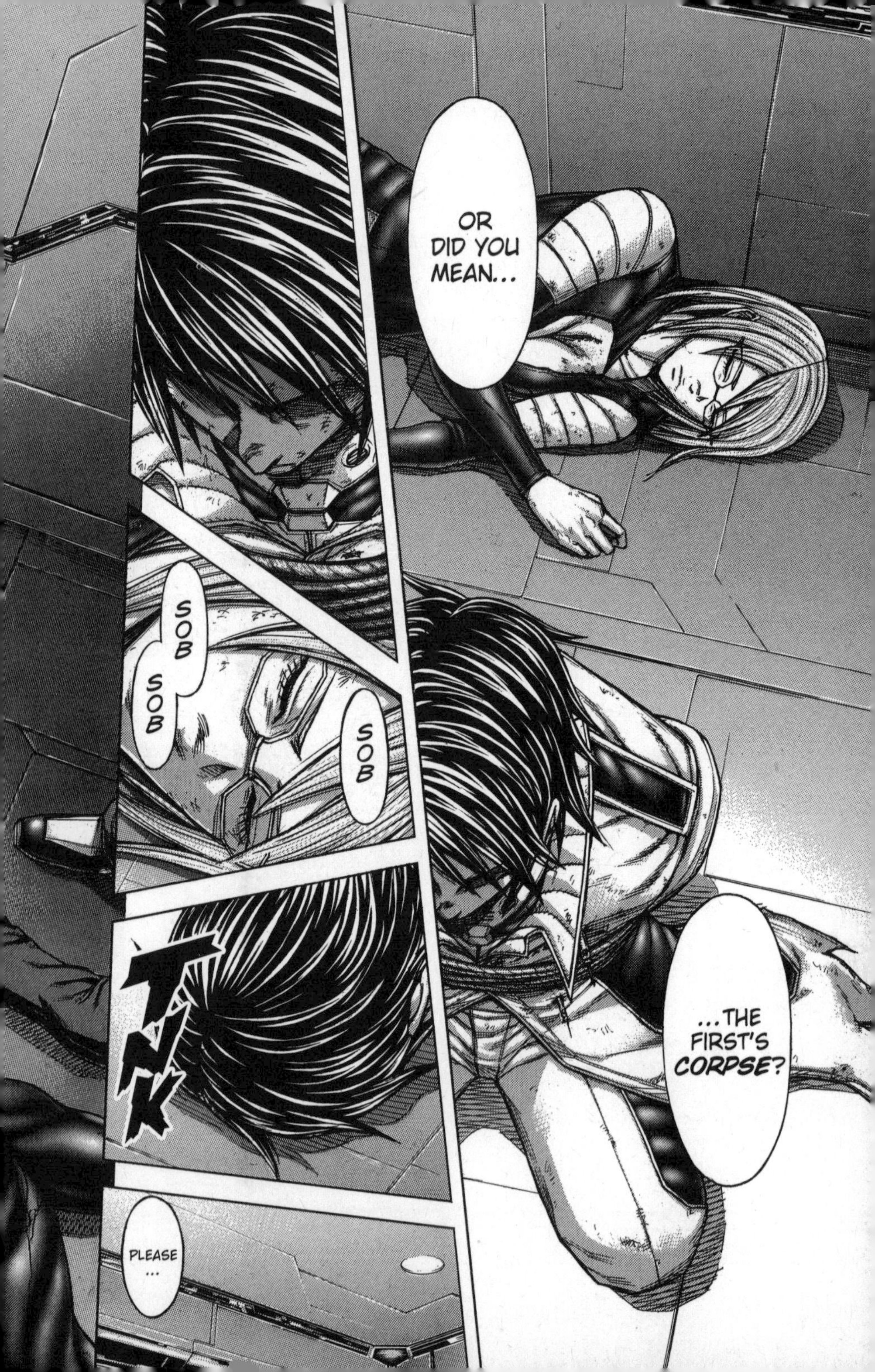
OR DID YOU MEAN...
...THE FIRST'S CORPSE?
SOB SOB
SOB
TNK
PLEASE ...

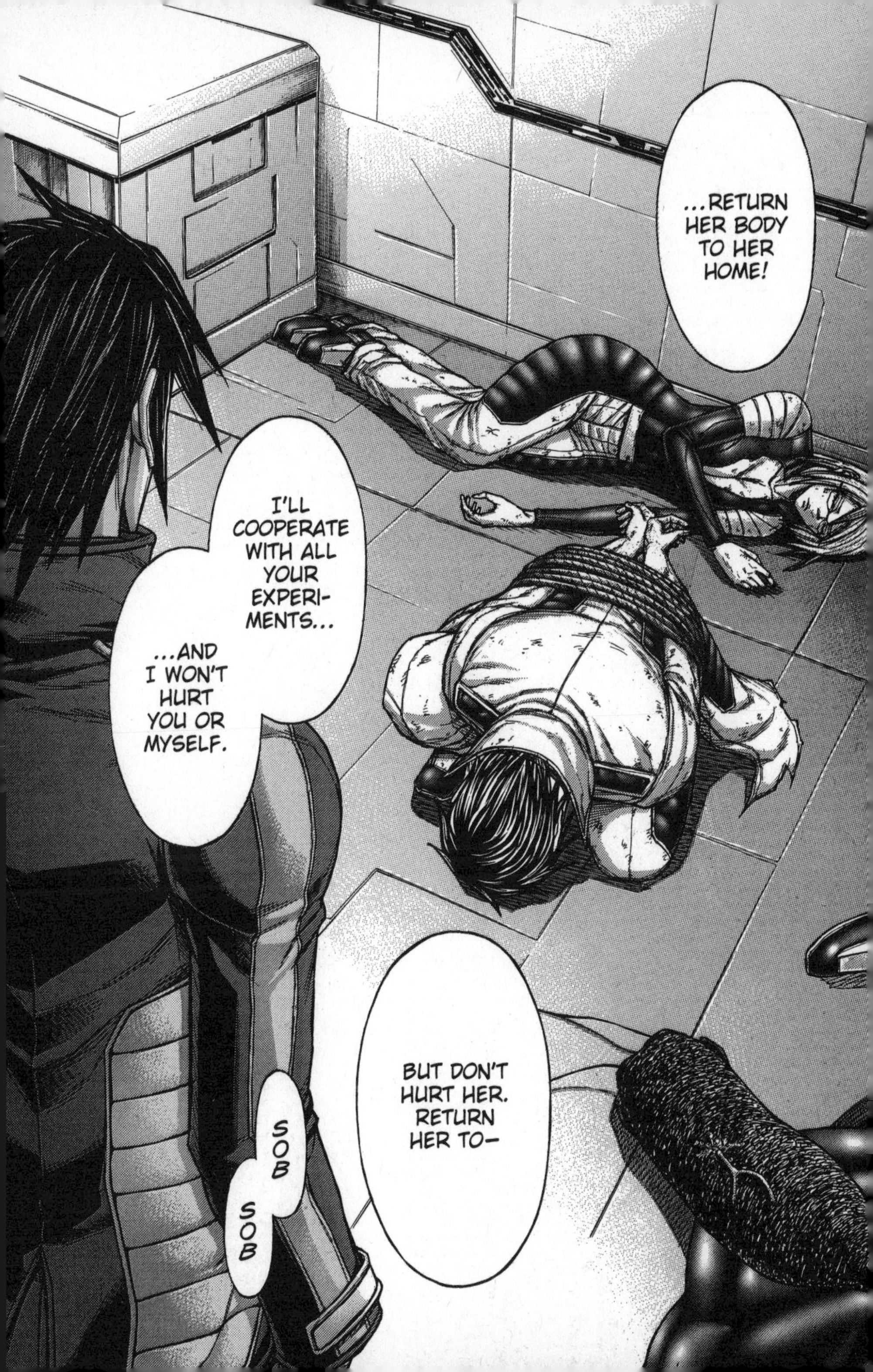
...RETURN HER BODY TO HER HOME!
I'LL COOPERATE WITH ALL YOUR EXPERIMENTS...
...AND I WON'T HURT YOU OR MYSELF.
BUT DON'T HURT HER. RETURN HER TO—
SOB
SOB

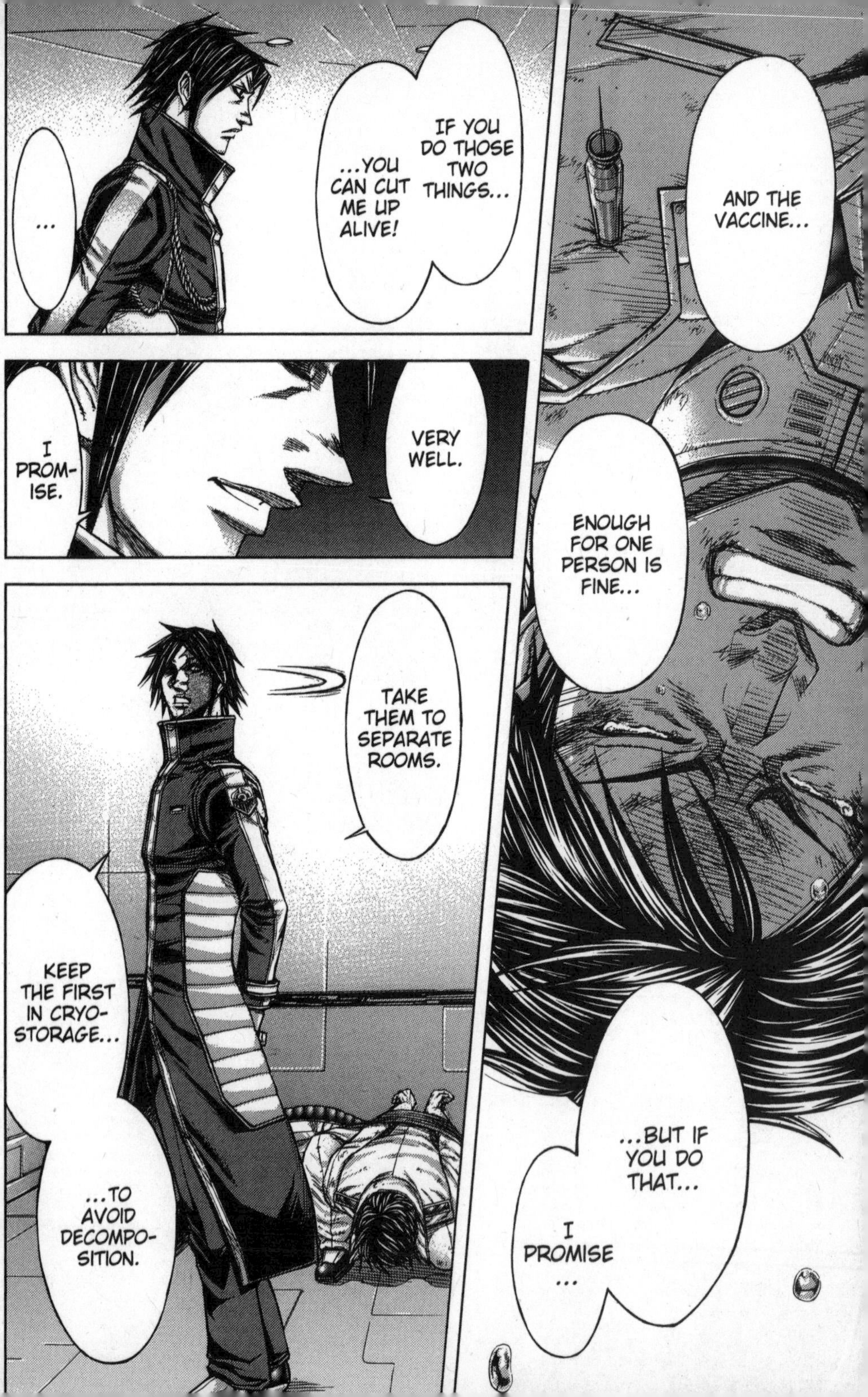
AND THE VACCINE...
ENOUGH FOR ONE PERSON IS FINE...
...BUT IF YOU DO THAT...
I PROMISE ...
IF YOU DO THOSE TWO THINGS...
...YOU CAN CUT ME UP ALIVE!
...
VERY WELL.
I PROMISE.
TAKE THEM TO SEPARATE ROOMS.
KEEP THE FIRST IN CRYO-STORAGE...
...TO AVOID DECOMPOSITION.

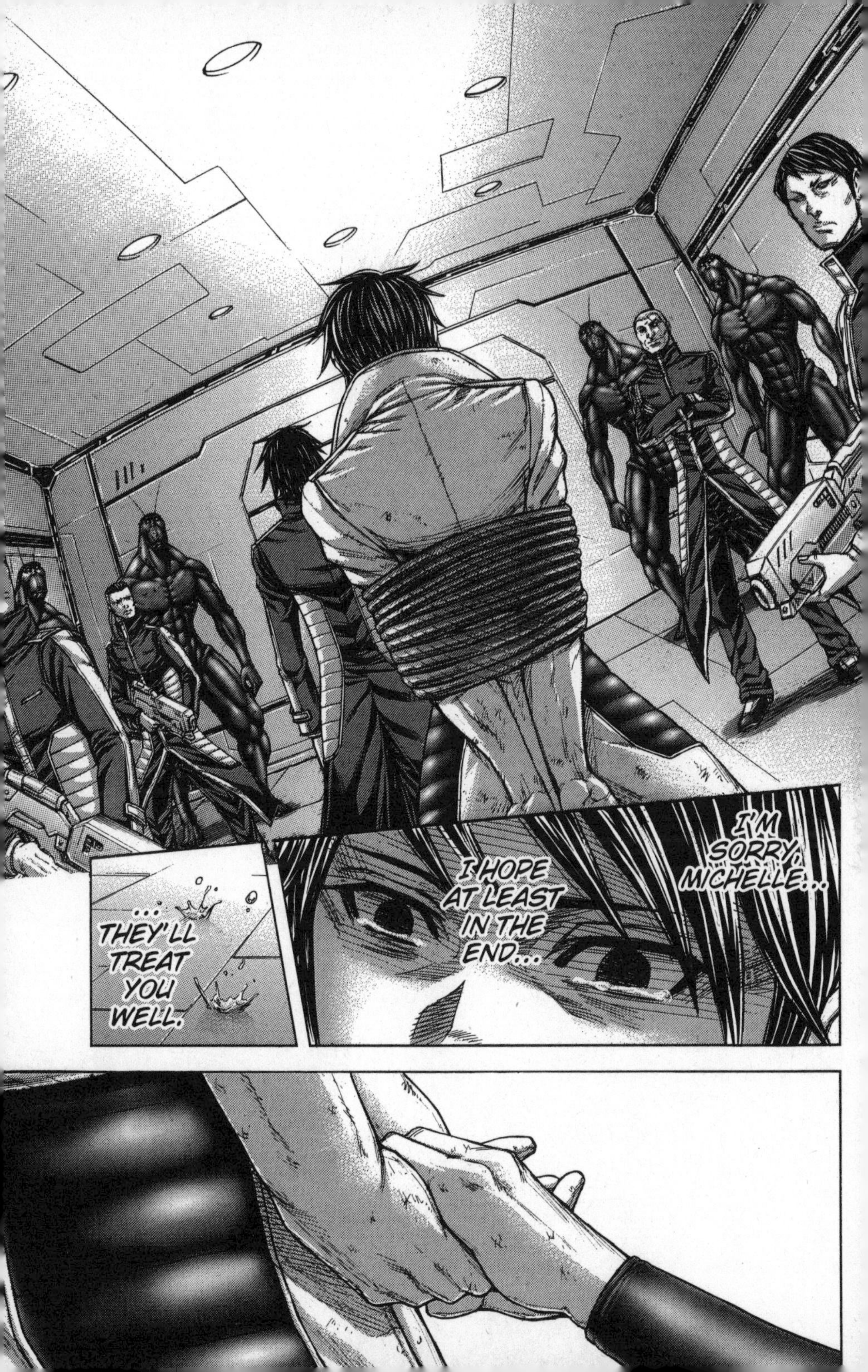
I'M SORRY, MICHELLE...
I HOPE AT LEAST IN THE END...
...THEY'LL TREAT YOU WELL.

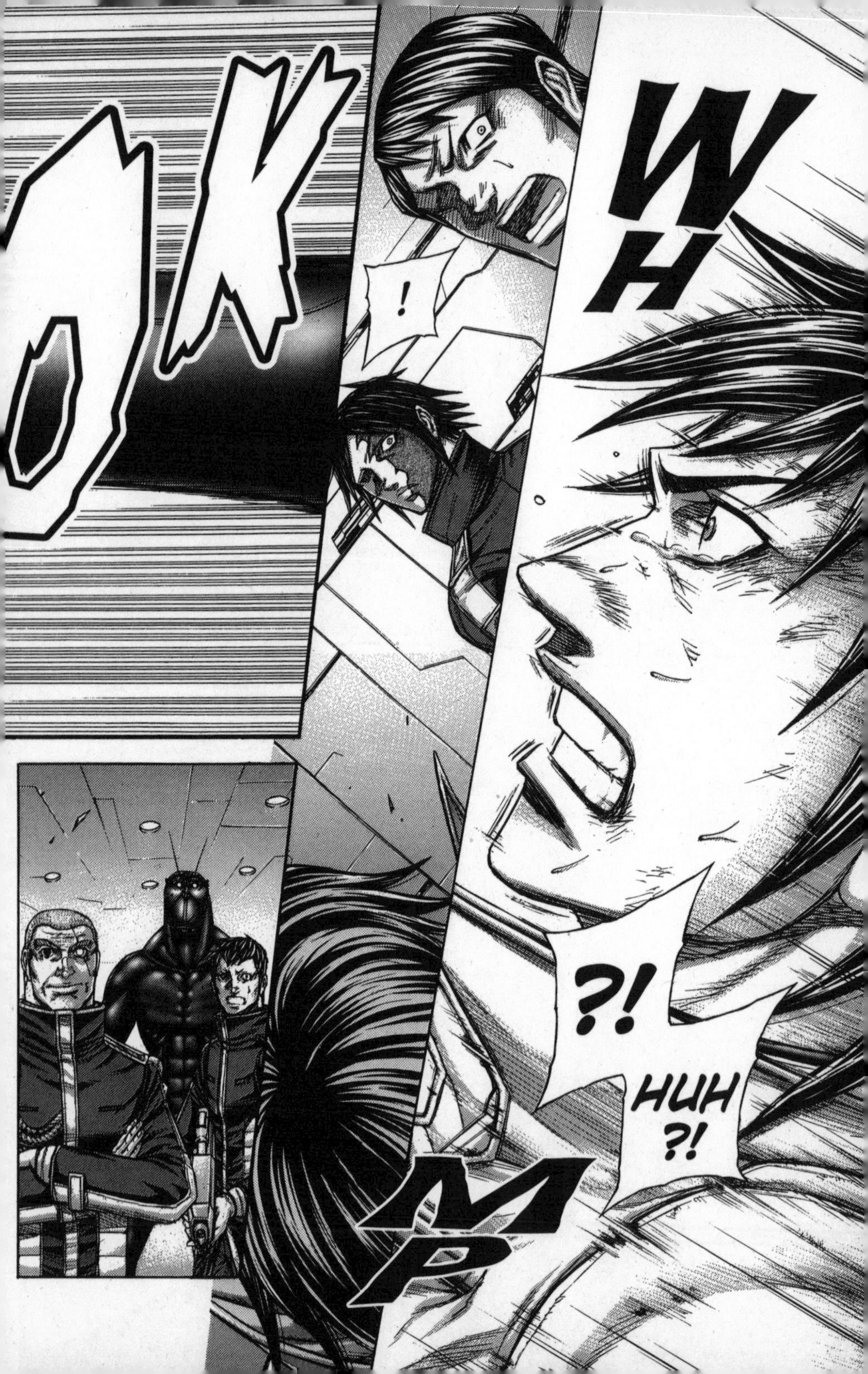

WH
?!
HUH ?!
!
MP
OK

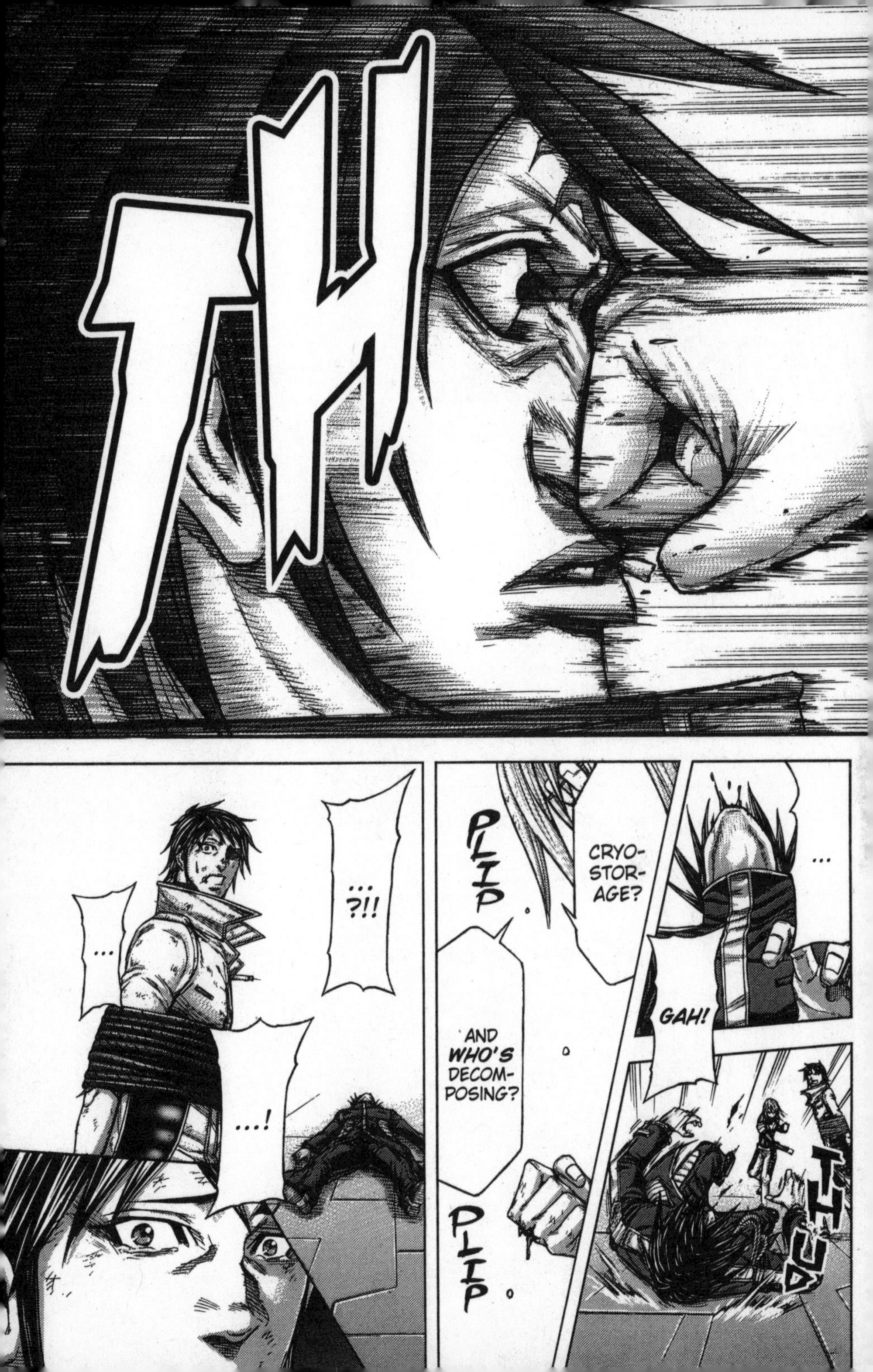
TH
...
GAH!
THUD
CRYO-STOR-AGE?
PLIP
AND *WHO'S* DECOM-POSING?
PLIP
...?!!
...
...!

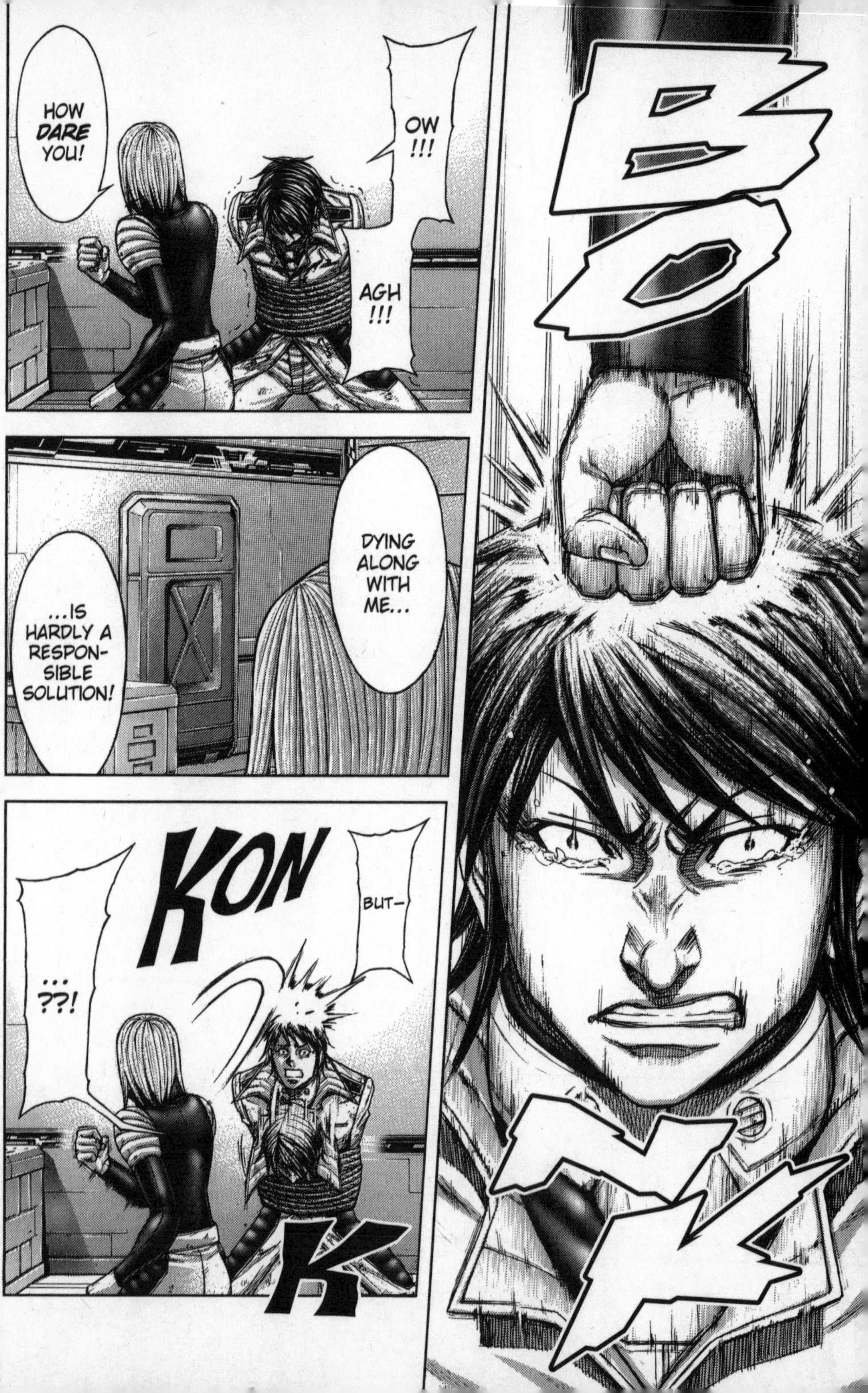
OW!!!
AGH!!!
HOW *DARE* YOU!
DYING ALONG WITH ME...
...IS HARDLY A RESPON-SIBLE SOLUTION!
BUT–
KON
... ??!
K

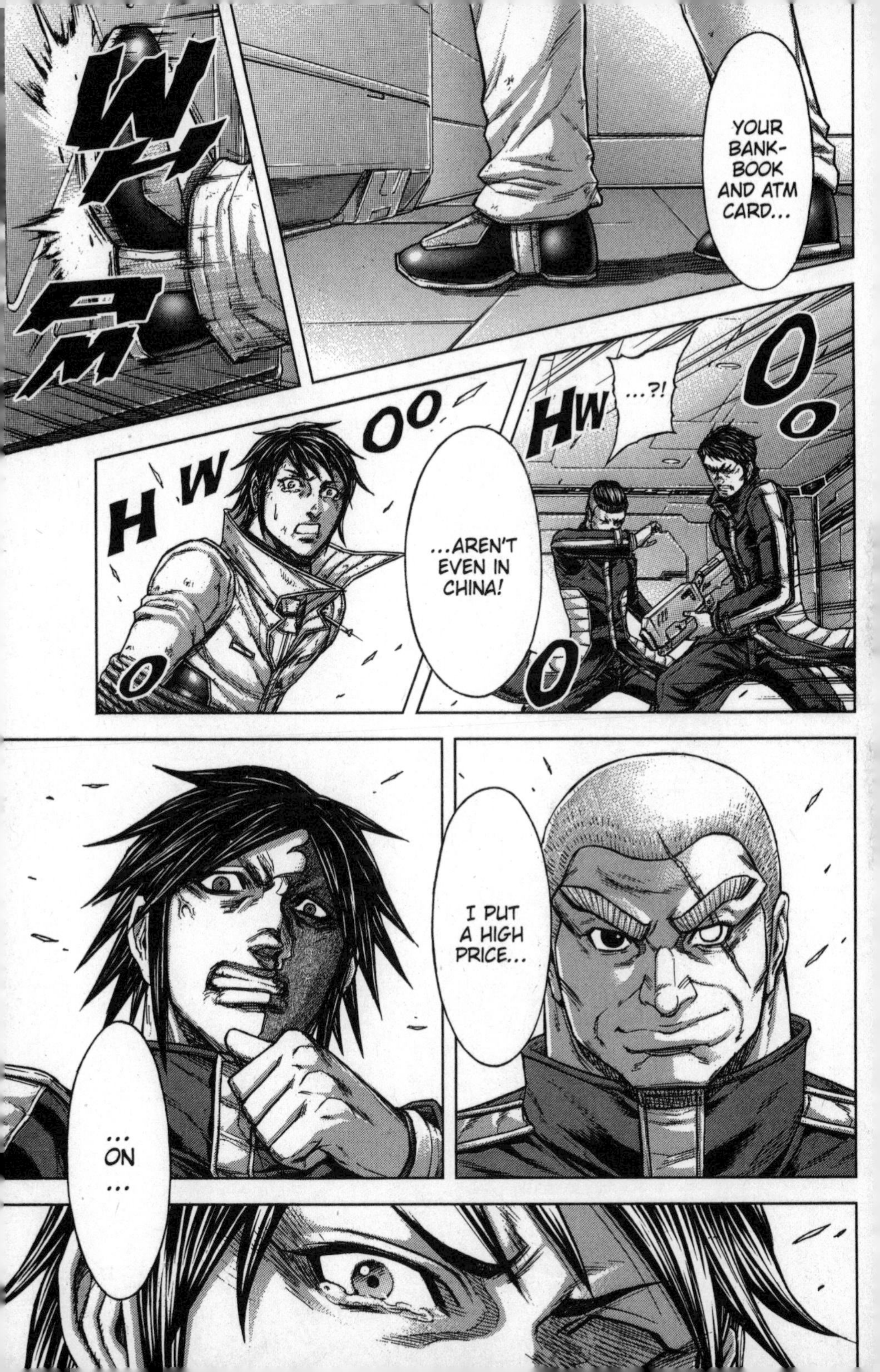
YOUR BANK-BOOK AND ATM CARD...
WHAM
HWOOO
...?!
HWOOO
...AREN'T EVEN IN CHINA!
I PUT A HIGH PRICE...
...ON...

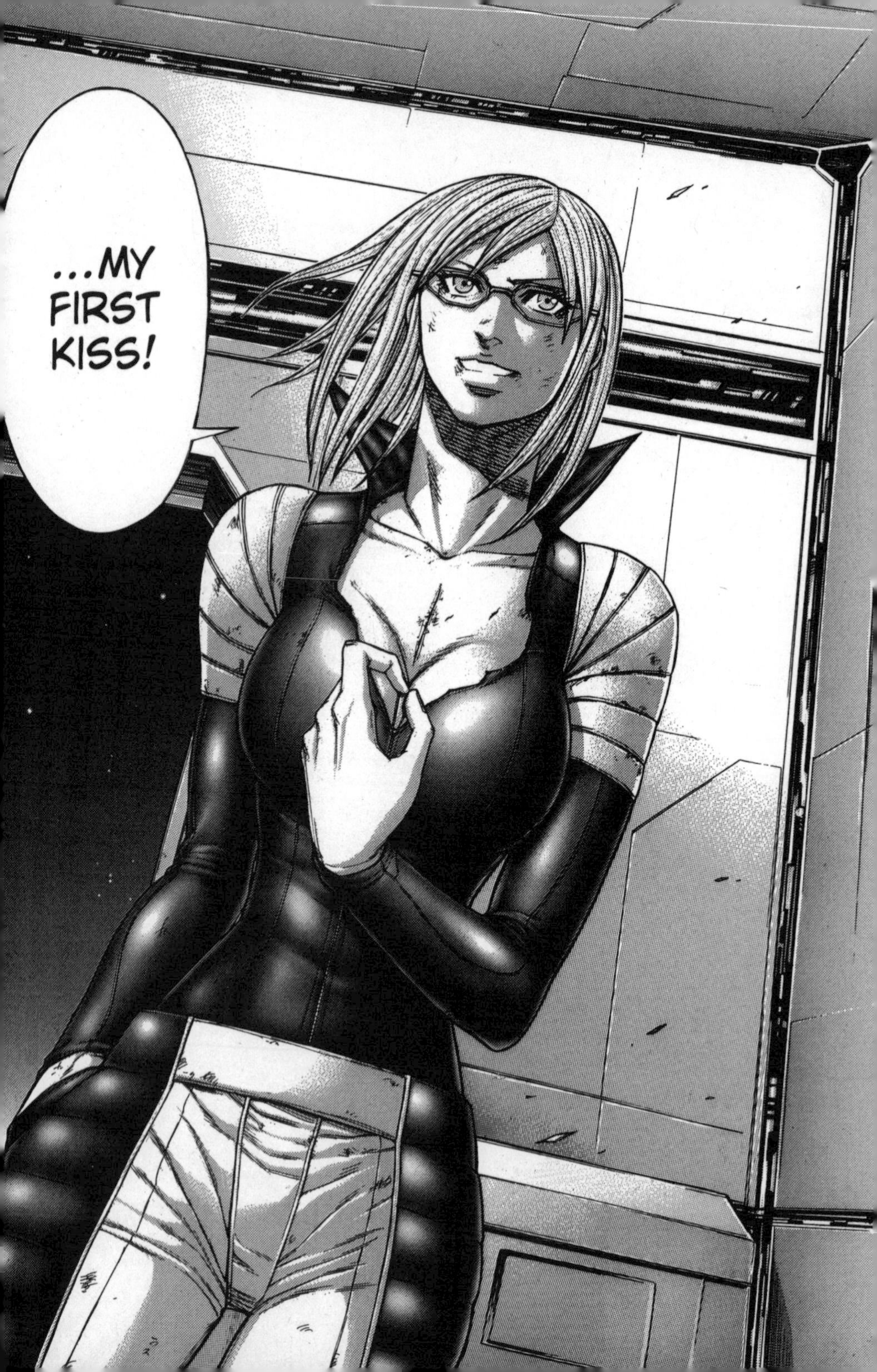
...MY FIRST KISS!

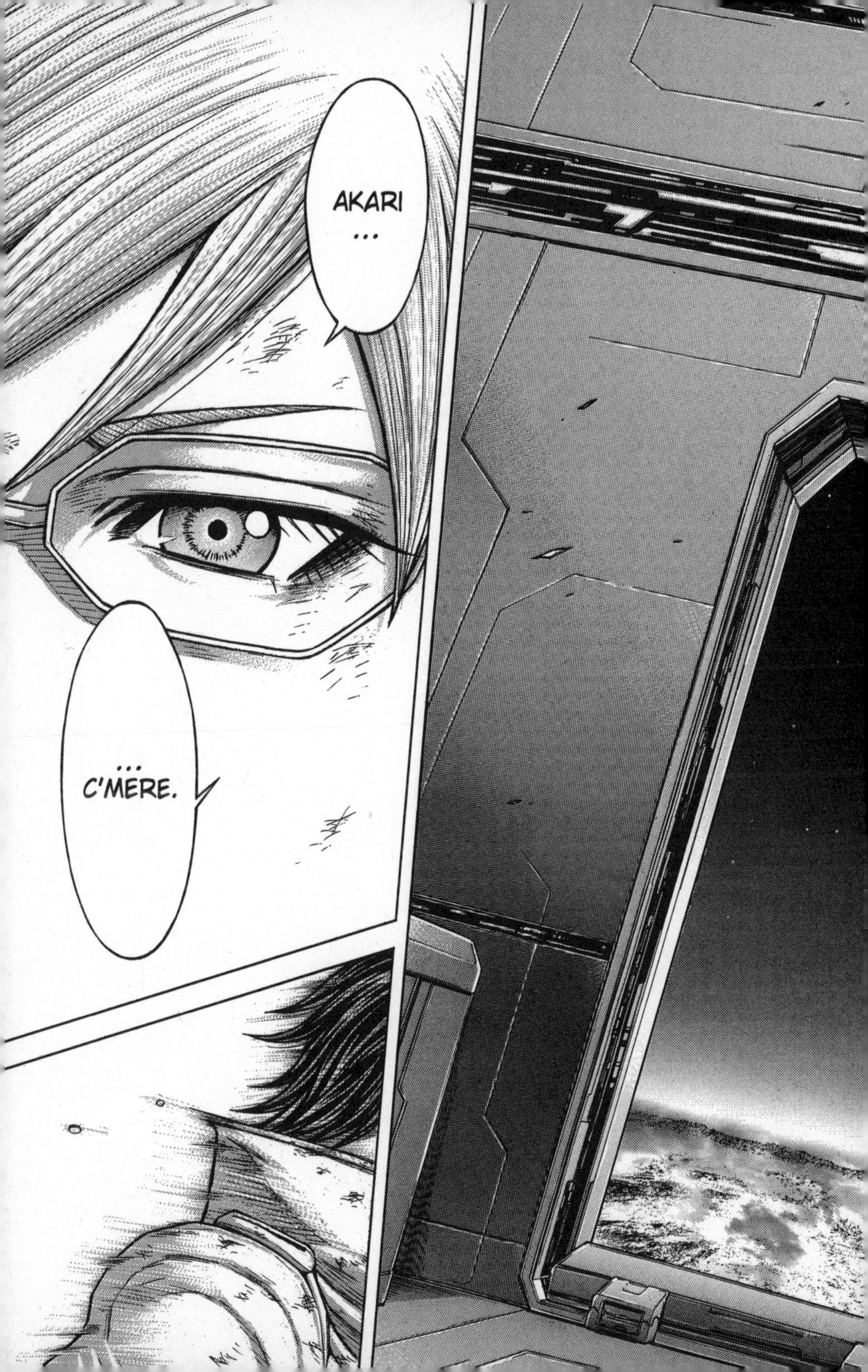
AKARI ...
... C'MERE.

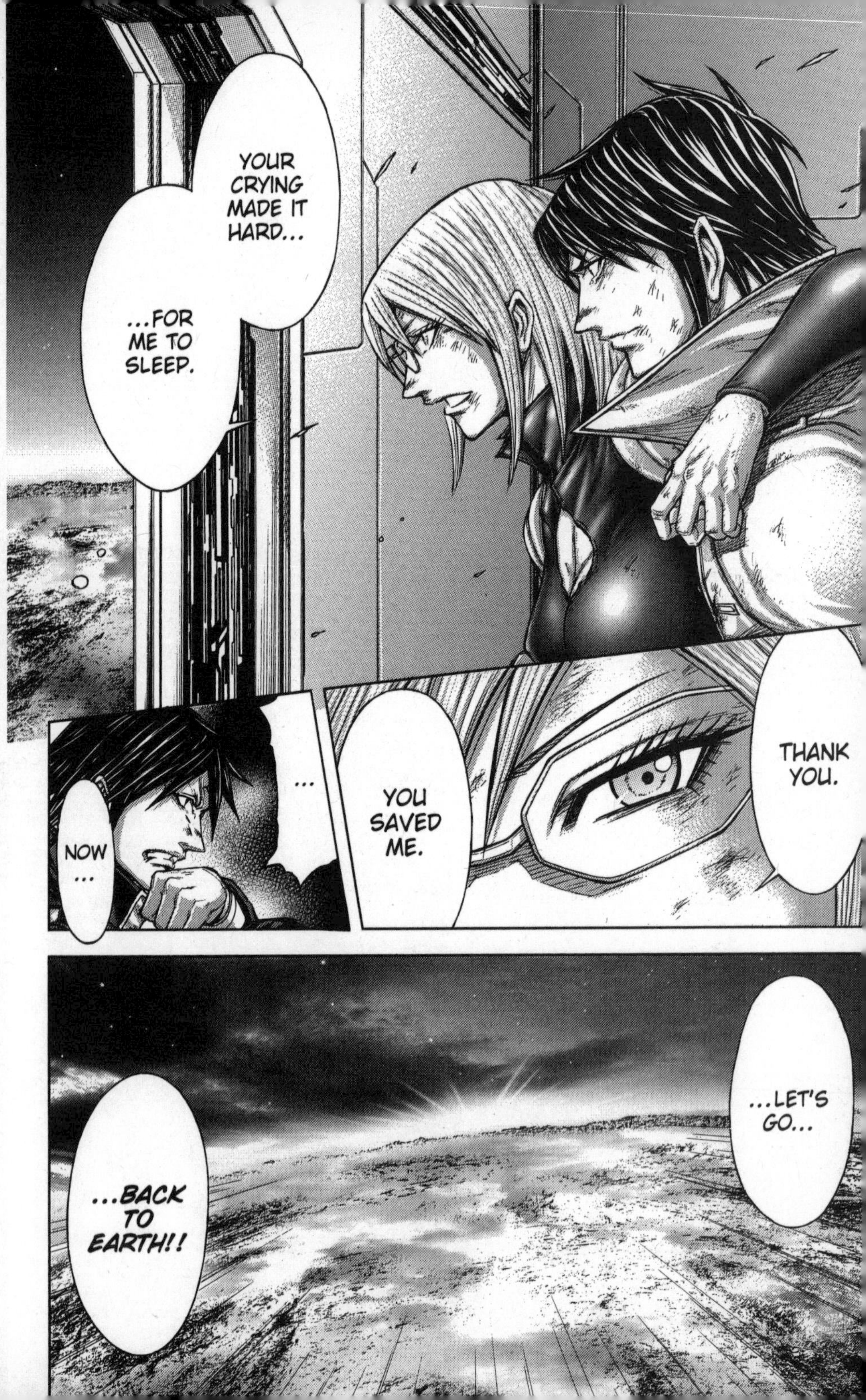
YOUR CRYING MADE IT HARD...
...FOR ME TO SLEEP.
THANK YOU.
YOU SAVED ME.
...
NOW ...
...LET'S GO...
...BACK TO EARTH!!

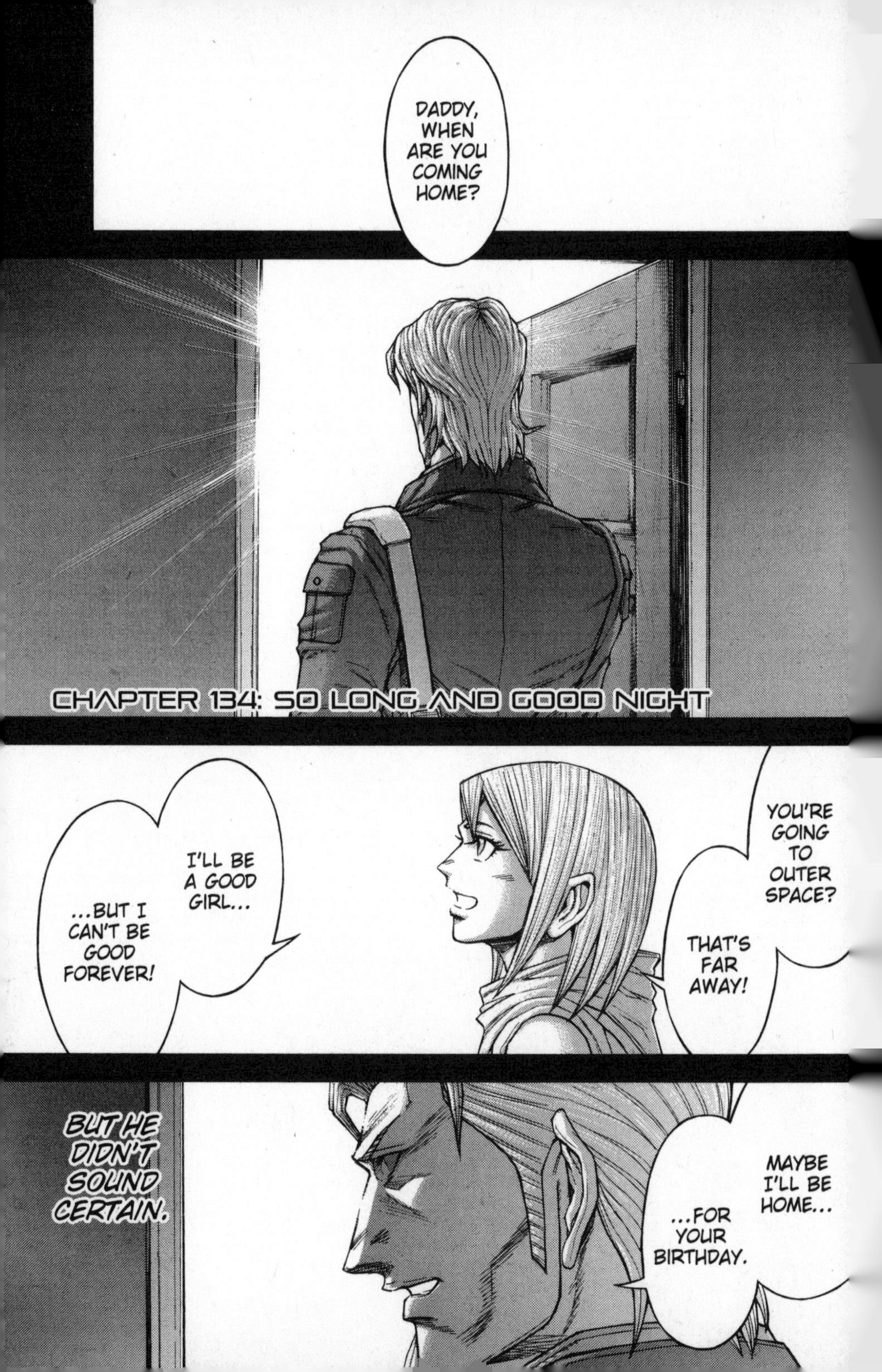
DADDY, WHEN ARE YOU COMING HOME?
CHAPTER 134: SO LONG AND GOOD NIGHT
YOU'RE GOING TO OUTER SPACE?
THAT'S FAR AWAY!
I'LL BE A GOOD GIRL...
...BUT I CAN'T BE GOOD FOREVER!
MAYBE I'LL BE HOME...
...FOR YOUR BIRTHDAY.
BUT HE DIDN'T SOUND CERTAIN.

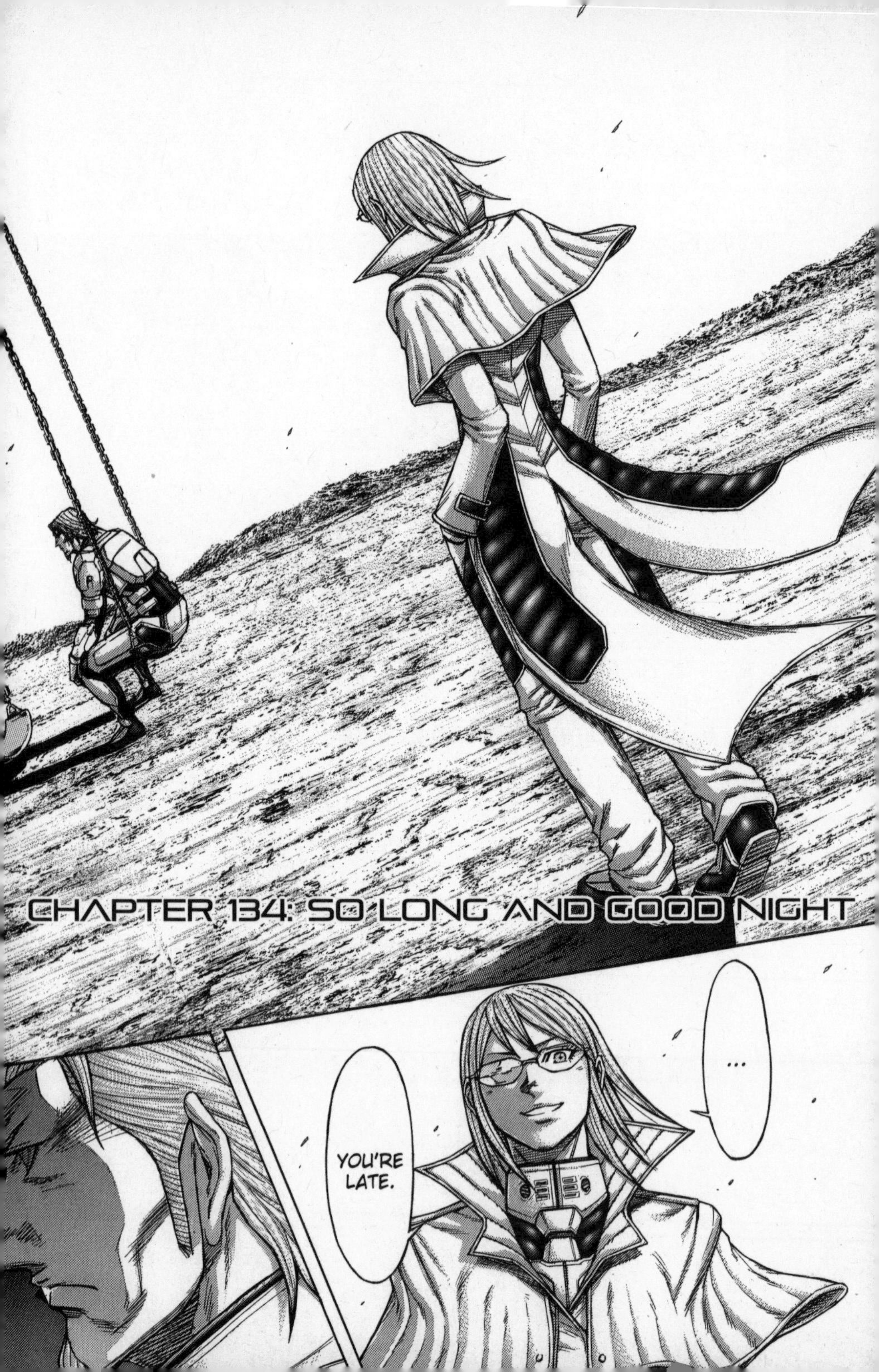
CHAPTER 134: SO LONG AND GOOD NIGHT
...
YOU'RE LATE.

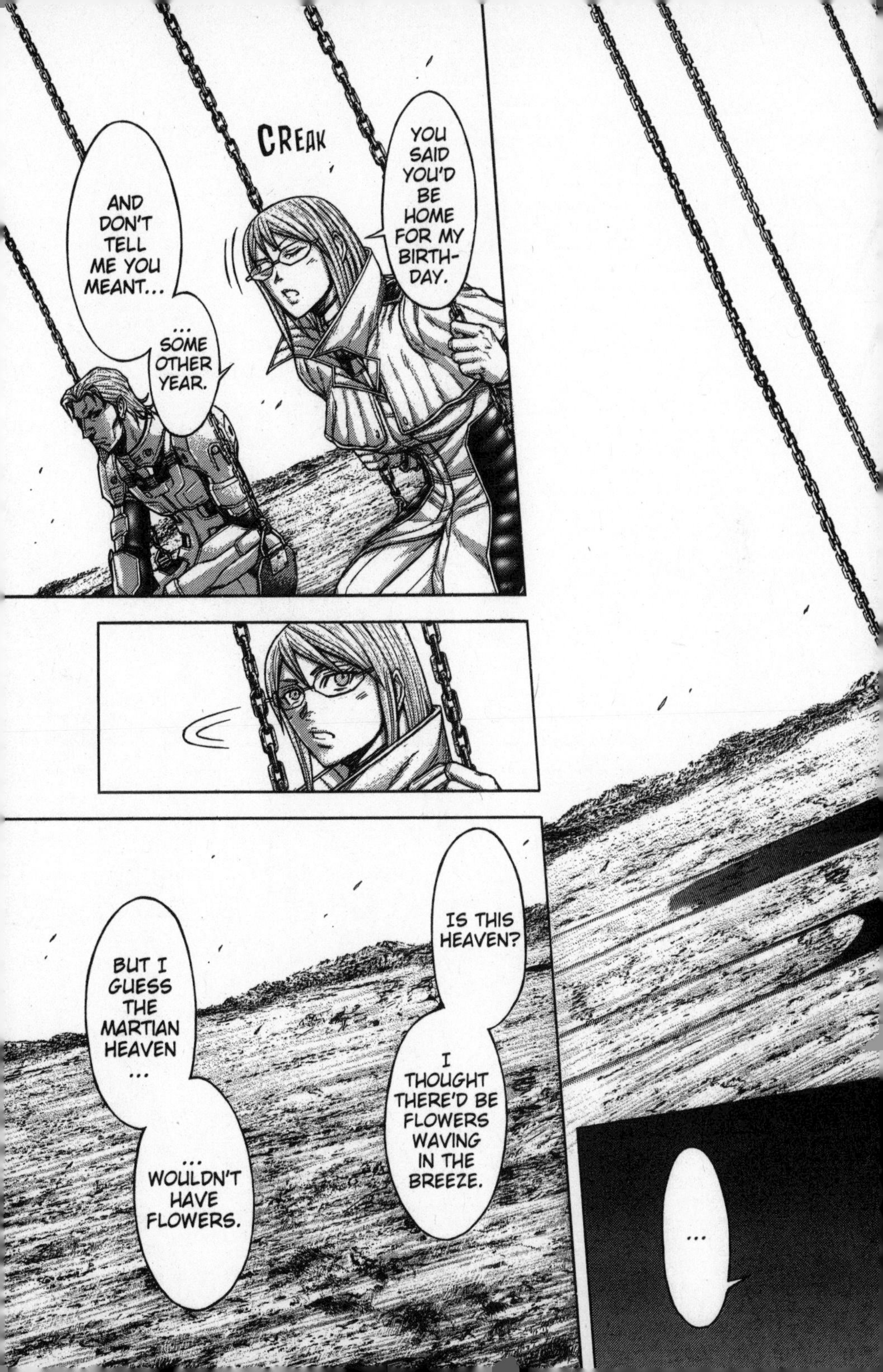
YOU SAID YOU'D BE HOME FOR MY BIRTH-DAY.
CREAK
AND DON'T TELL ME YOU MEANT...
...SOME OTHER YEAR.
IS THIS HEAVEN?
I THOUGHT THERE'D BE FLOWERS WAVING IN THE BREEZE.
BUT I GUESS THE MARTIAN HEAVEN...
...WOULDN'T HAVE FLOWERS.
...

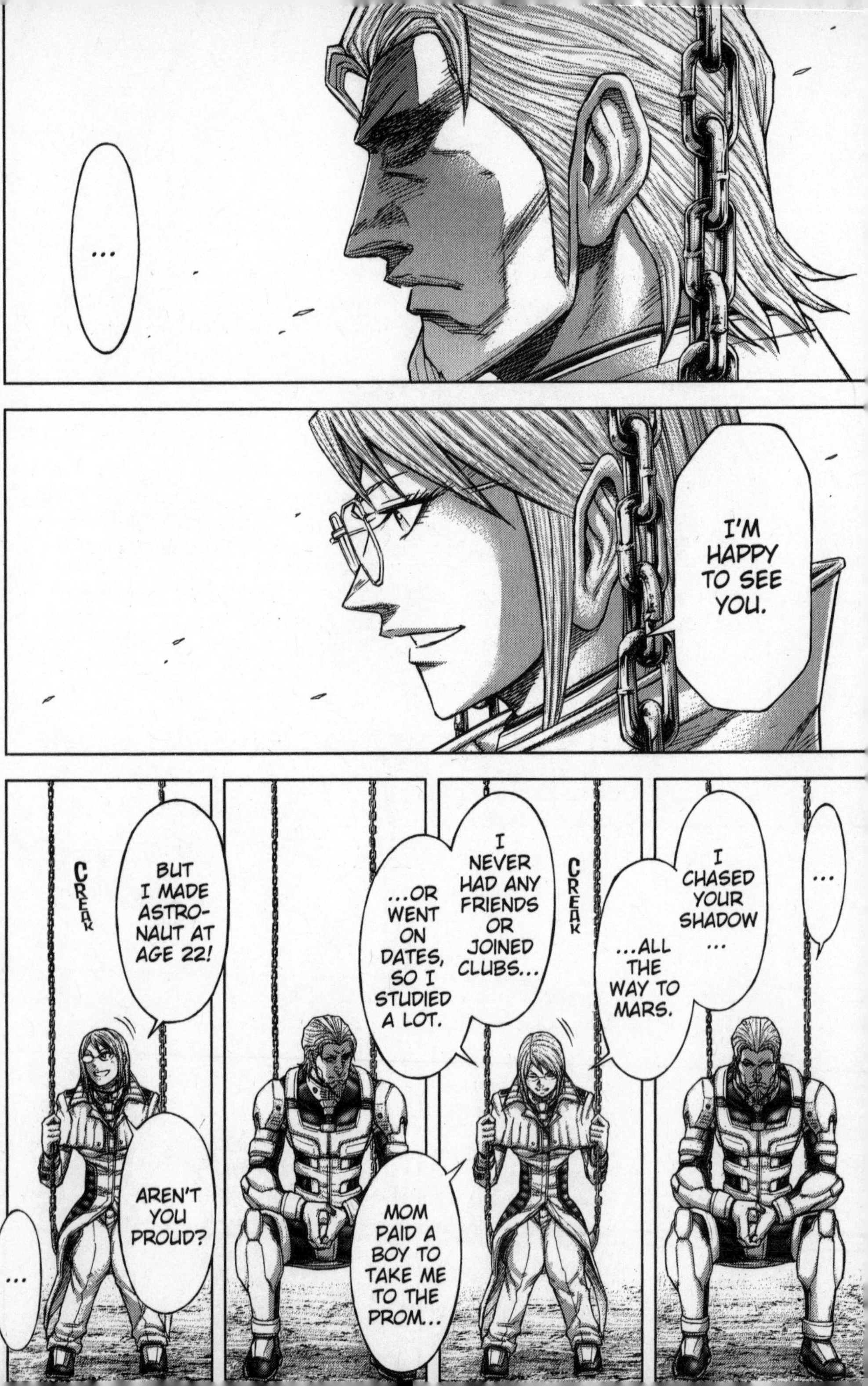
...
I'M HAPPY TO SEE YOU.
...
I CHASED YOUR SHADOW ...
...ALL THE WAY TO MARS.
I NEVER HAD ANY FRIENDS OR JOINED CLUBS...
CREAK
...OR WENT ON DATES, SO I STUDIED A LOT.
MOM PAID A BOY TO TAKE ME TO THE PROM...
BUT I MADE ASTRONAUT AT AGE 22!
CREAK
AREN'T YOU PROUD?
...

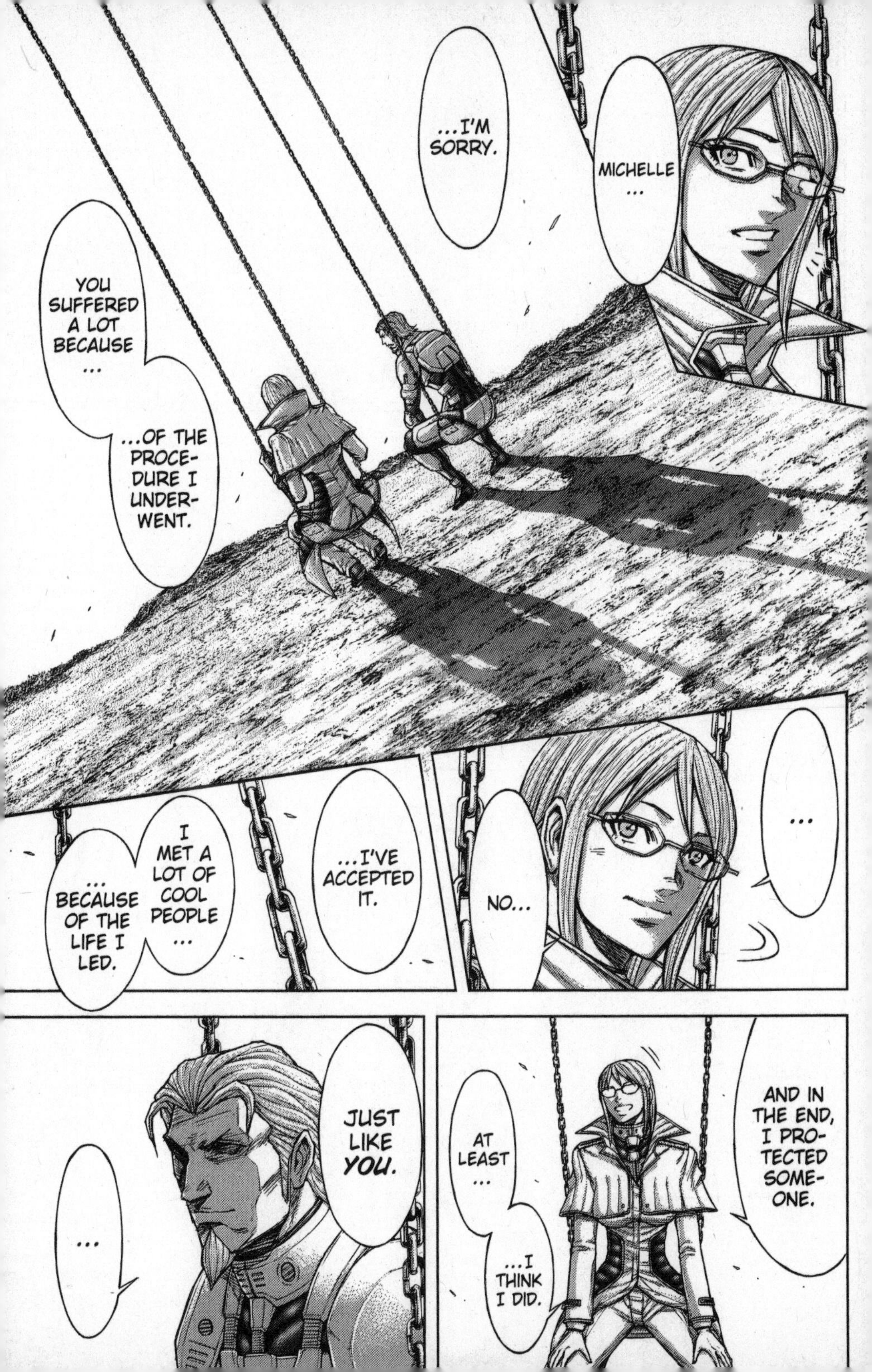
MICHELLE ...
...I'M SORRY.
YOU SUFFERED A LOT BECAUSE ...
...OF THE PROCEDURE I UNDERWENT.
...
NO...
...I'VE ACCEPTED IT.
I MET A LOT OF COOL PEOPLE ...
... BECAUSE OF THE LIFE I LED.
AND IN THE END, I PROTECTED SOMEONE.
AT LEAST ...
...I THINK I DID.
JUST LIKE *YOU*.
...

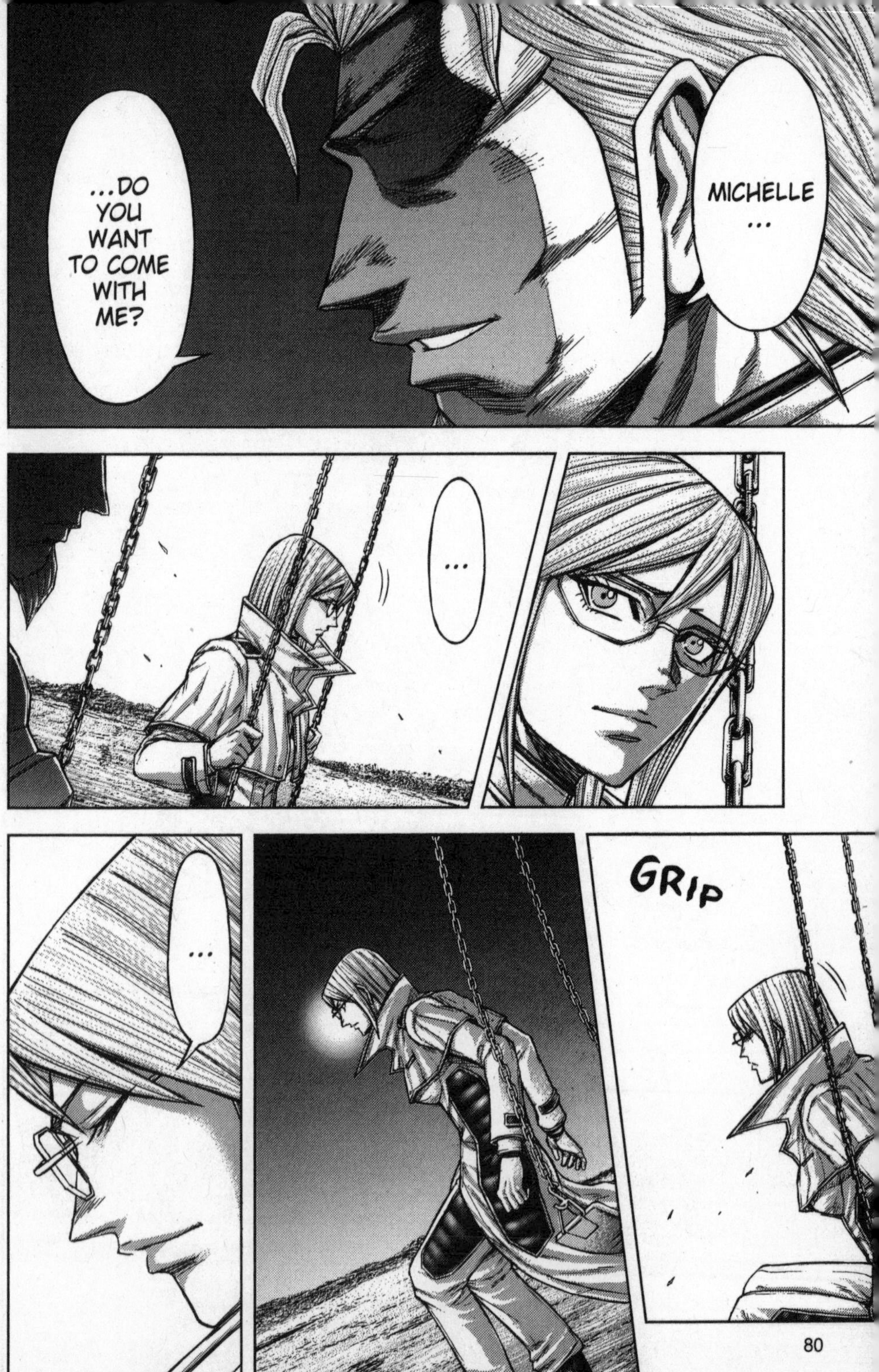
MICHELLE...
...DO YOU WANT TO COME WITH ME?
...
GRIP
...

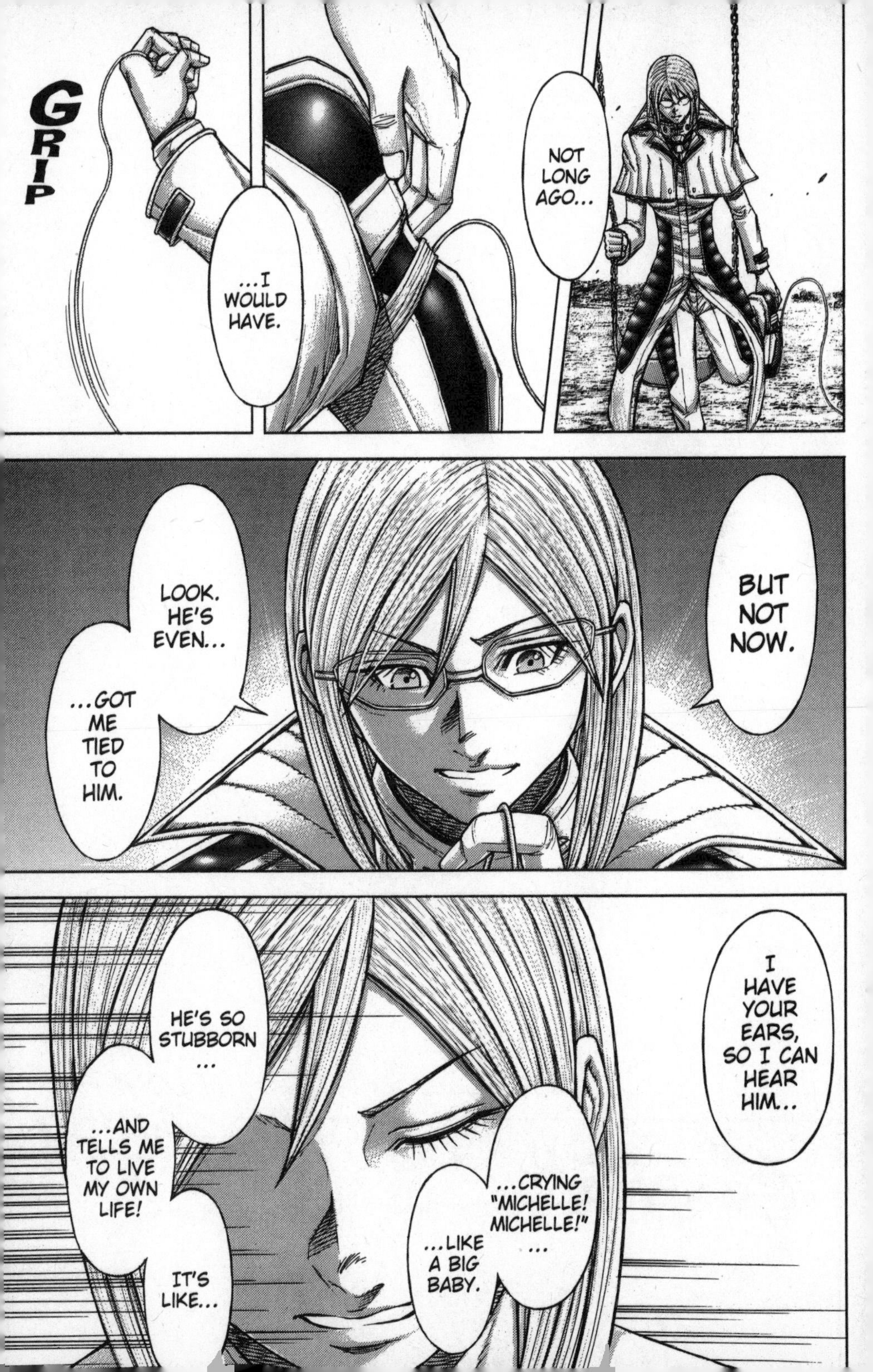
NOT LONG AGO...
...I WOULD HAVE.
GRIP
BUT NOT NOW.
LOOK. HE'S EVEN...
...GOT ME TIED TO HIM.
I HAVE YOUR EARS, SO I CAN HEAR HIM...
...CRYING "MICHELLE! MICHELLE!"...
...LIKE A BIG BABY.
HE'S SO STUBBORN...
...AND TELLS ME TO LIVE MY OWN LIFE!
IT'S LIKE...

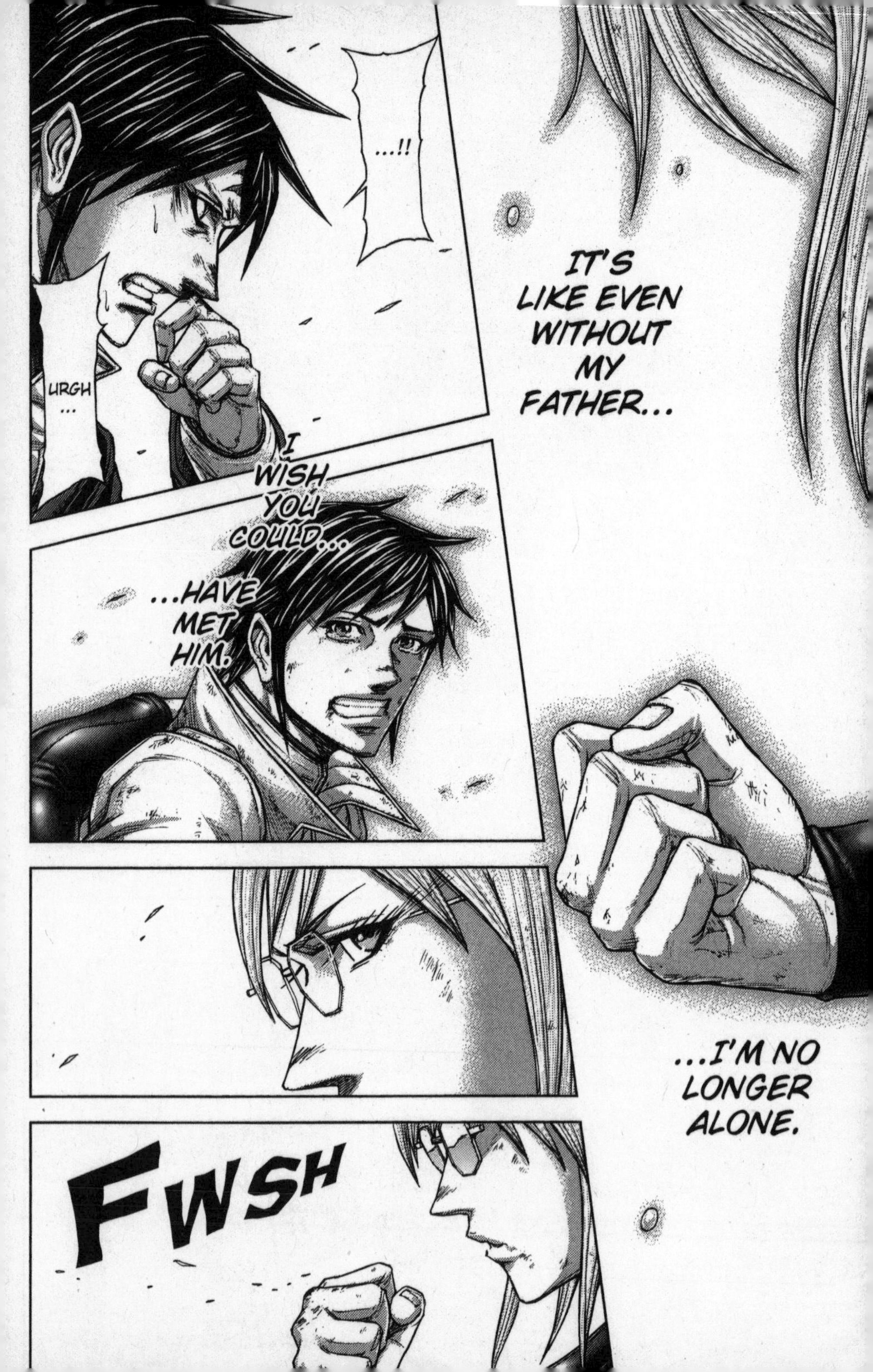
IT'S LIKE EVEN WITHOUT MY FATHER...
...I'M NO LONGER ALONE.
...!!
URGH ...
I WISH YOU COULD...
...HAVE MET HIM.
FWSH

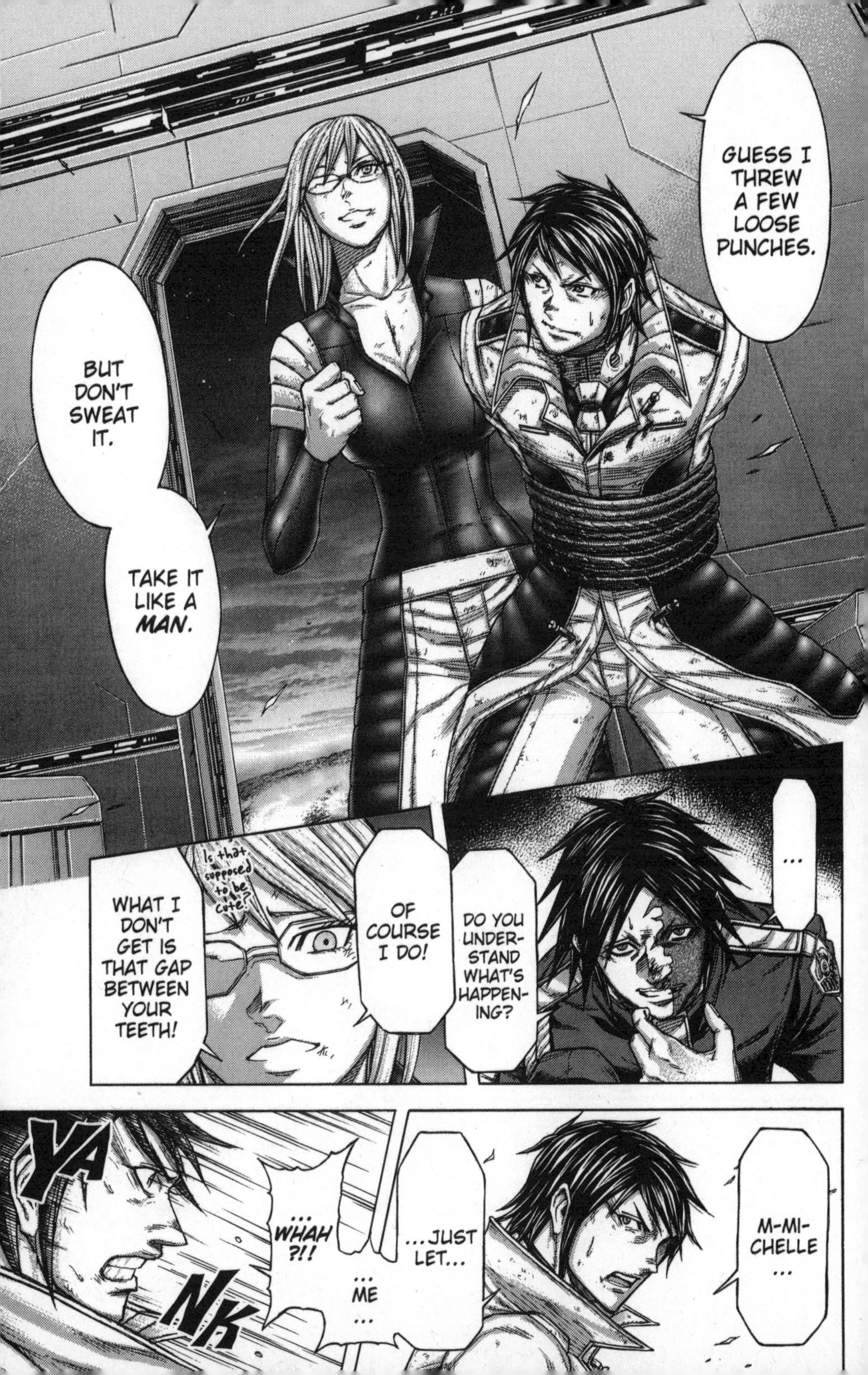
GUESS I THREW A FEW LOOSE PUNCHES.
BUT DON'T SWEAT IT.
TAKE IT LIKE A *MAN*.
...
DO YOU UNDER-STAND WHAT'S HAPPEN-ING?
OF COURSE I DO!
Is that supposed to be cute?
WHAT I DON'T GET IS THAT GAP BETWEEN YOUR TEETH!
M-MI-CHELLE ...
...JUST LET...
...ME...
...WHAH ?!!
YANK

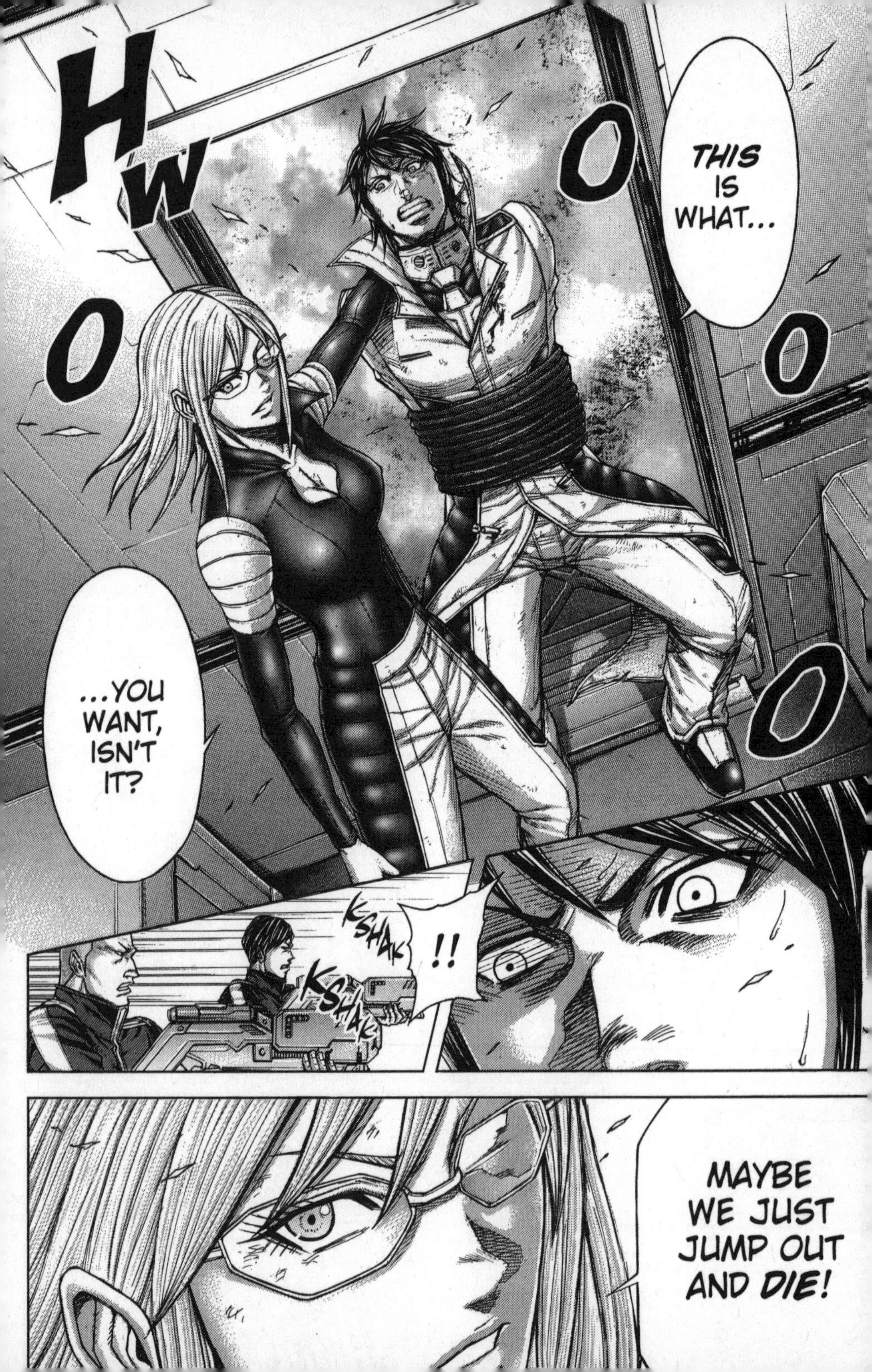
HWOOOOO
THIS IS WHAT...
...YOU WANT, ISN'T IT?
!!
KSHAK
KSHAK
MAYBE WE JUST JUMP OUT AND DIE!

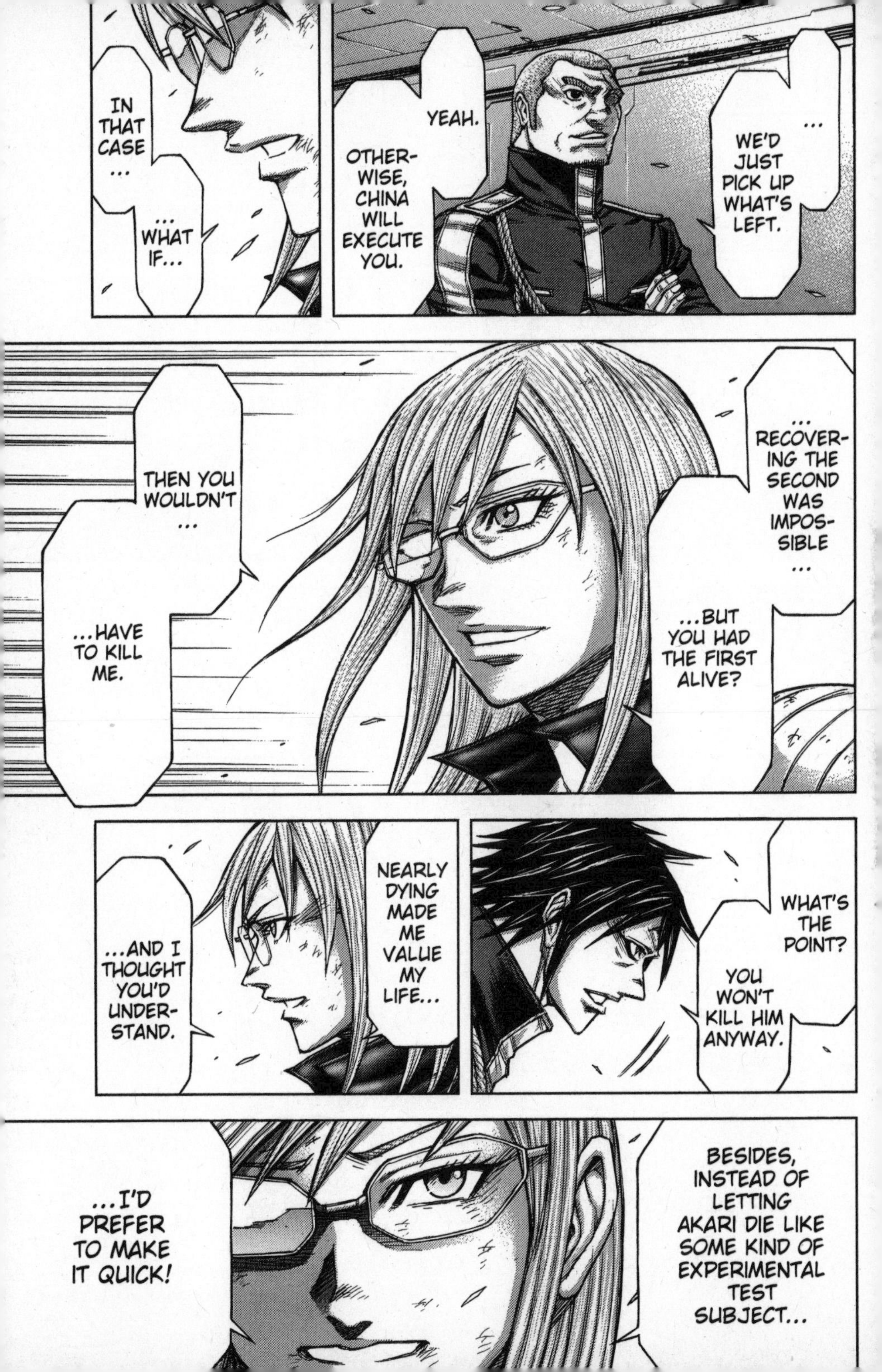
...
WE'D JUST PICK UP WHAT'S LEFT.
YEAH.
OTHERWISE, CHINA WILL EXECUTE YOU.
IN THAT CASE...
...WHAT IF...
...RECOVERING THE SECOND WAS IMPOSSIBLE...
...BUT YOU HAD THE FIRST ALIVE?
THEN YOU WOULDN'T...
...HAVE TO KILL ME.
WHAT'S THE POINT?
YOU WON'T KILL HIM ANYWAY.
NEARLY DYING MADE ME VALUE MY LIFE...
...AND I THOUGHT YOU'D UNDERSTAND.
BESIDES, INSTEAD OF LETTING AKARI DIE LIKE SOME KIND OF EXPERIMENTAL TEST SUBJECT...
...I'D PREFER TO MAKE IT QUICK!

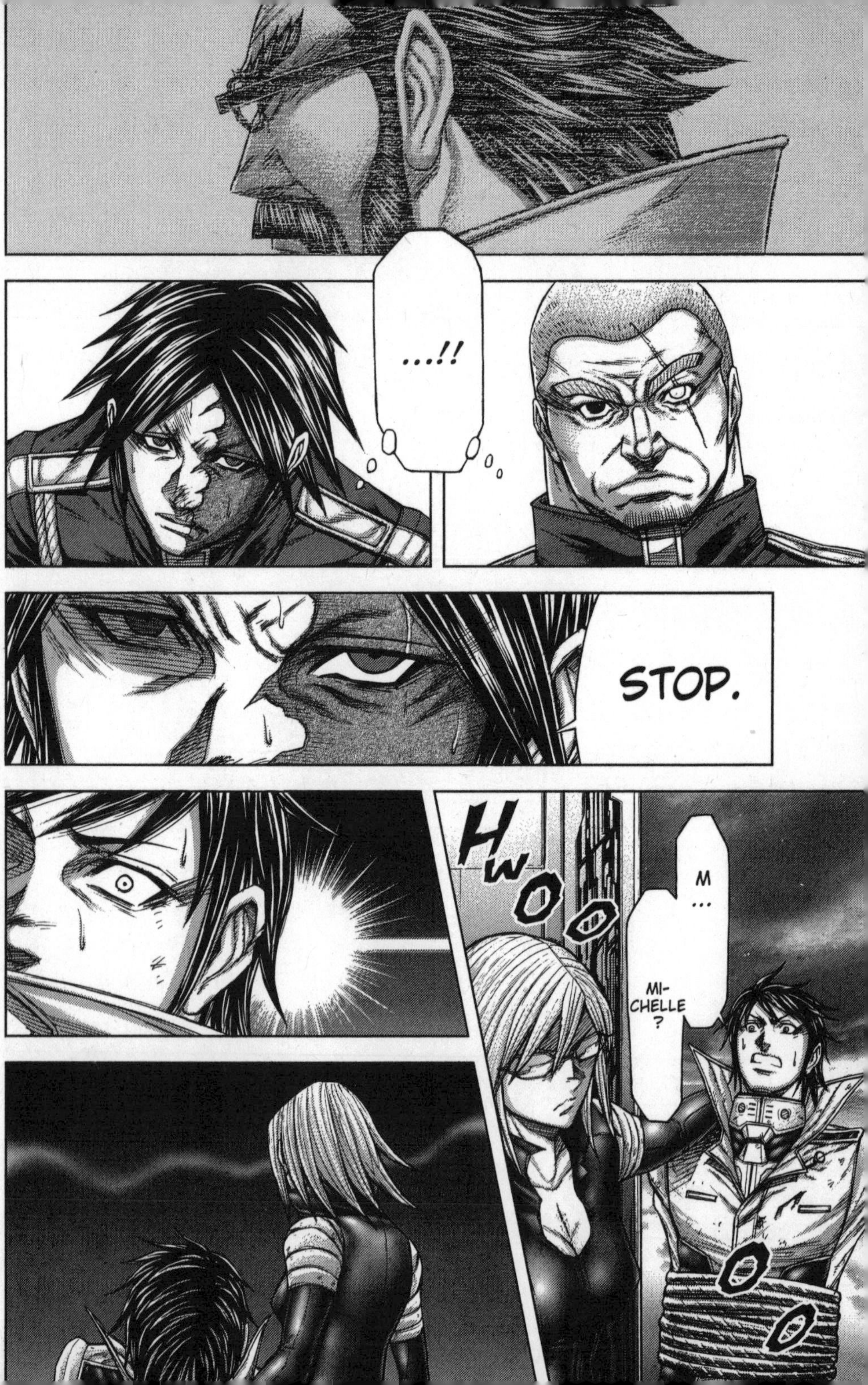
...!!
STOP.
HWOOO
M...
MI-CHELLE?
OO

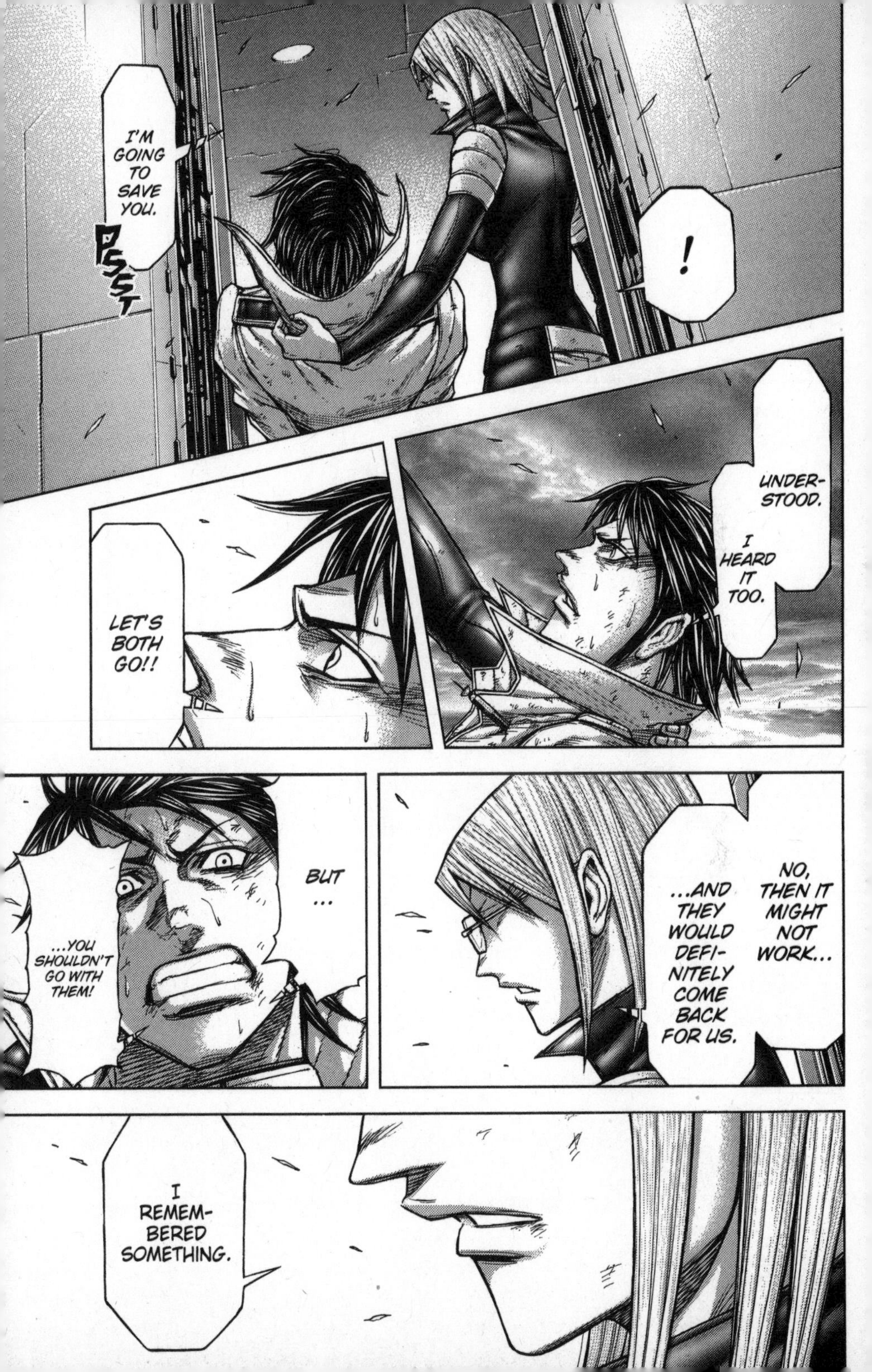
I'M GOING TO SAVE YOU.
PSSST
!
UNDER-STOOD.
I HEARD IT TOO.
LET'S BOTH GO!!
NO, THEN IT MIGHT NOT WORK...
...AND THEY WOULD DEFI-NITELY COME BACK FOR US.
BUT...
...YOU SHOULDN'T GO WITH THEM!
I REMEM-BERED SOMETHING.

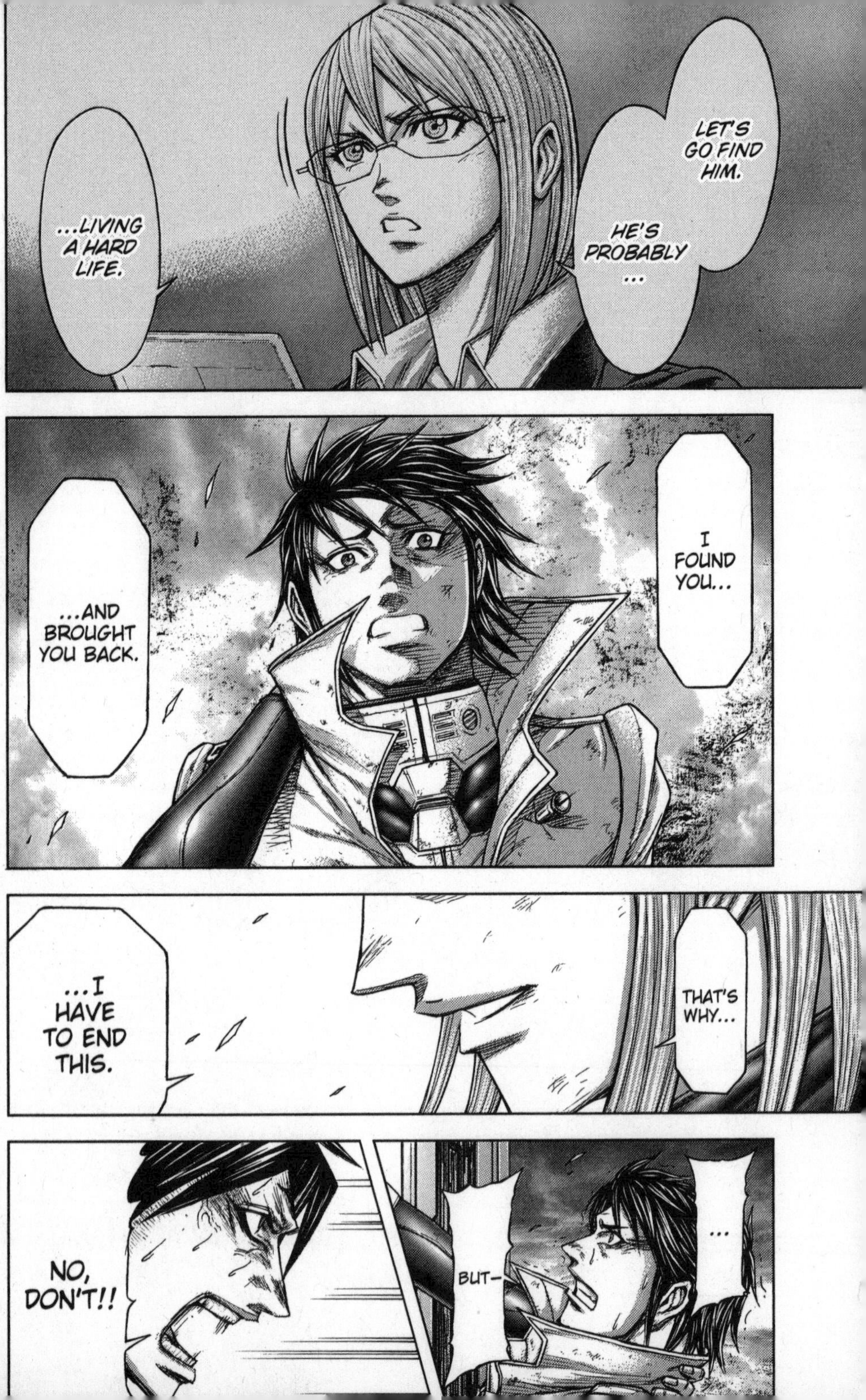
LET'S GO FIND HIM.
HE'S PROBABLY ...
...LIVING A HARD LIFE.
I FOUND YOU...
...AND BROUGHT YOU BACK.
THAT'S WHY...
...I HAVE TO END THIS.
...
BUT—
NO, DON'T!!

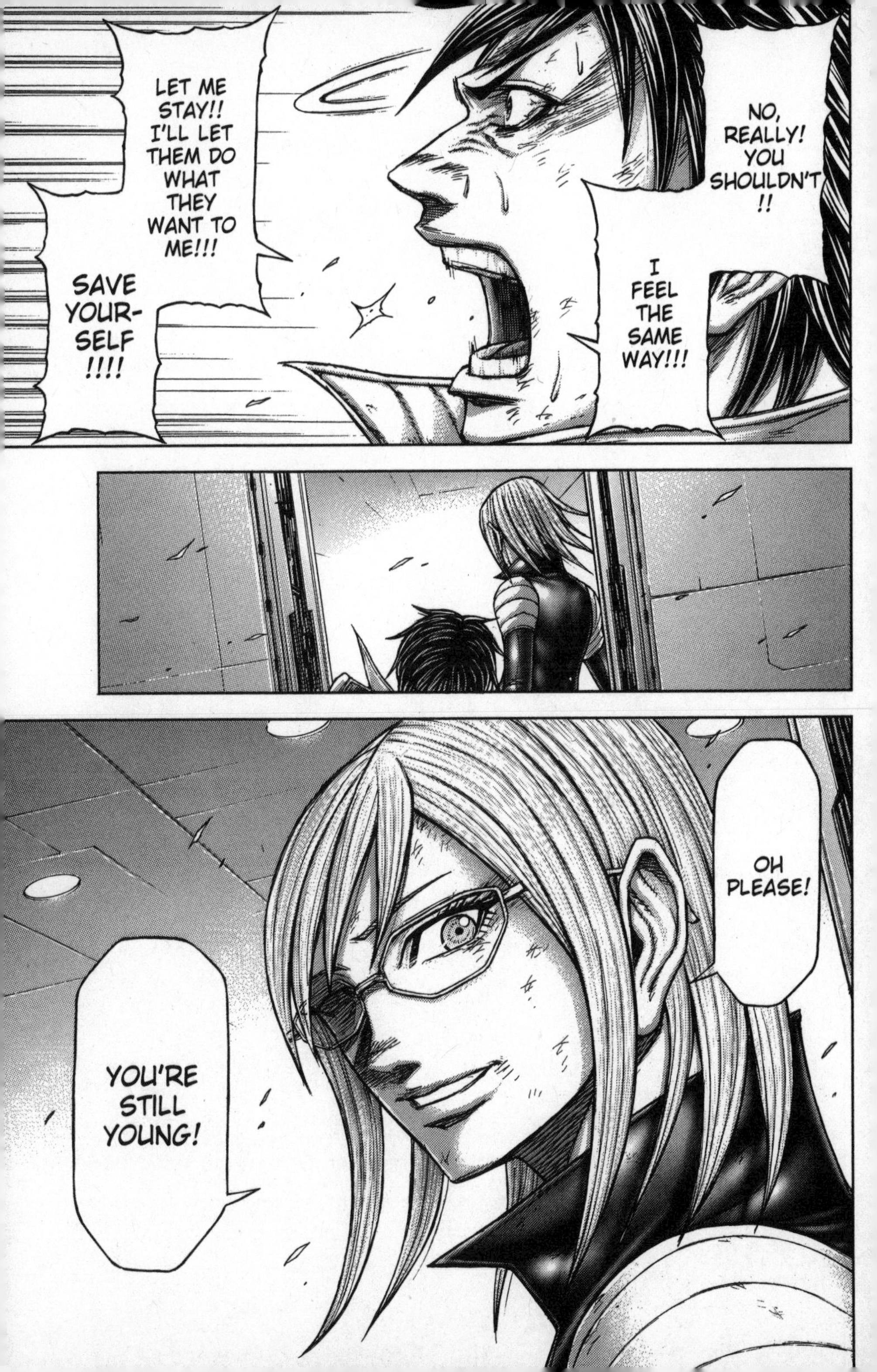
NO, REALLY! YOU SHOULDN'T!!
I FEEL THE SAME WAY!!!
LET ME STAY!! I'LL LET THEM DO WHAT THEY WANT TO ME!!!
SAVE YOUR-SELF!!!!
OH PLEASE!
YOU'RE STILL YOUNG!

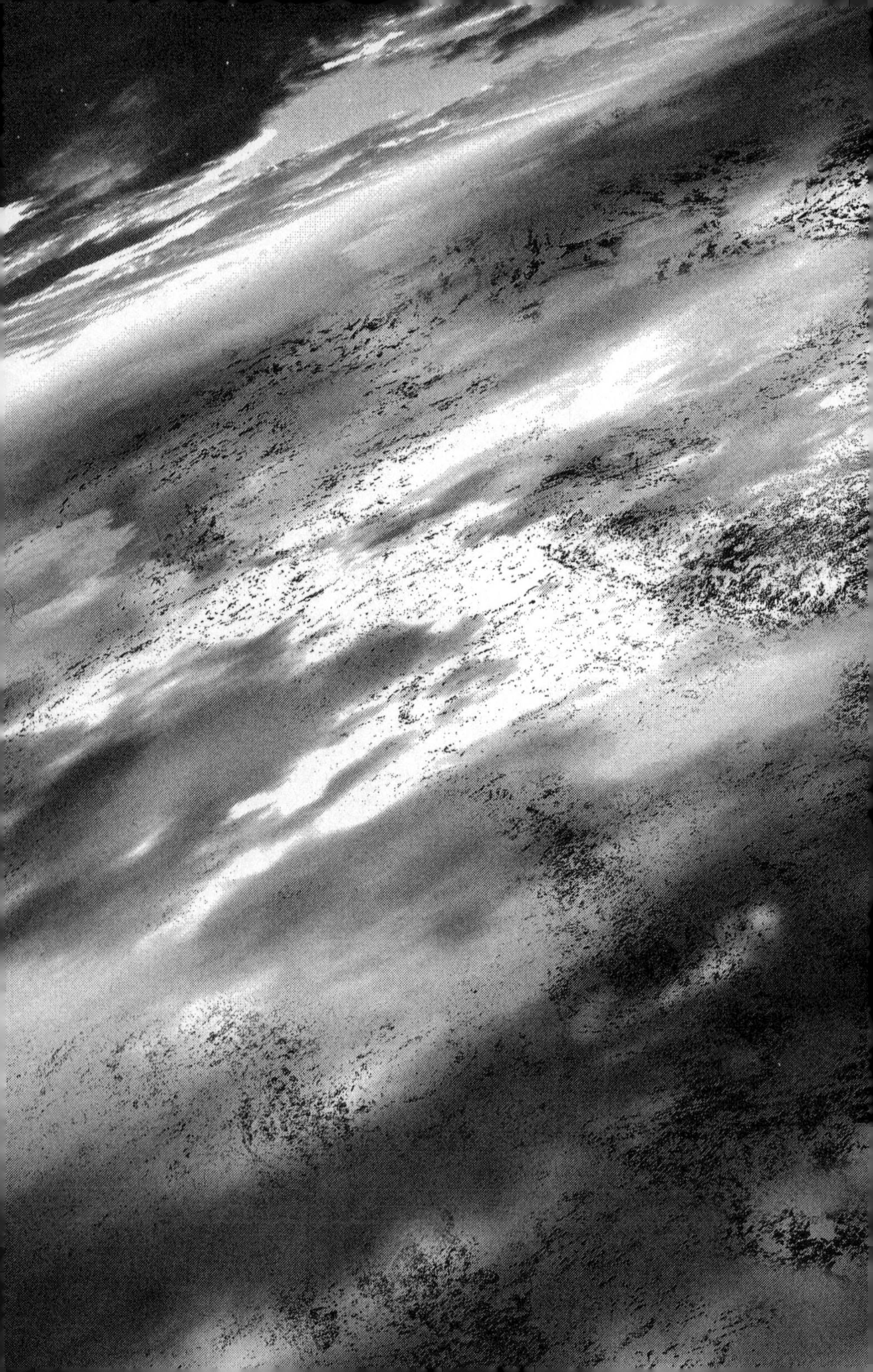

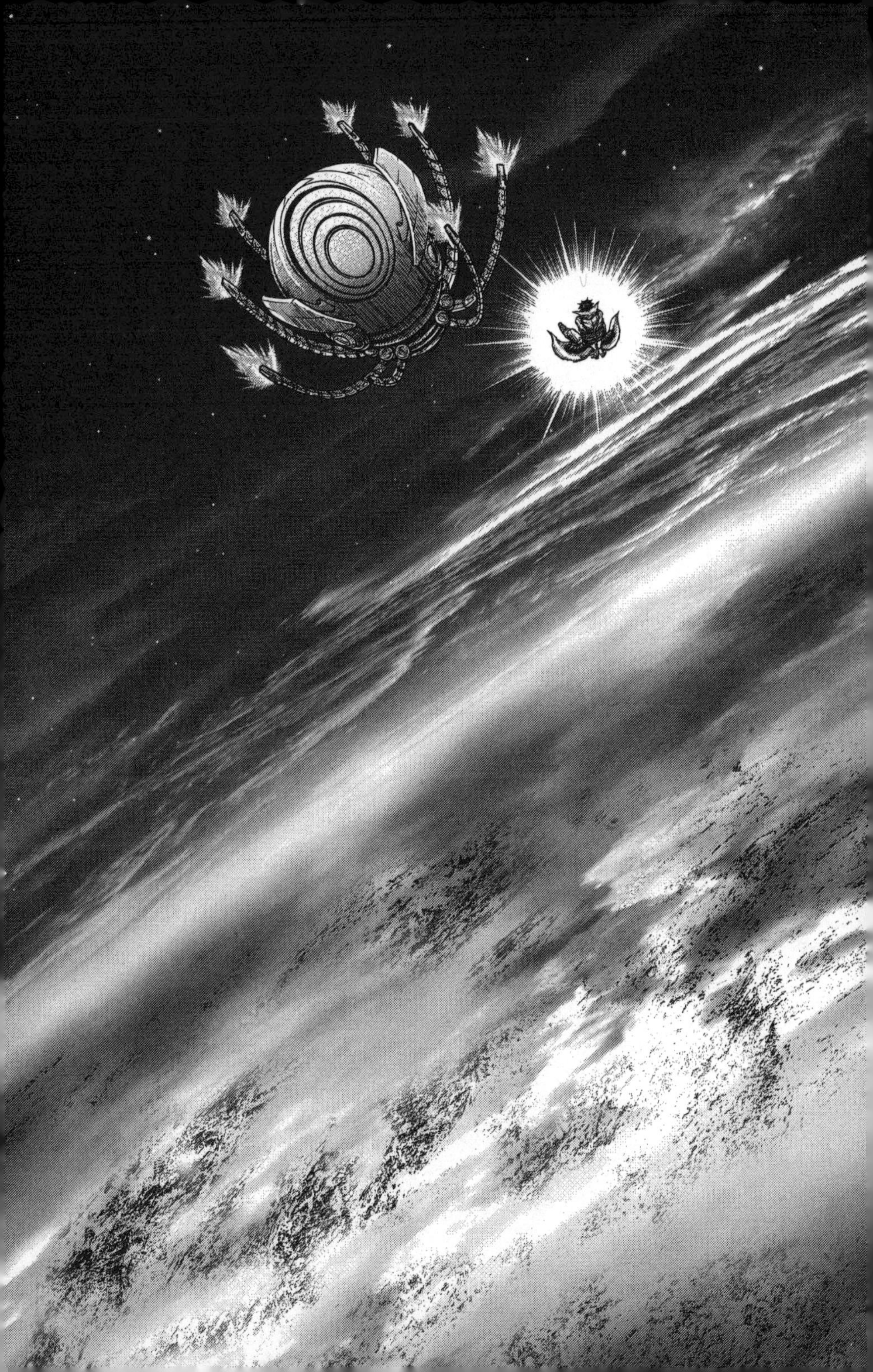

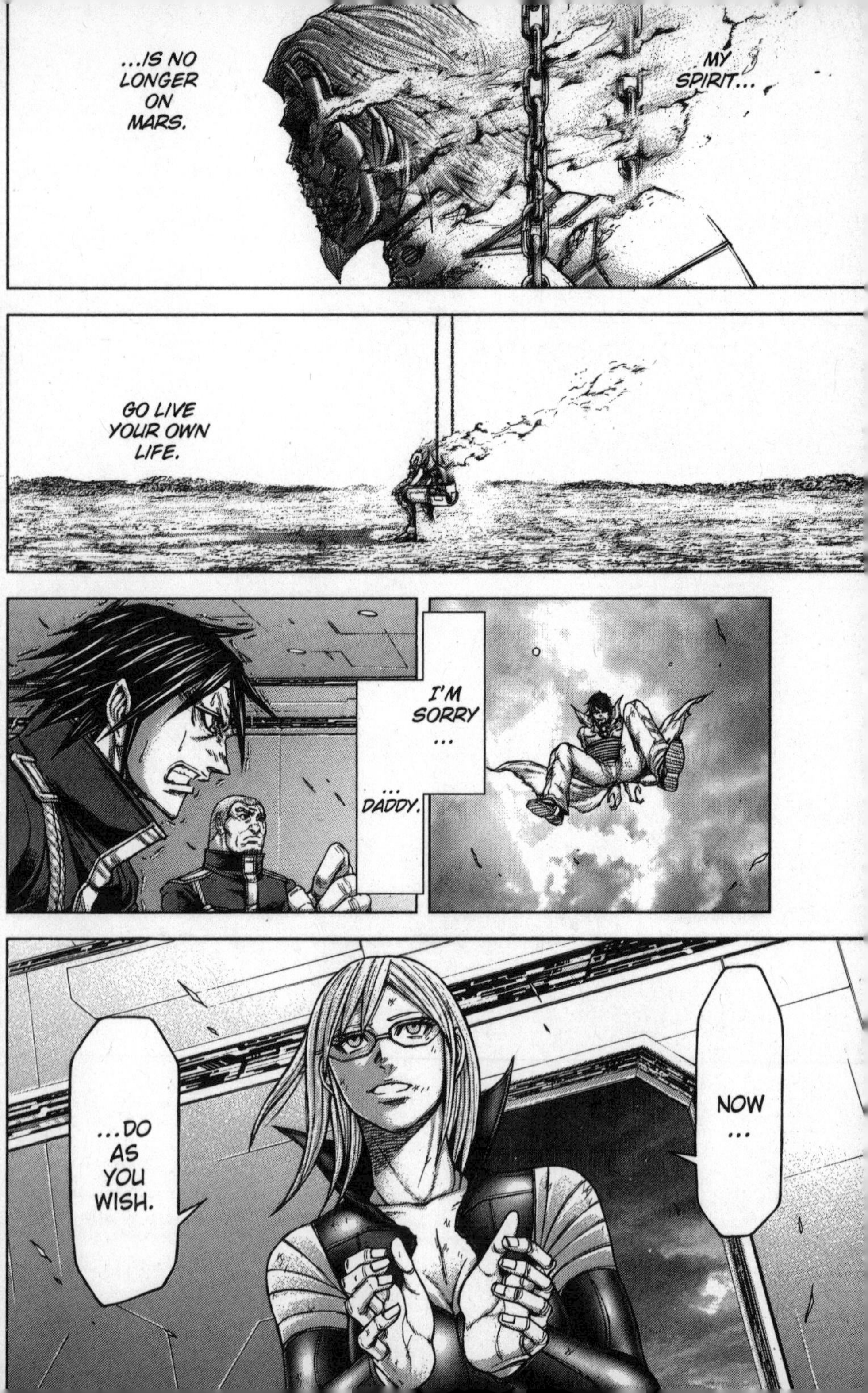
MY SPIRIT...
...IS NO LONGER ON MARS.
GO LIVE YOUR OWN LIFE.
I'M SORRY ...
... DADDY.
NOW ...
...DO AS YOU WISH.

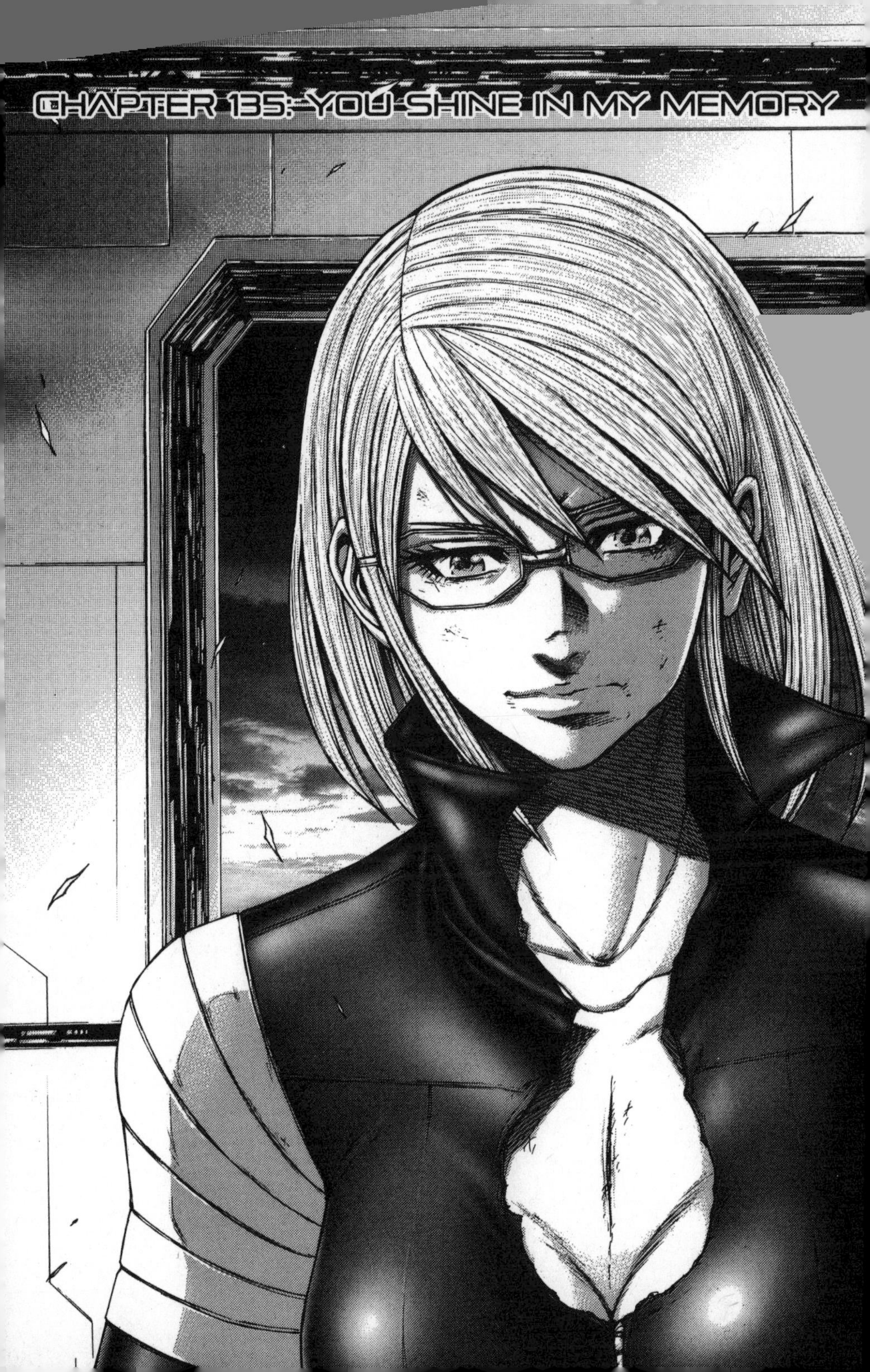
CHAPTER 135: YOU SHINE IN MY MEMORY

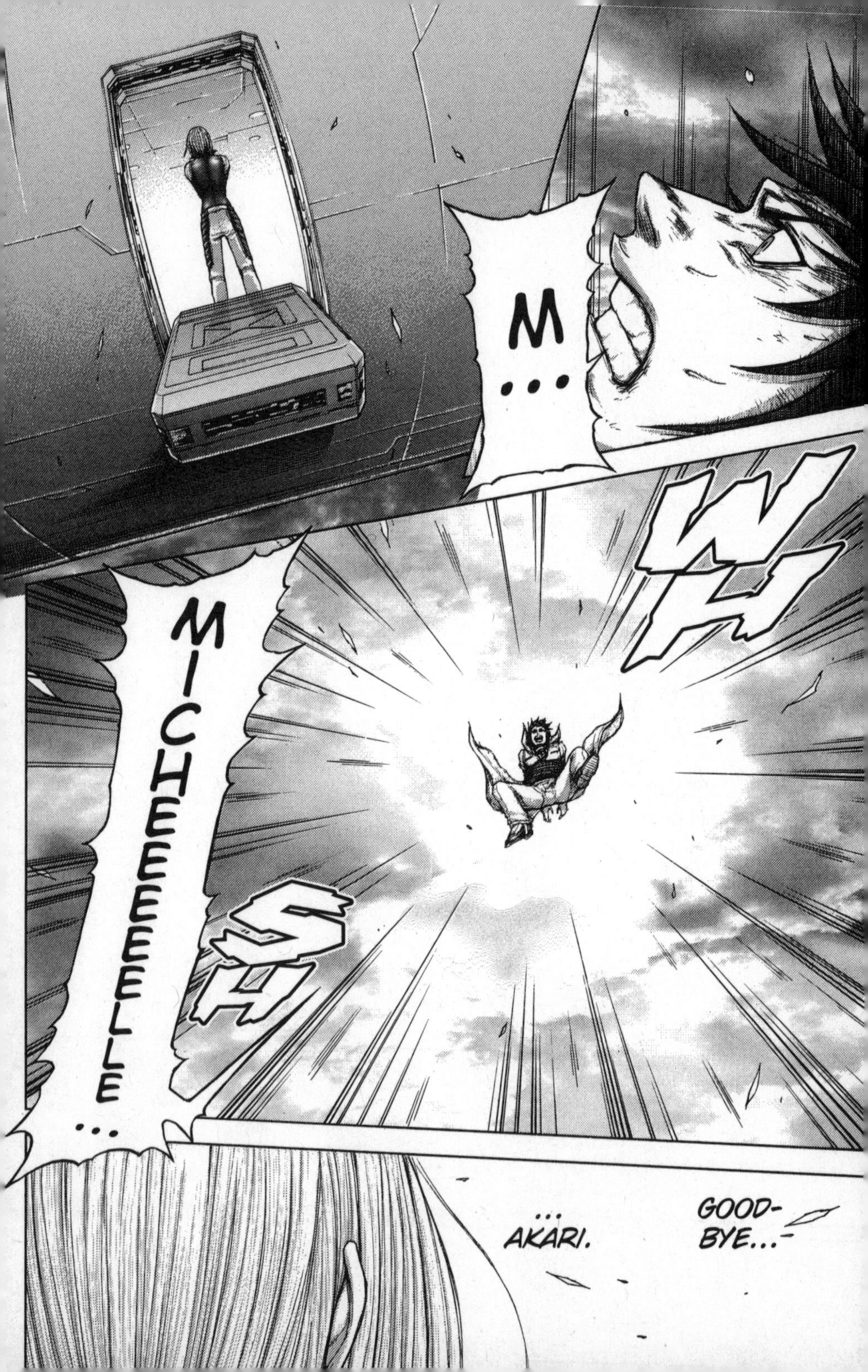
M...
WH
MICHEEEEEELLE...
SH
GOOD-BYE...
...AKARI.

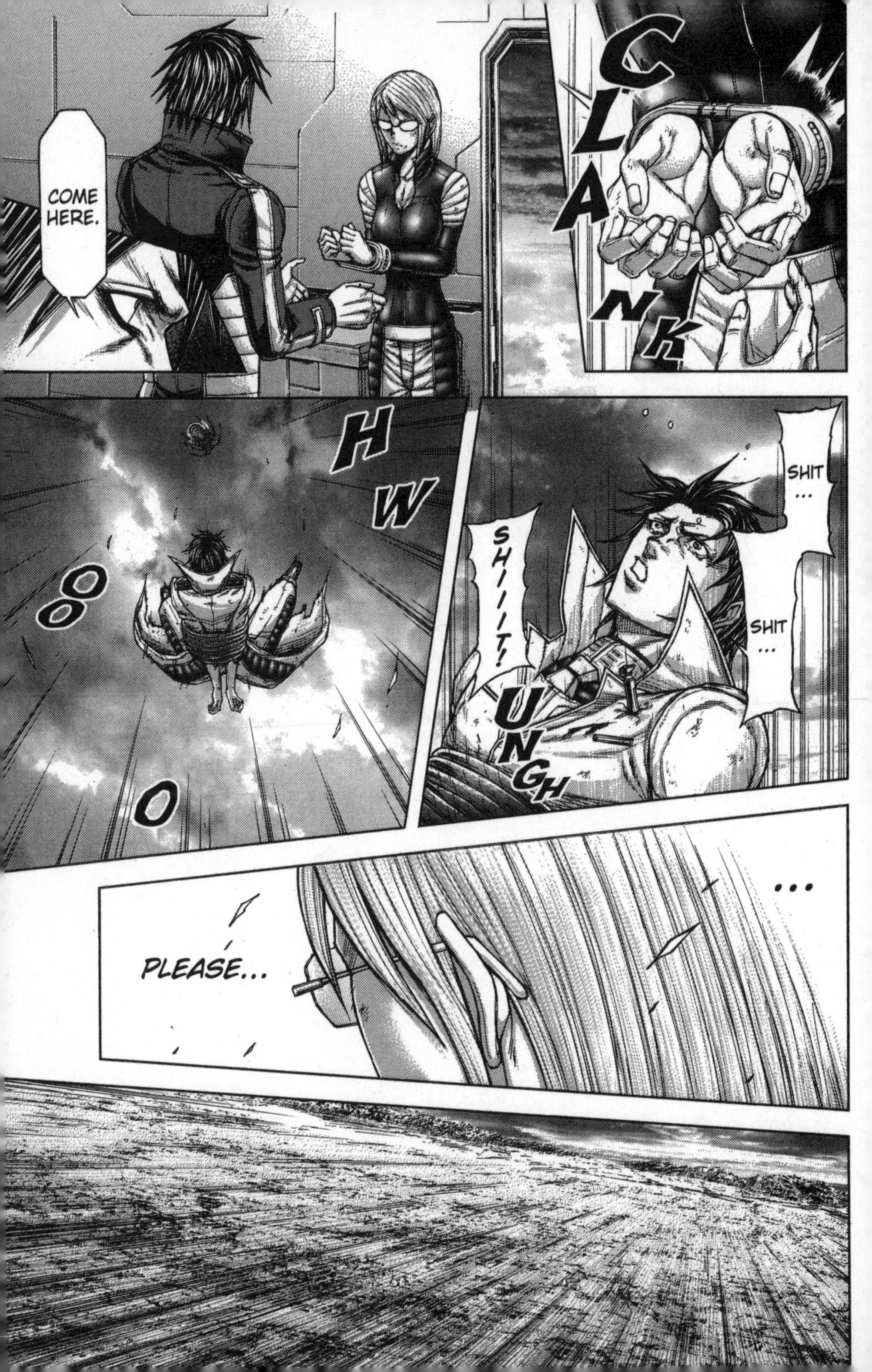
CLANK
COME HERE.
SHIT...
SHIIIT!
SHIT...
UNGH
HWOOO
...
PLEASE...

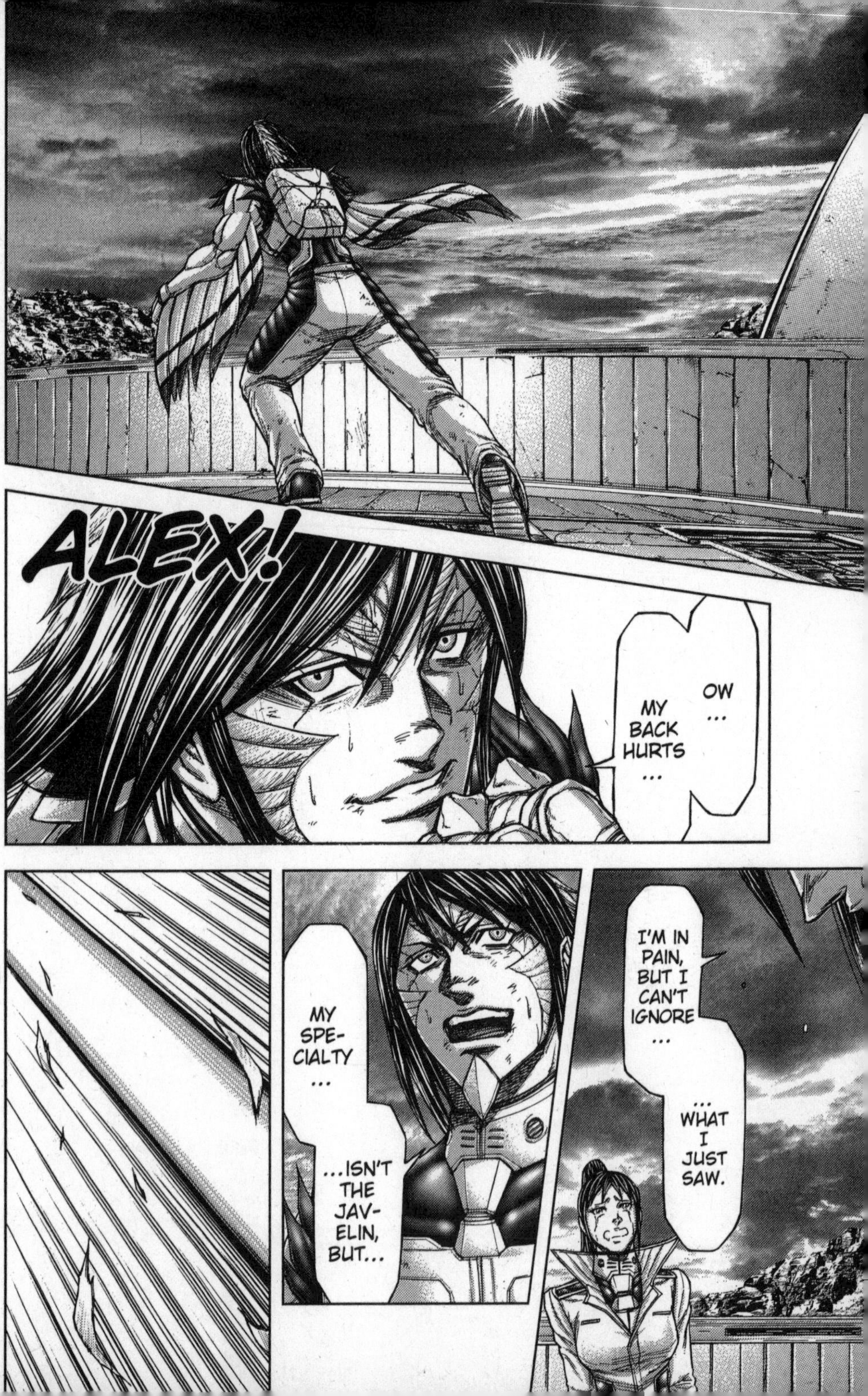
ALEX!
OW ... MY BACK HURTS ...
I'M IN PAIN, BUT I CAN'T IGNORE ...
... WHAT I JUST SAW.
MY SPE-CIALTY ...
...ISN'T THE JAV-ELIN, BUT...

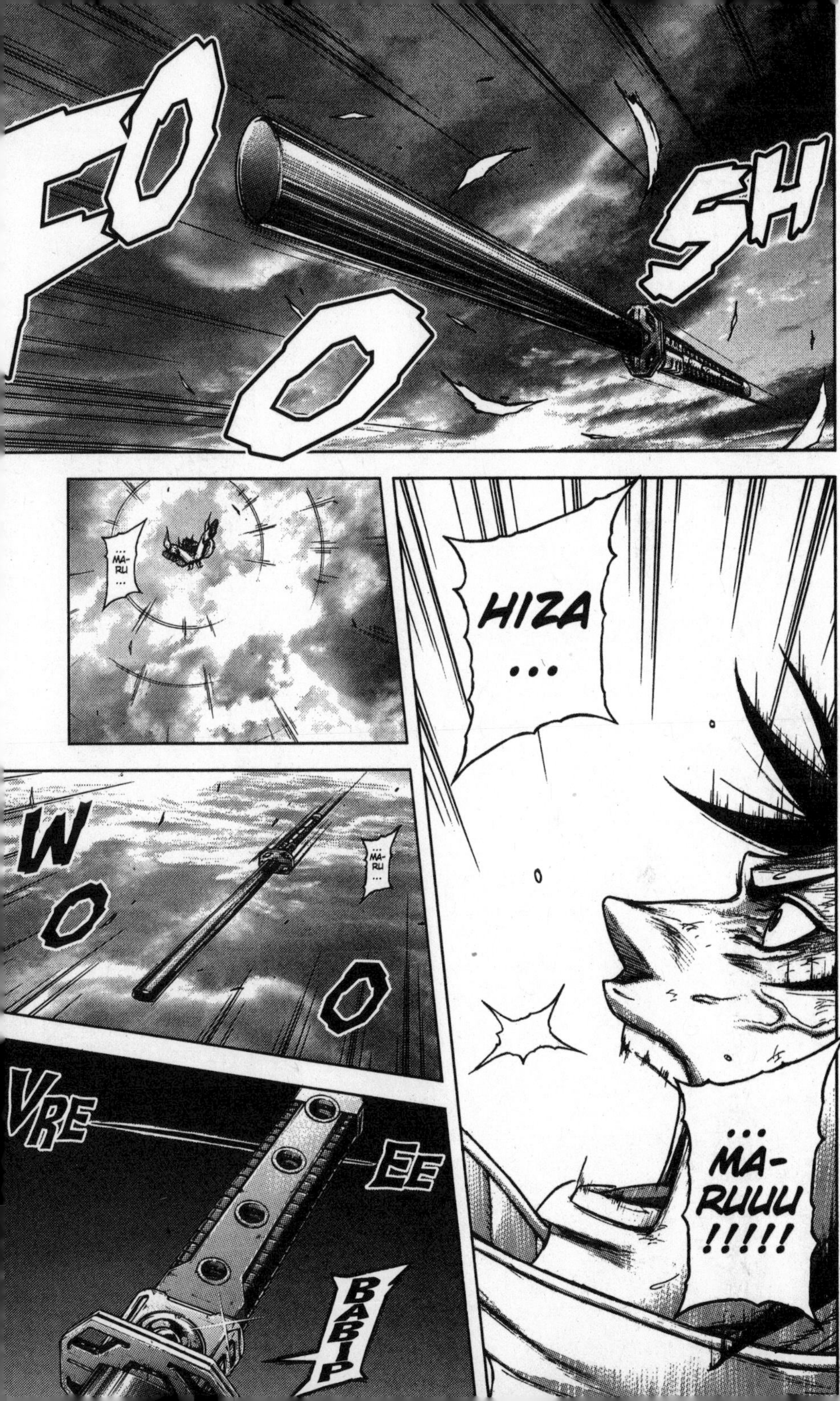
O
O
SH
HIZA ...
...MA-RUUU!!!!!
...MA-RU...
WOO
...MA-RU...
VRE-EE
BABIP

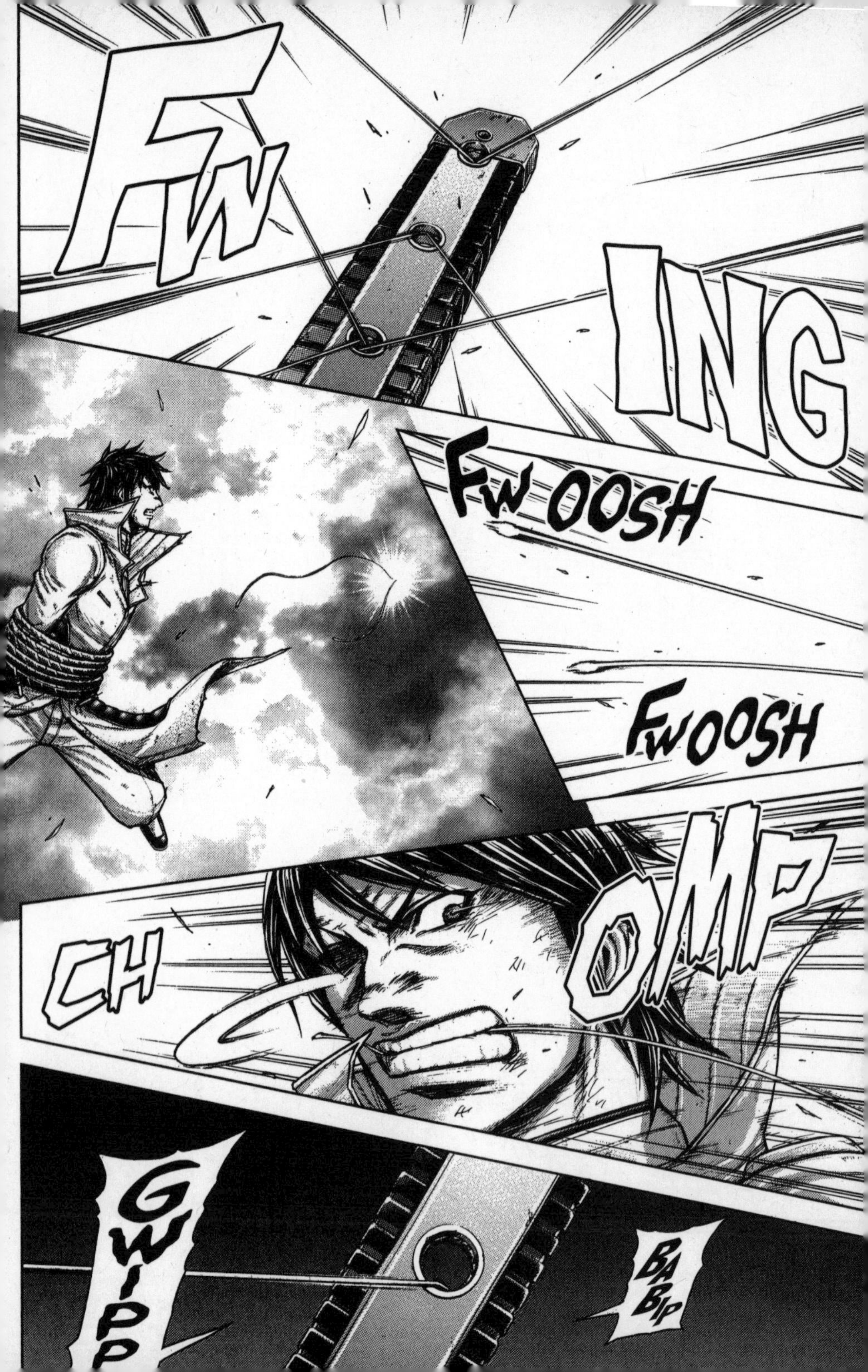
FW
ING
FWOOSH
FWOOSH
CH
OMP
BABIP
GWIPP

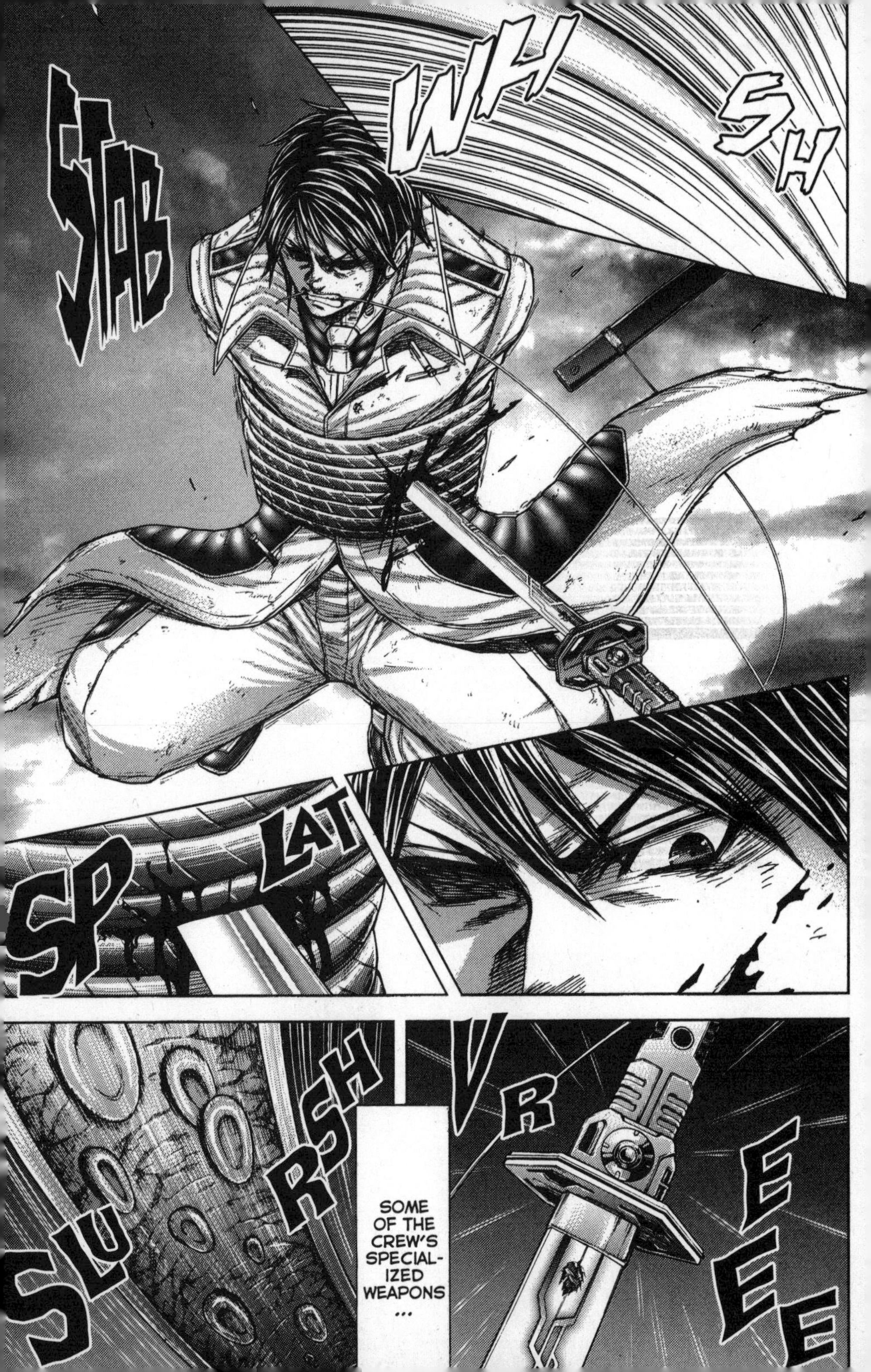
WHSH
STAB
SPLAT
VREEE
SOME OF THE CREW'S SPECIAL-IZED WEAPONS...
SLURSH

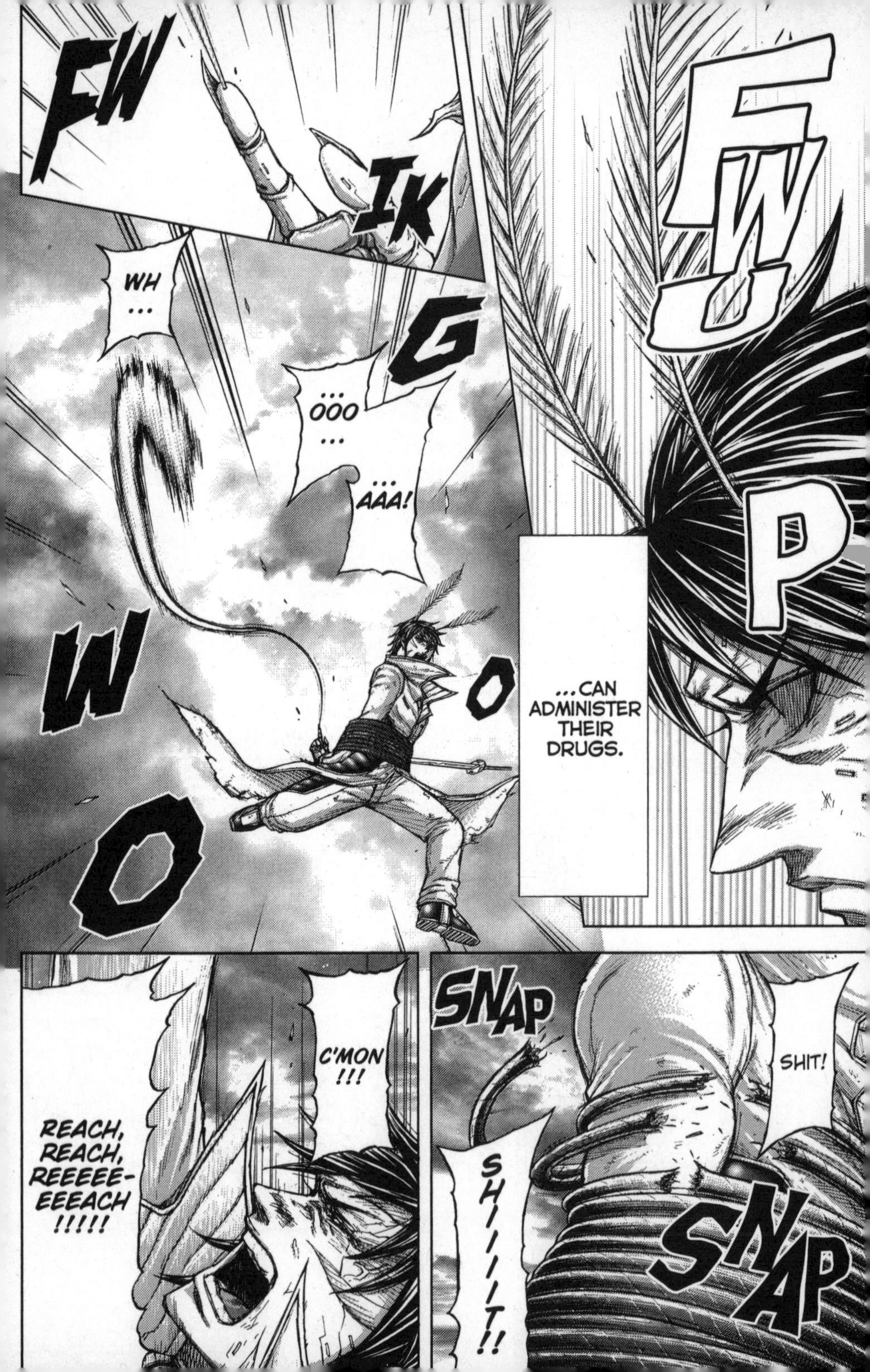
FWUP
...CAN ADMINISTER THEIR DRUGS.
FWIK
WH...
...ÖOO... ...ÄAA!
SNAP
SHIT!
SHIIIIIT!!
SNAP
C'MON!!!
REACH, REACH, REEEEEEEEEACH!!!!!

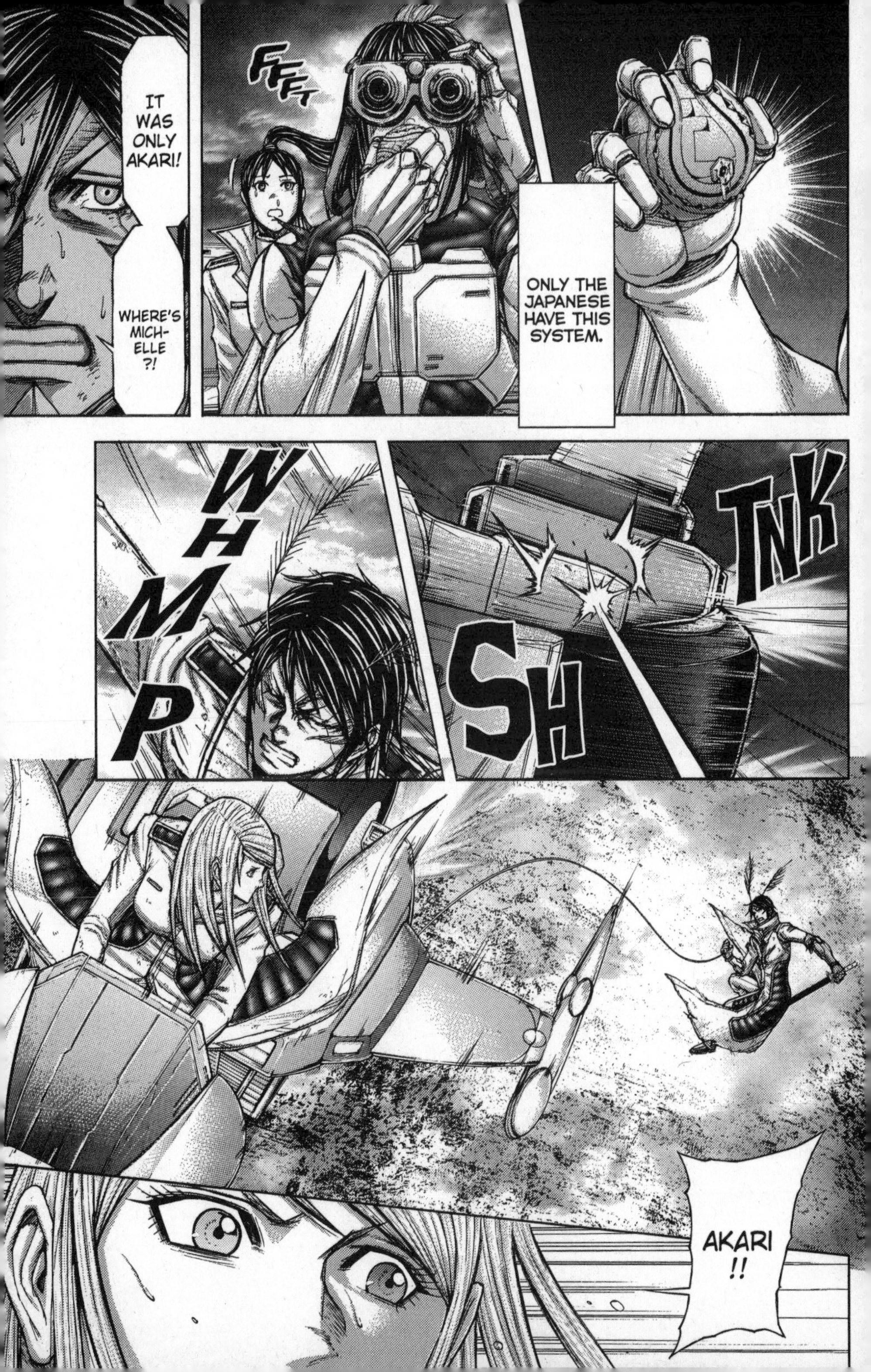
ONLY THE JAPANESE HAVE THIS SYSTEM.
FFFT
IT WAS ONLY AKARI!
WHERE'S MICHELLE?!
TNK
SH
WHMP
AKARI!!

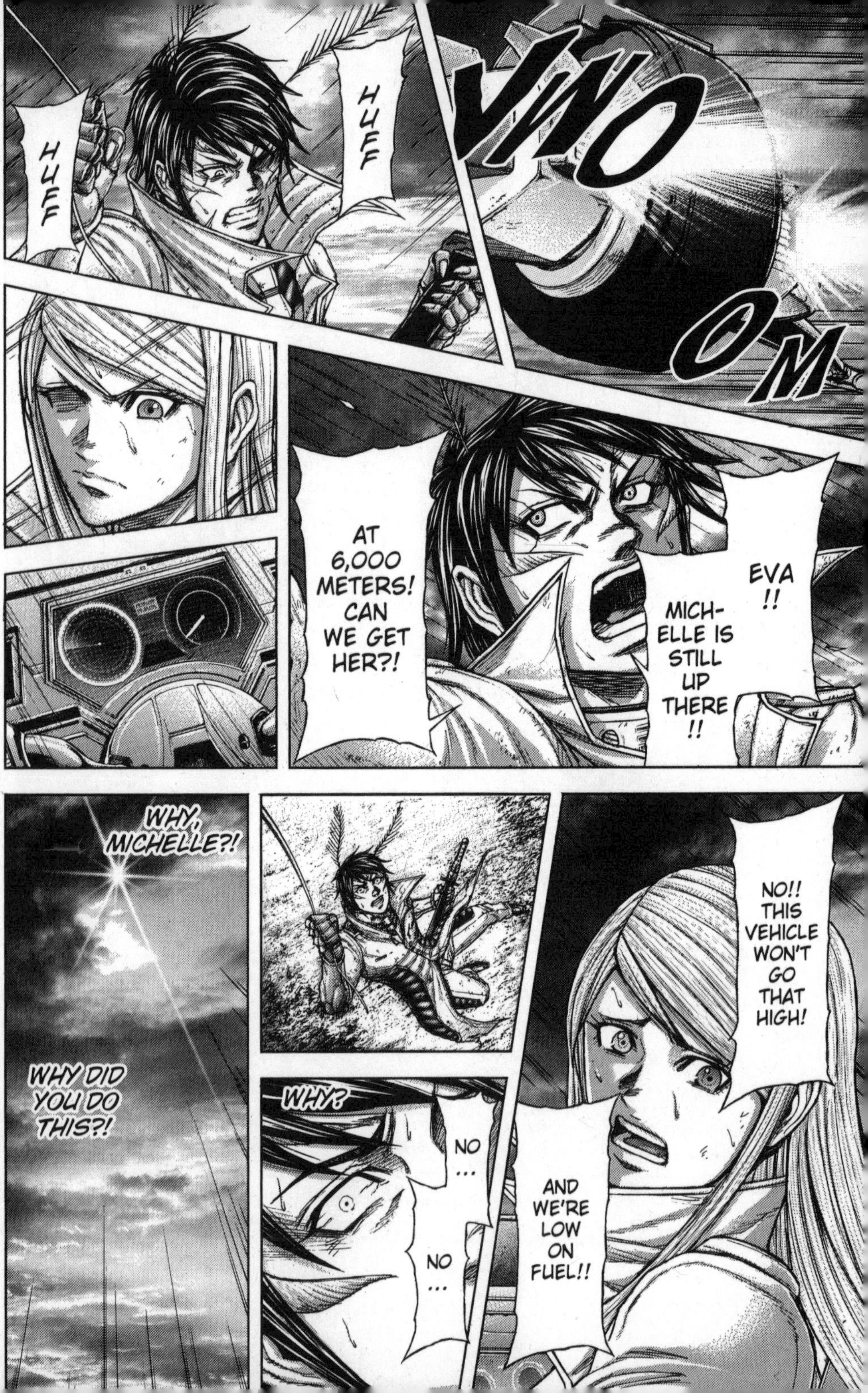
VNOOM
HUFF
HUFF
EVA!!
MICHELLE IS STILL UP THERE!!
AT 6,000 METERS! CAN WE GET HER?!
NO!! THIS VEHICLE WON'T GO THAT HIGH!
AND WE'RE LOW ON FUEL!!
NO...
WHY?
NO...
WHY, MICHELLE?!
WHY DID YOU DO THIS?!

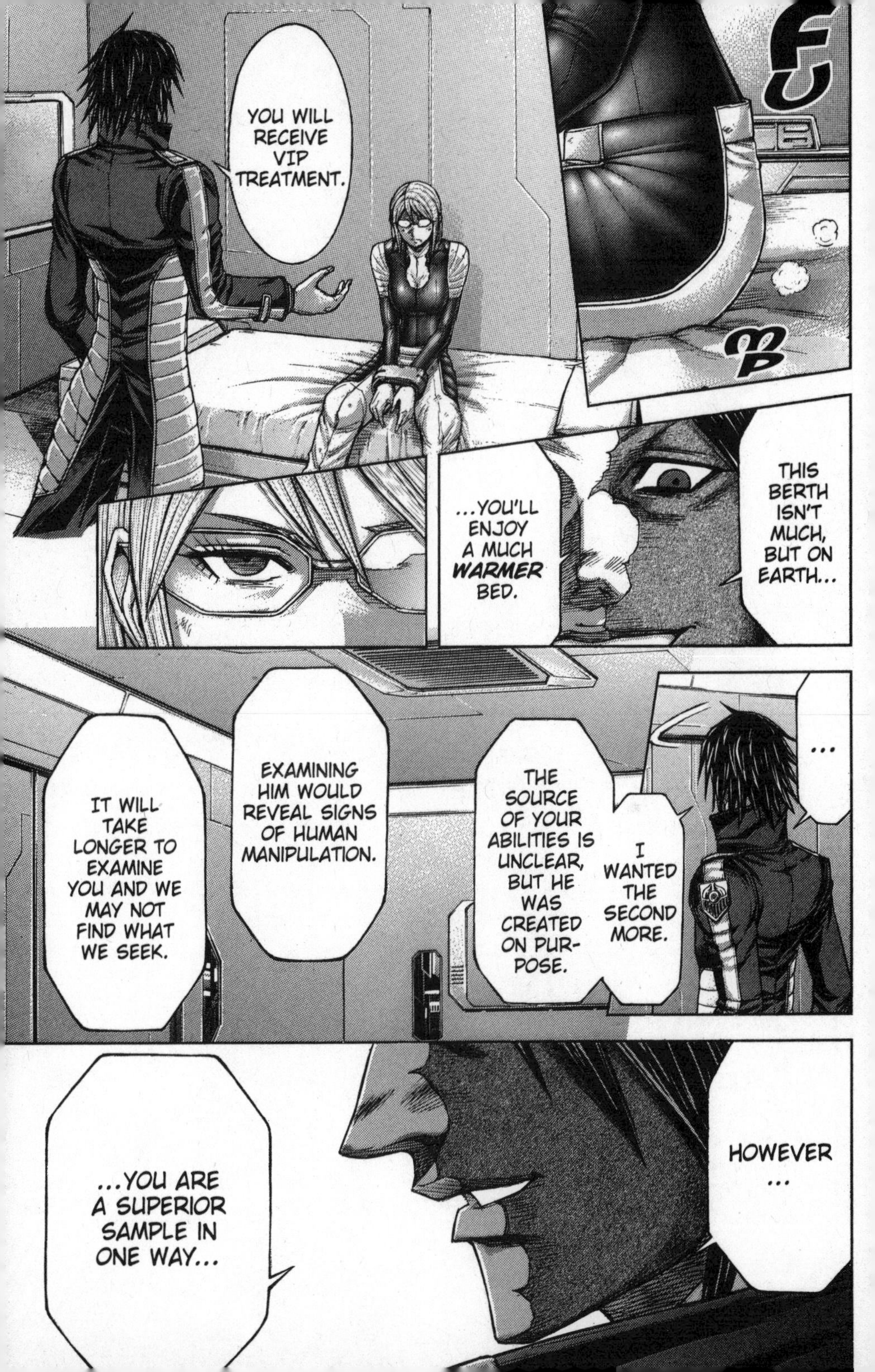
FU
MP
YOU WILL RECEIVE VIP TREATMENT.
THIS BERTH ISN'T MUCH, BUT ON EARTH...
...YOU'LL ENJOY A MUCH **WARMER** BED.
...
I WANTED THE SECOND MORE.
THE SOURCE OF YOUR ABILITIES IS UNCLEAR, BUT HE WAS CREATED ON PUR-POSE.
EXAMINING HIM WOULD REVEAL SIGNS OF HUMAN MANIPULATION.
IT WILL TAKE LONGER TO EXAMINE YOU AND WE MAY NOT FIND WHAT WE SEEK.
HOWEVER ...
...YOU ARE A SUPERIOR SAMPLE IN ONE WAY...

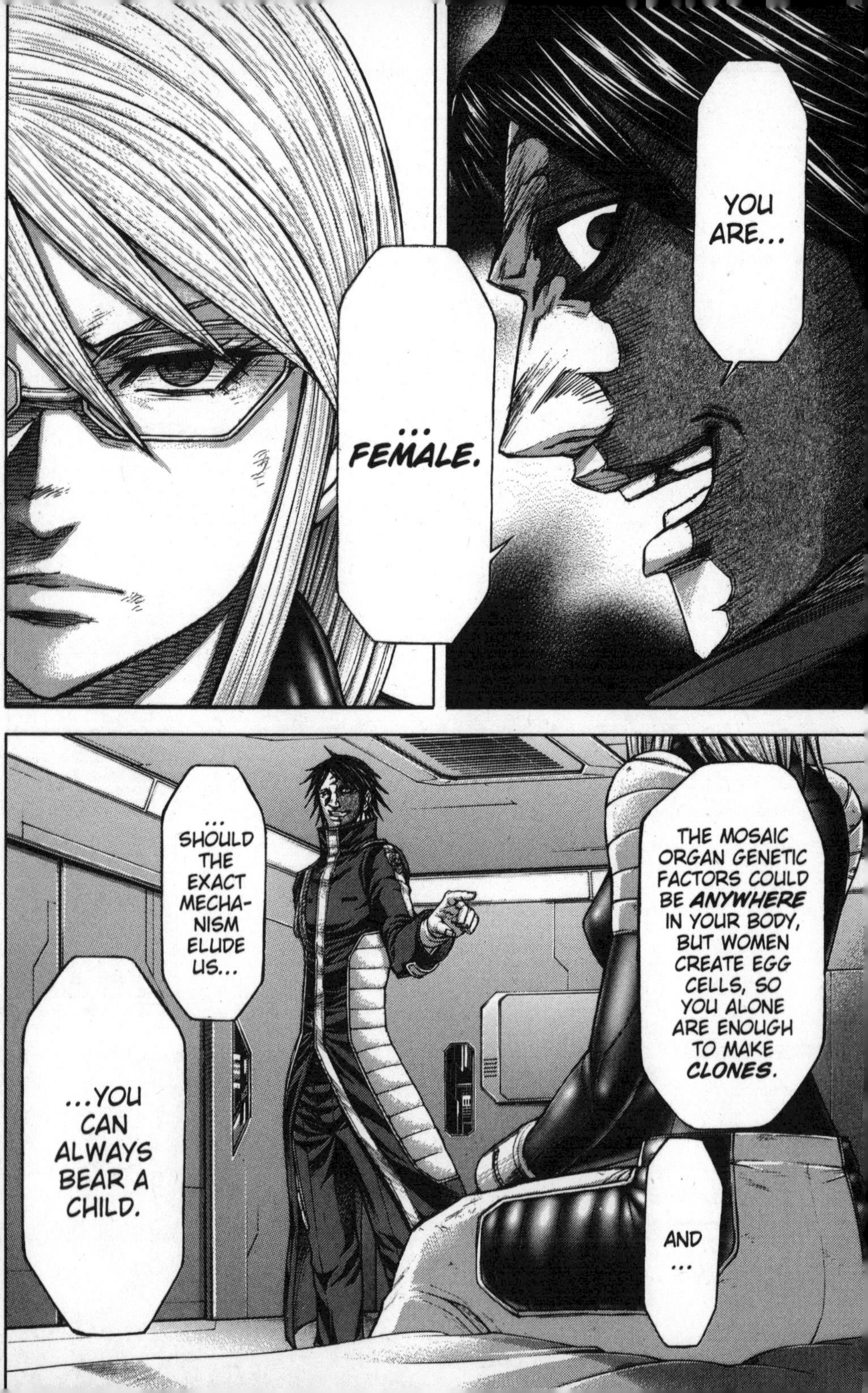
YOU ARE...
...FEMALE.
THE MOSAIC ORGAN GENETIC FACTORS COULD BE ANYWHERE IN YOUR BODY, BUT WOMEN CREATE EGG CELLS, SO YOU ALONE ARE ENOUGH TO MAKE CLONES.
AND...
...SHOULD THE EXACT MECHA-NISM ELUDE US...
...YOU CAN ALWAYS BEAR A CHILD.

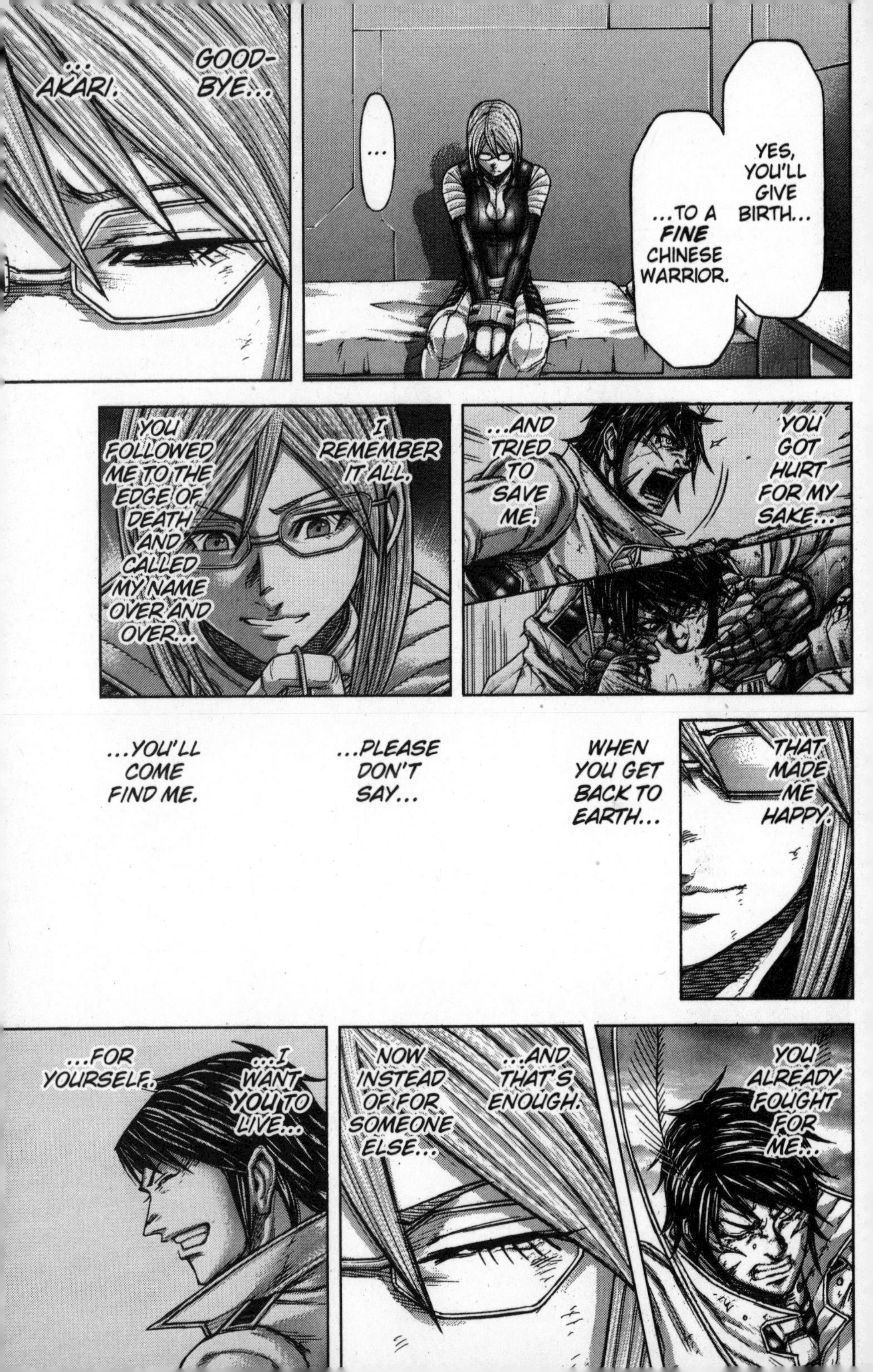
YES, YOU'LL GIVE BIRTH...
...TO A FINE CHINESE WARRIOR.
...
GOOD-BYE...
...AKARI.
YOU GOT HURT FOR MY SAKE...
...AND TRIED TO SAVE ME.
I REMEMBER IT ALL.
YOU FOLLOWED ME TO THE EDGE OF DEATH AND CALLED MY NAME OVER AND OVER...
THAT MADE ME HAPPY.
WHEN YOU GET BACK TO EARTH...
...PLEASE DON'T SAY...
...YOU'LL COME FIND ME.
YOU ALREADY FOUGHT FOR ME...
...AND THAT'S ENOUGH.
NOW INSTEAD OF FOR SOMEONE ELSE...
...I WANT YOU TO LIVE...
...FOR YOURSELF.

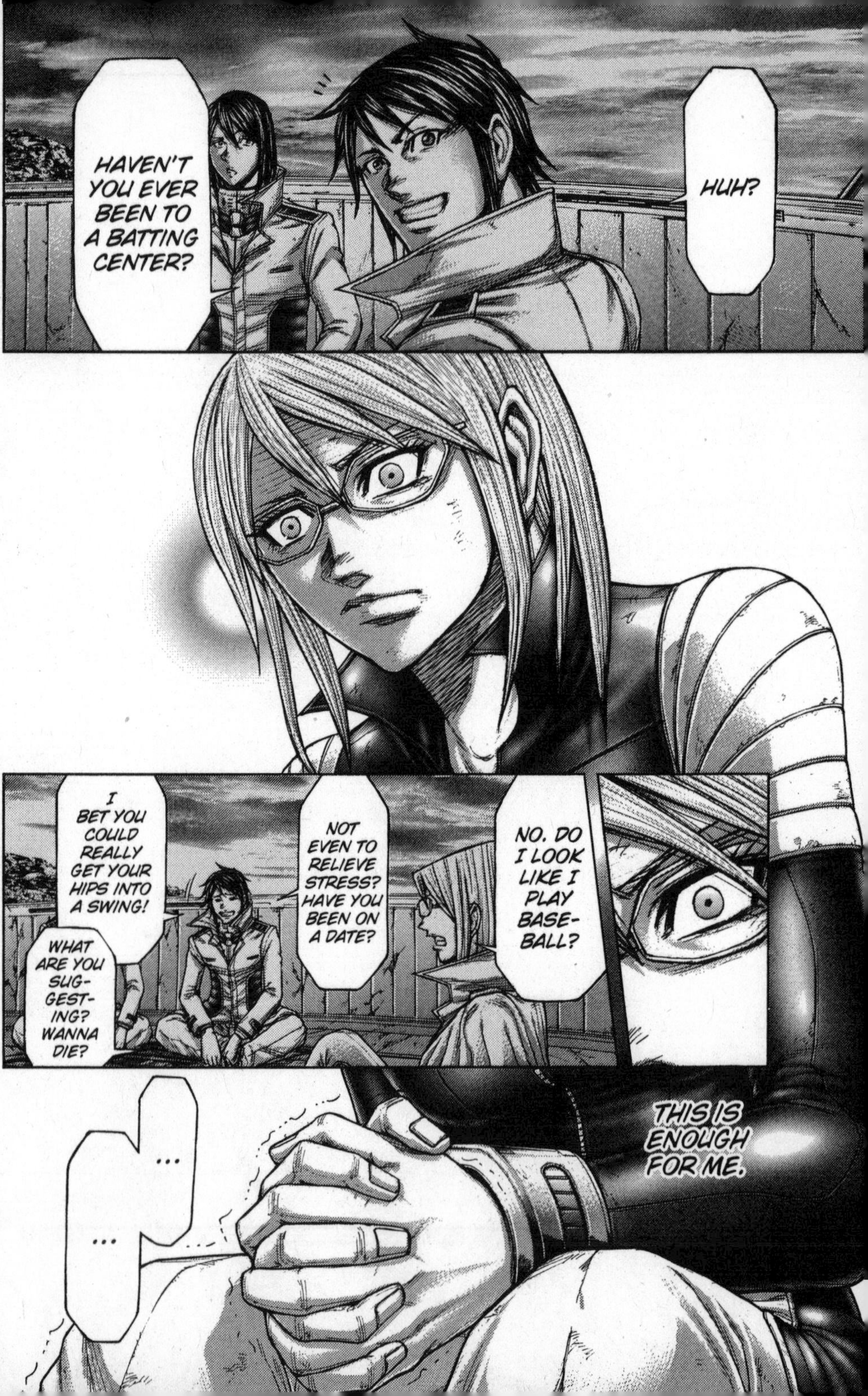
HUH?
HAVEN'T YOU EVER BEEN TO A BATTING CENTER?
NO. DO I LOOK LIKE I PLAY BASE-BALL?
NOT EVEN TO RELIEVE STRESS? HAVE YOU BEEN ON A DATE?
I BET YOU COULD REALLY GET YOUR HIPS INTO A SWING!
WHAT ARE YOU SUG-GEST-ING? WANNA DIE?
THIS IS ENOUGH FOR ME.
... ...

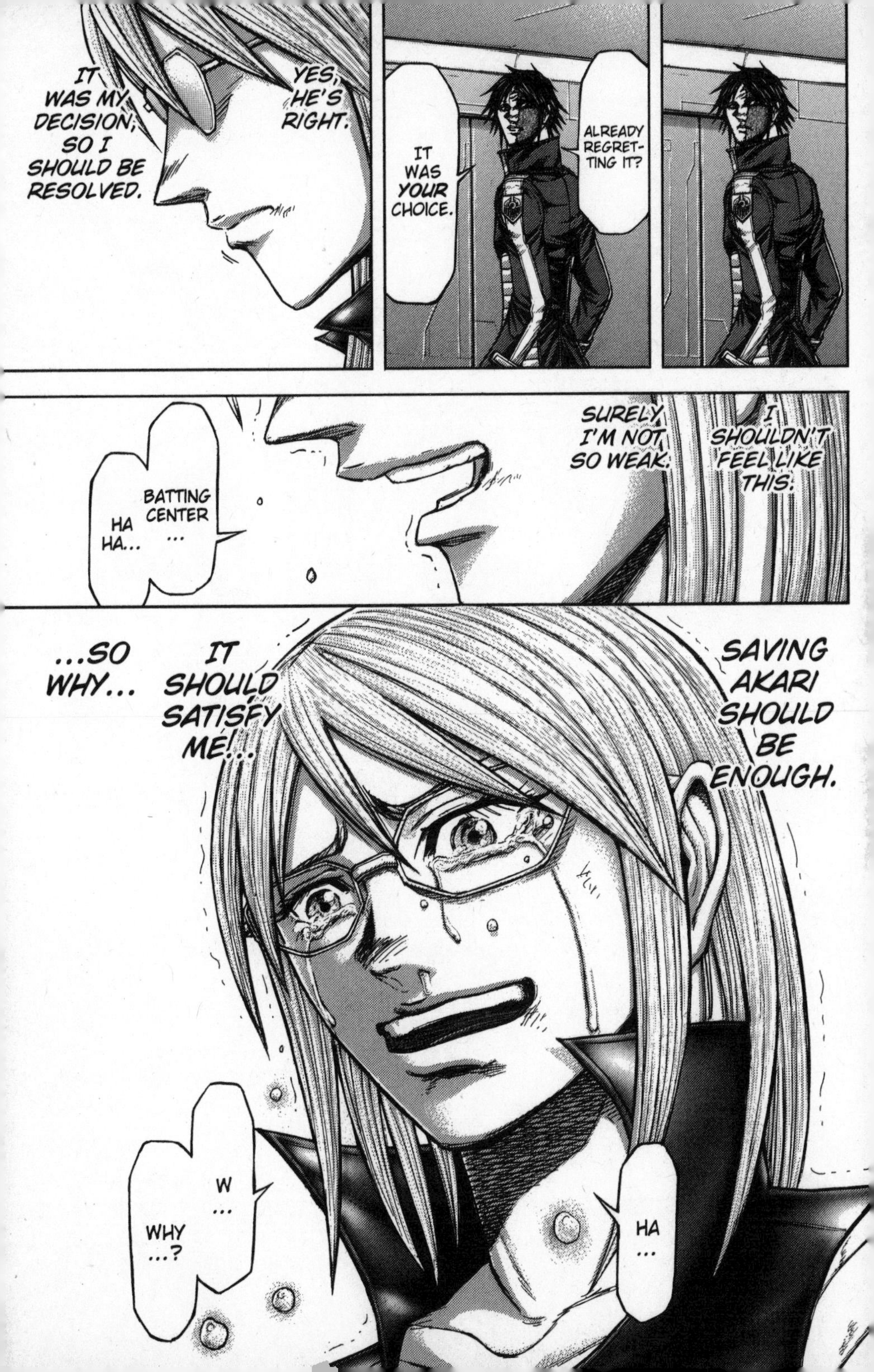
ALREADY REGRET-TING IT?
IT WAS YOUR CHOICE.
YES, HE'S RIGHT.
IT WAS MY DECISION, SO I SHOULD BE RESOLVED.
I SHOULDN'T FEEL LIKE THIS.
SURELY, I'M NOT SO WEAK.
BATTING CENTER ...
HA HA...
SAVING AKARI SHOULD BE ENOUGH.
IT SHOULD SATISFY ME!...
...SO WHY...
HA ...
W ... WHY ...?

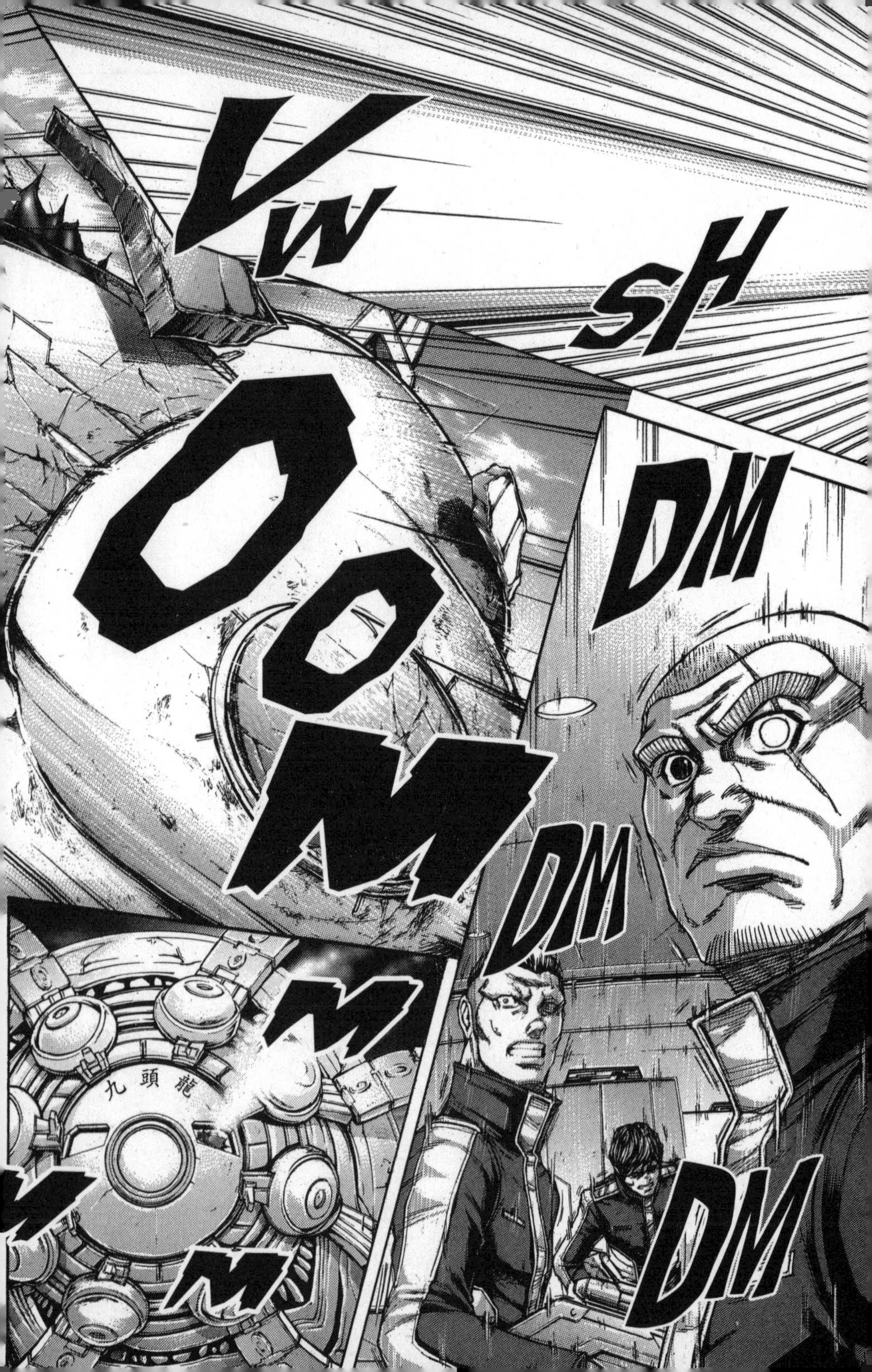
VWSH
OOM
DM
DM
DM
M
M
九頭龍

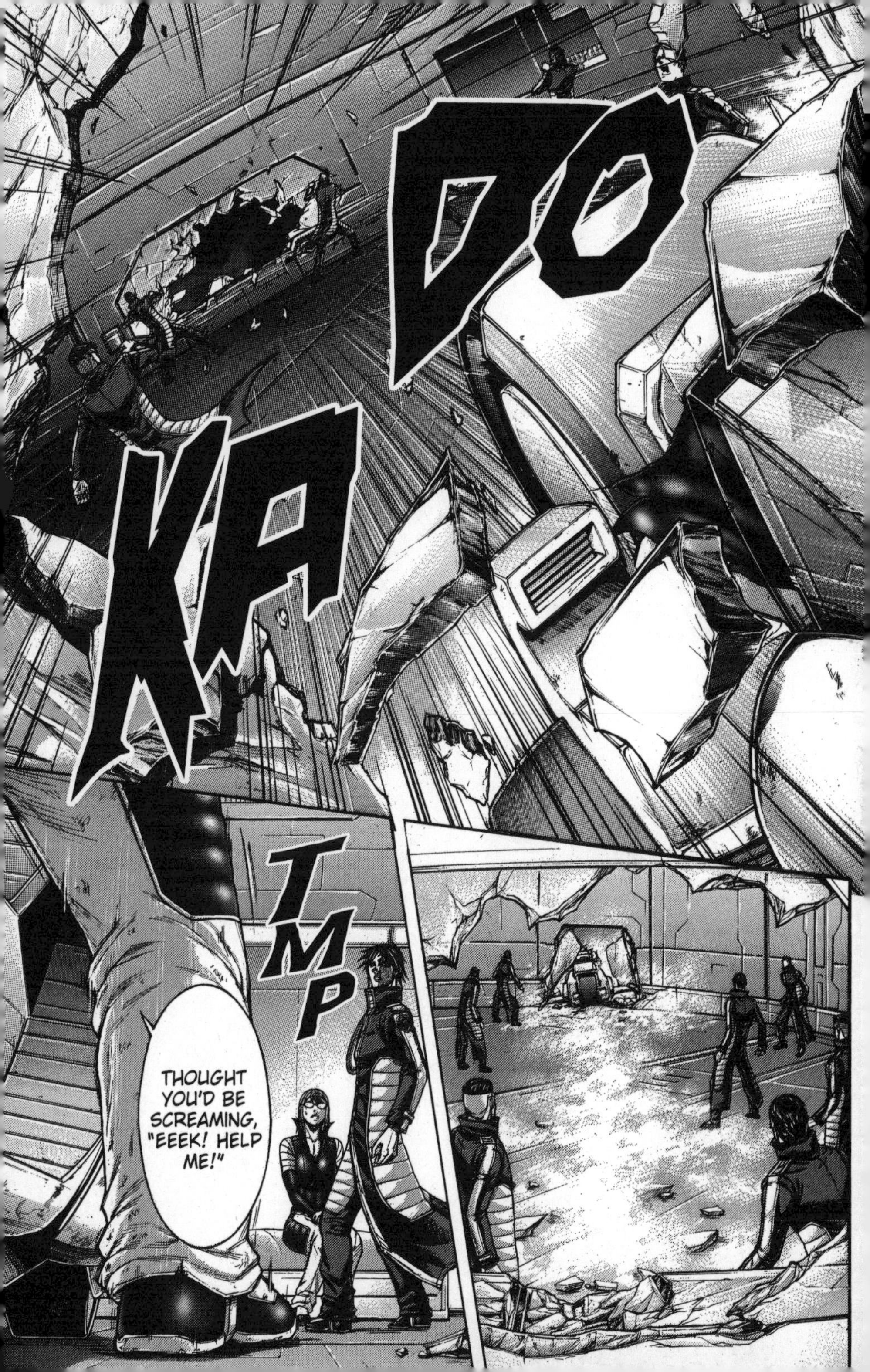
DO
KA
TMP
THOUGHT YOU'D BE SCREAMING, "EEEK! HELP ME!"

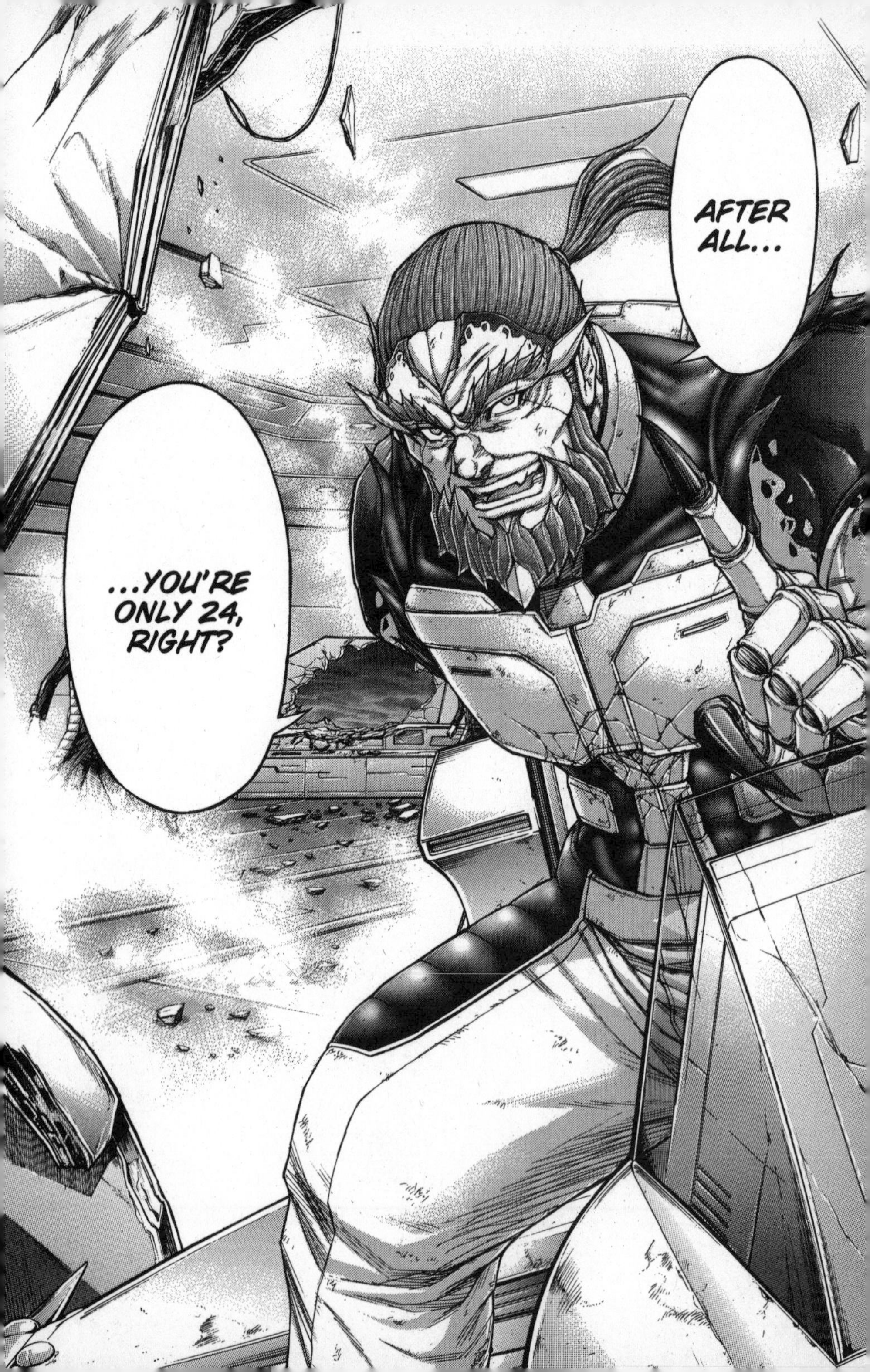
AFTER ALL...
...YOU'RE ONLY 24, RIGHT?

Welcome to the Land of Bears and Magic!

Harigimi Sea Land

Closed in 2602.

A direct monorail from Sapporo Station is still in operation for the people of Harigimi City.

Delightful Mascot Characters

Melon is quite the hunk.

Melona is sorta Melon's girlfriend—and she's been through a lot.

A single transformation requires inhaling three to four balls, and that takes time.

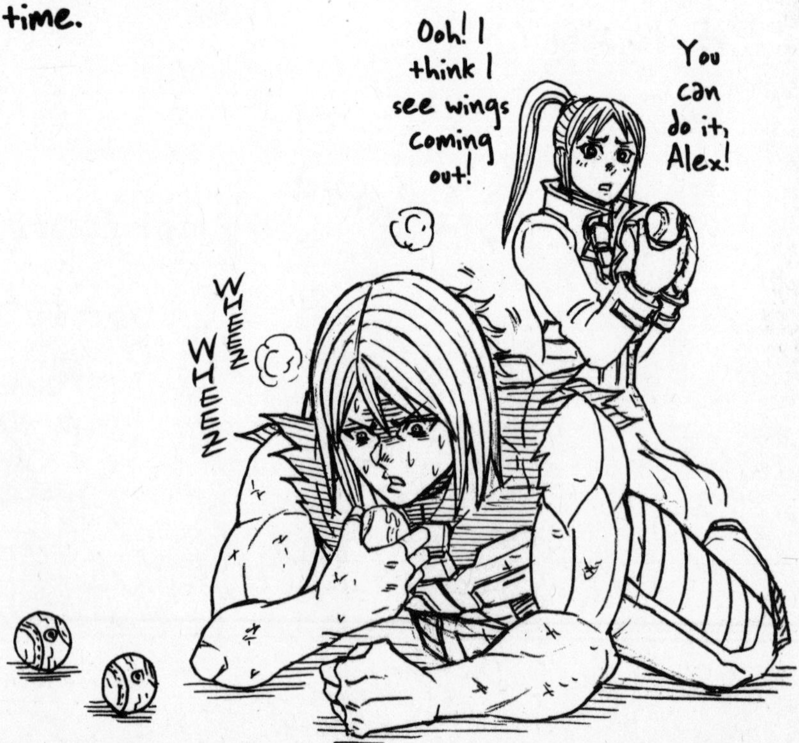
You can do it, Alex!
Ooh! I think I see wings coming out!
WHEEZ
WHEEZ

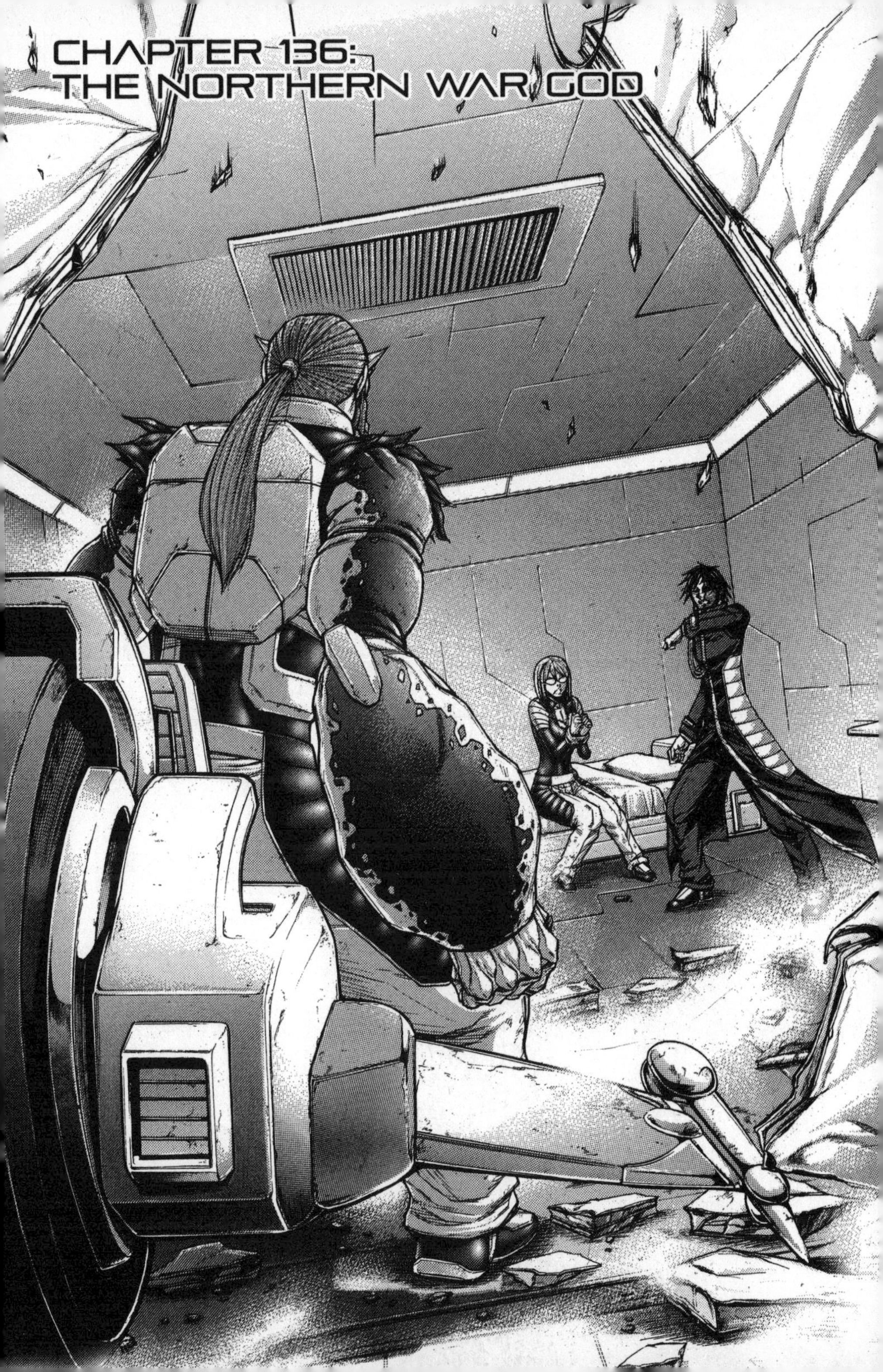
CHAPTER 136:
THE NORTHERN WAR GOD

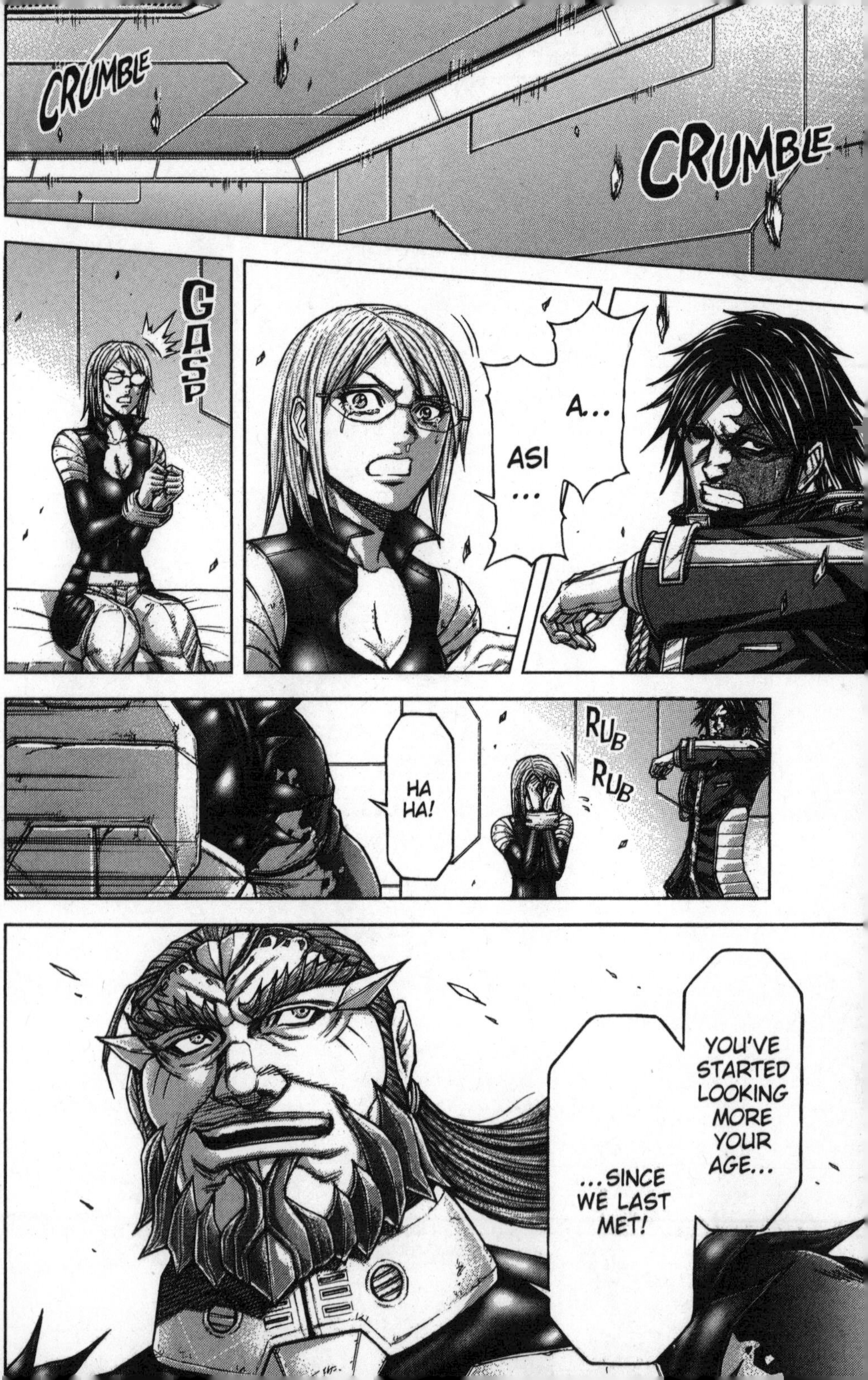
CRUMBLE
CRUMBLE
A...
ASI
...
GASP
RUB
RUB
HA HA!
YOU'VE STARTED LOOKING MORE YOUR AGE...
...SINCE WE LAST MET!

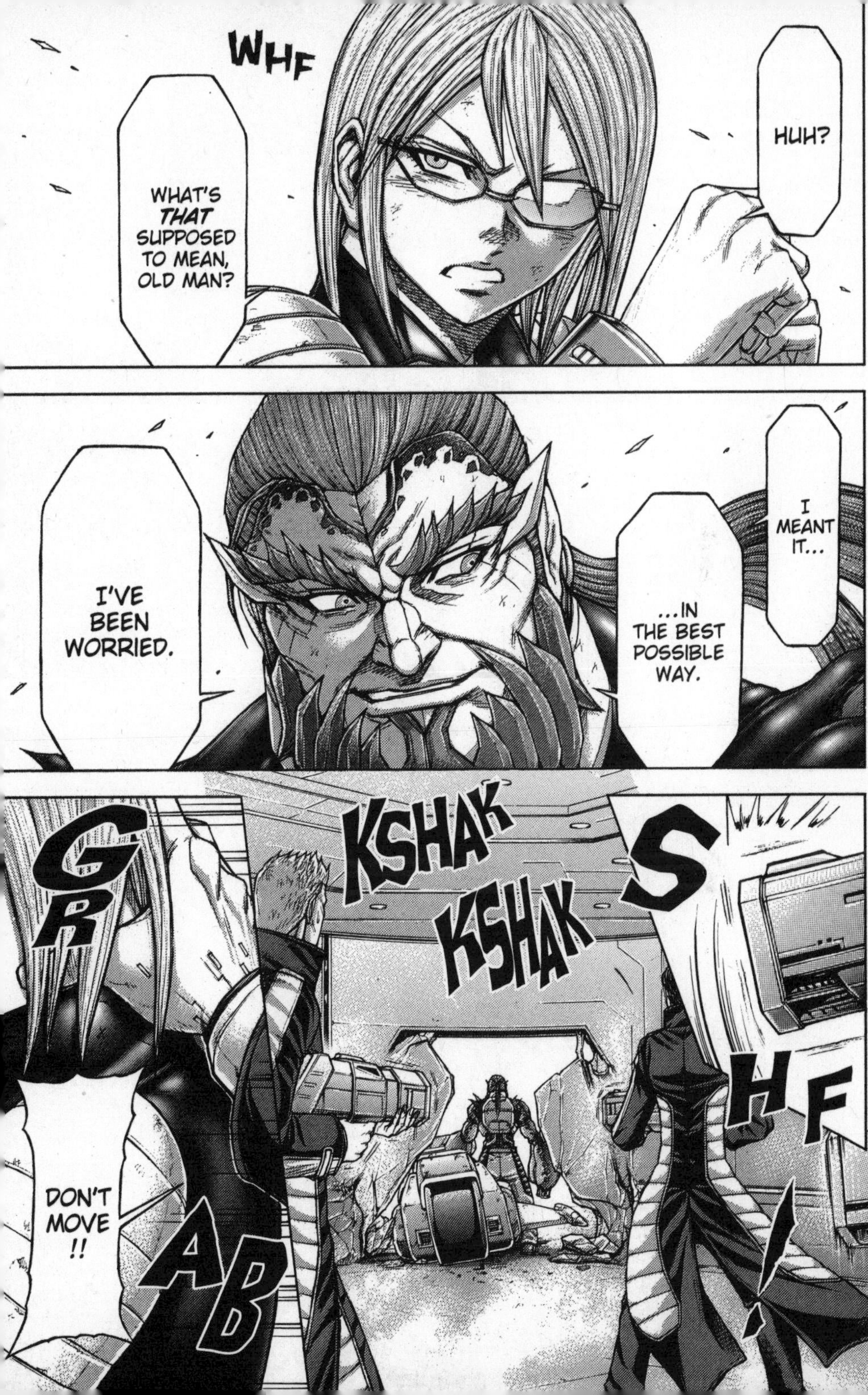
HUH?
WHF
WHAT'S *THAT* SUPPOSED TO MEAN, OLD MAN?
I MEANT IT...
...IN THE BEST POSSIBLE WAY.
I'VE BEEN WORRIED.
SHF
!
KSHAK
KSHAK
GRAB
DON'T MOVE !!

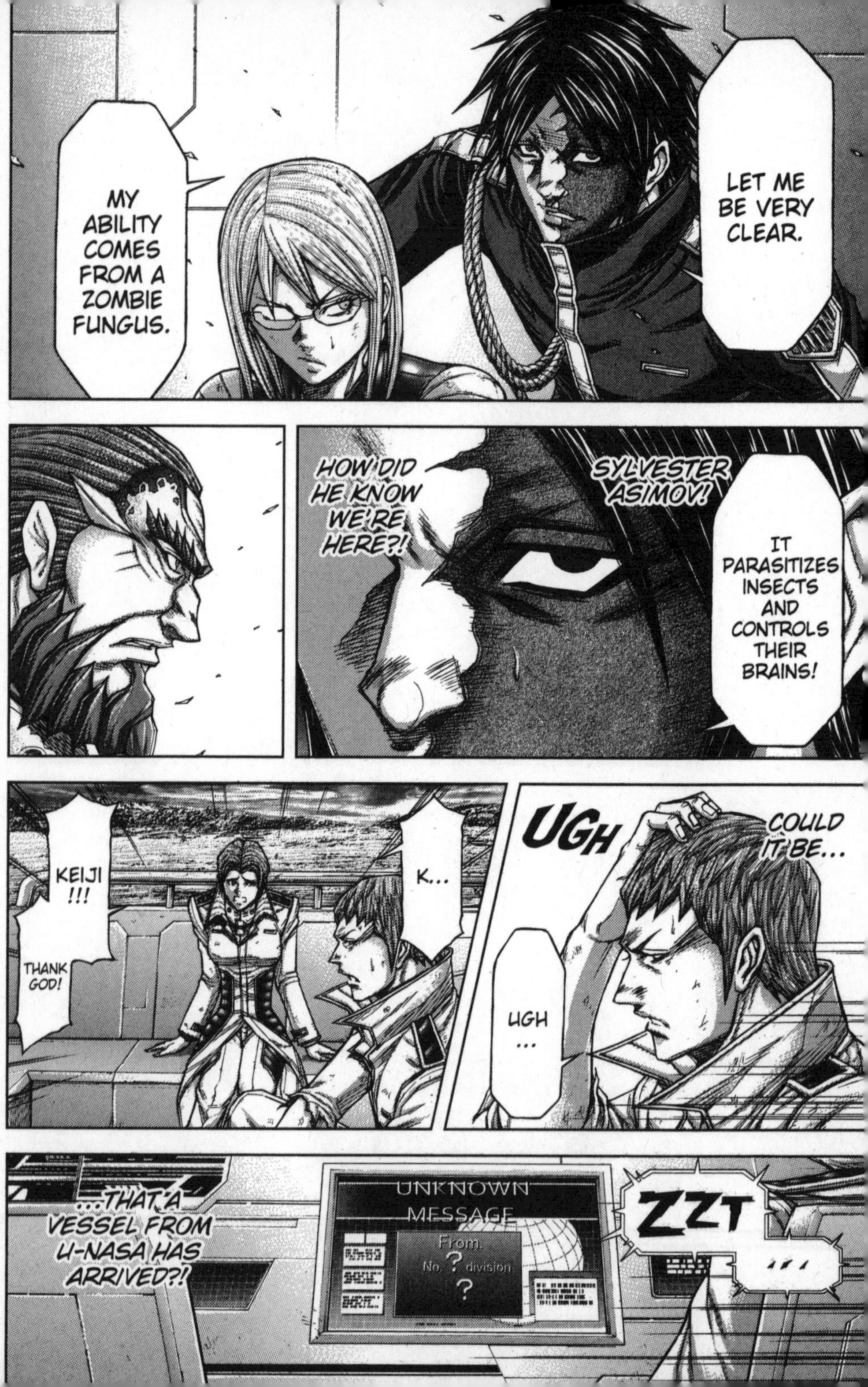
LET ME BE VERY CLEAR.
MY ABILITY COMES FROM A ZOMBIE FUNGUS.
IT PARASITIZES INSECTS AND CONTROLS THEIR BRAINS!
SYLVESTER ASIMOV!
HOW DID HE KNOW WE'RE HERE?!
COULD IT BE...
UGH
UGH ...
K...
KEIJI !!!
THANK GOD!
ZZT
...
UNKNOWN MESSAGE
From.
No. ? division
?
...THAT A VESSEL FROM U-NASA HAS ARRIVED?!

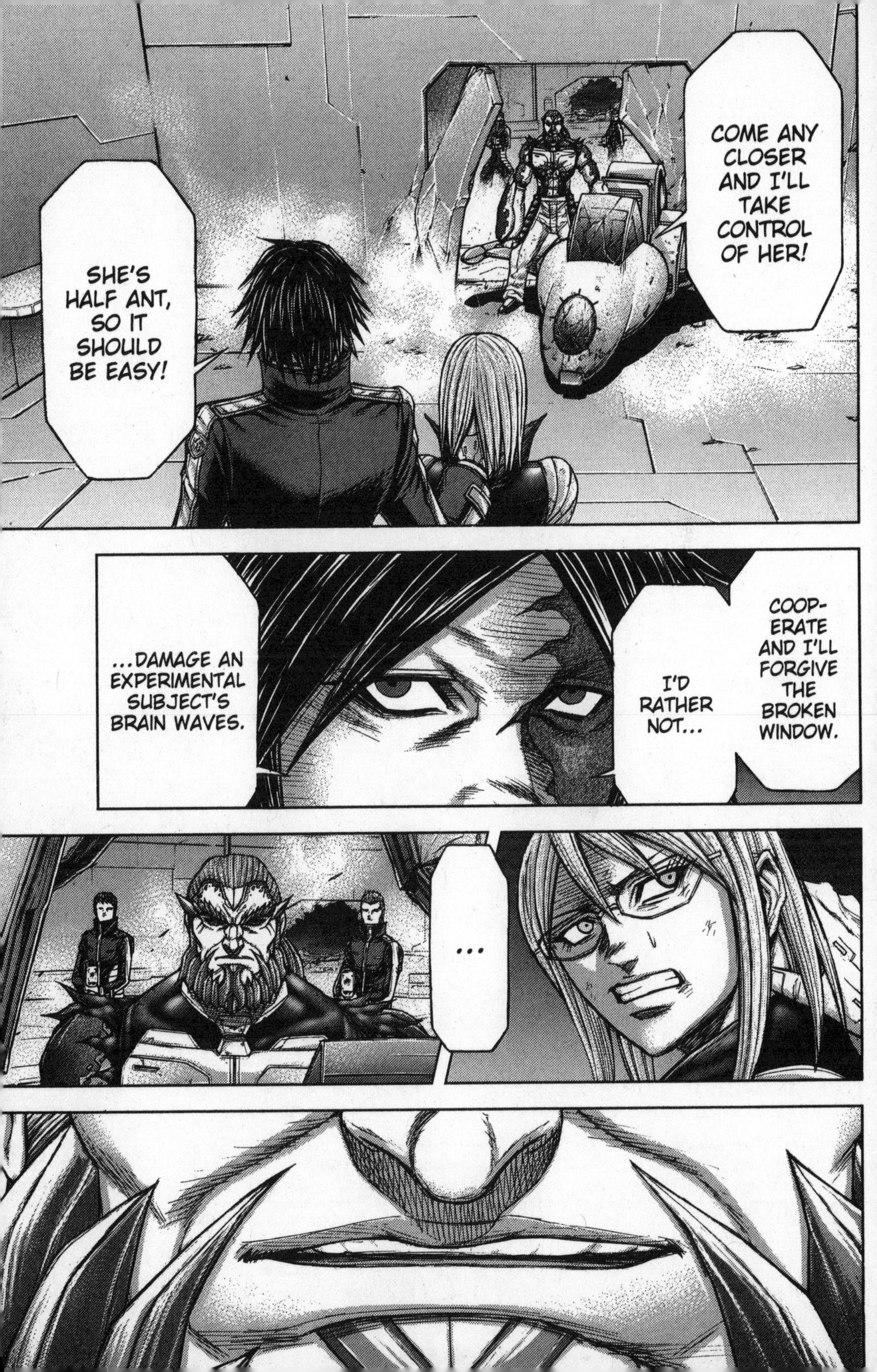
COME ANY CLOSER AND I'LL TAKE CONTROL OF HER!
SHE'S HALF ANT, SO IT SHOULD BE EASY!
COOP-ERATE AND I'LL FORGIVE THE BROKEN WINDOW.
I'D RATHER NOT...
...DAMAGE AN EXPERIMENTAL SUBJECT'S BRAIN WAVES.
...

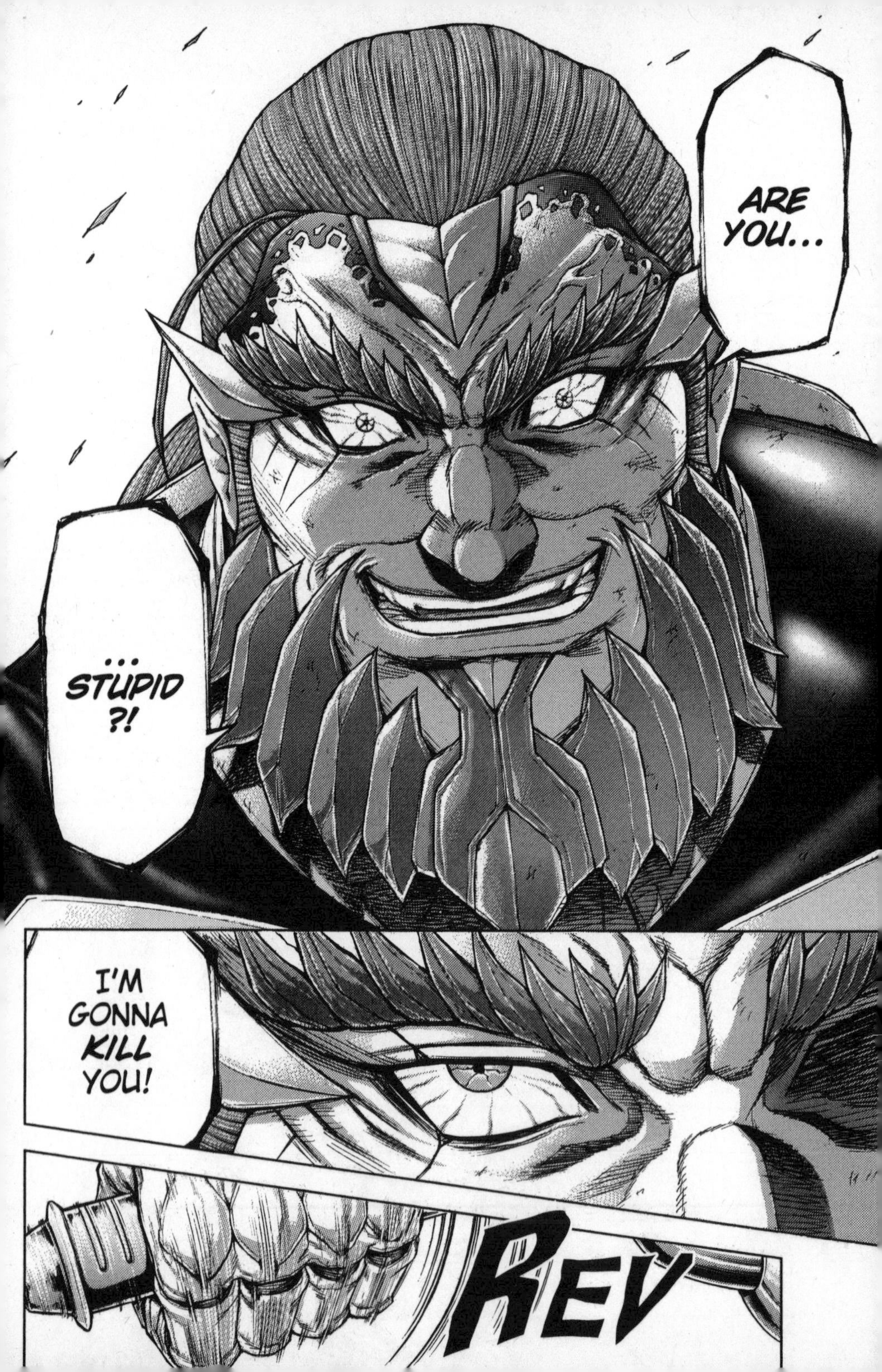
ARE YOU...
... STÜPID ?!
I'M GONNA KILL YOU!
REV

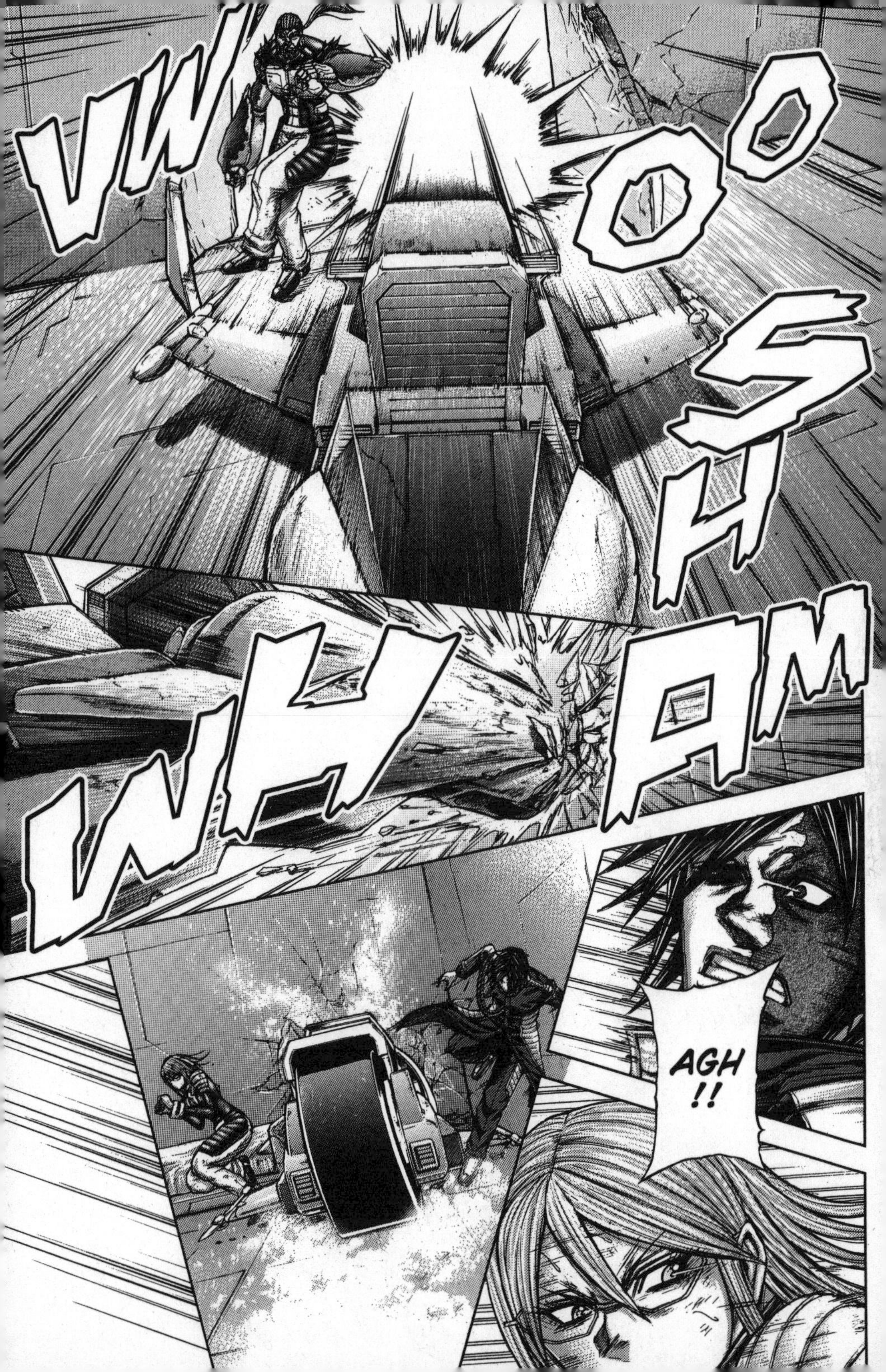
VWOOOSH
WHAM
AGH !!

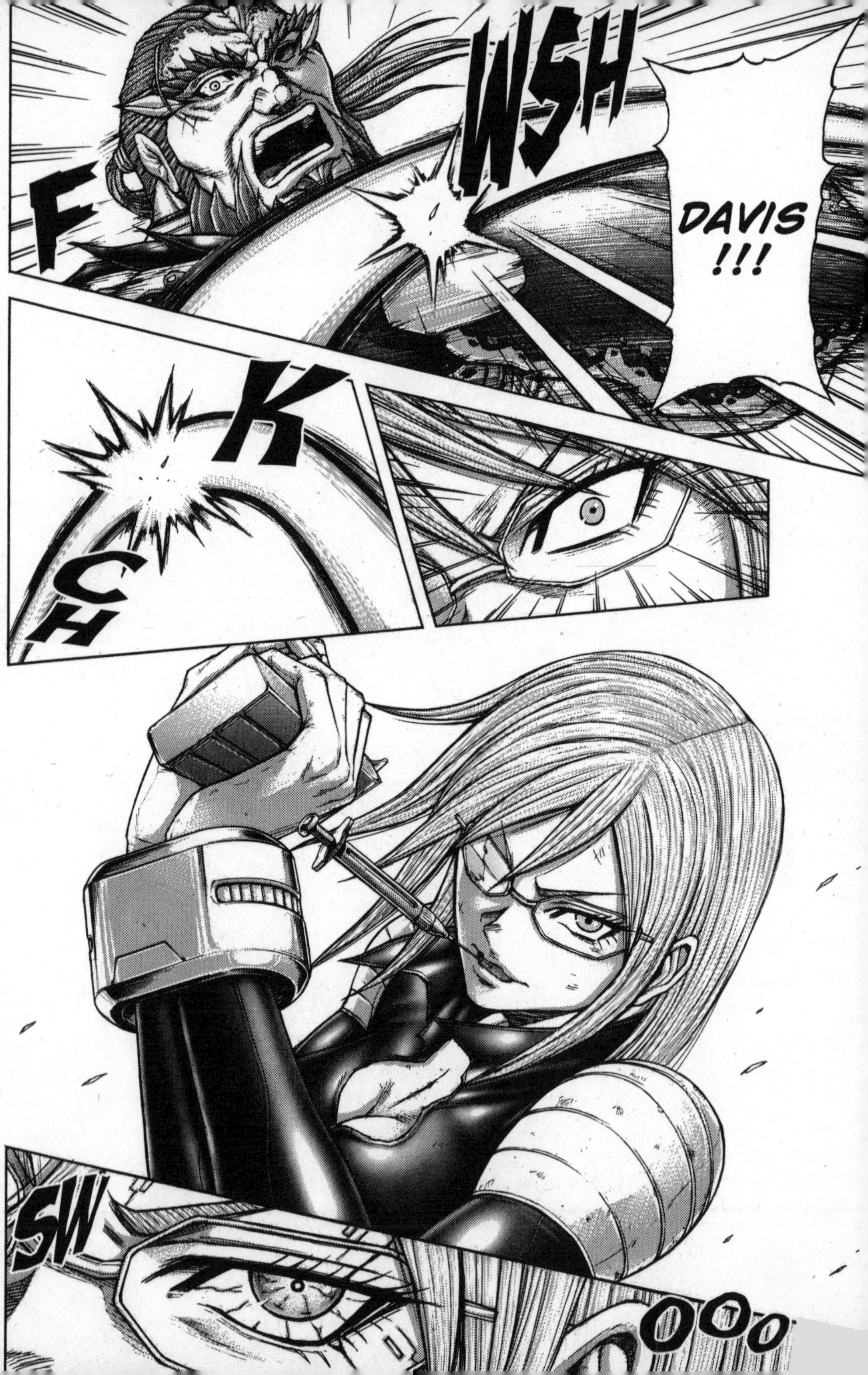
DAVIS !!!
WSH
F
K
CH
OOO
SW

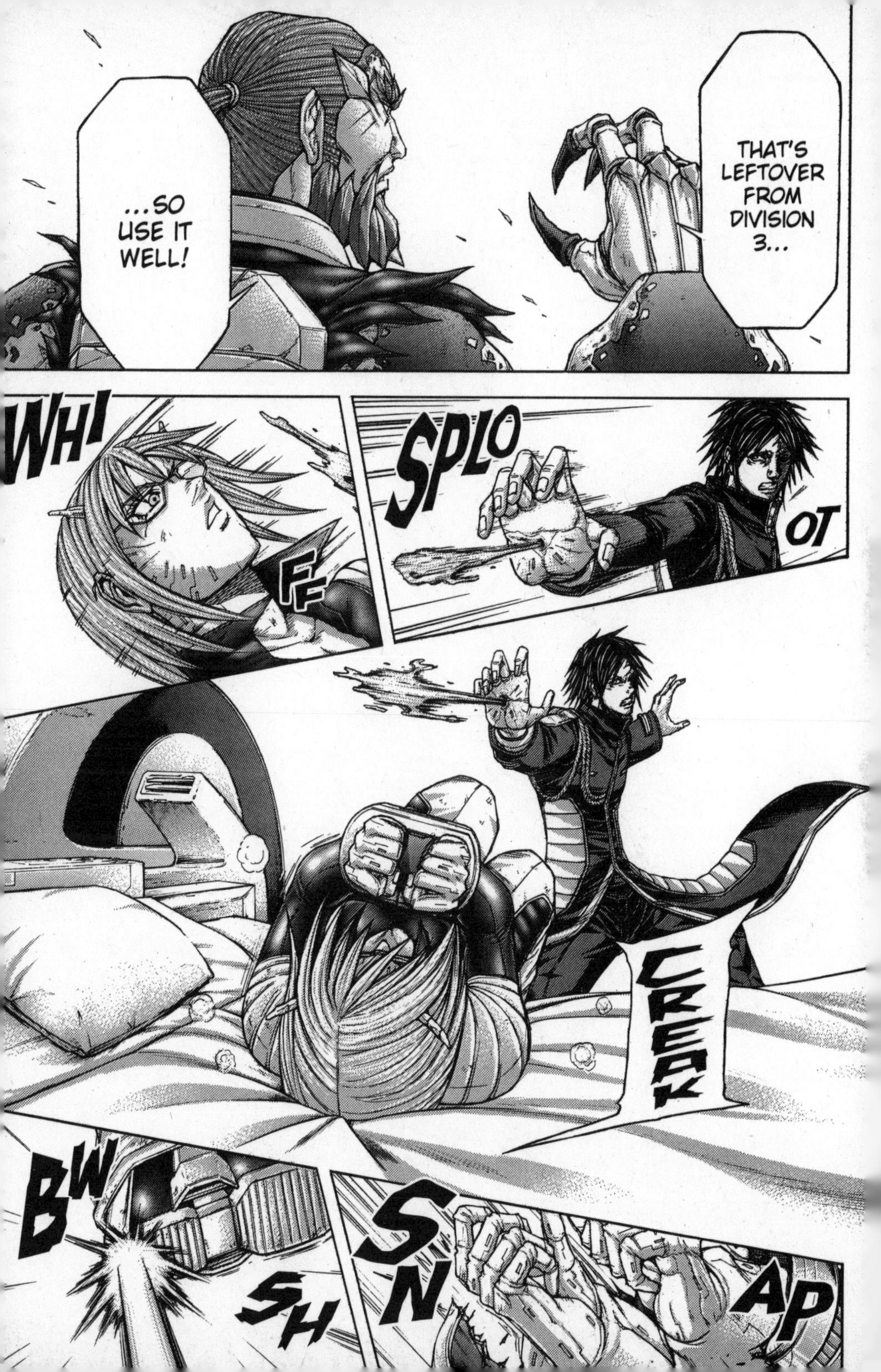
THAT'S LEFTOVER FROM DIVISION 3...
...SO USE IT WELL!
SPLO
OT
WHI
FF
CREAK
S
N
AP
BW
SH

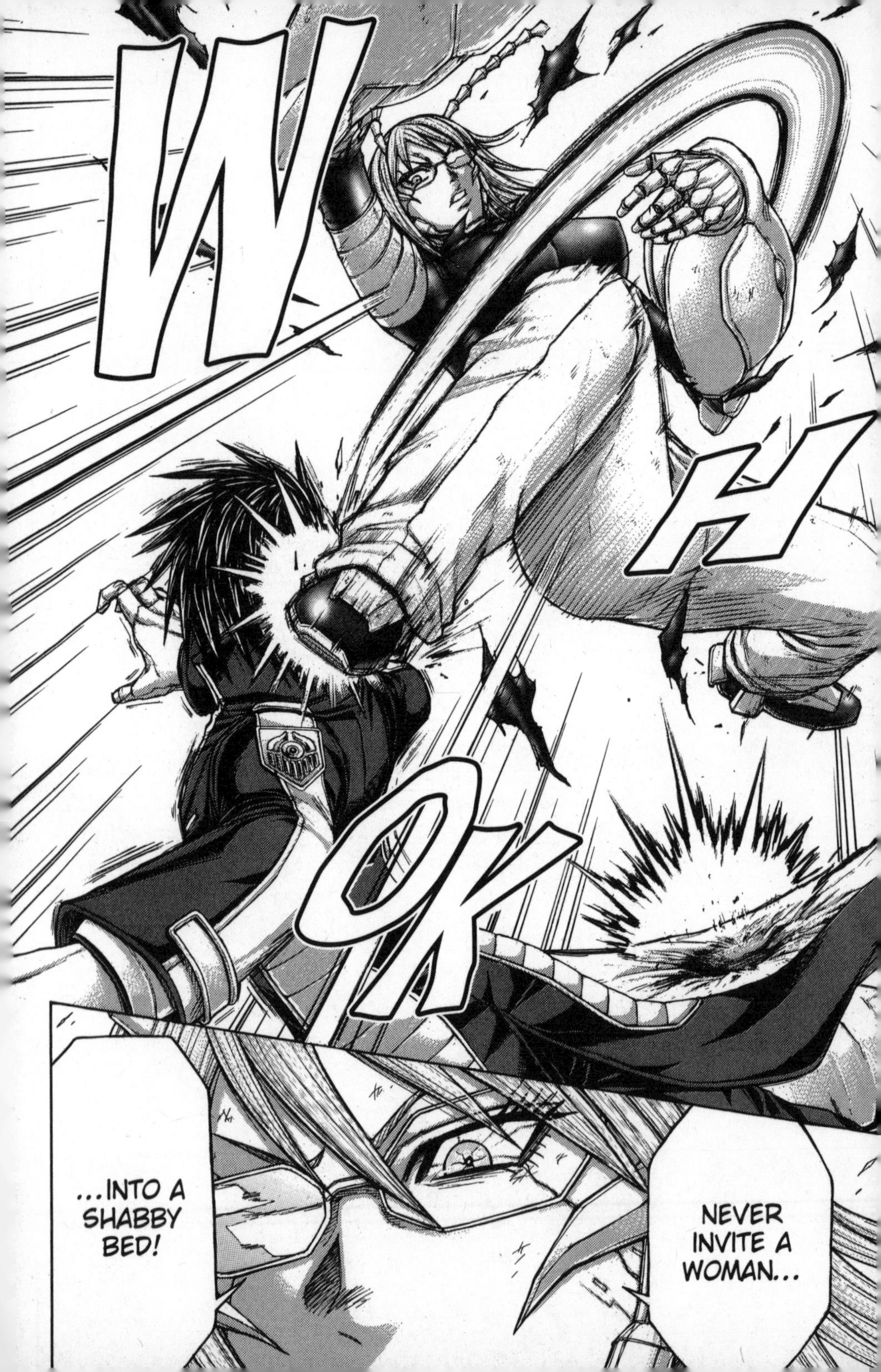
WHOK
NEVER INVITE A WOMAN...
...INTO A SHABBY BED!

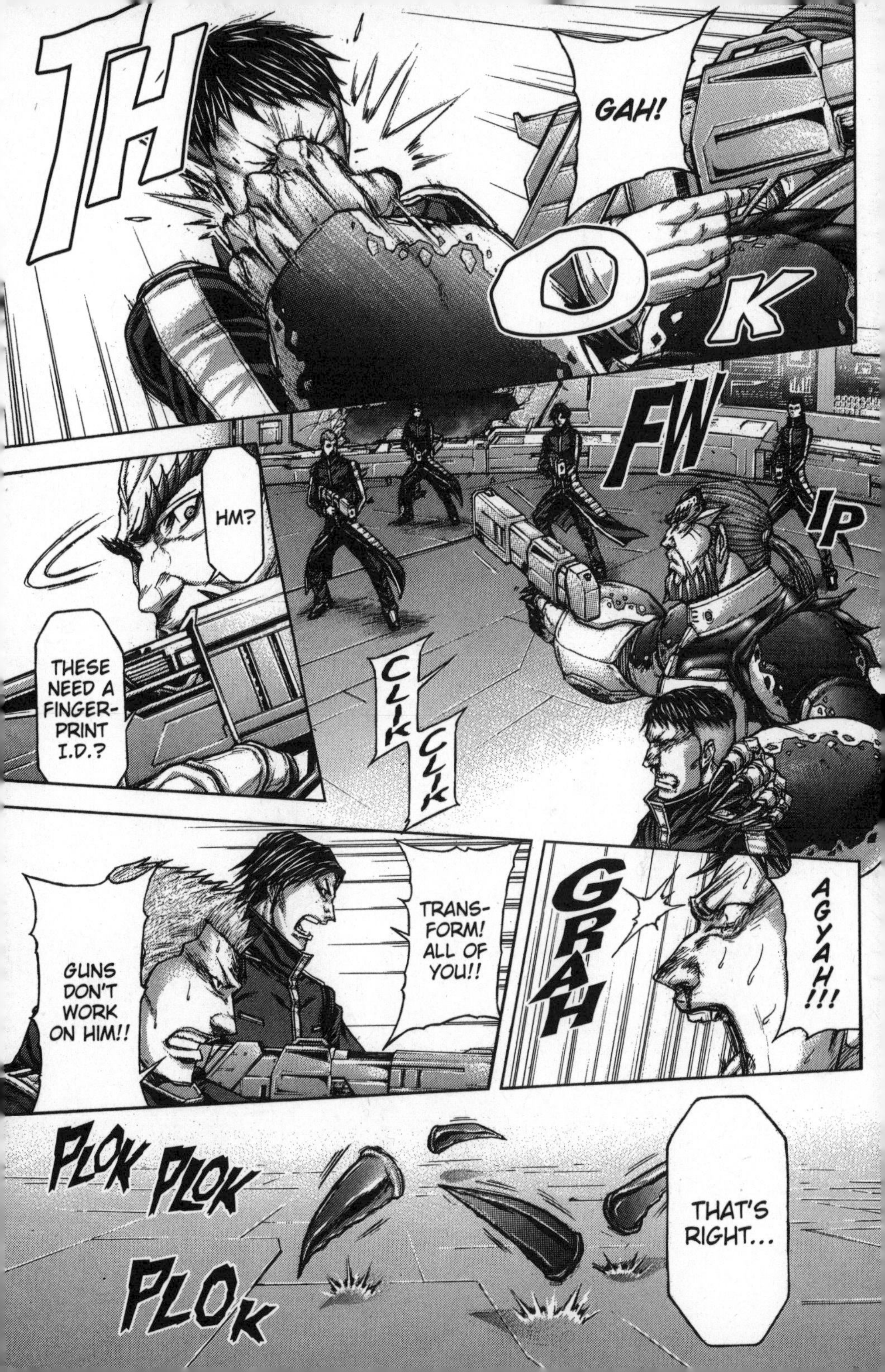
GAH!
THOK
FWIP
CLIK
CLIK
HM?
THESE NEED A FINGER-PRINT I.D.?
AGYAH!!!
GRAH
TRANS-FORM! ALL OF YOU!!
GUNS DON'T WORK ON HIM!!
THAT'S RIGHT...
PLOK PLOK
PLOK

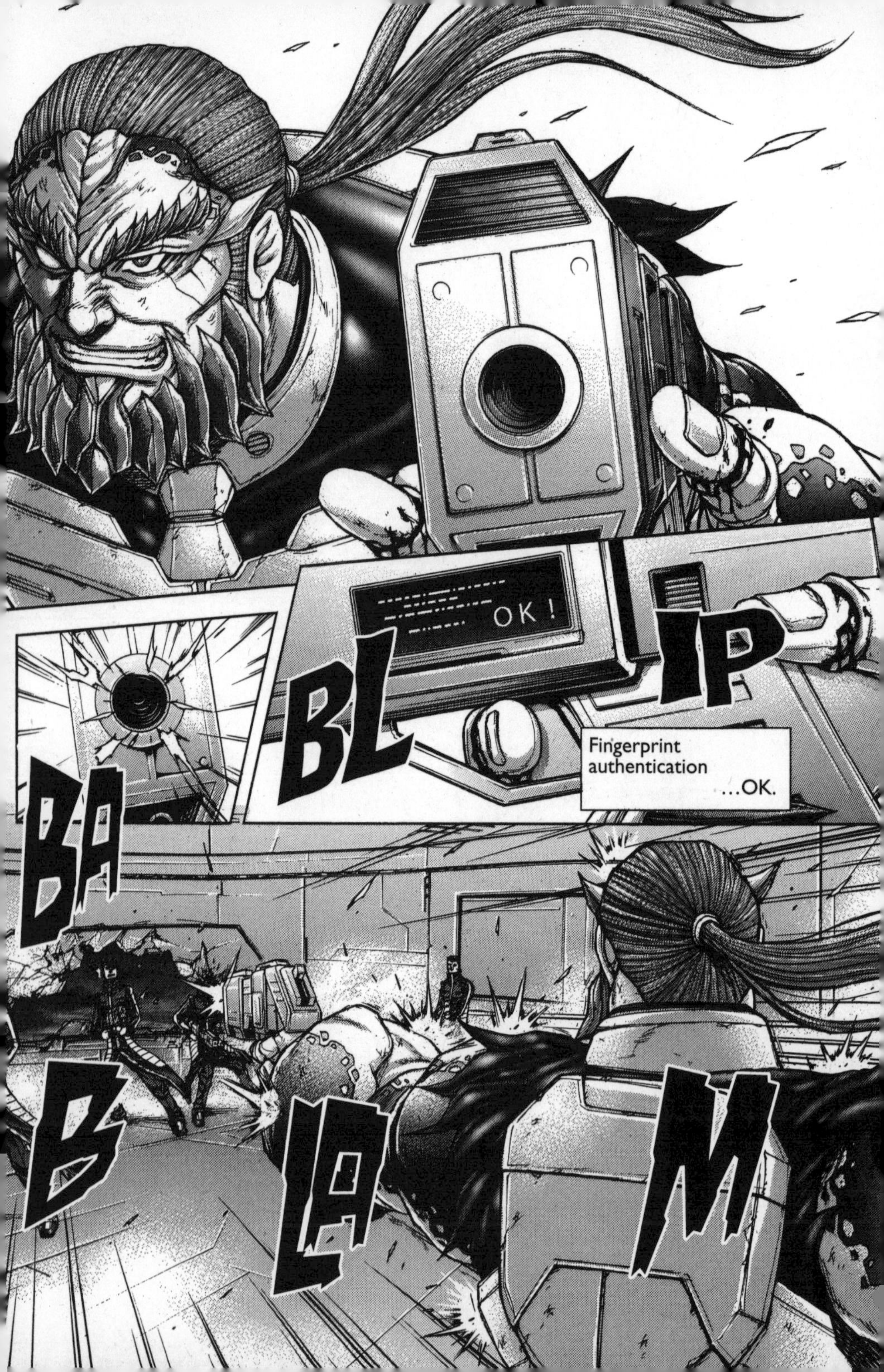
OK !
BLIP
Fingerprint authentication ...OK.
BA
BLAM

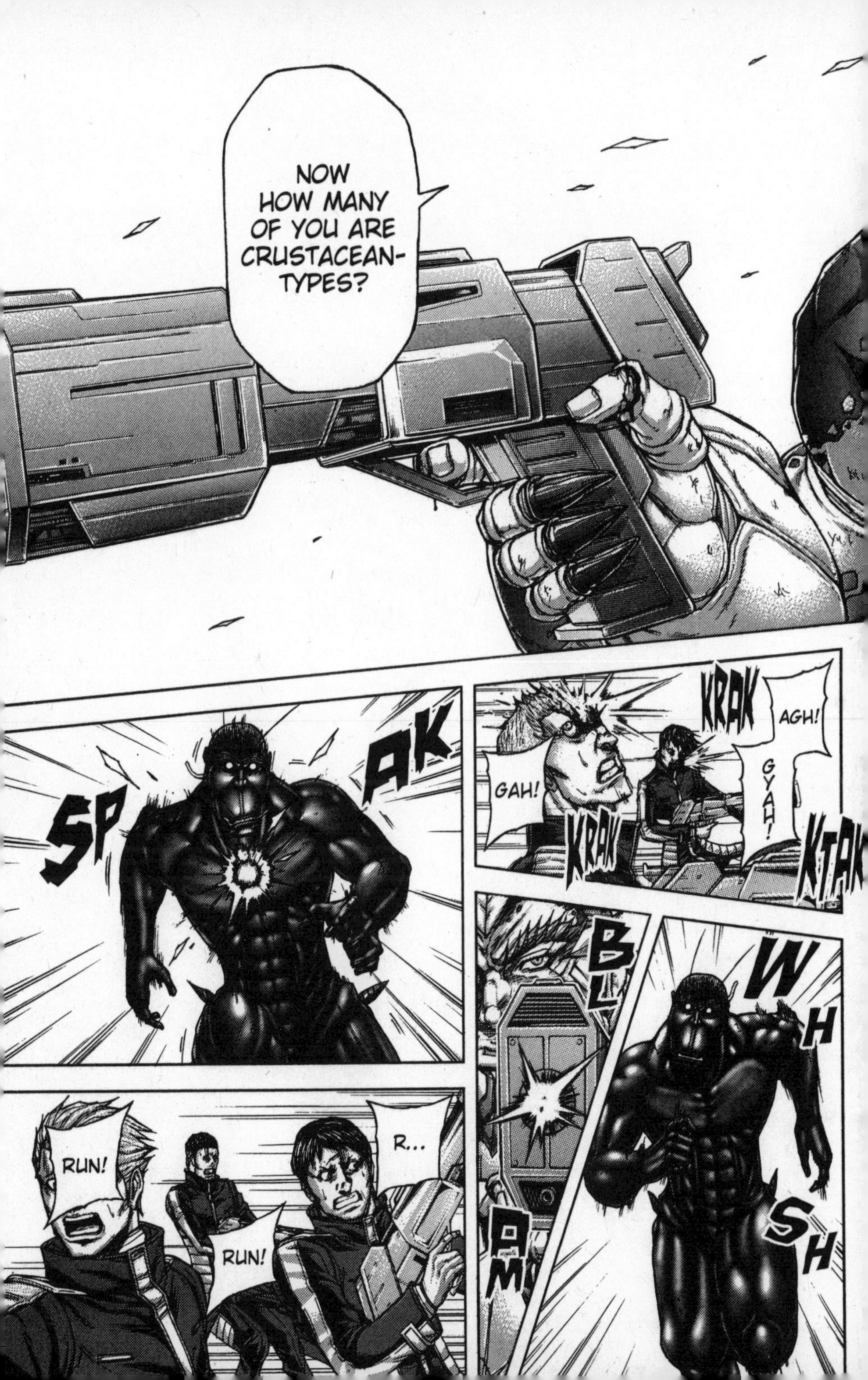

NOW HOW MANY OF YOU ARE CRUSTACEAN-TYPES?
KRAK
AGH!
GYAH!
GAH!
KRAK
KTAK
SP
AK
WH
SH
BL
AM
R...
RUN!
RUN!

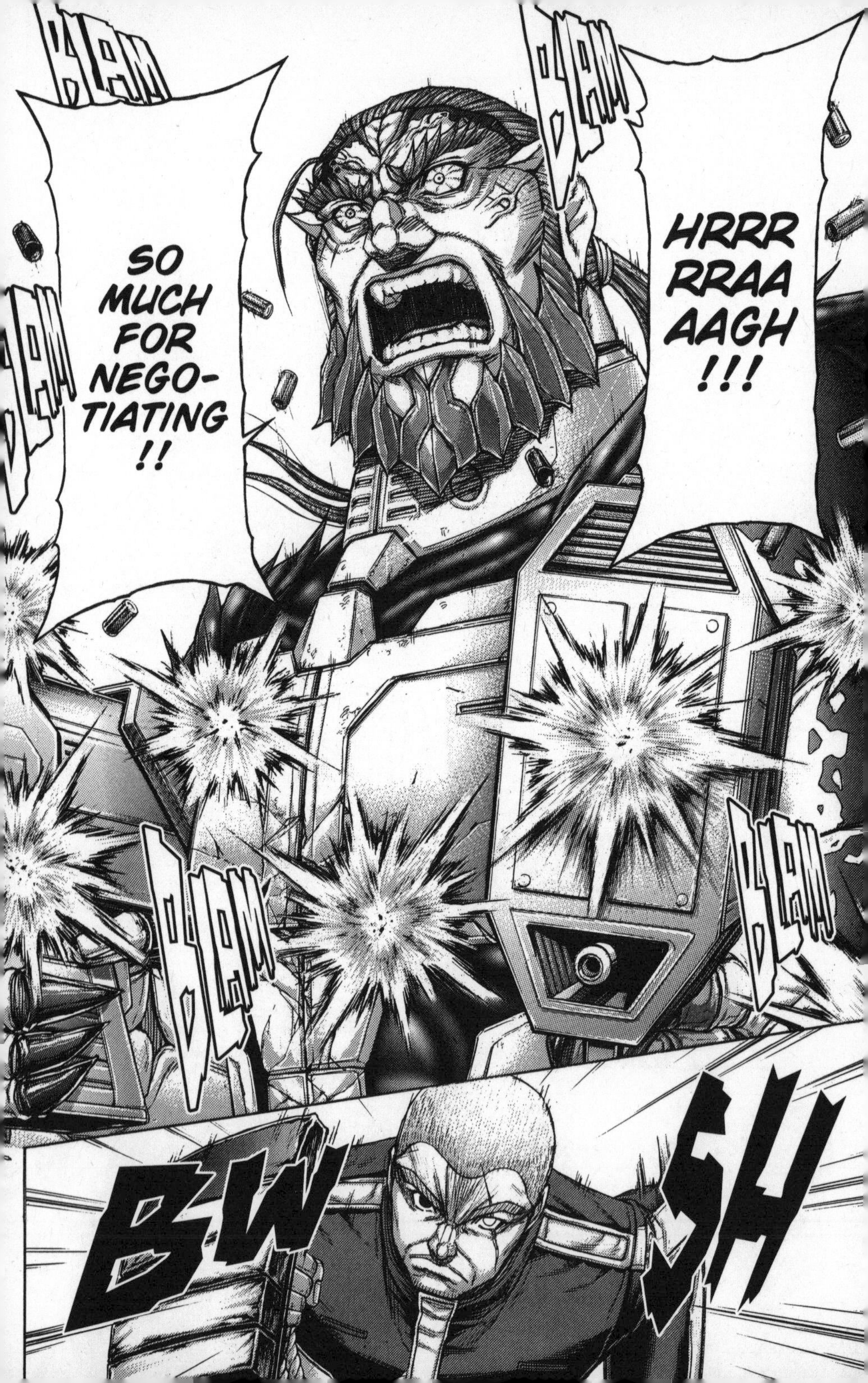
BLAM
HRRR RRAA AAGH!!!
BLAM
SO MUCH FOR NEGO-TIATING!!
BLAM
BLAM
BLAM
BLAM
BWSH

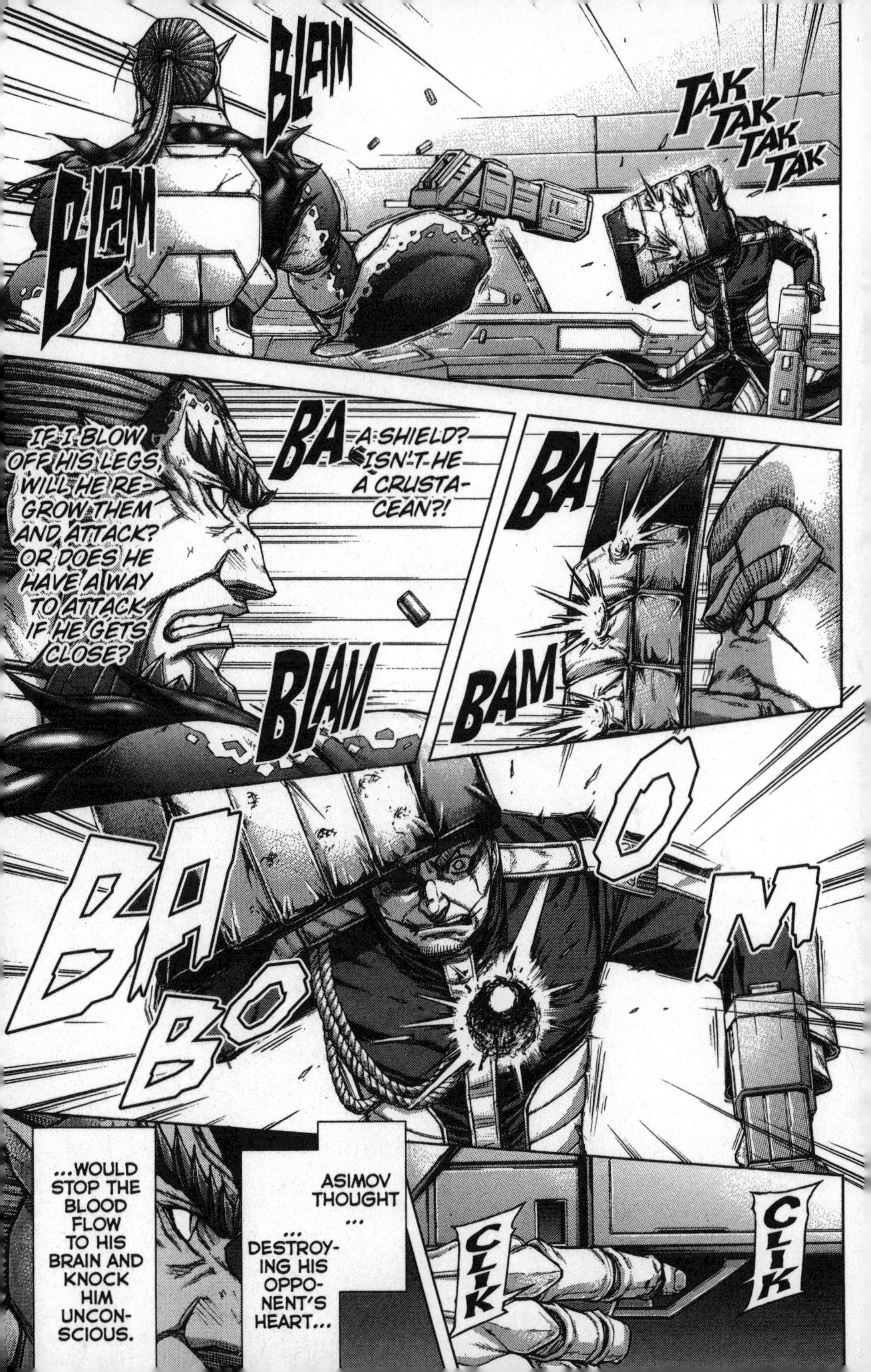

TAK TAK TAK TAK
BLAM
BLAM
BA
BAM
A SHIELD? ISN'T HE A CRUSTA-CEAN?!
BA
IF I BLOW OFF HIS LEGS, WILL HE RE-GROW THEM AND ATTACK? OR DOES HE HAVE A WAY TO ATTACK IF HE GETS CLOSE?
BLAM
BA BO O M
CLIK
CLIK
ASIMOV THOUGHT ... DESTROYING HIS OPPONENT'S HEART...
...WOULD STOP THE BLOOD FLOW TO HIS BRAIN AND KNOCK HIM UNCONSCIOUS.

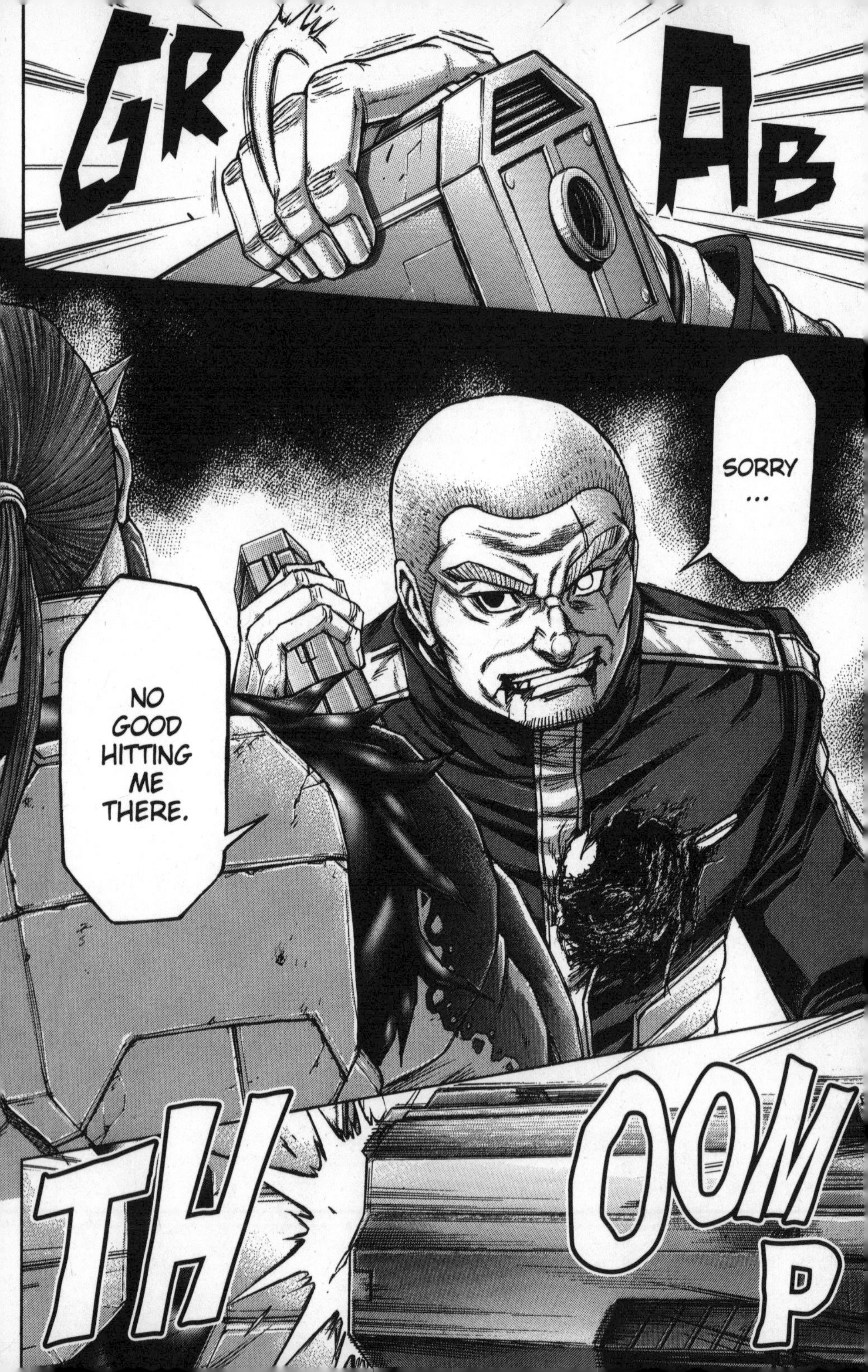
GRAB
SORRY ...
NO GOOD HITTING ME THERE.
THOOMP

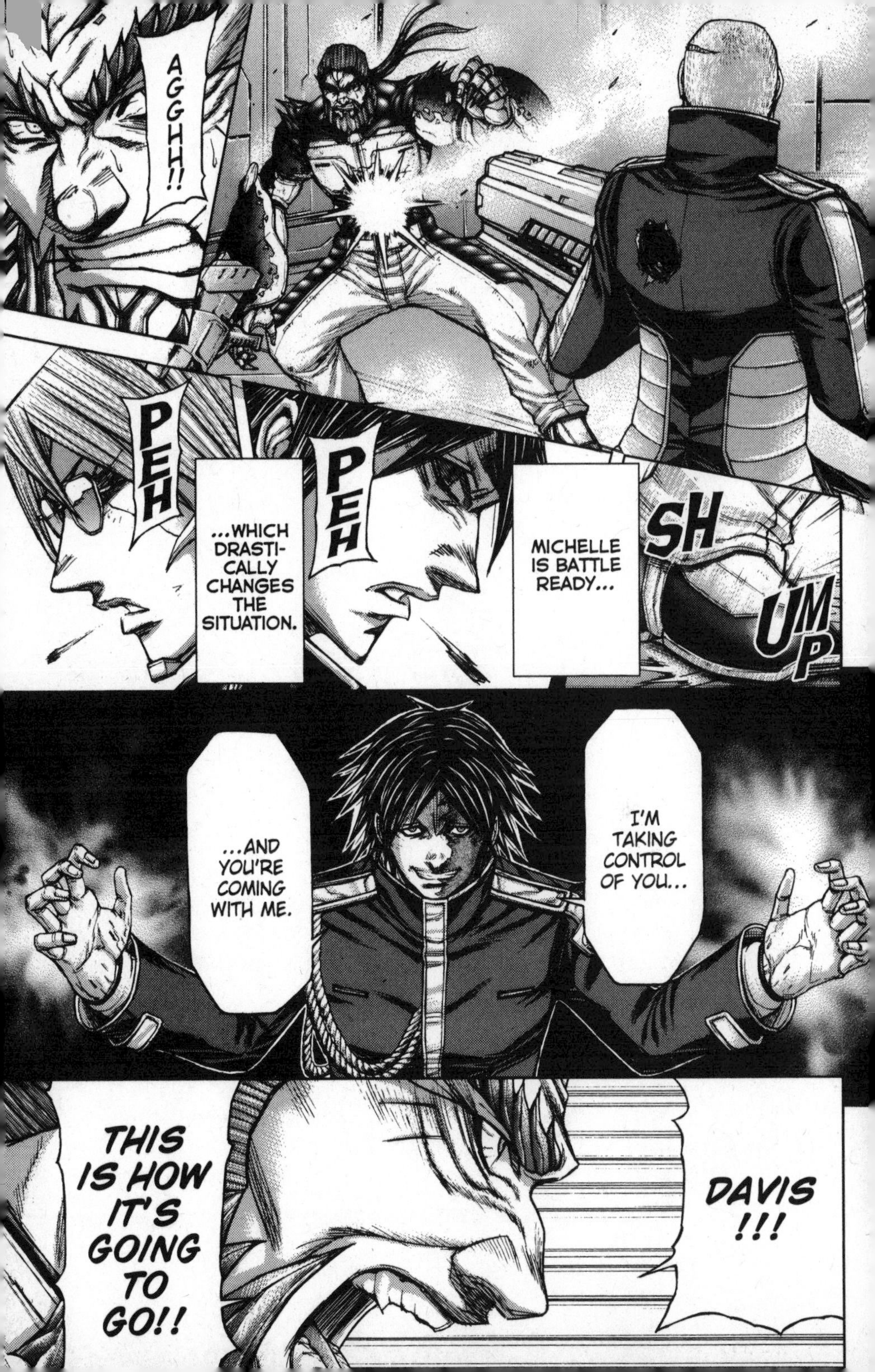
AGGHH!!
SHUMUP
MICHELLE IS BATTLE READY...
PEH
...WHICH DRASTICALLY CHANGES THE SITUATION.
PEH
I'M TAKING CONTROL OF YOU...
...AND YOU'RE COMING WITH ME.
DAVIS!!!
THIS IS HOW IT'S GOING TO GO!!

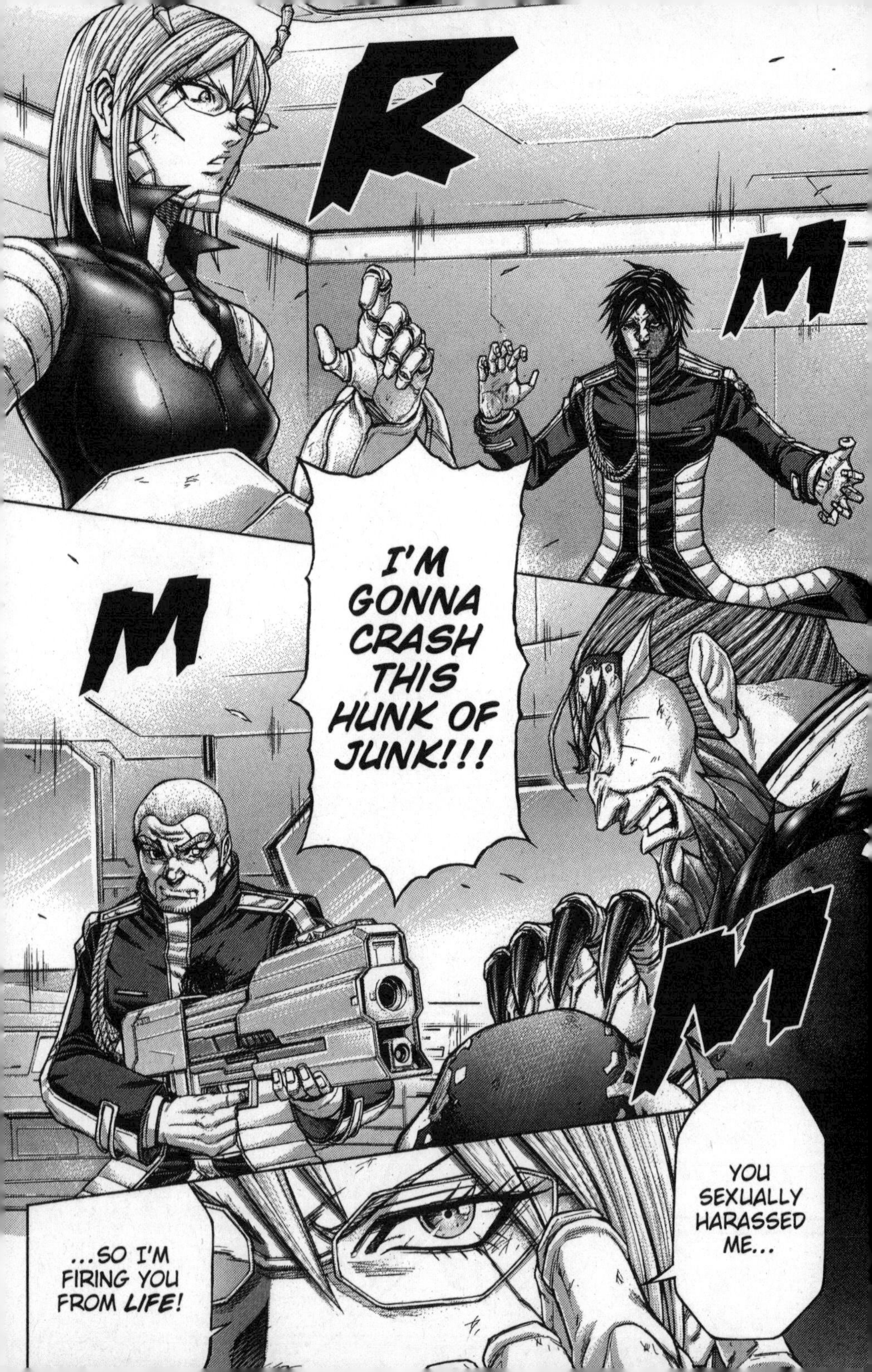
R
M
M
I'M GONNA CRASH THIS HUNK OF JUNK!!!
M
YOU SEXUALLY HARASSED ME...
...SO I'M FIRING YOU FROM *LIFE*!

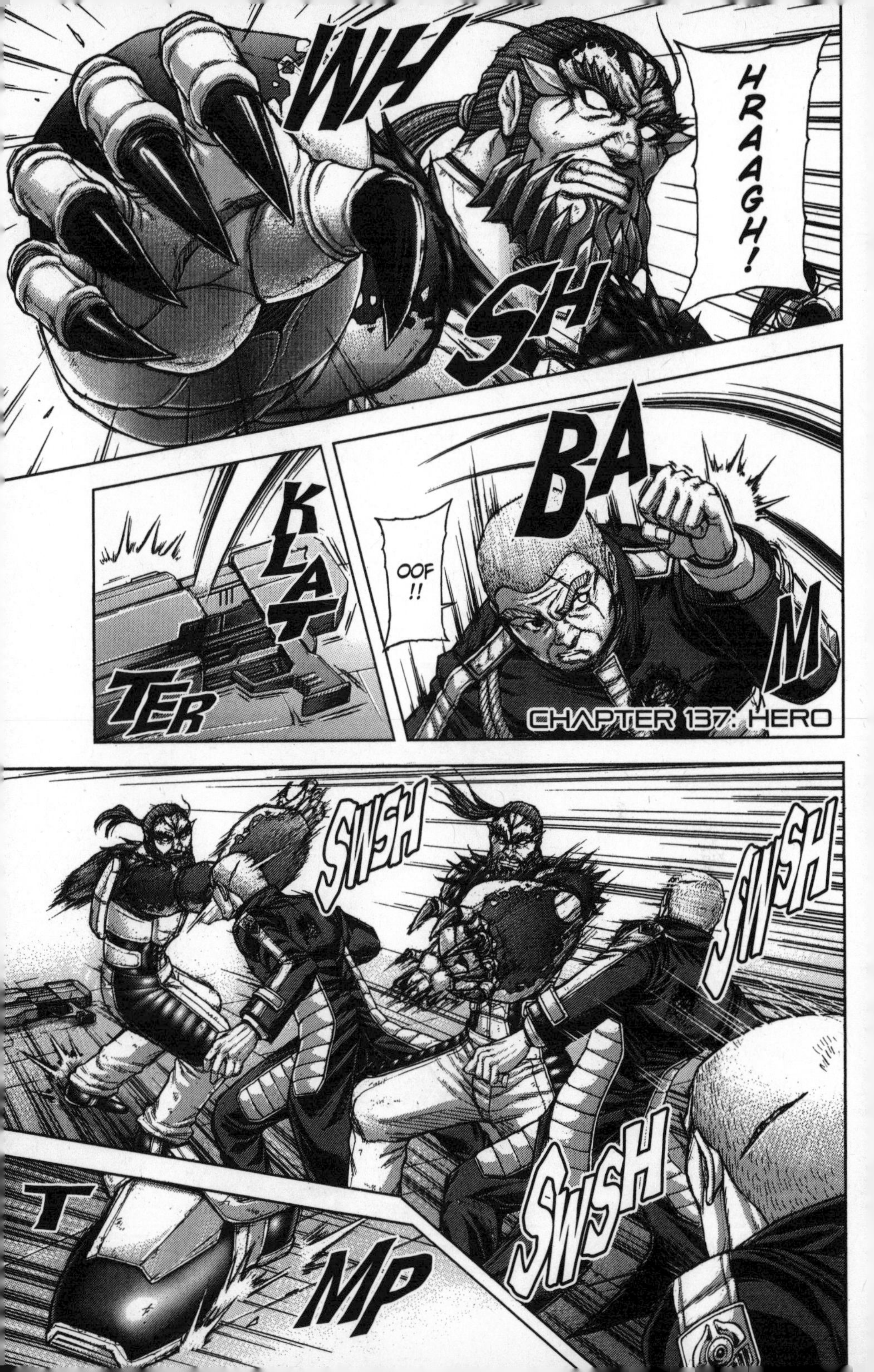
HRAAGH!
WHSH
BAM
OOF!!
CHAPTER 137: HERO
KLATTER
SWSH
SWSH
SWSH
TMP

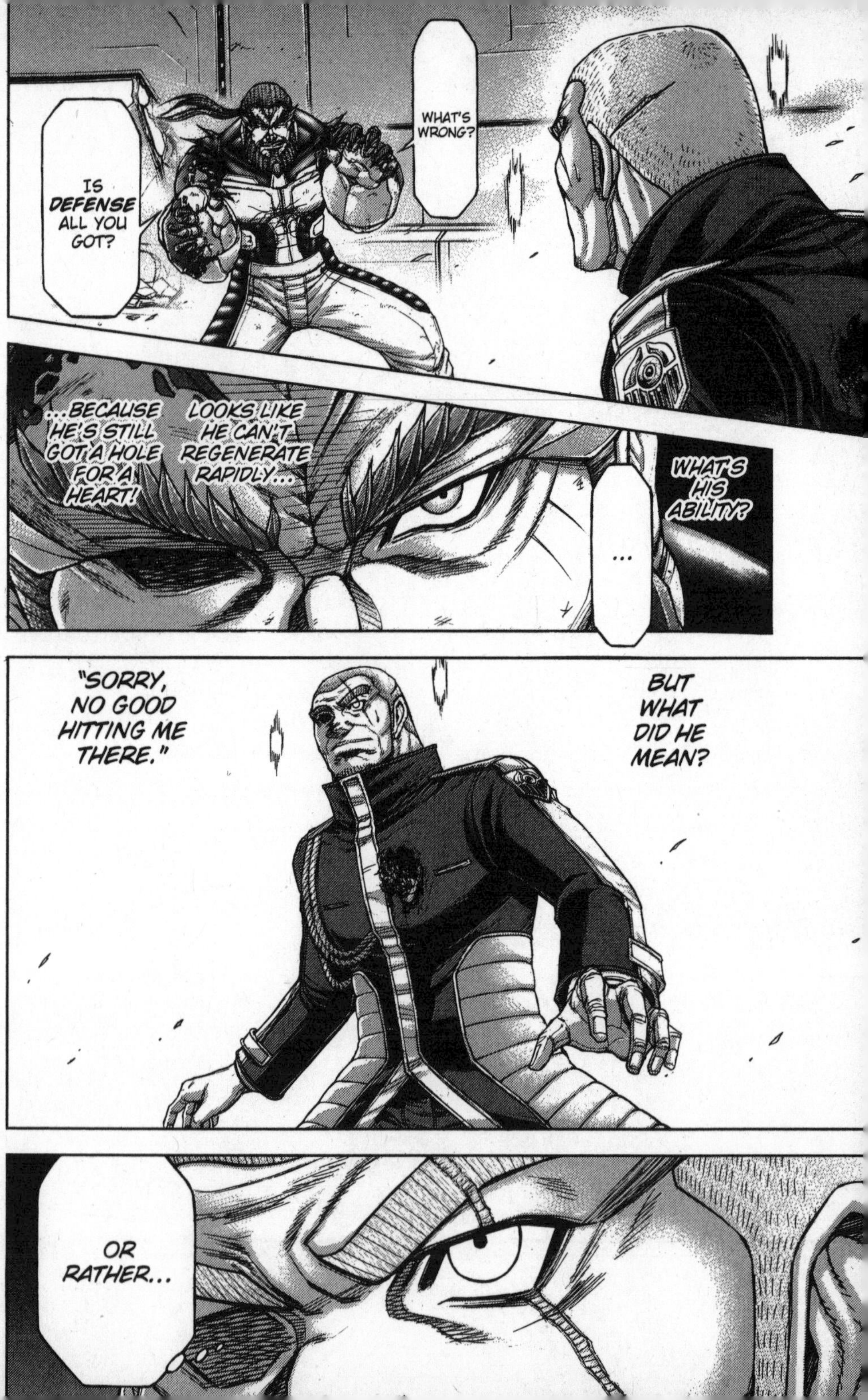
WHAT'S WRONG?
IS **DEFENSE** ALL YOU GOT?
WHAT'S HIS ABILITY?
...
LOOKS LIKE HE CAN'T REGENERATE RAPIDLY...
...BECAUSE HE'S STILL GOT A HOLE FOR A HEART!
BUT WHAT DID HE MEAN?
"SORRY, NO GOOD HITTING ME THERE."
OR RATHER...

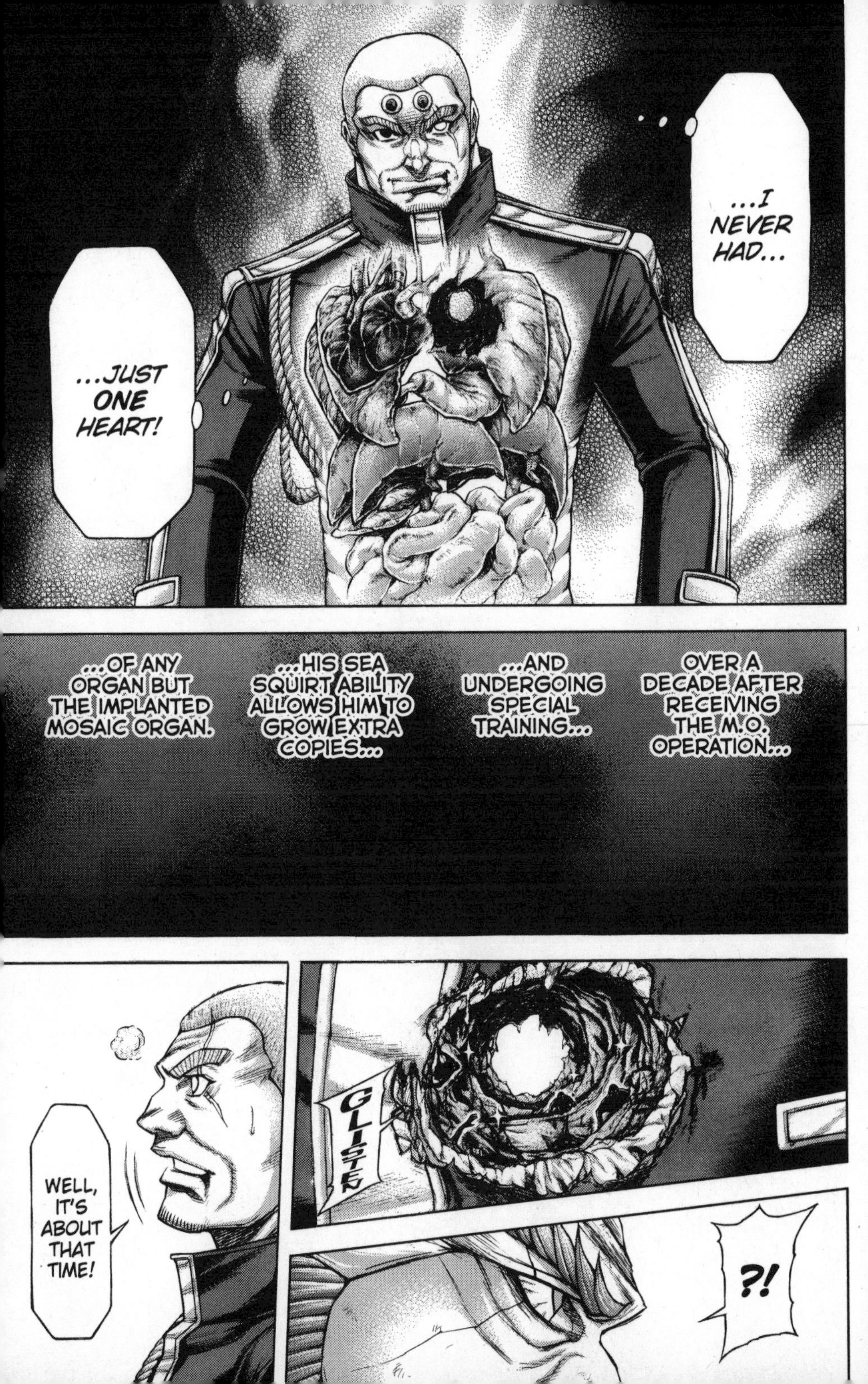
...I NEVER HAD...
...JUST ONE HEART!
OVER A DECADE AFTER RECEIVING THE M.O. OPERATION...
...AND UNDERGOING SPECIAL TRAINING...
...HIS SEA SQUIRT ABILITY ALLOWS HIM TO GROW EXTRA COPIES...
...OF ANY ORGAN BUT THE IMPLANTED MOSAIC ORGAN.
GLISTEN
?!
WELL, IT'S ABOUT THAT TIME!

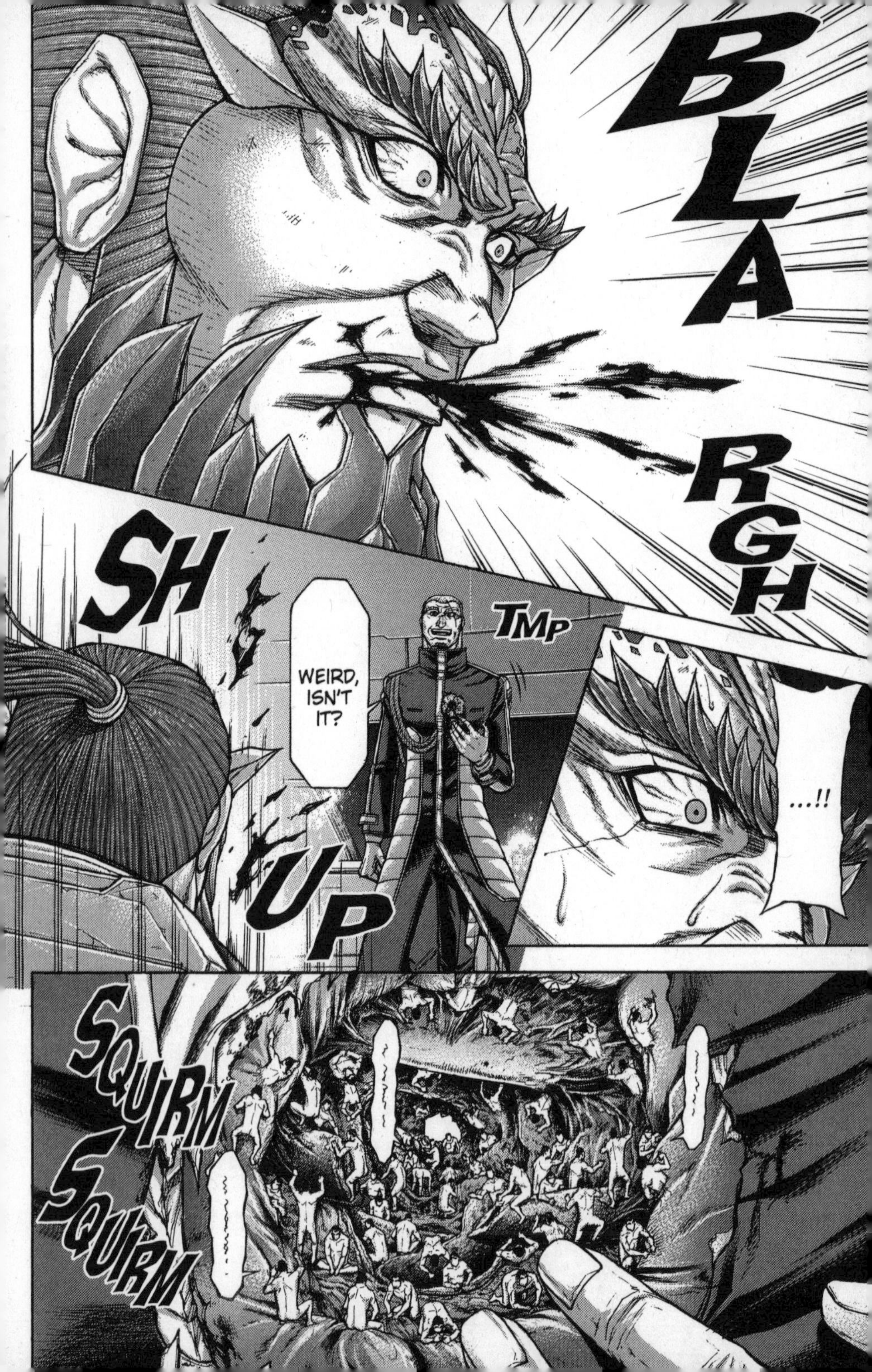
BLARGH
...!!
TMP
WEIRD, ISN'T IT?
SH
UP
SQUIRM
SQUIRM

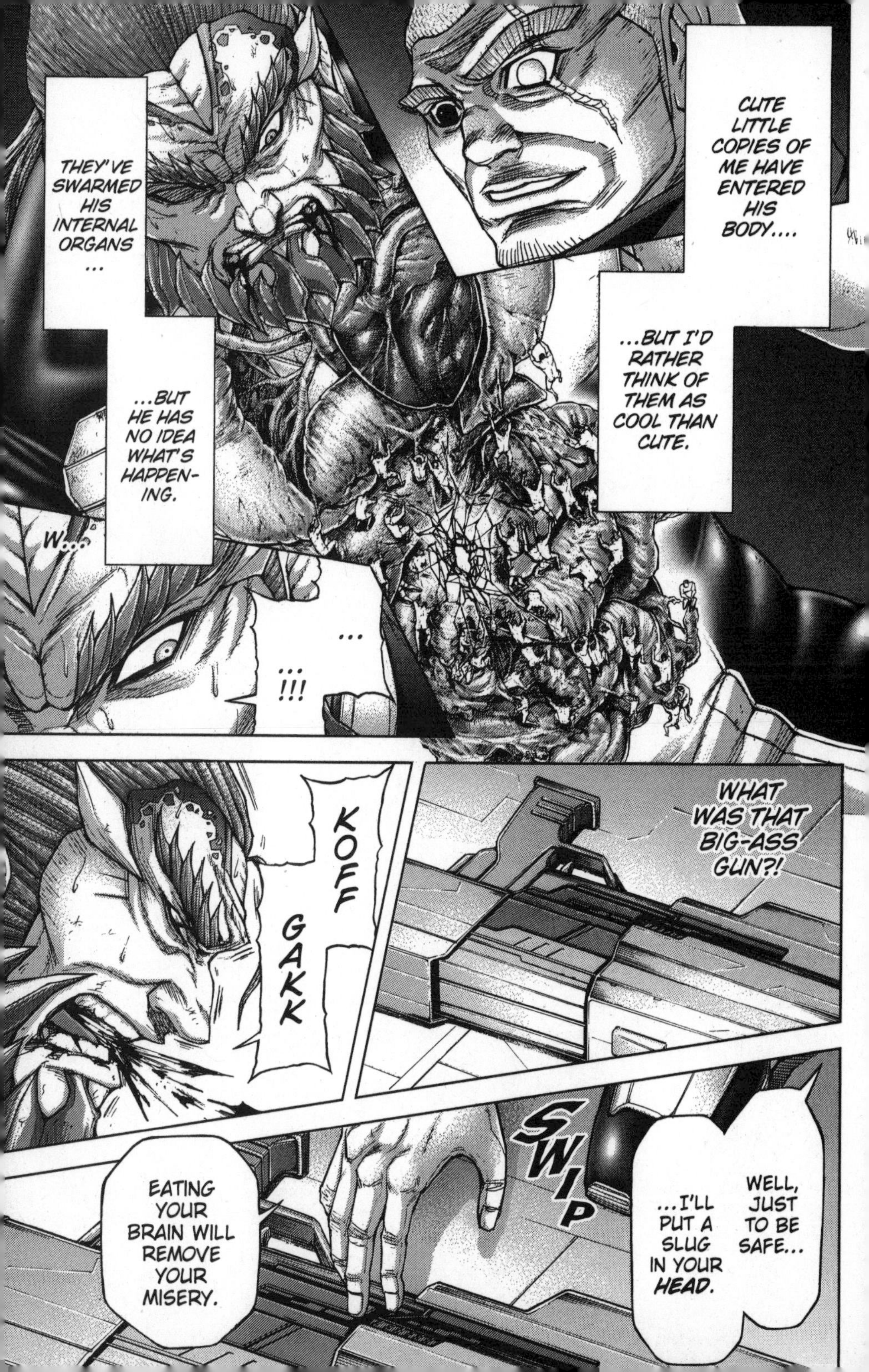
CUTE LITTLE COPIES OF ME HAVE ENTERED HIS BODY....
...BUT I'D RATHER THINK OF THEM AS COOL THAN CUTE.
THEY'VE SWARMED HIS INTERNAL ORGANS ...
...BUT HE HAS NO IDEA WHAT'S HAPPEN-ING.
W...
...
... !!!
WHAT WAS THAT BIG-ASS GUN?!
KOFF
GAKK
SWIP
WELL, JUST TO BE SAFE...
...I'LL PUT A SLUG IN YOUR HEAD.
EATING YOUR BRAIN WILL REMOVE YOUR MISERY.

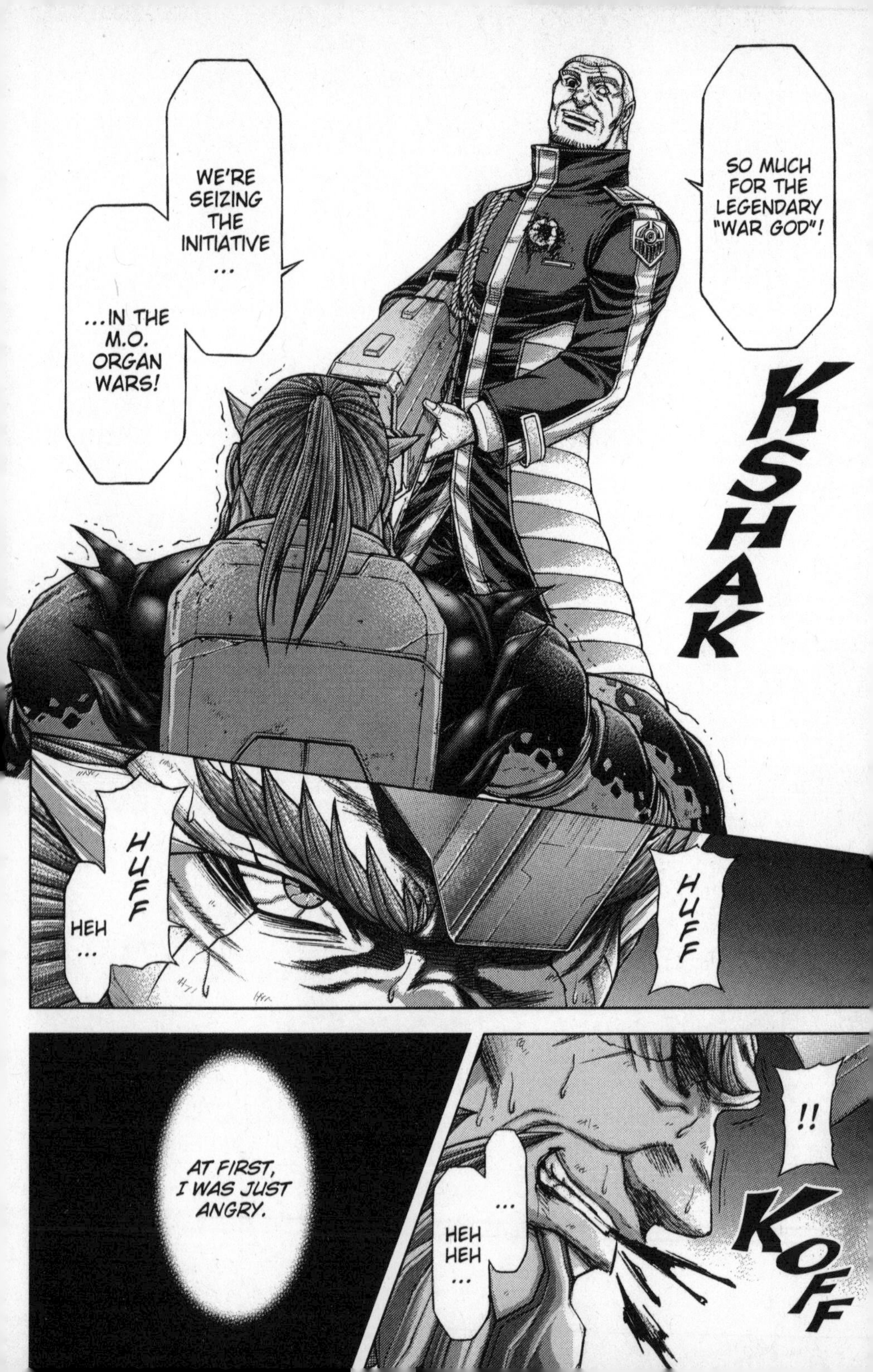
SO MUCH FOR THE LEGENDARY "WAR GOD"!
WE'RE SEIZING THE INITIATIVE ...
...IN THE M.O. ORGAN WARS!
KSHAK
HUFF HUFF
HUFF
HEH ...
!!
KOFF
... HEH HEH ...
AT FIRST, I WAS JUST ANGRY.

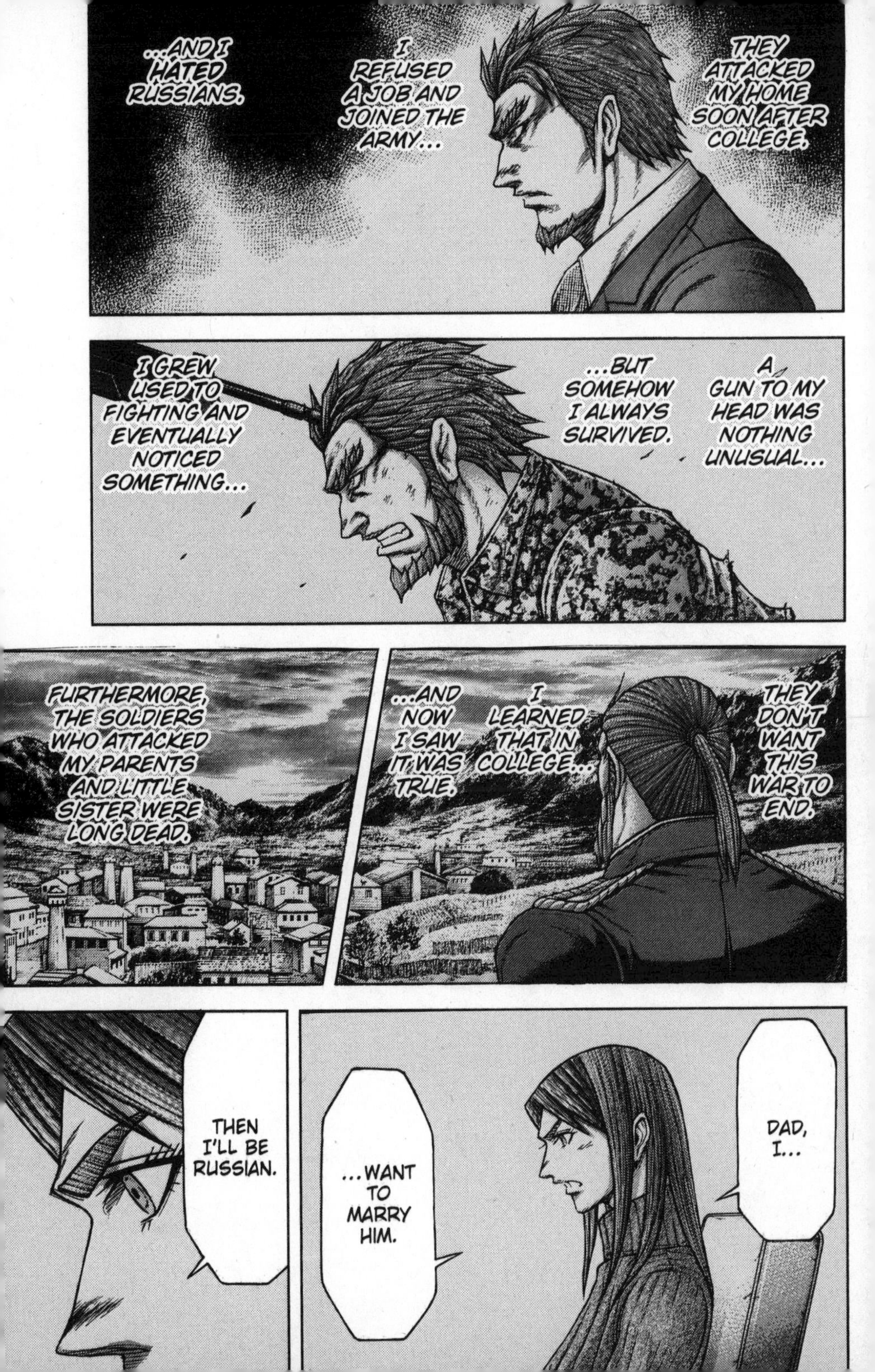
THEY ATTACKED MY HOME SOON AFTER COLLEGE.
I REFUSED A JOB AND JOINED THE ARMY...
...AND I HATED RUSSIANS.
A GUN TO MY HEAD WAS NOTHING UNUSUAL...
...BUT SOMEHOW I ALWAYS SURVIVED.
I GREW USED TO FIGHTING AND EVENTUALLY NOTICED SOMETHING...
THEY DON'T WANT THIS WAR TO END.
I LEARNED THAT IN COLLEGE...
...AND NOW I SAW IT WAS TRUE.
FURTHERMORE, THE SOLDIERS WHO ATTACKED MY PARENTS AND LITTLE SISTER WERE LONG DEAD.
DAD, I...
...WANT TO MARRY HIM.
THEN I'LL BE RUSSIAN.

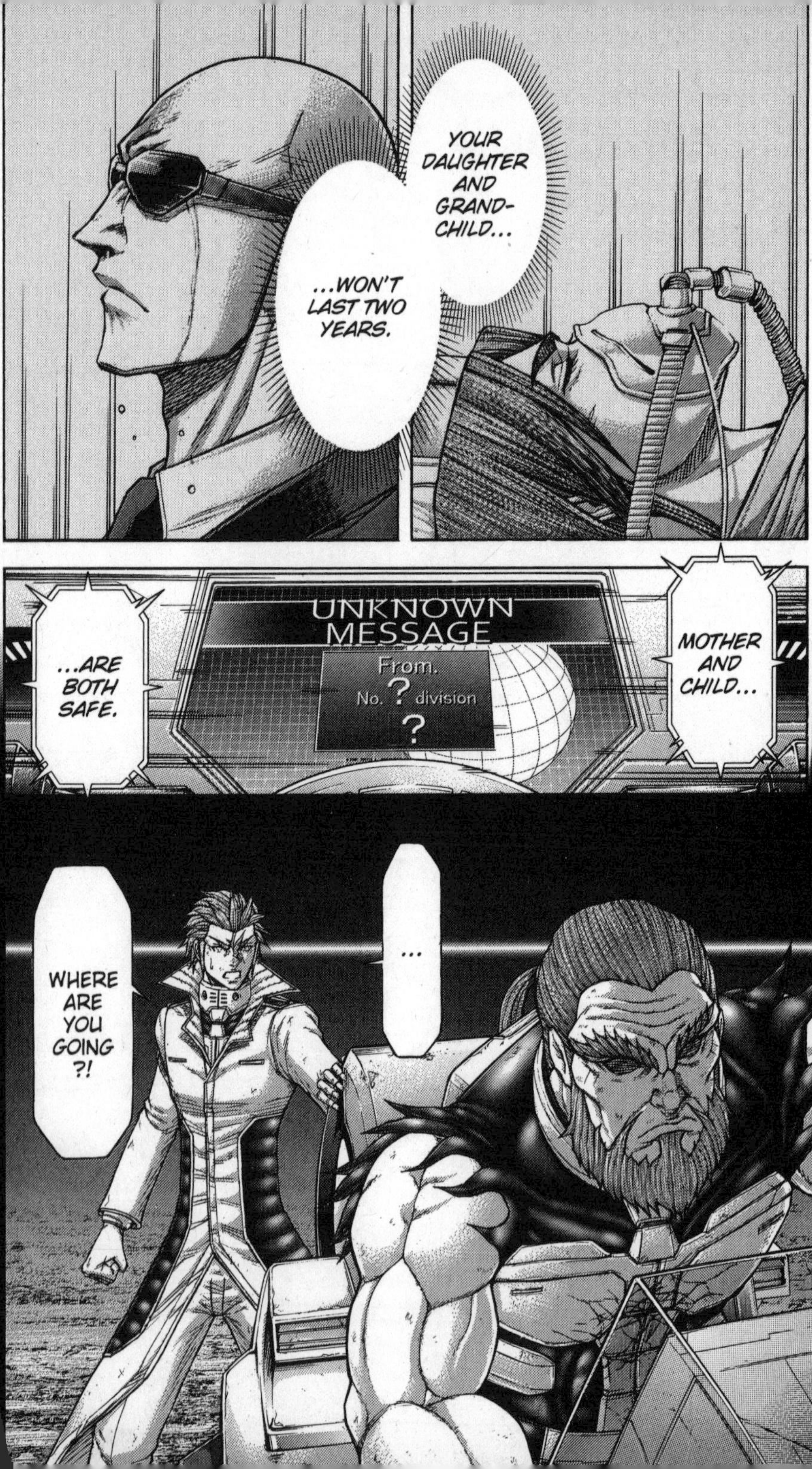
YOUR DAUGHTER AND GRAND-CHILD...
...WON'T LAST TWO YEARS.
MOTHER AND CHILD...
UNKNOWN MESSAGE
From.
No. ? division
?
...ARE BOTH SAFE.
...
WHERE ARE YOU GOING ?!

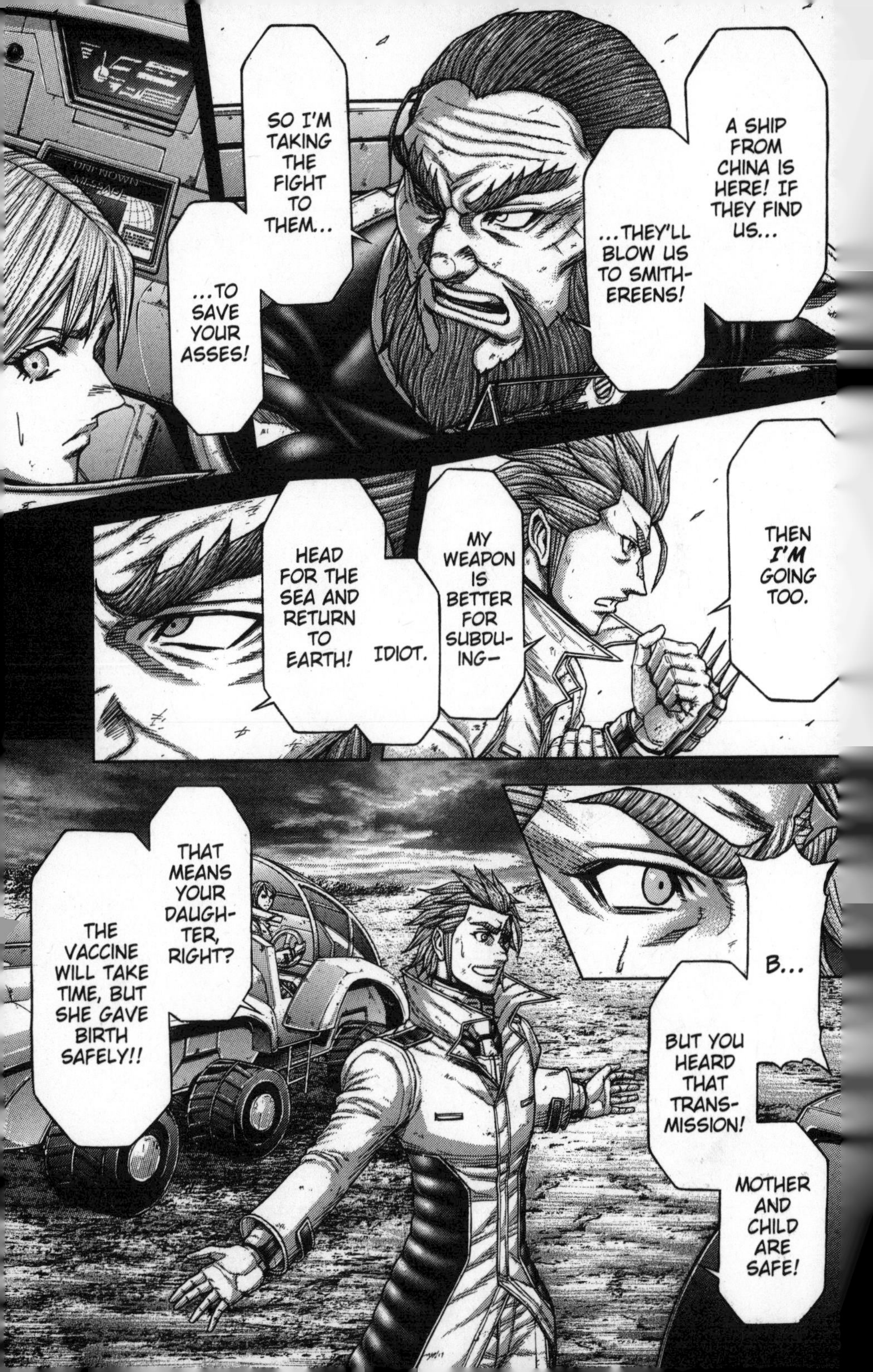
A SHIP FROM CHINA IS HERE! IF THEY FIND US...
...THEY'LL BLOW US TO SMITH-EREENS!
SO I'M TAKING THE FIGHT TO THEM...
...TO SAVE YOUR ASSES!
THEN *I'M* GOING TOO.
MY WEAPON IS BETTER FOR SUBDU-ING—
IDIOT.
HEAD FOR THE SEA AND RETURN TO EARTH!
B...
BUT YOU HEARD THAT TRANS-MISSION!
MOTHER AND CHILD ARE SAFE!
THAT MEANS YOUR DAUGH-TER, RIGHT?
THE VACCINE WILL TAKE TIME, BUT SHE GAVE BIRTH SAFELY!!

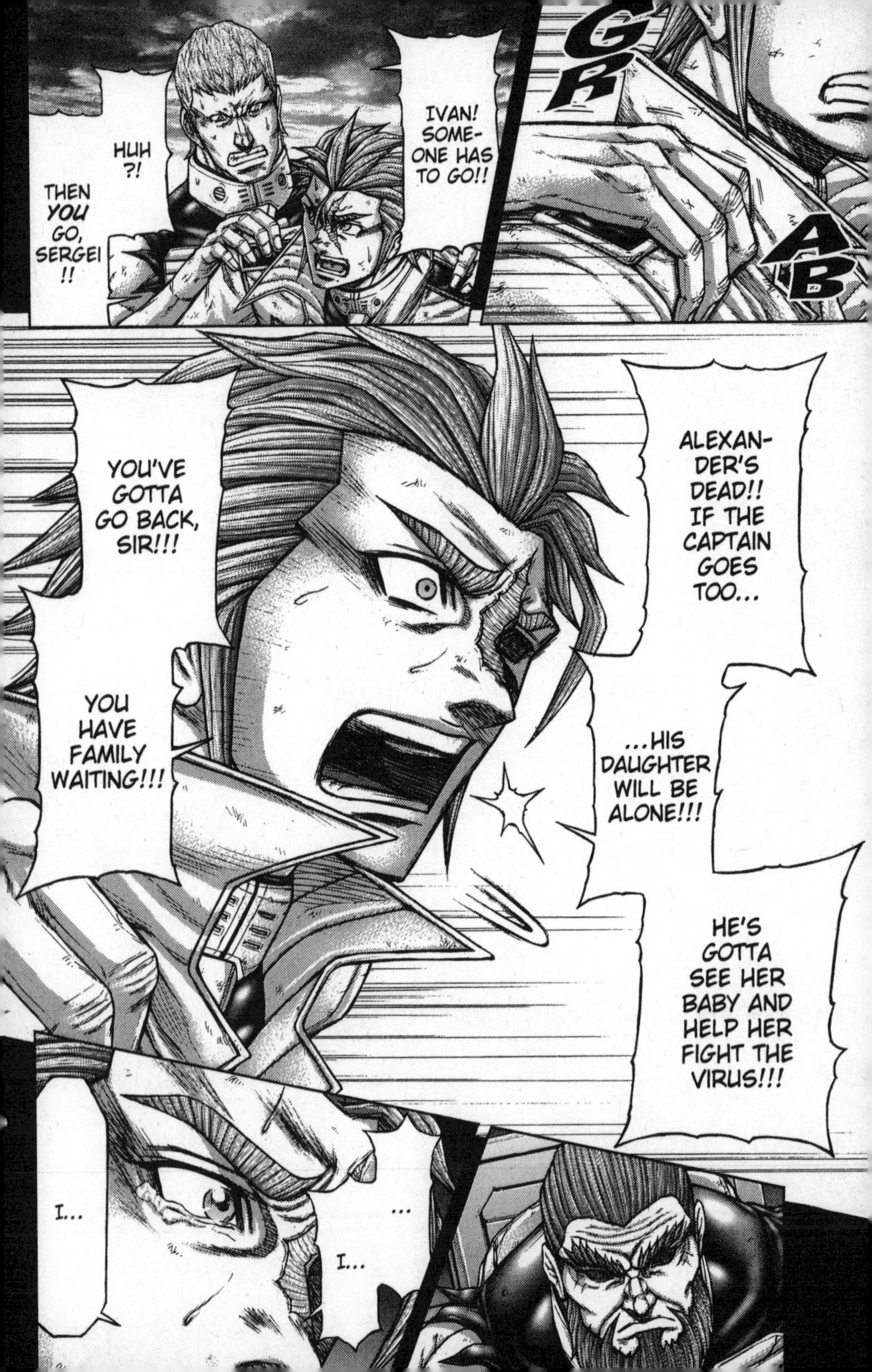
GRAB
IVAN! SOME-ONE HAS TO GO!!
HUH ?!
THEN *YOU* GO, SERGEI !!
ALEXAN-DER'S DEAD!! IF THE CAPTAIN GOES TOO...
...HIS DAUGHTER WILL BE ALONE!!!
HE'S GOTTA SEE HER BABY AND HELP HER FIGHT THE VIRUS!!!
YOU'VE GOTTA GO BACK, SIR!!!
YOU HAVE FAMILY WAITING!!!
...
I...
I...

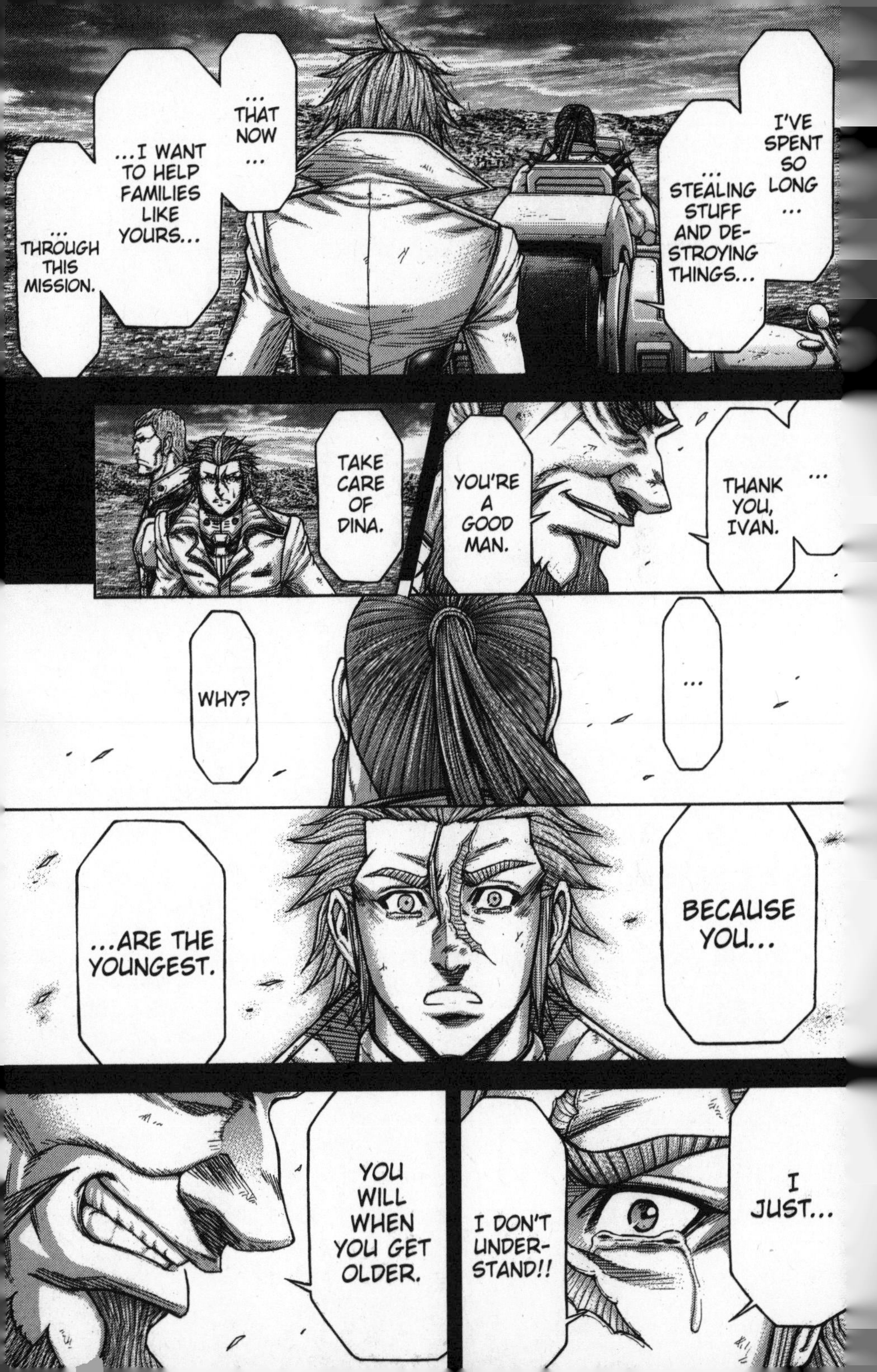
I'VE SPENT SO LONG...
...STEALING STUFF AND DE-STROYING THINGS...
...THAT NOW...
...I WANT TO HELP FAMILIES LIKE YOURS...
...THROUGH THIS MISSION.
...
THANK YOU, IVAN.
YOU'RE A GOOD MAN.
TAKE CARE OF DINA.
...
WHY?
BECAUSE YOU...
...ARE THE YOUNGEST.
I JUST...
I DON'T UNDER-STAND!!
YOU WILL WHEN YOU GET OLDER.

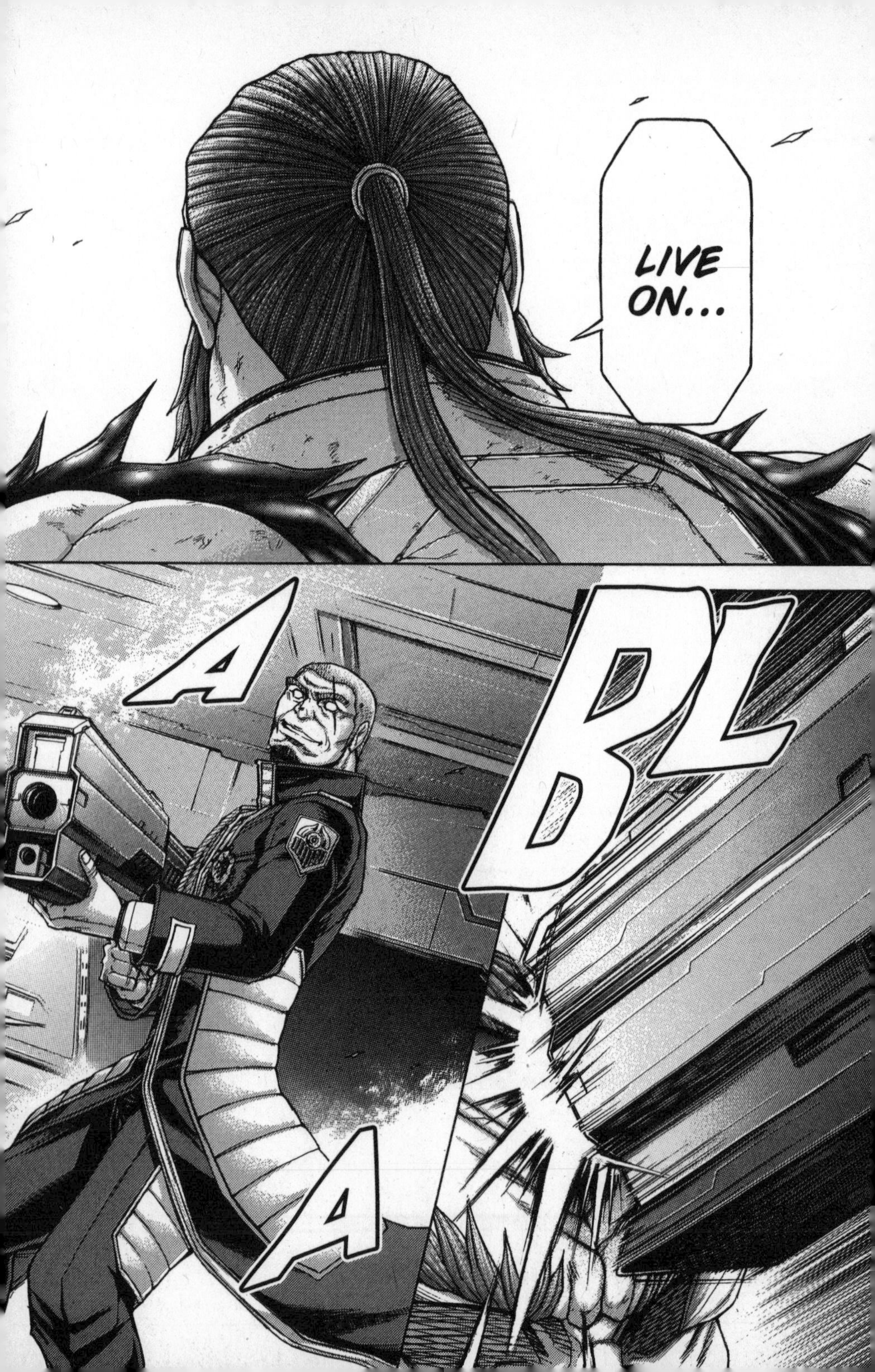
LIVE ON...
BLAA

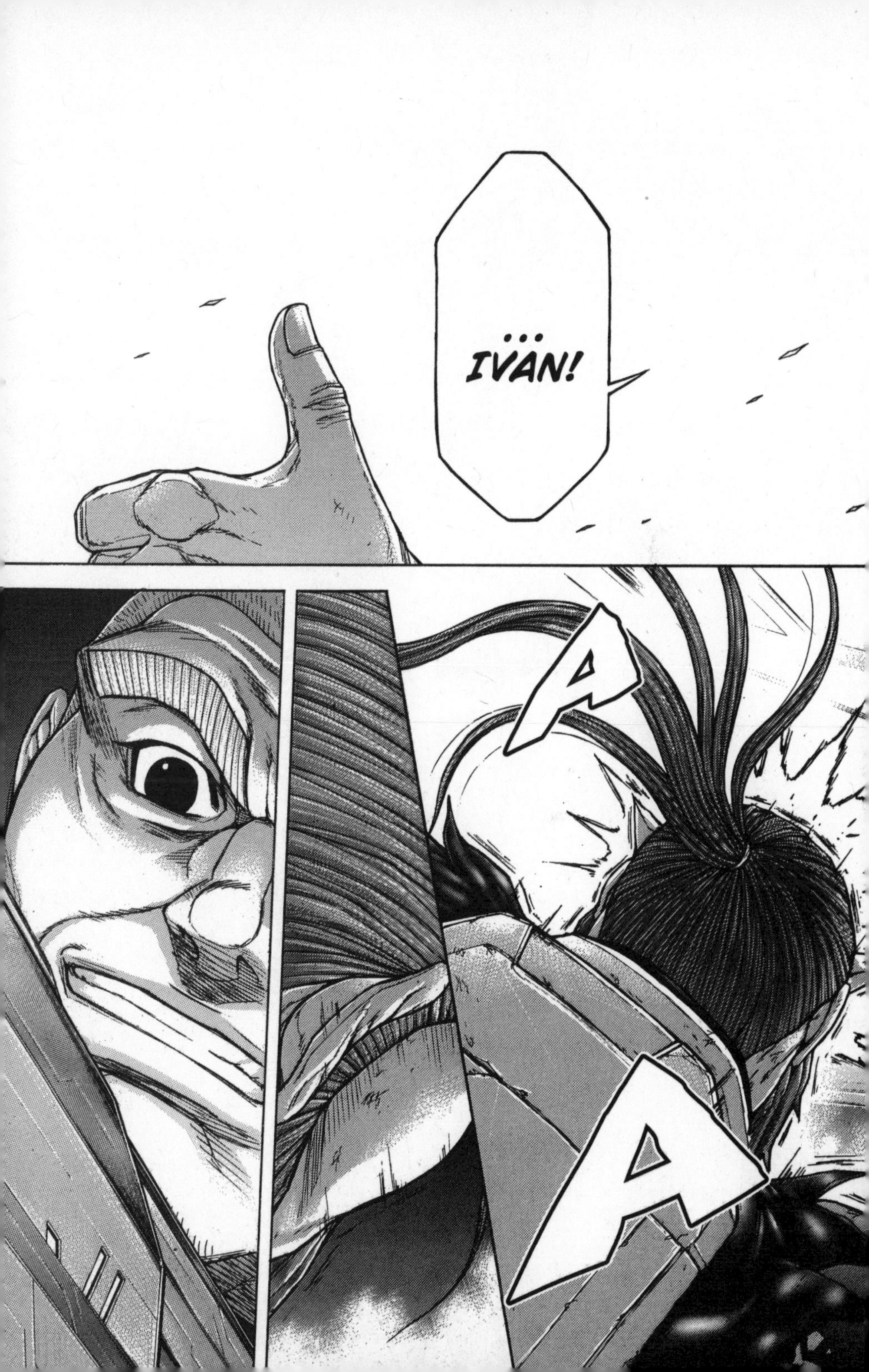
...IVÄN!

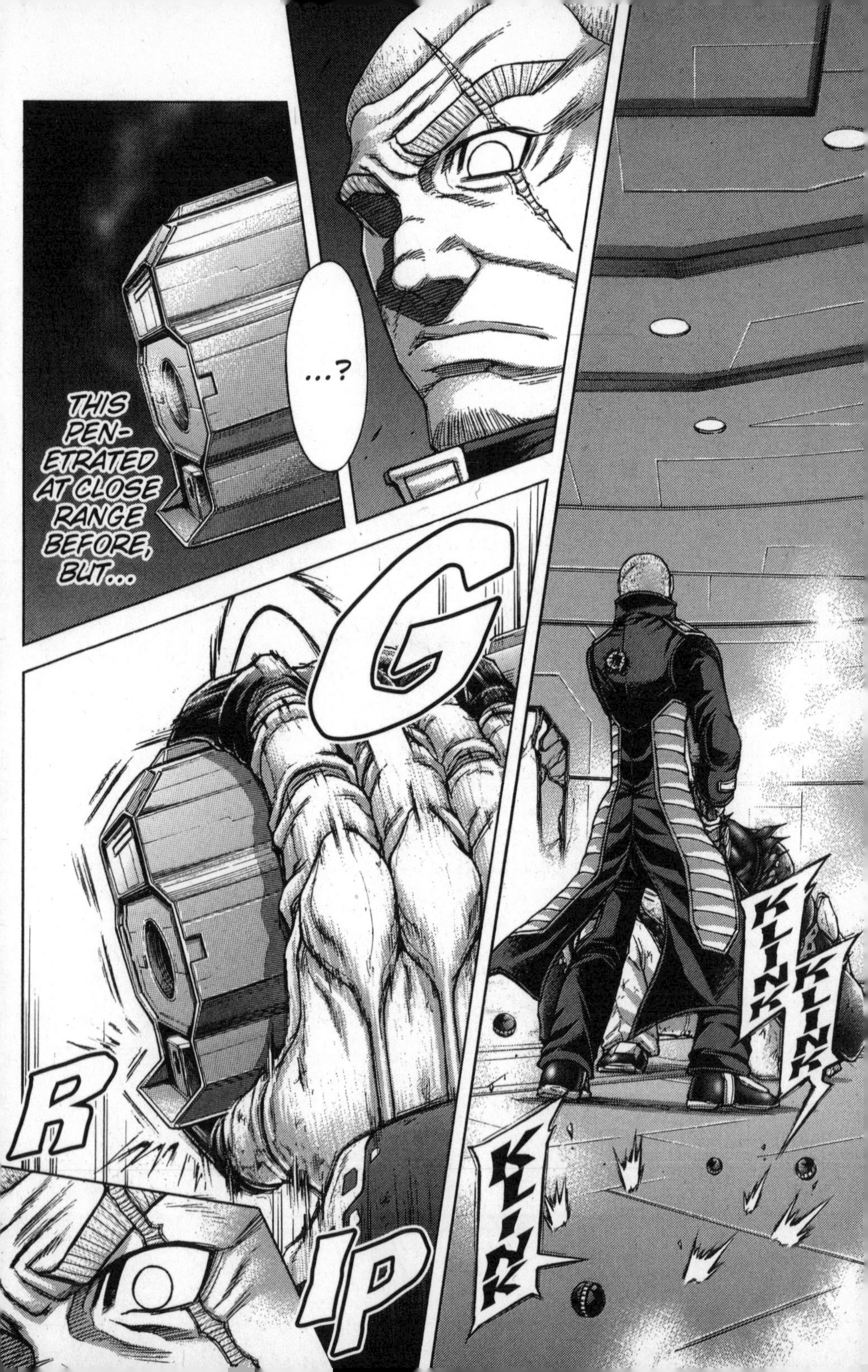
KLINK
KLINK
KLINK
...?
THIS PEN-ETRATED AT CLOSE RANGE BEFORE, BUT...
G
R
I
P

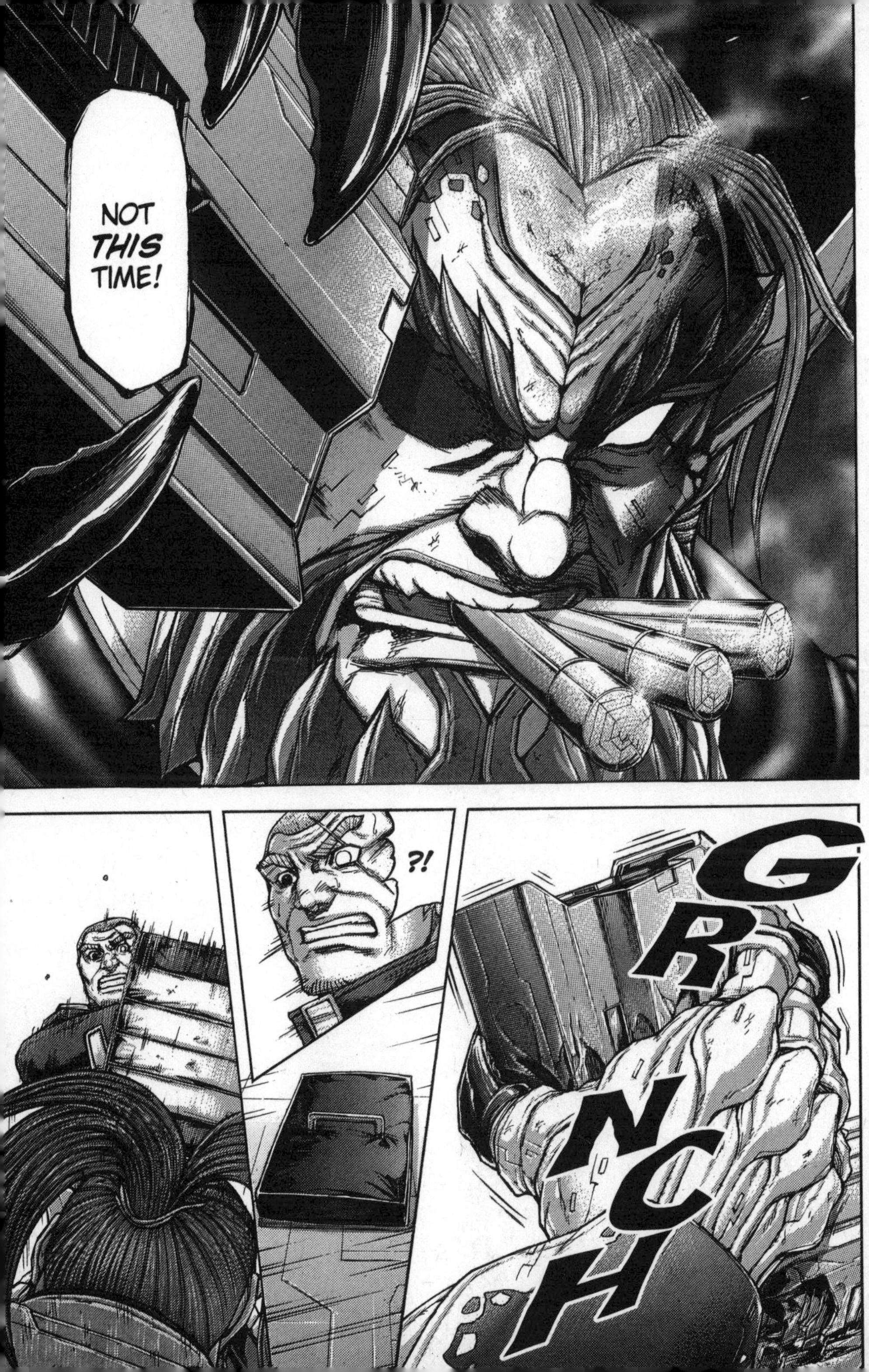
NOT *THIS* TIME!
GRNCH
?!

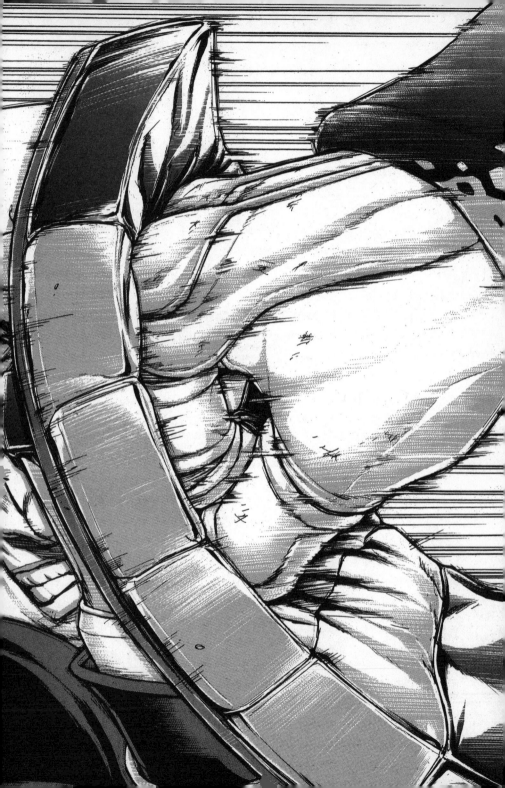

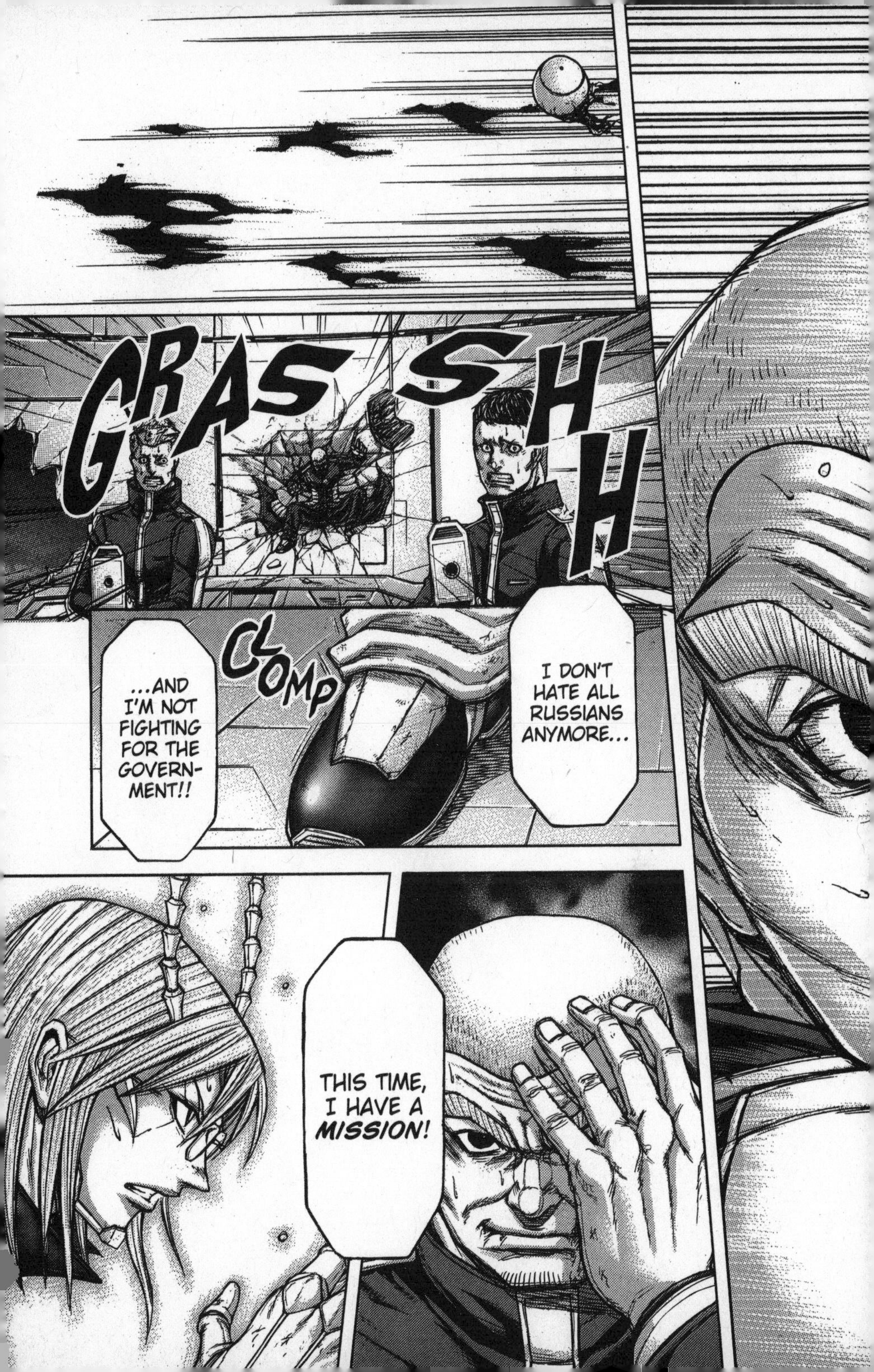
GRASSHH
I DON'T HATE ALL RUSSIANS ANYMORE...
CLOMP
...AND I'M NOT FIGHTING FOR THE GOVERN-MENT!!
THIS TIME, I HAVE A *MISSION*!

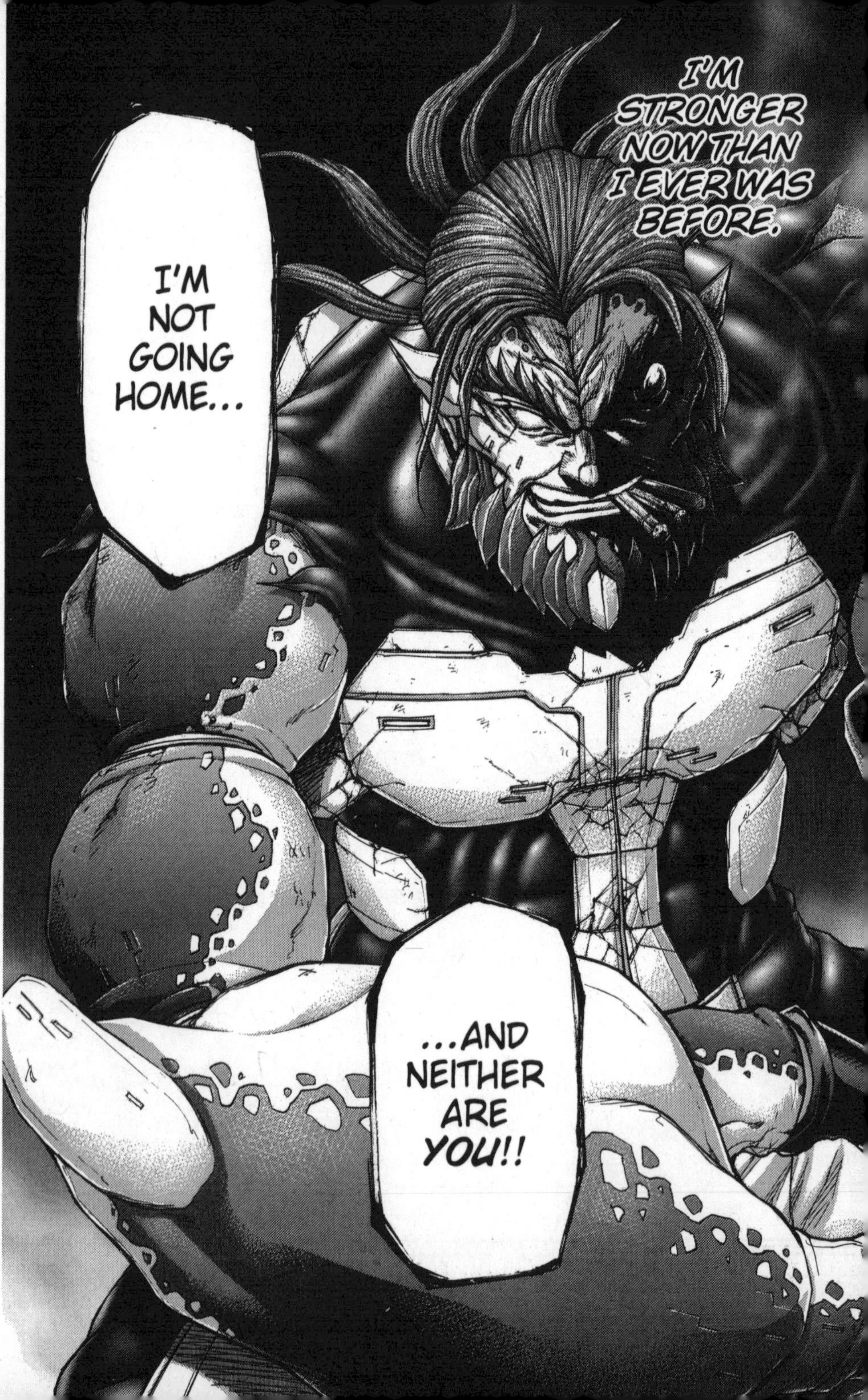
I'M STRONGER NOW THAN I EVER WAS BEFORE.
I'M NOT GOING HOME...
...AND NEITHER ARE YOU!!

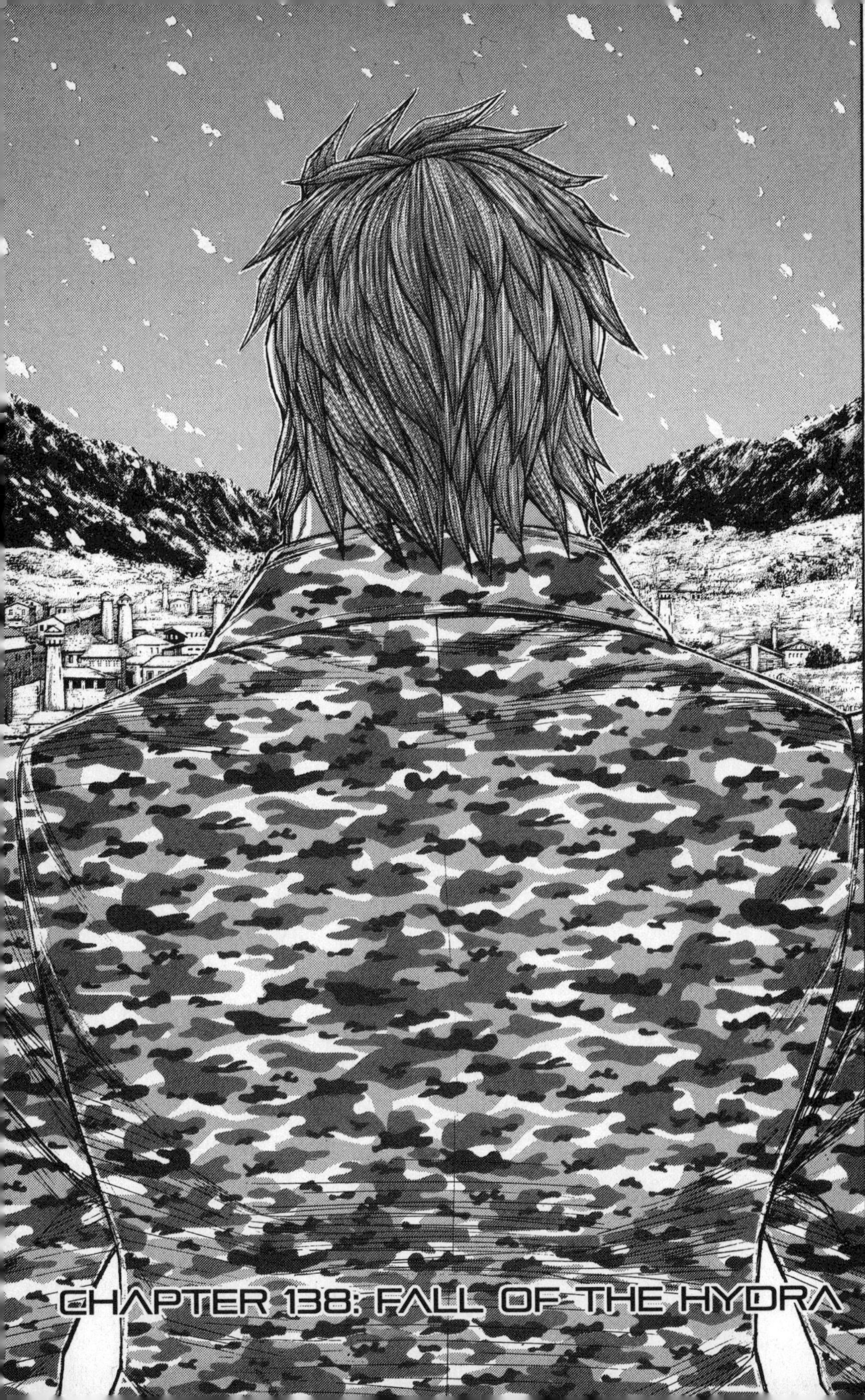
CHAPTER 138: FALL OF THE HYDRA

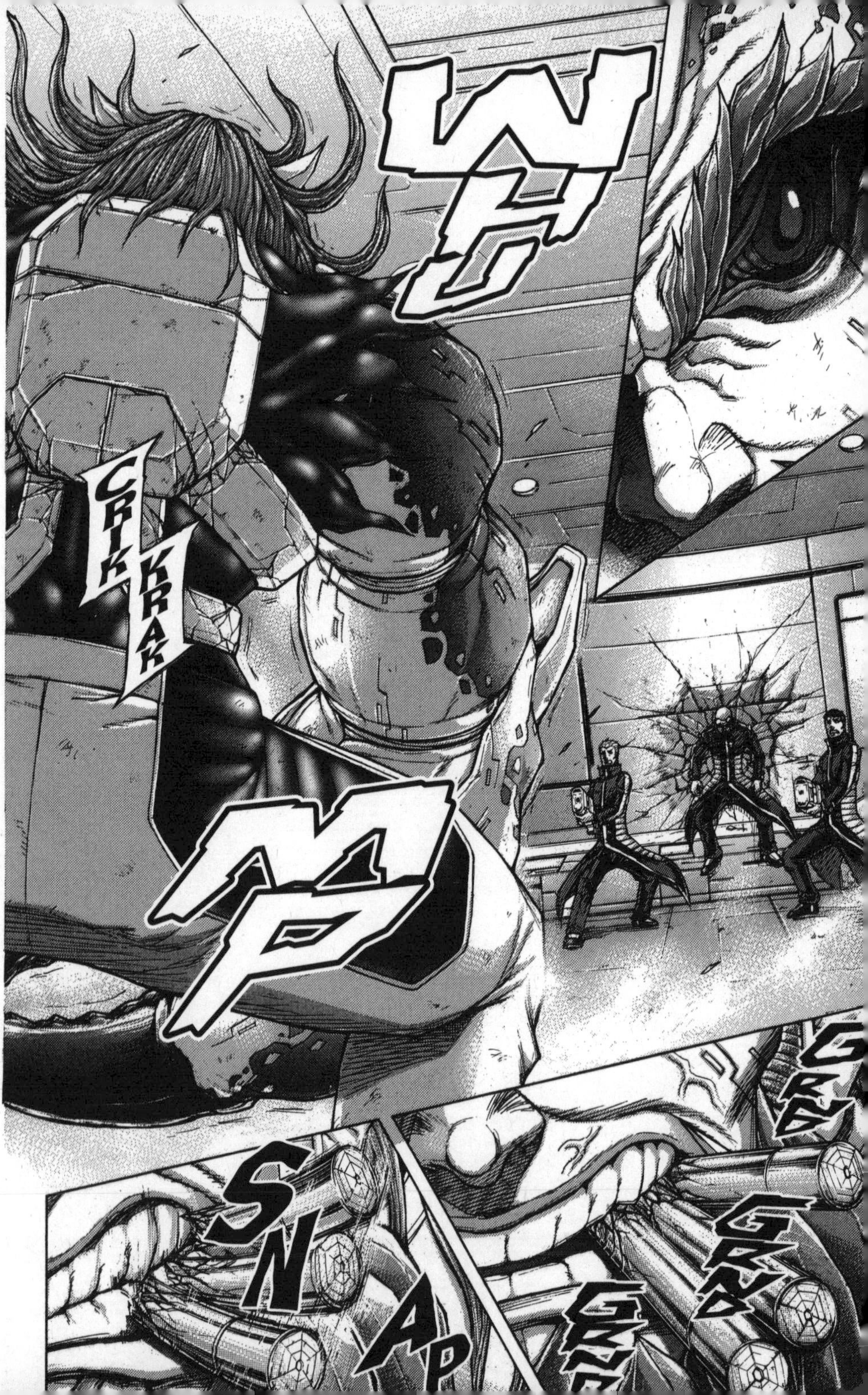
WHUMP
CRIK KRAK
GRND
GRND
SNAP

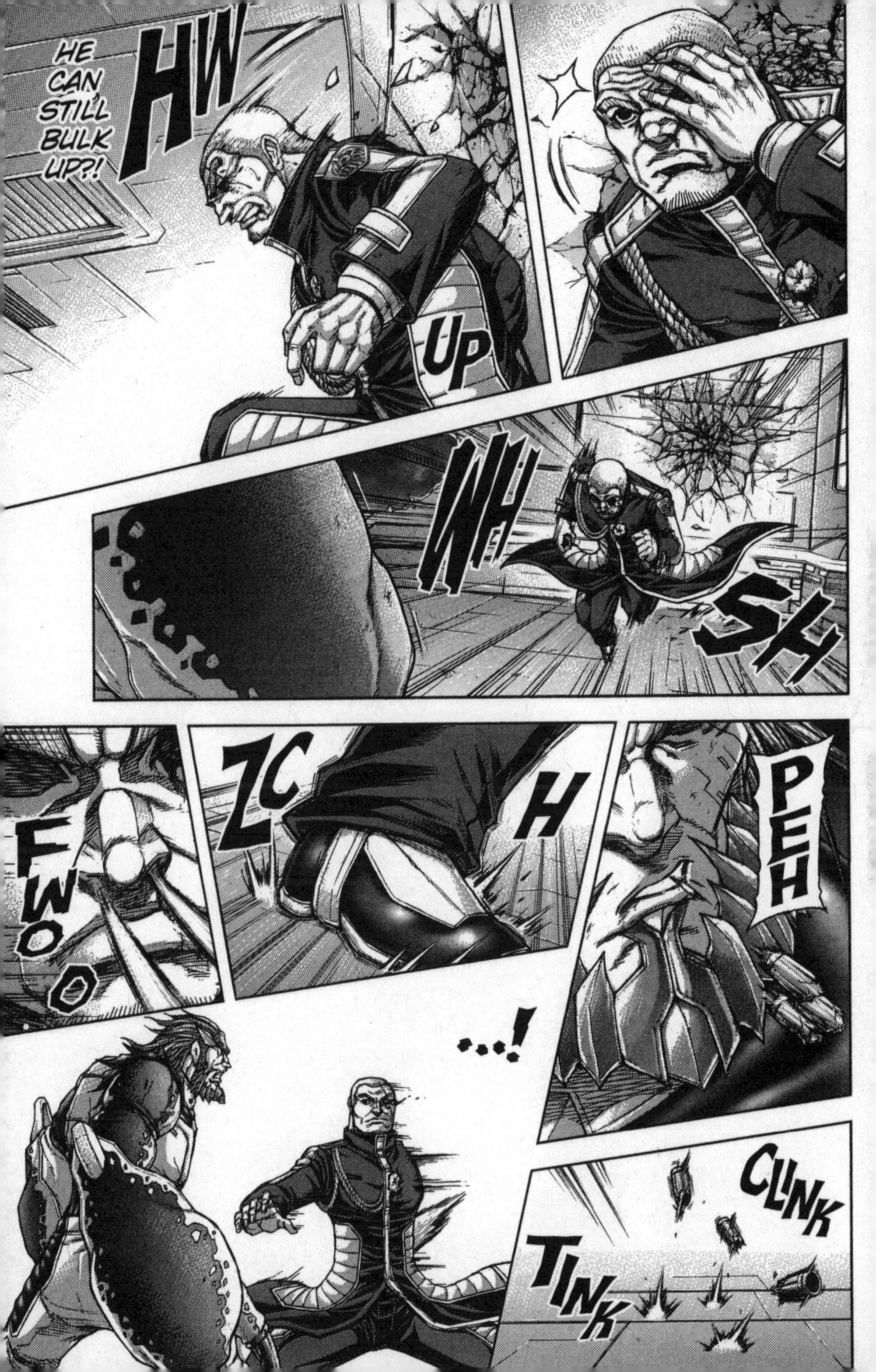

HE CAN STILL BULK UP?!
HW
UP
WH
SH
PEH
ZC
H
FWO
O
CLINK
TINK
...!

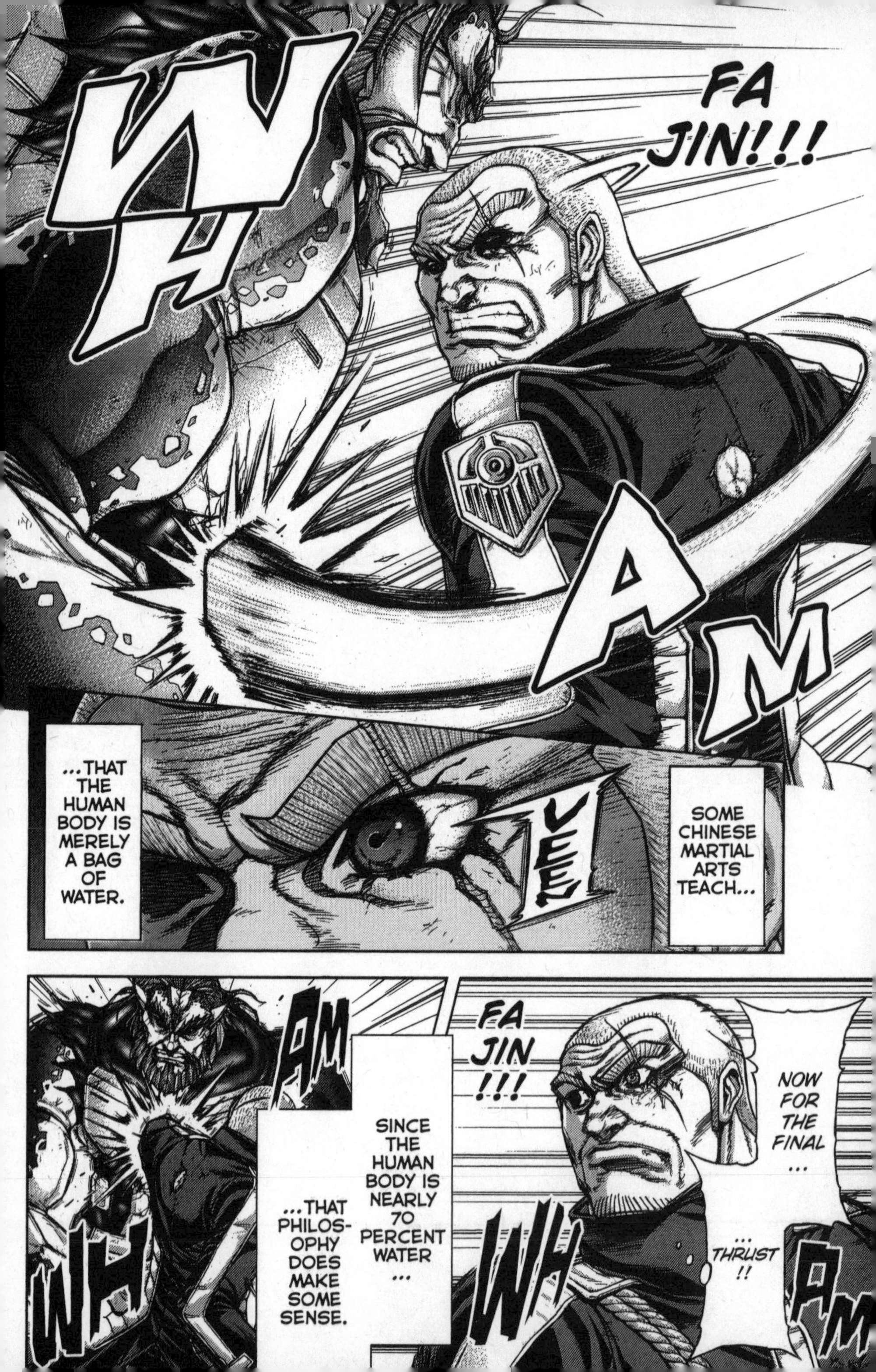
FA JIN!!!
WH
AM
SOME CHINESE MARTIAL ARTS TEACH...
VEEEN
...THAT THE HUMAN BODY IS MERELY A BAG OF WATER.
NOW FOR THE FINAL ...
FA JIN !!!
... THRUST !!
WH
PAM
SINCE THE HUMAN BODY IS NEARLY 70 PERCENT WATER ...
...THAT PHILOSOPHY DOES MAKE SOME SENSE.
AM
WH

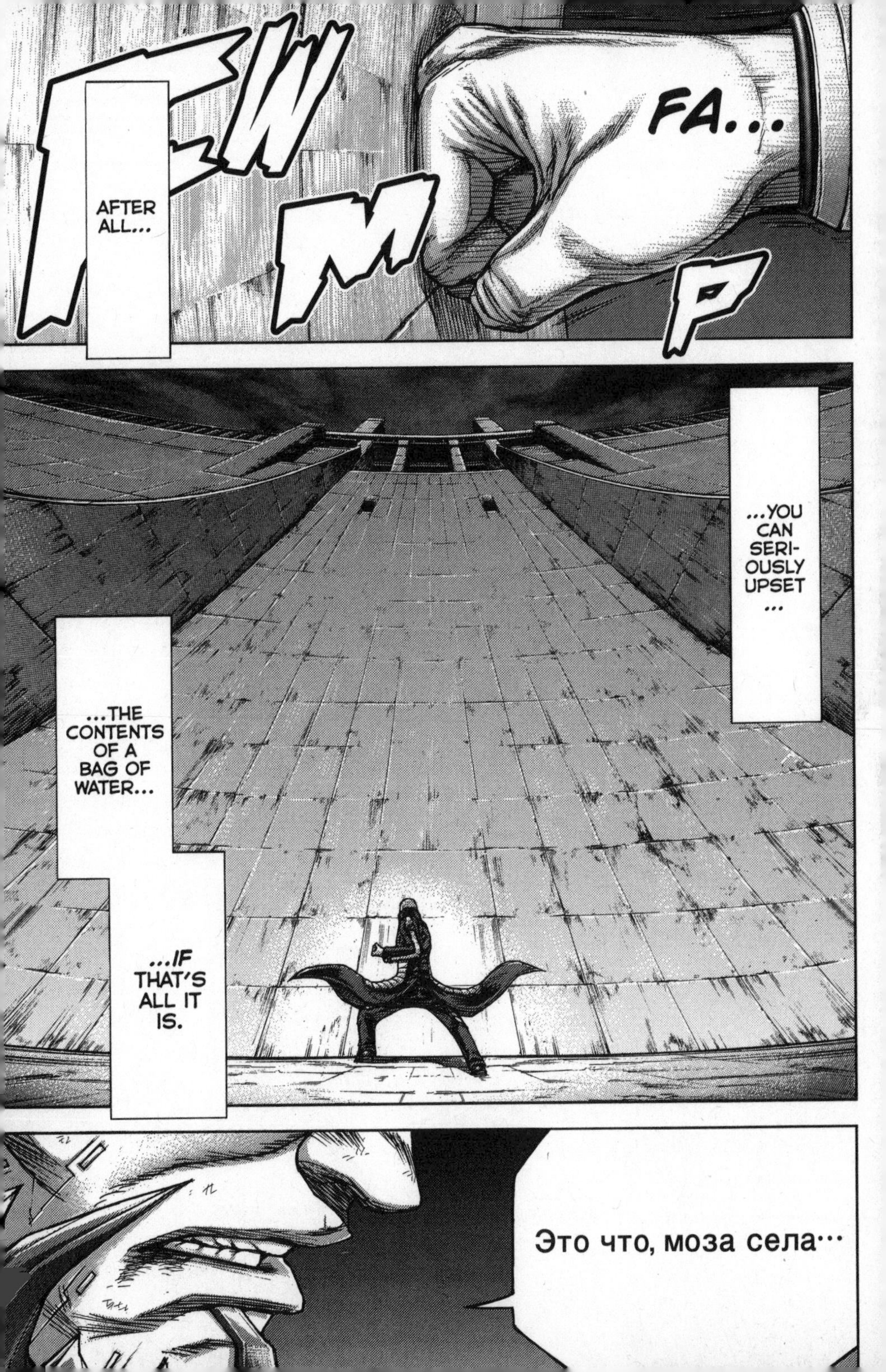
FA...
FWMP
AFTER ALL...
...YOU CAN SERI-OUSLY UPSET...
...THE CONTENTS OF A BAG OF WATER...
...IF THAT'S ALL IT IS.
Это что, моза села···

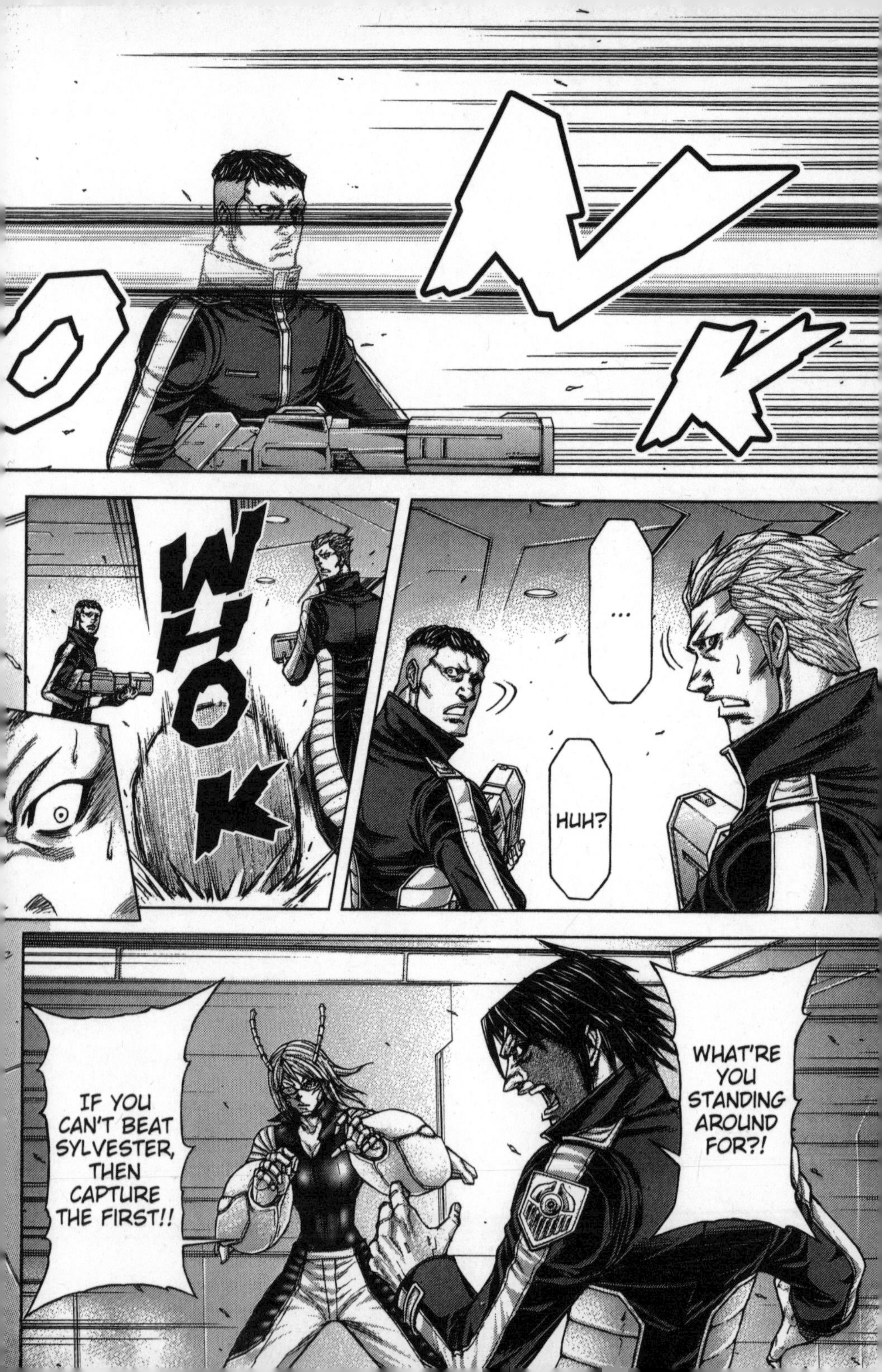
ONK
...
HUH?
WHOK
WHAT'RE YOU STANDING AROUND FOR?!
IF YOU CAN'T BEAT SYLVESTER, THEN CAPTURE THE FIRST!!

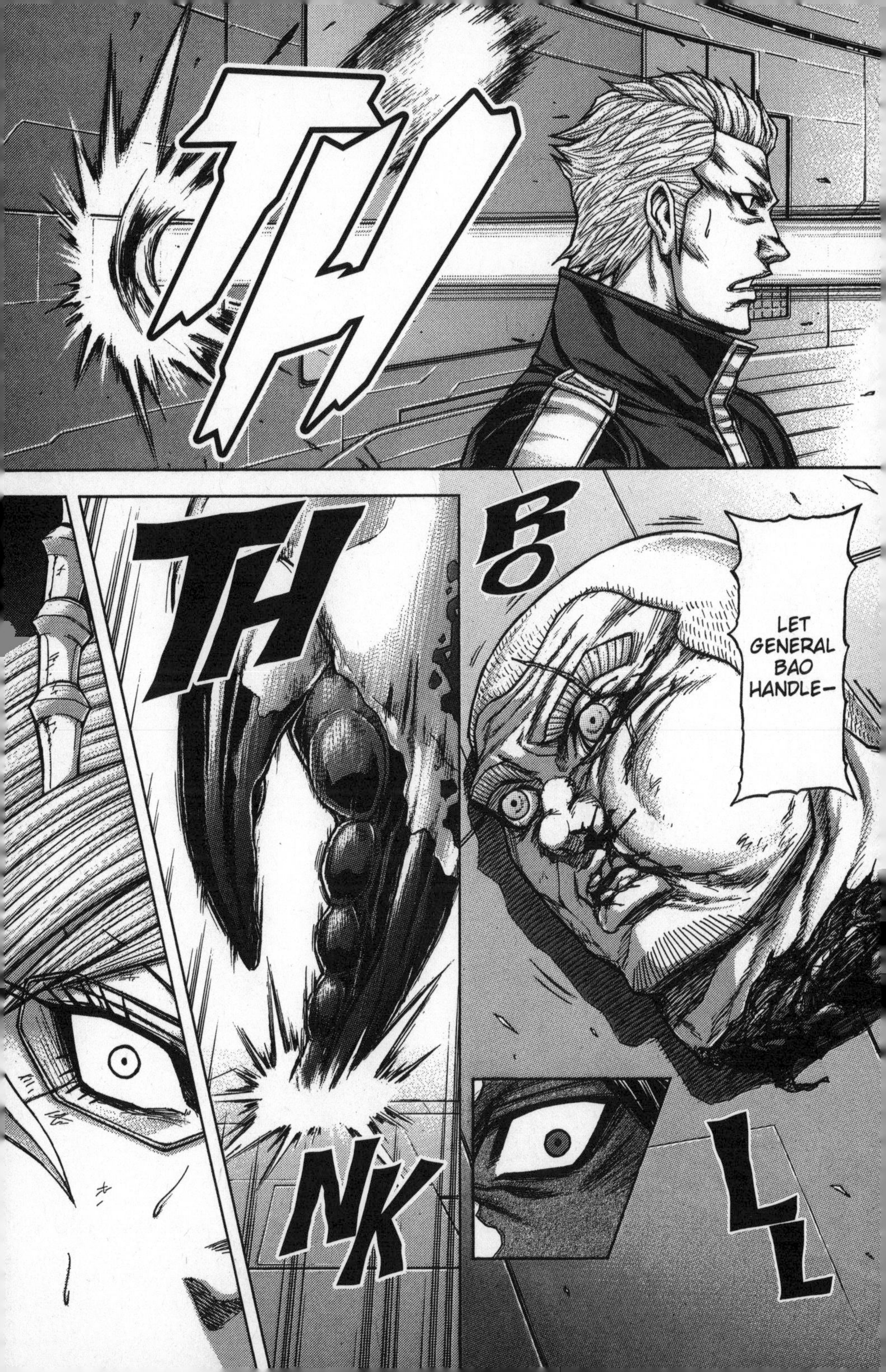
TH
BO
LET GENERAL BAO HANDLE—
LL
TH
NK

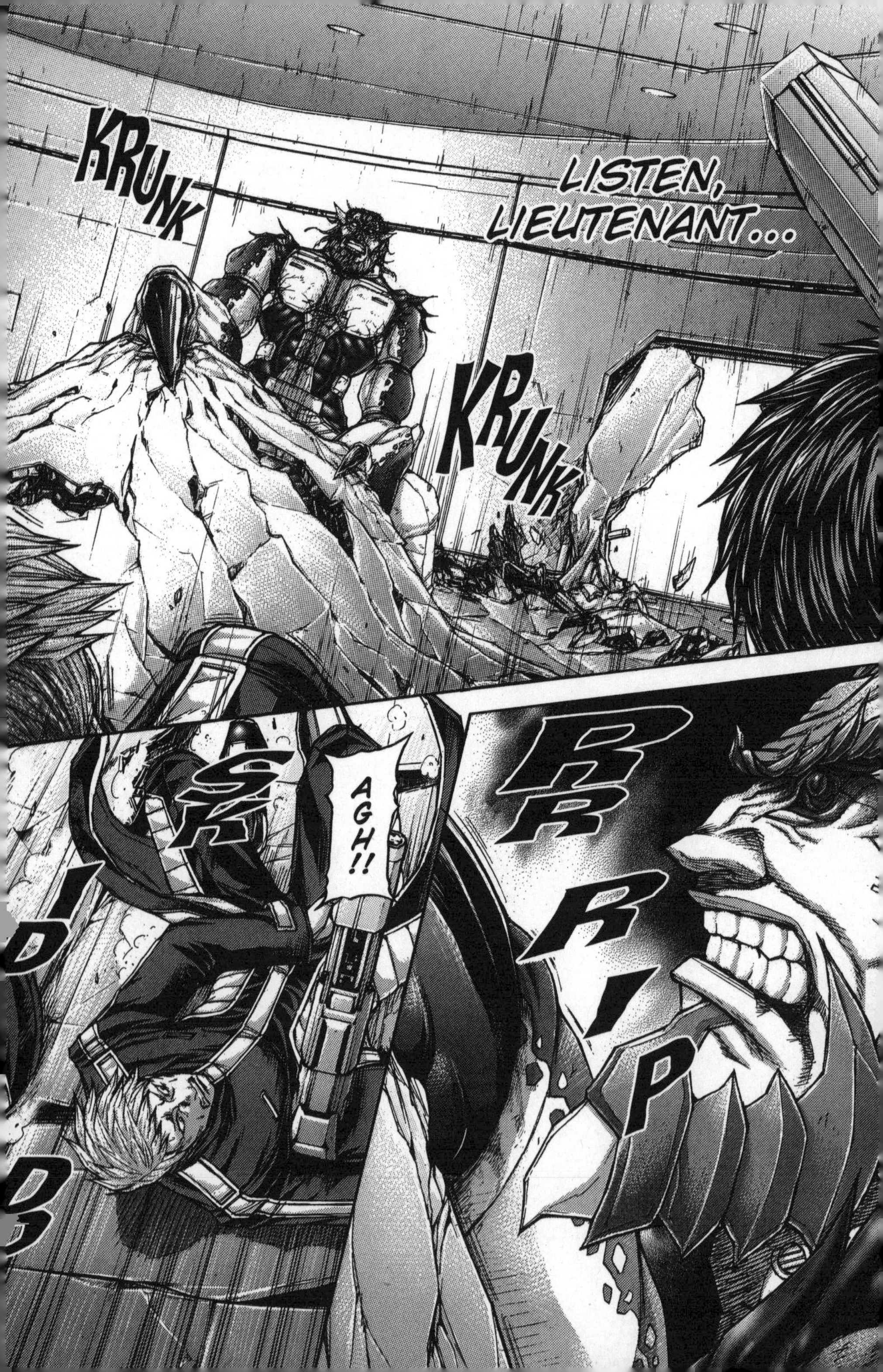
LISTEN, LIEUTENANT...
KRUNK
KRUNK
RRRIP
AGH!!
SK

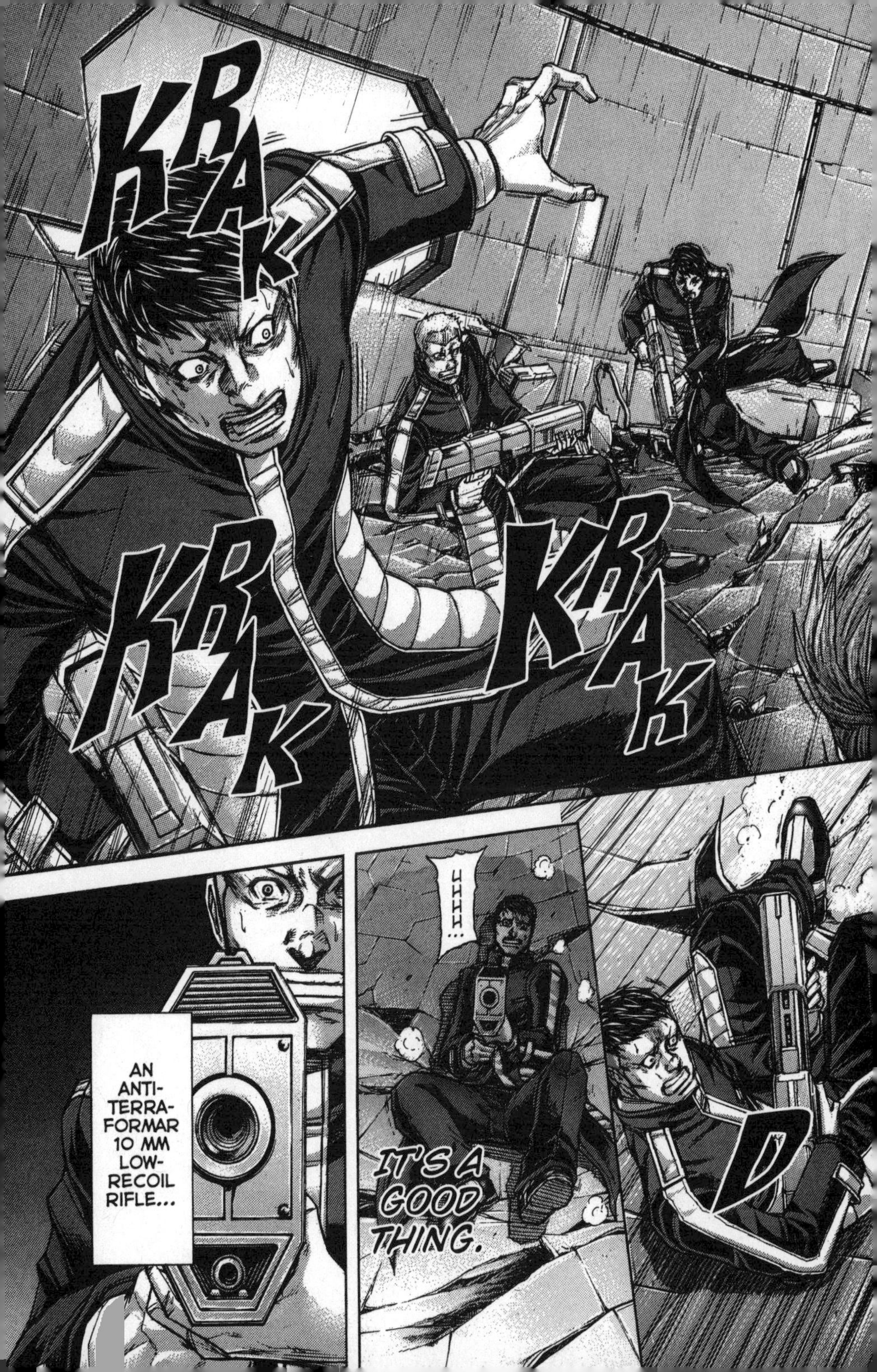
KRAK
KRAK
KRAK
D
UHHH...!!
IT'S A GOOD THING.
AN ANTI-TERRAFORMAR 10 MM LOW-RECOIL RIFLE...

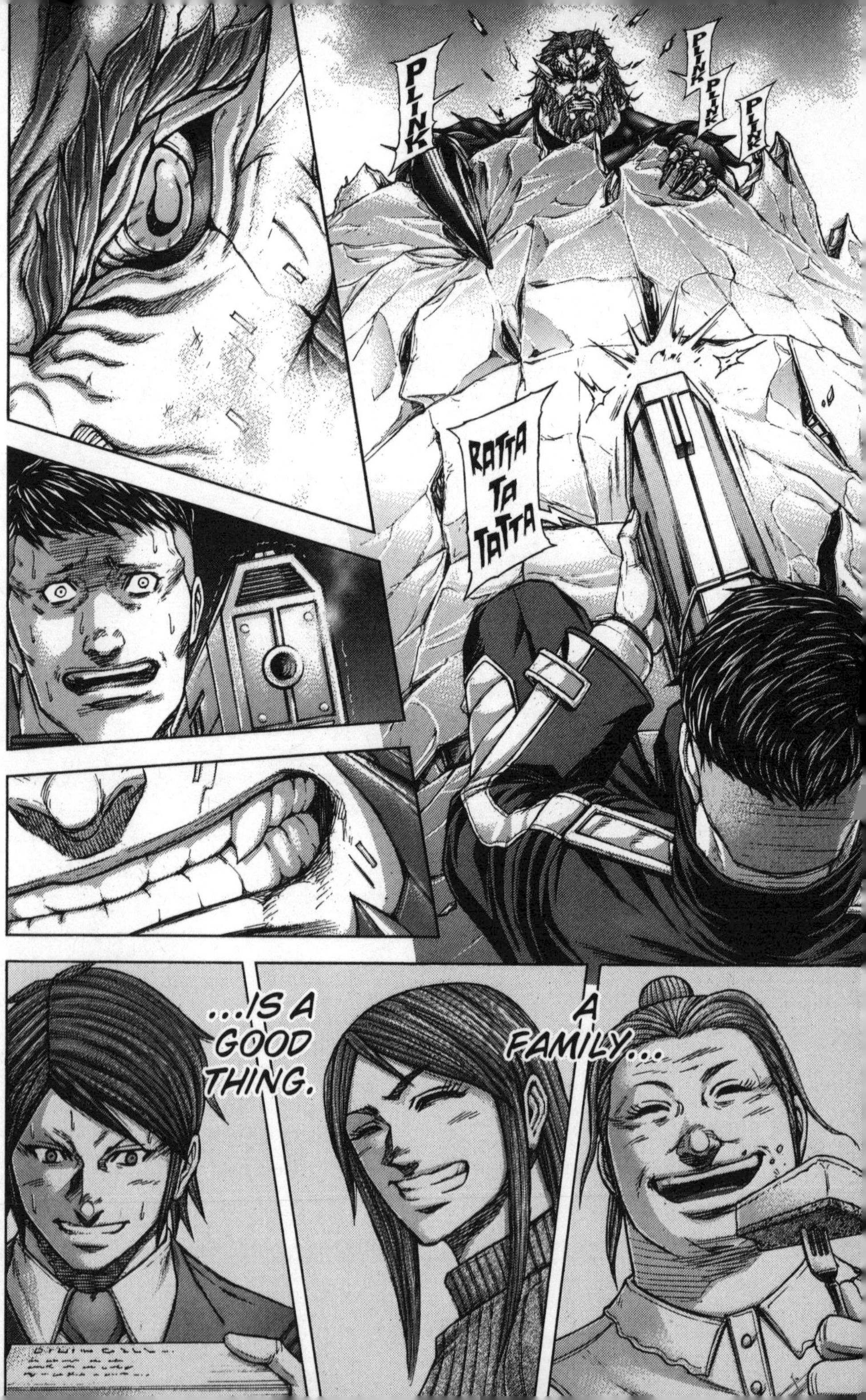
PLINK PLINK
PLINK
PLINK
PLINK
RATTA TA TATTA
A FAMILY...
...IS A GOOD THING.

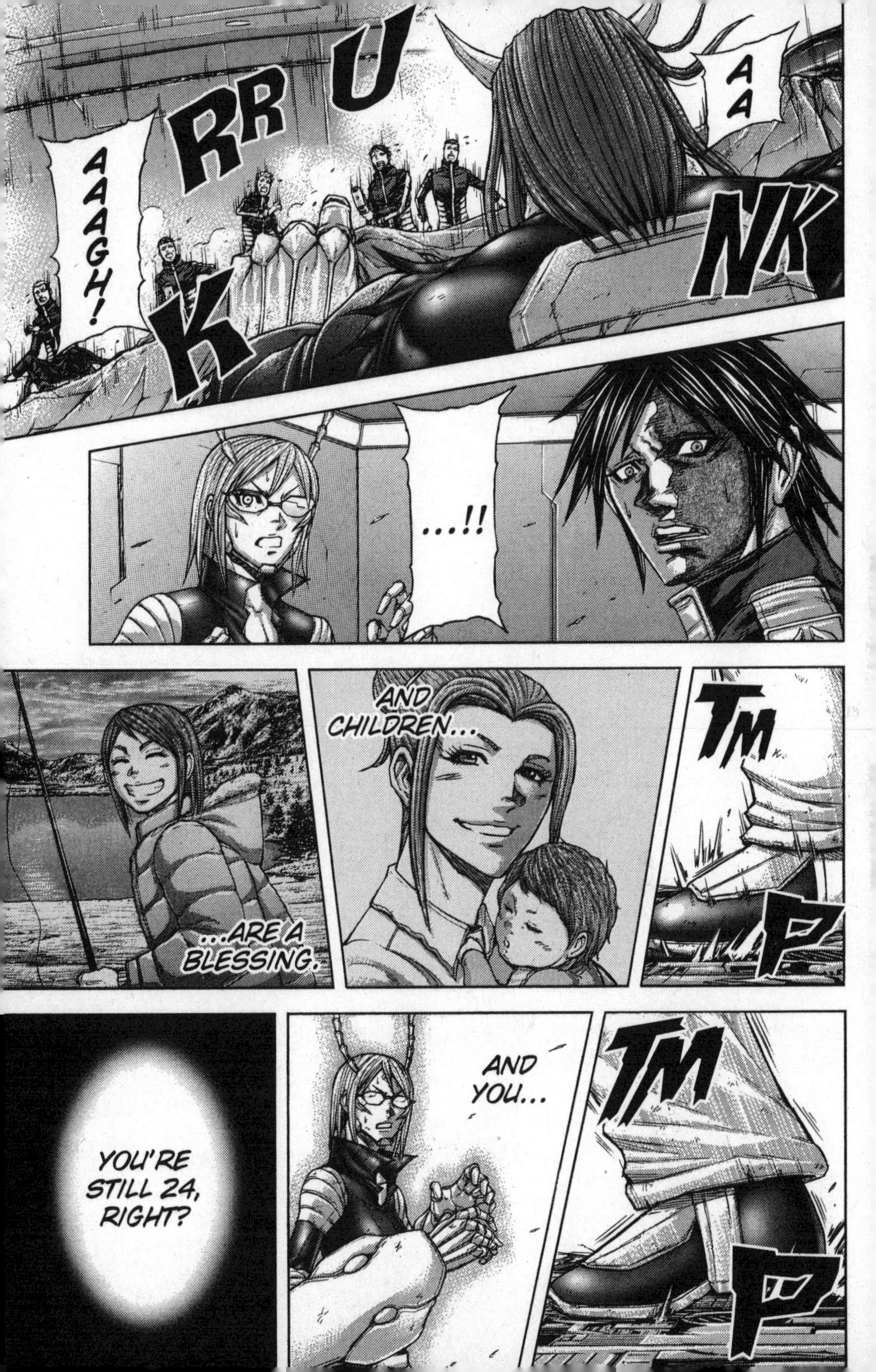
AA
KRRUNK
AAAAGH!
...!!
TMP
AND CHILDREN...
...ARE A BLESSING.
TMP
AND YOU...
YOU'RE STILL 24, RIGHT?

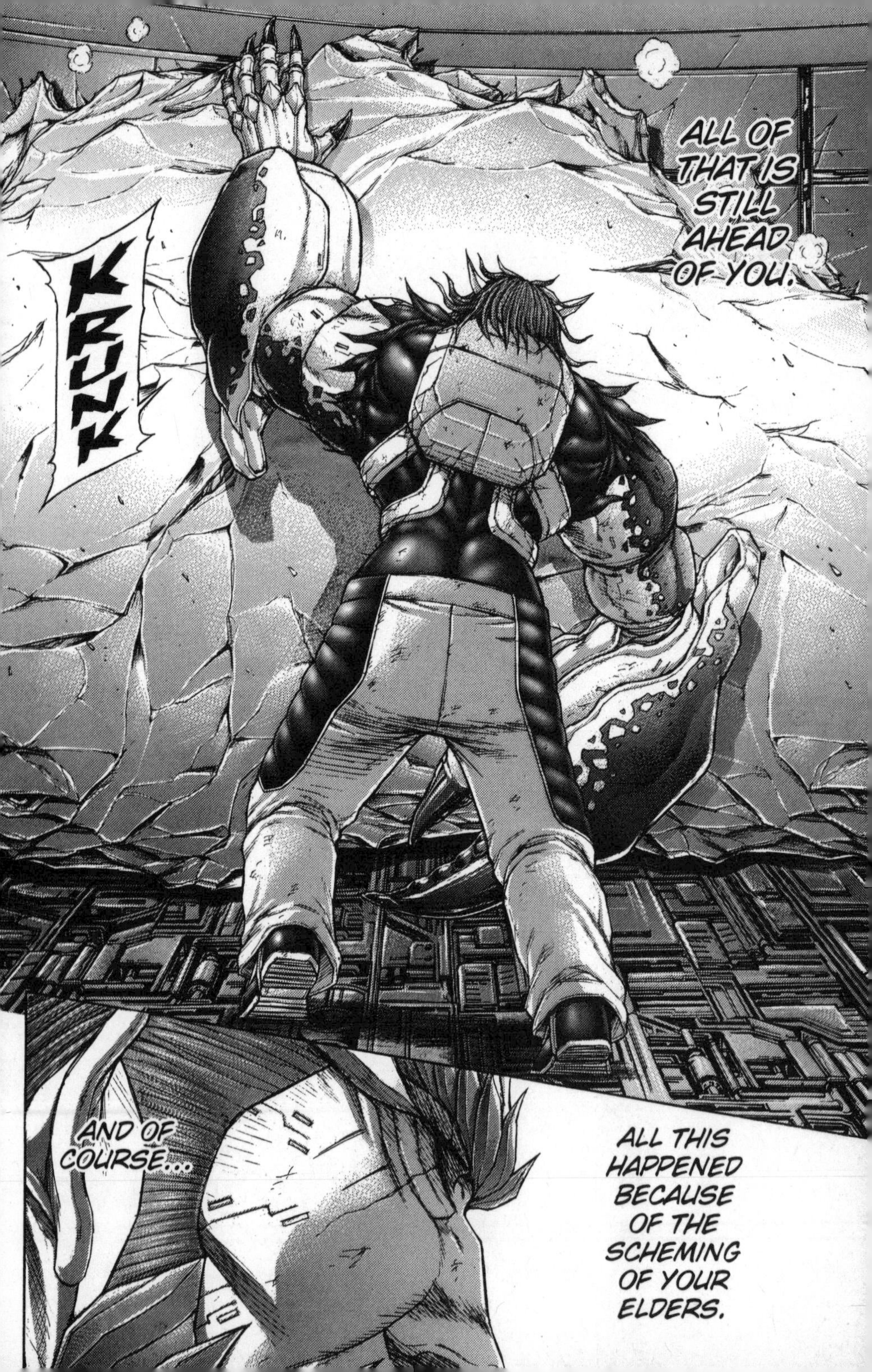
ALL OF THAT IS STILL AHEAD OF YOU.
KRUNK
AND OF COURSE...
ALL THIS HAPPENED BECAUSE OF THE SCHEMING OF YOUR ELDERS.

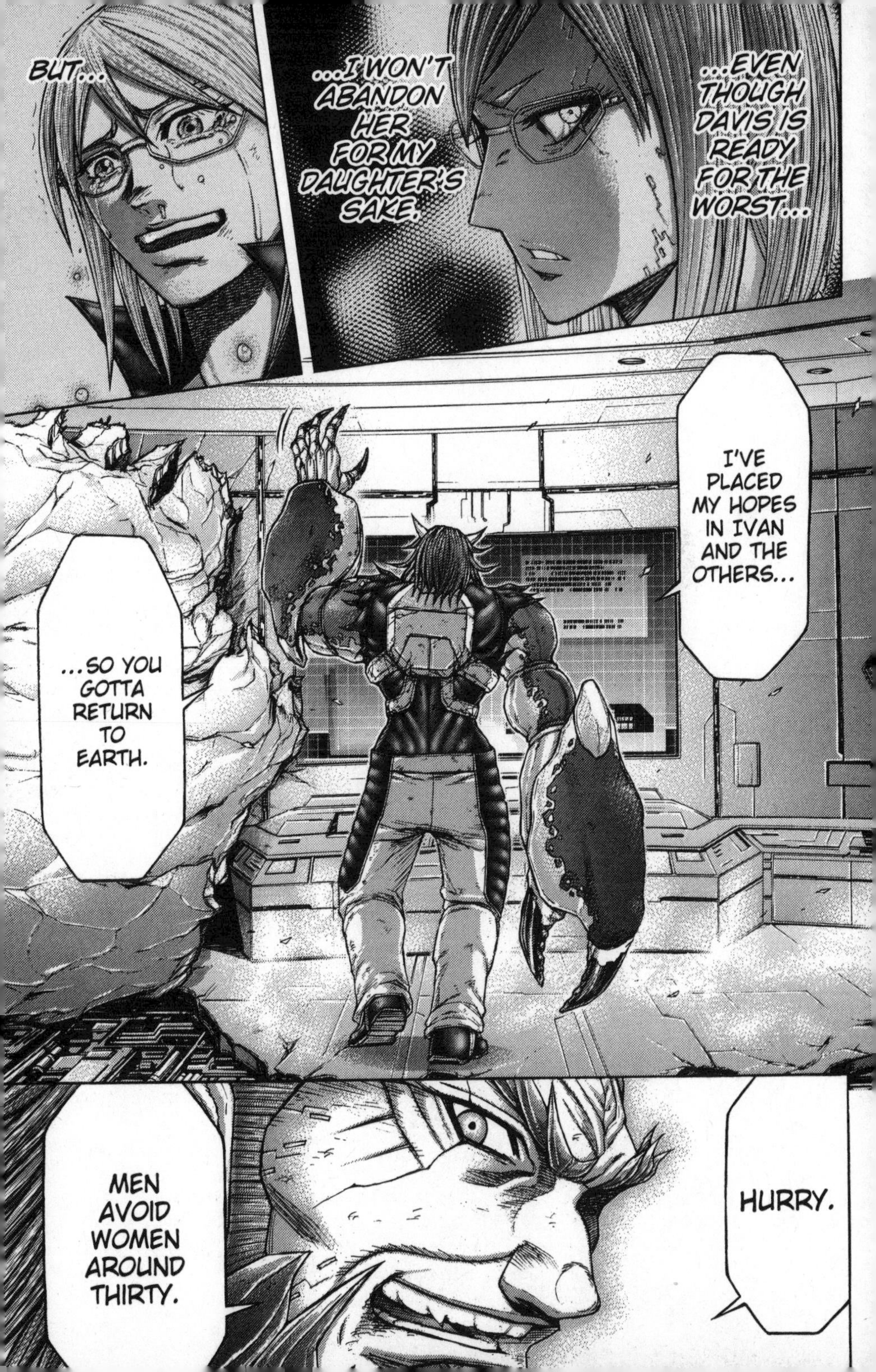
...EVEN THOUGH DAVIS IS READY FOR THE WORST...
...I WON'T ABANDON HER FOR MY DAUGHTER'S SAKE.
BUT...
I'VE PLACED MY HOPES IN IVAN AND THE OTHERS...
...SO YOU GOTTA RETURN TO EARTH.
HURRY.
MEN AVOID WOMEN AROUND THIRTY.

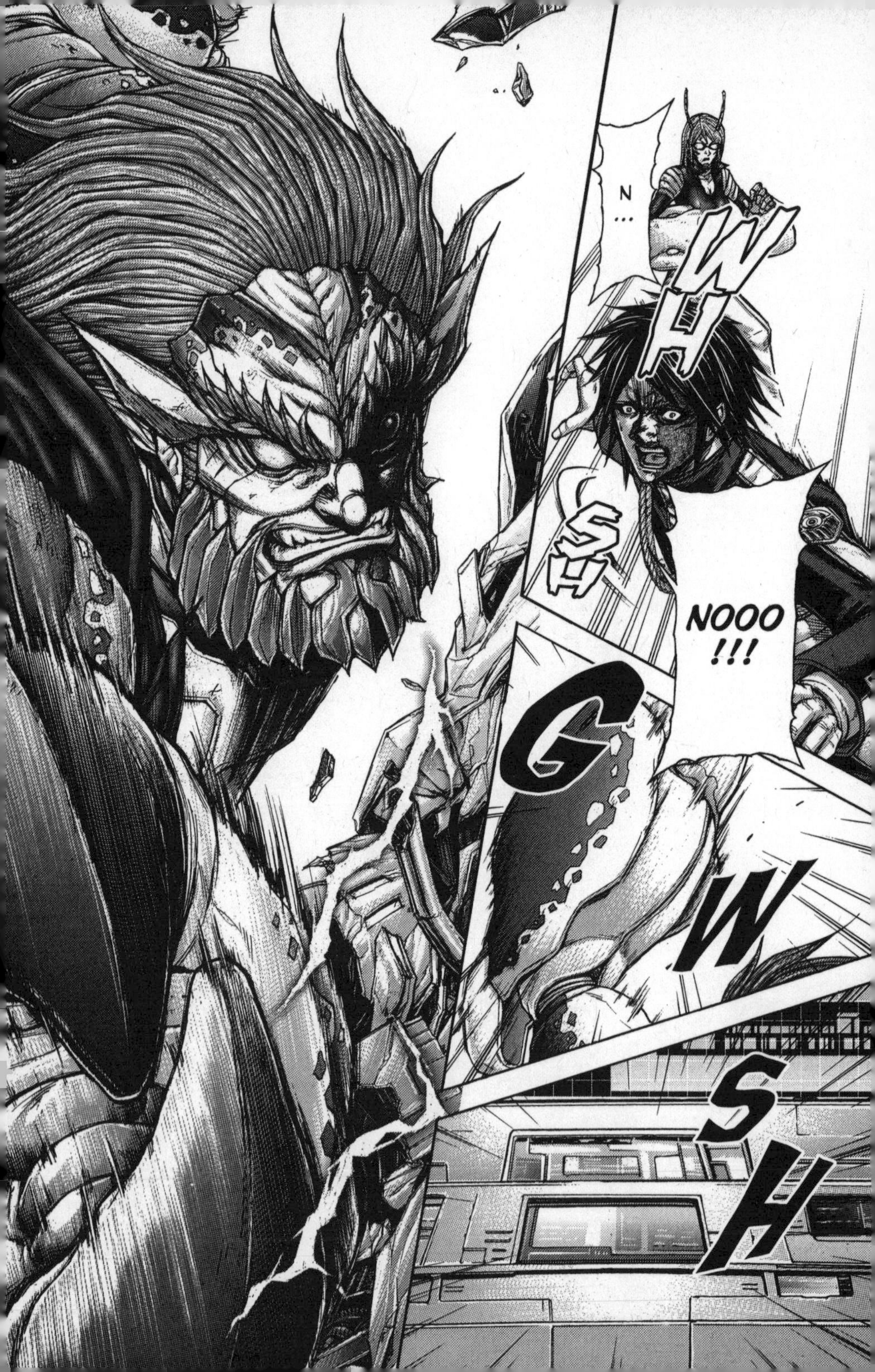
N...
WH
SH
NOOO!!!
GW
SH

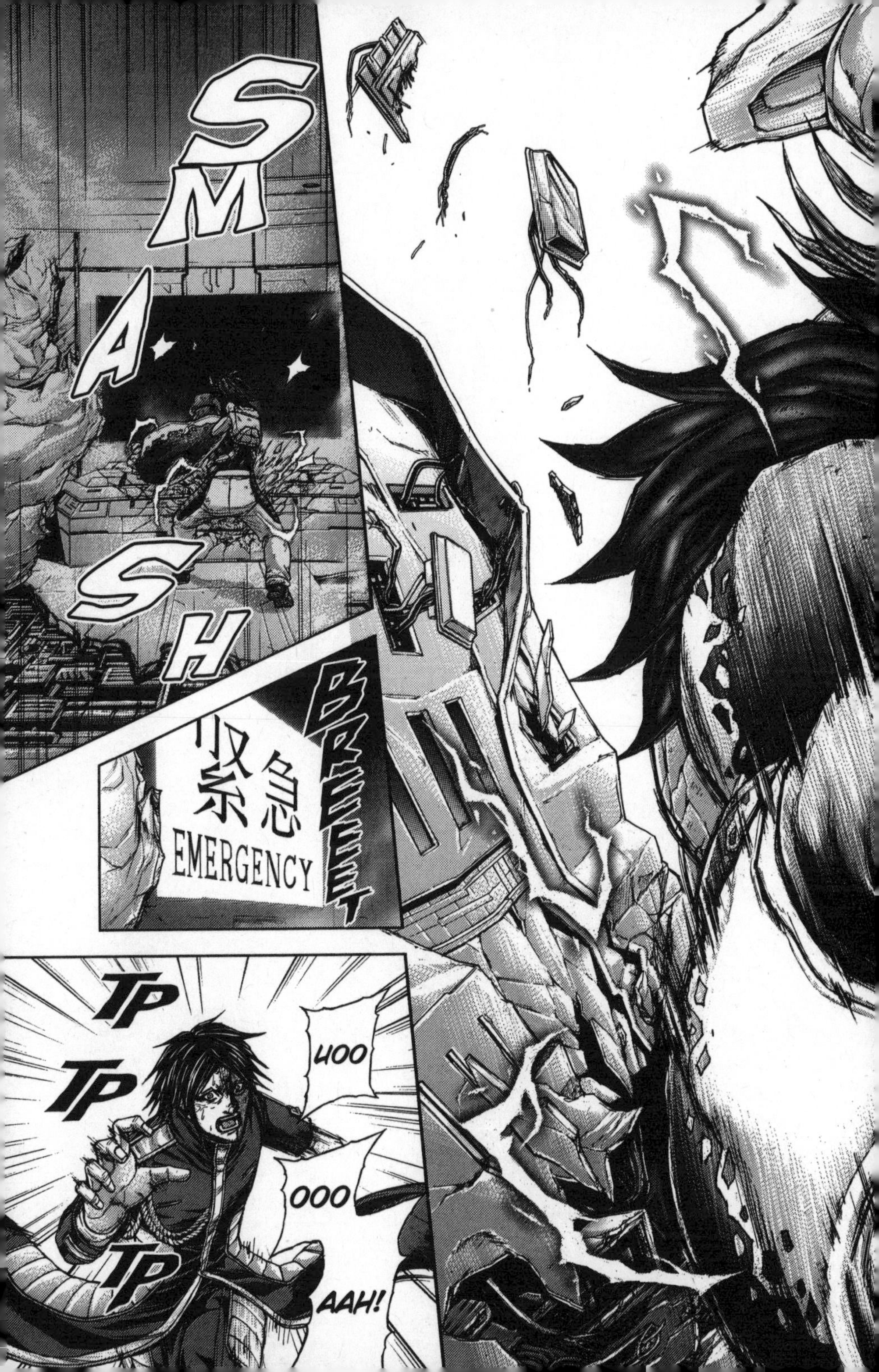
SMASH
BREEET
紧急
EMERGENCY
TP TP TP
UOO
OOO
AAH!

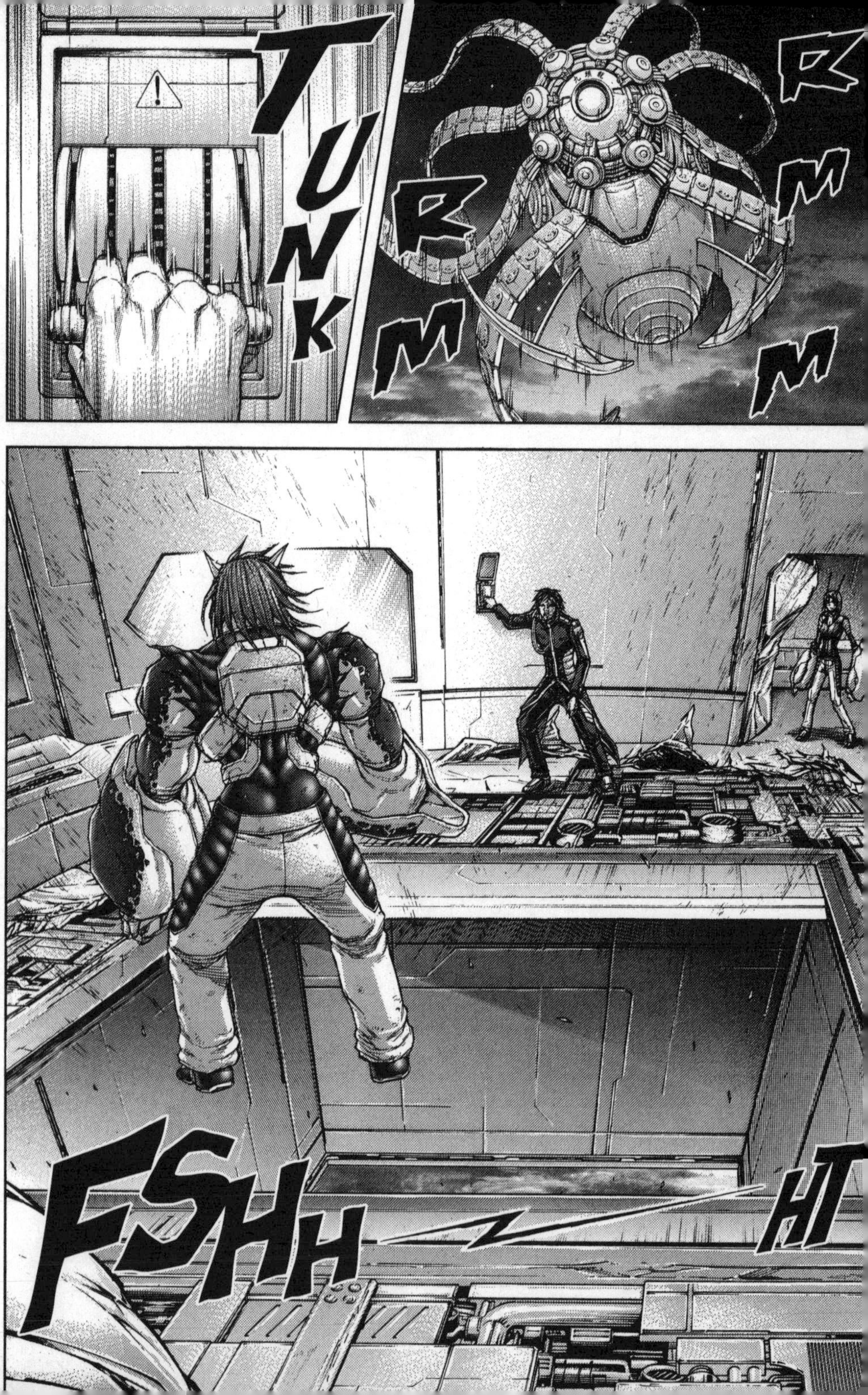
RMM
RM
TUNK
FSHH—HT

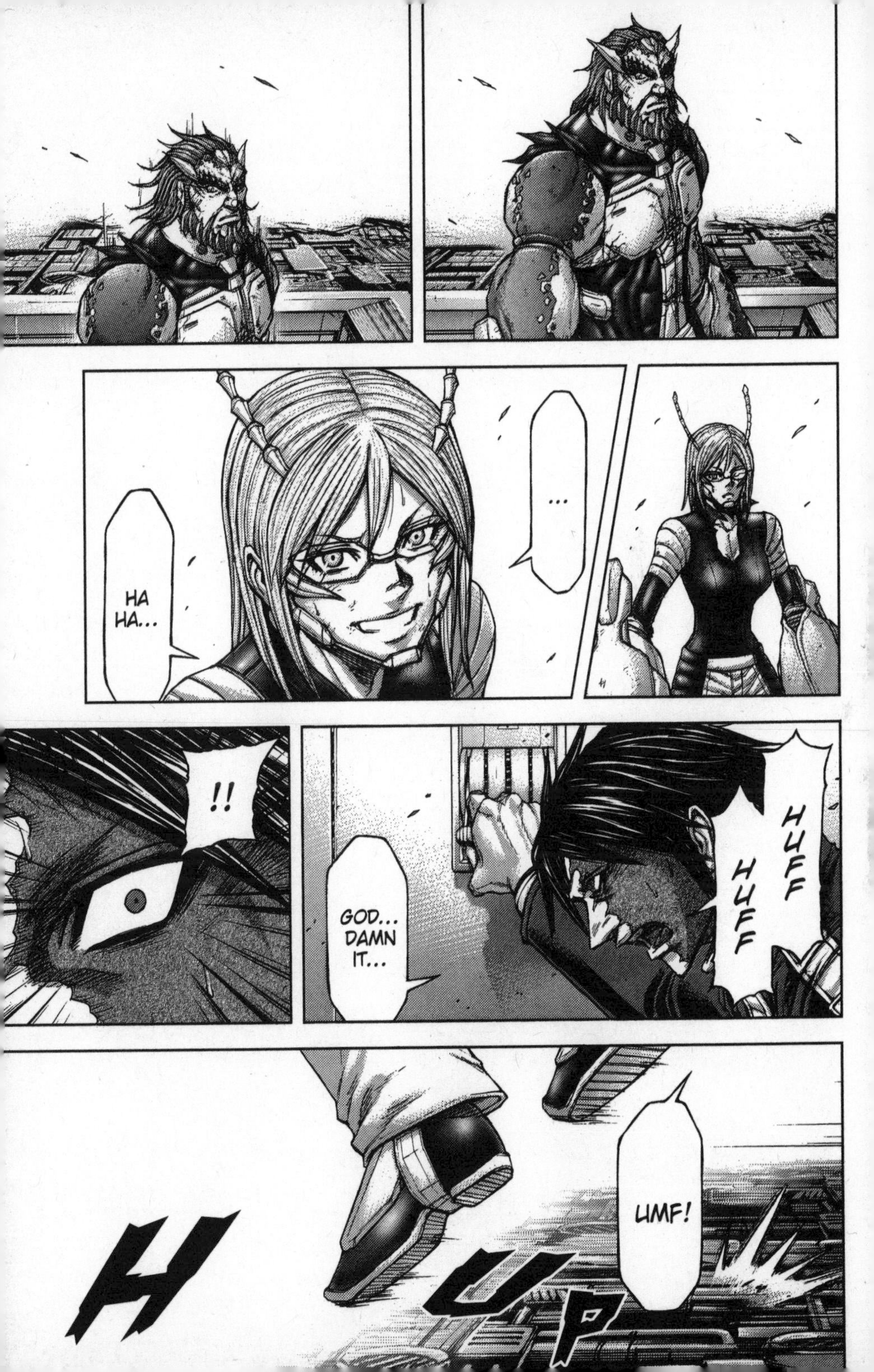
...
HA HA...
HUFF HUFF
GOD... DAMN IT...
!!
UMF!
HUP

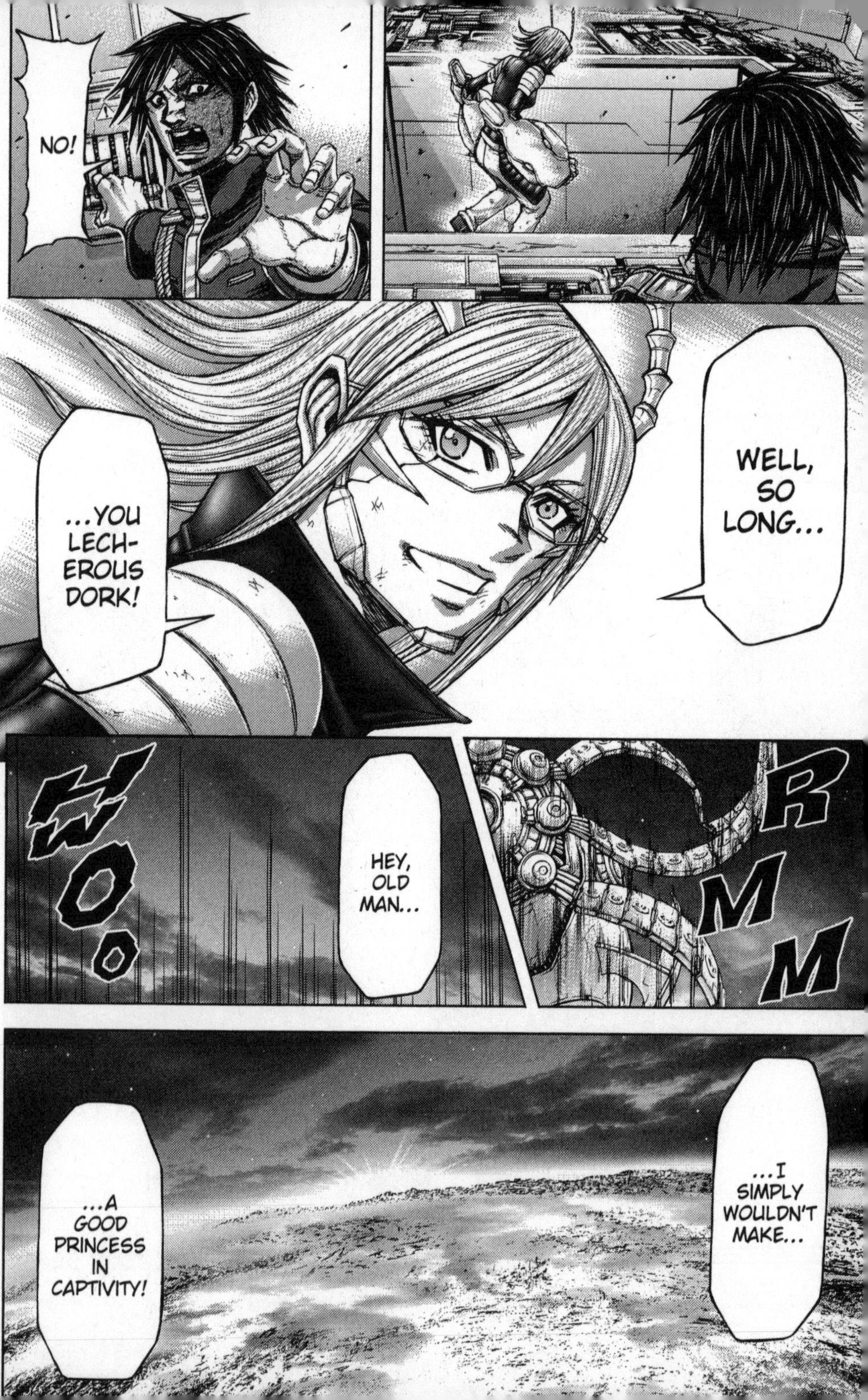
NO!
WELL, SO LONG...
...YOU LECH-EROUS DORK!
RMMM
HEY, OLD MAN...
WOo
...I SIMPLY WOULDN'T MAKE...
...A GOOD PRINCESS IN CAPTIVITY!

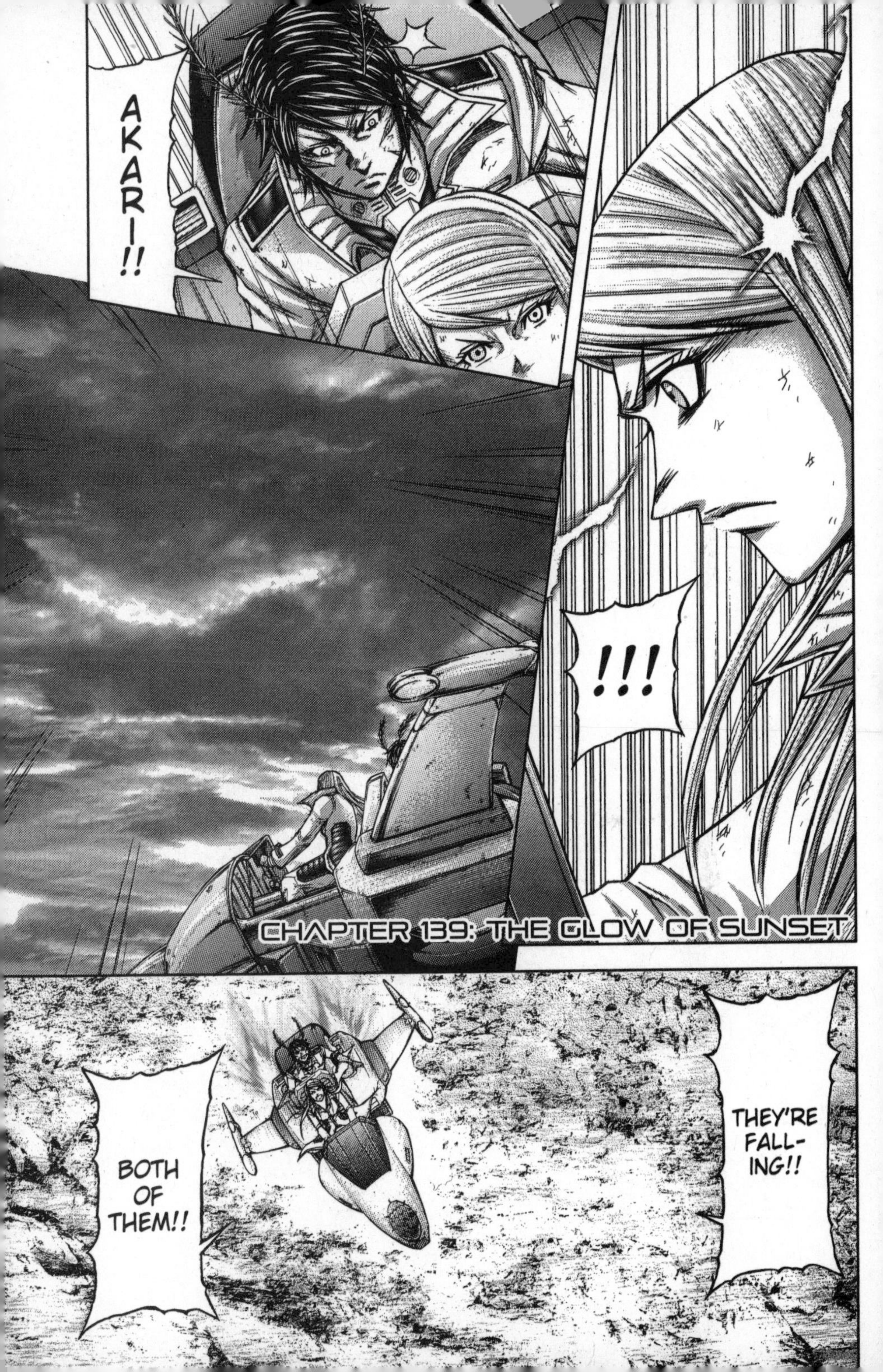
!!!
AKARI!!
CHAPTER 139: THE GLOW OF SUNSET
THEY'RE FALL-ING!!
BOTH OF THEM!!

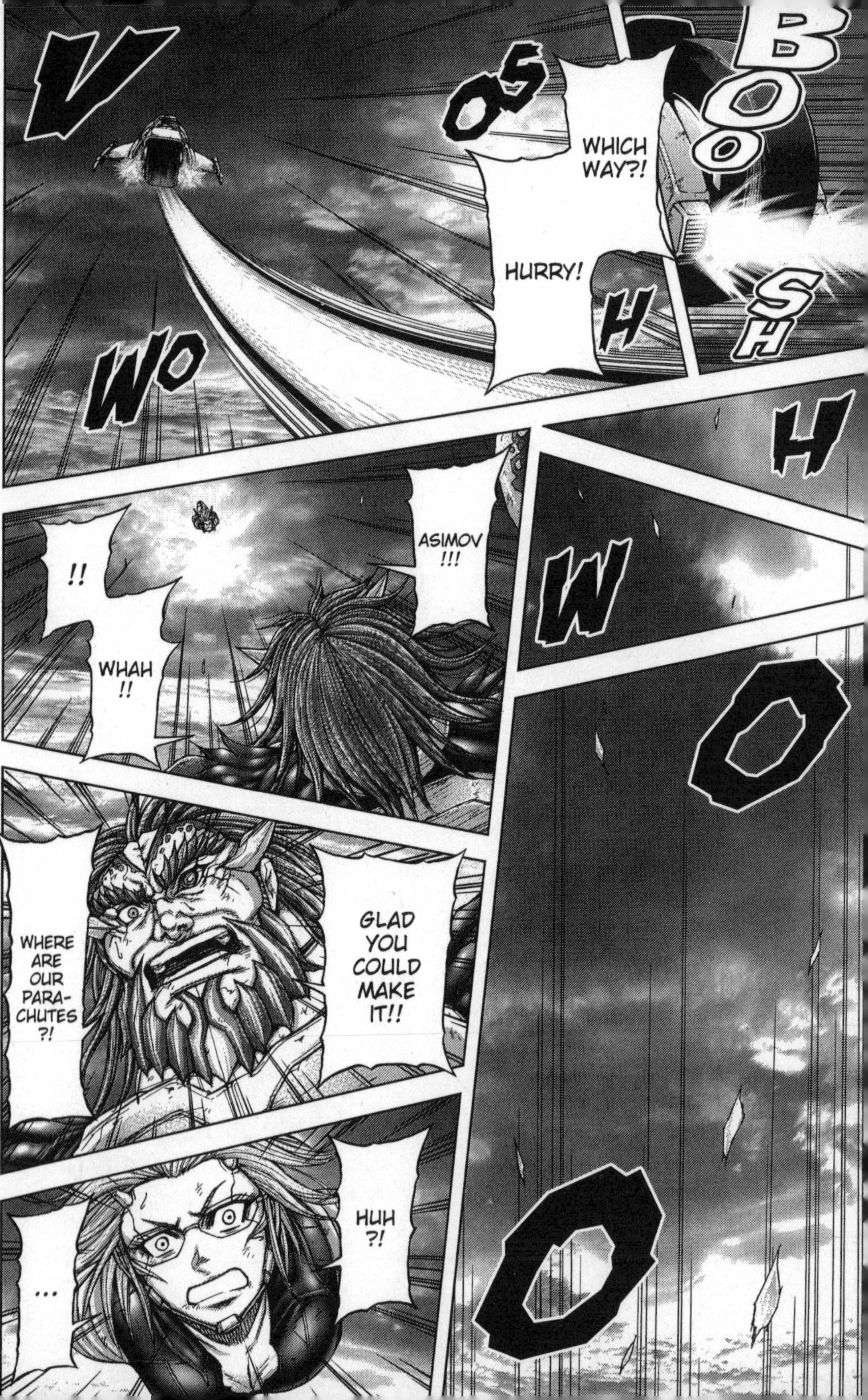

BOOOSH
WHICH WAY?!
HURRY!
V
WO
OS
H
H
W
O
O
ASIMOV!!!
!!
WHAH!!
GLAD YOU COULD MAKE IT!!
WHERE ARE OUR PARA-CHUTES?!
HUH?!
...

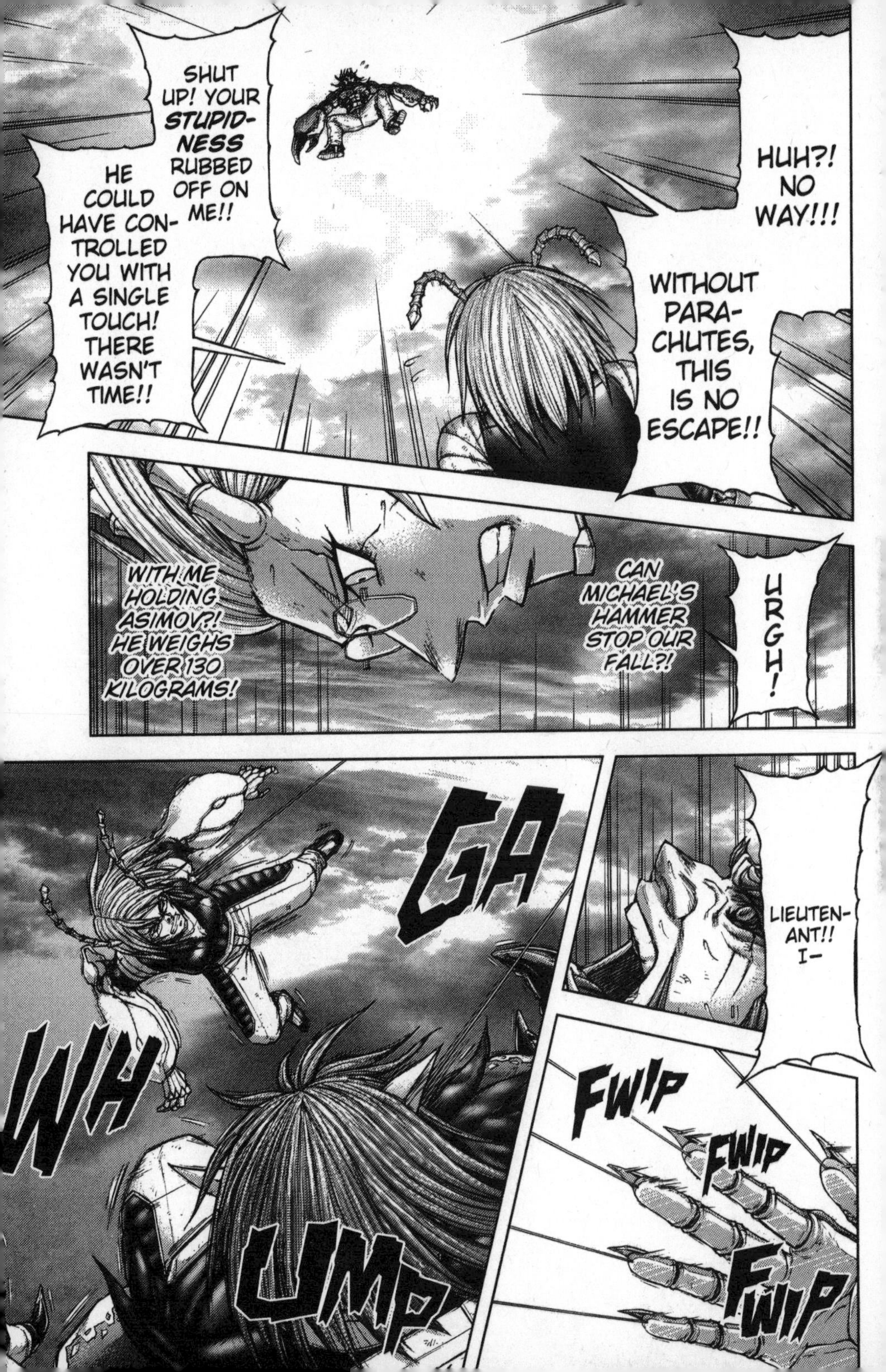
HUH?! NO WAY!!!
WITHOUT PARA-CHUTES, THIS IS NO ESCAPE!!
SHUT UP! YOUR STUPID-NESS RUBBED OFF ON ME!!
HE COULD HAVE CON-TROLLED YOU WITH A SINGLE TOUCH! THERE WASN'T TIME!!
URGH!
CAN MICHAEL'S HAMMER STOP OUR FALL?!
WITH ME HOLDING ASIMOV?! HE WEIGHS OVER 130 KILOGRAMS!
LIEUTEN-ANT!! I—
FWIP
FWIP
FWIP
GA
WH
UMP

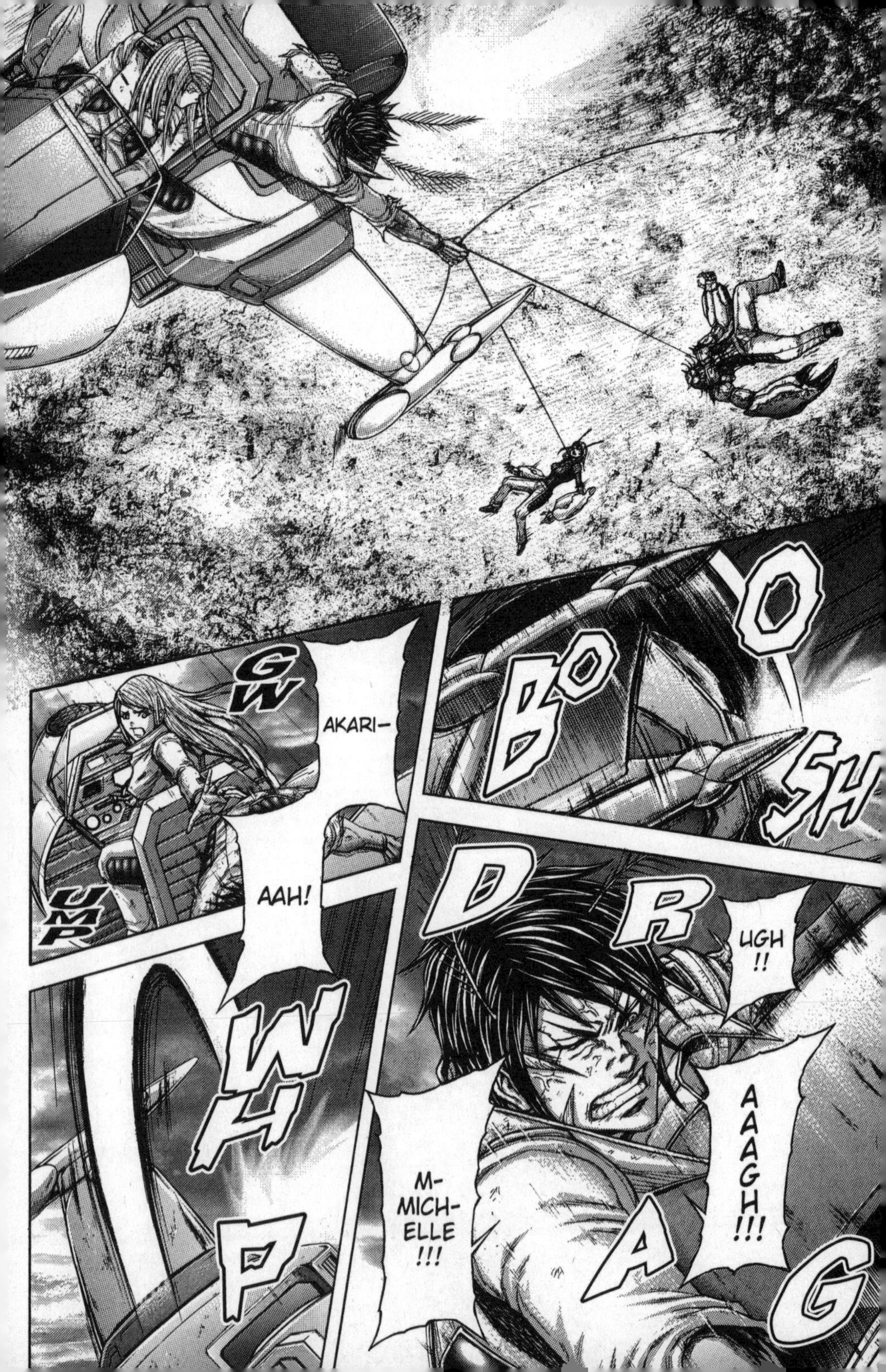
BOOSH
GWUMP
AKARI-
AAH!
DRAG
UGH!!
AAAGH!!!
M-MICHELLE!!!
WHP

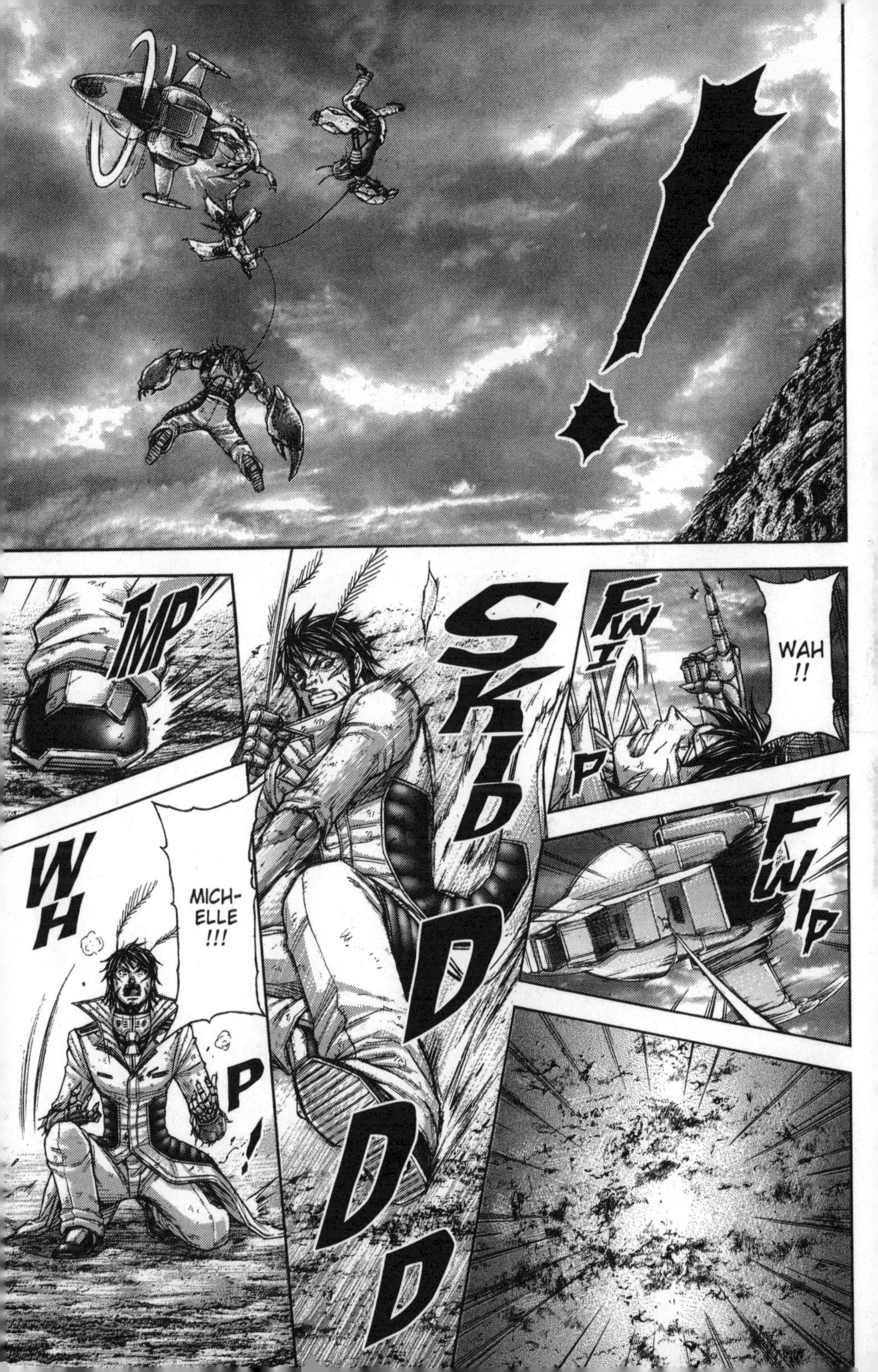
!
WAH!!
FWIP
FWIP
SKIDDDD
TMP
MICHELLE!!!
WHP!

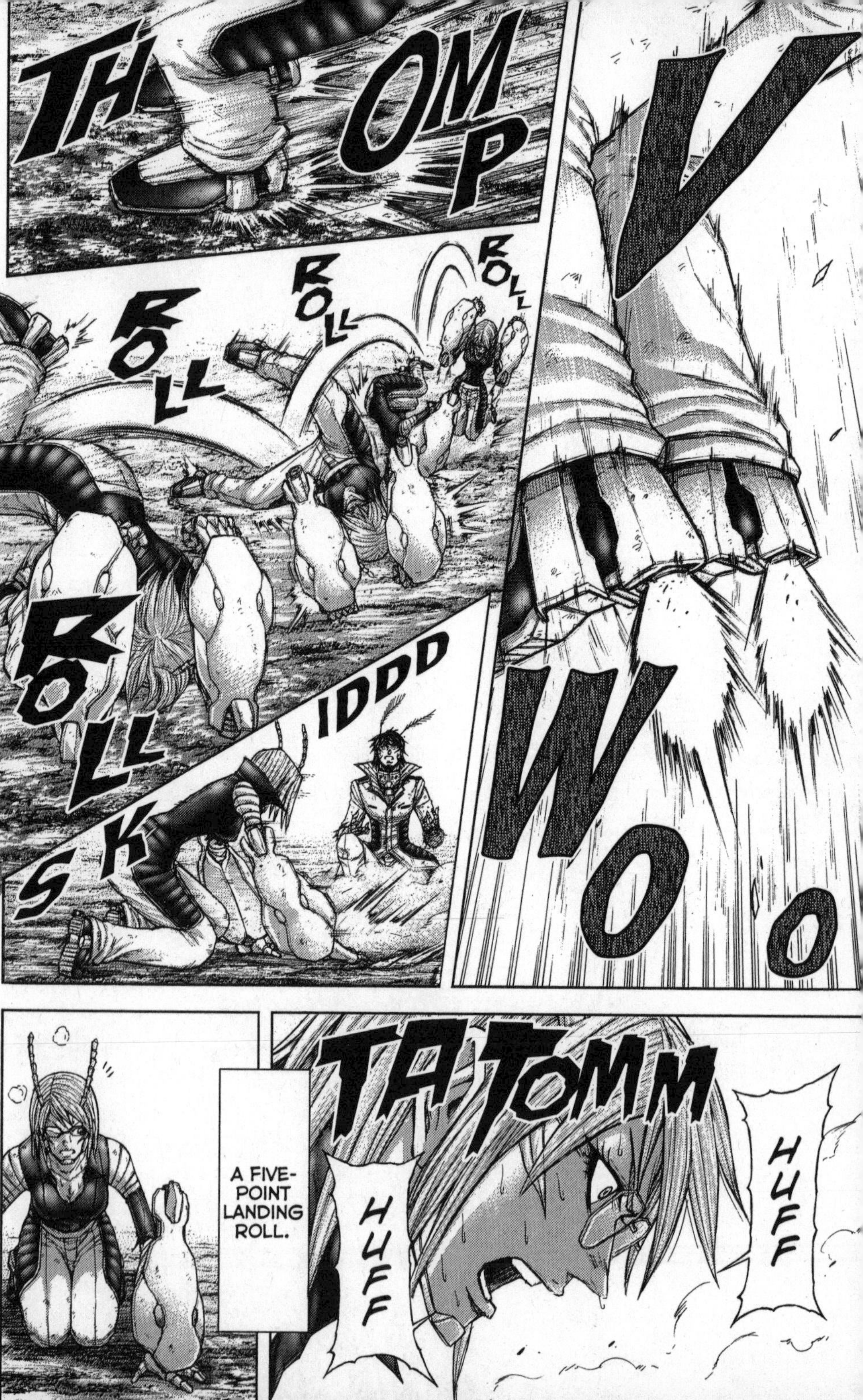
VWOOO
THOMP
ROLL
ROLL
ROLL
ROLL
SKIDDD
TATOMM
HUFF
HUFF
A FIVE-POINT LANDING ROLL.

... W ...

WHERE'S ASIMOV?!

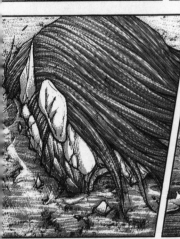

!!!

ASIMOV ...

... SAVED ME!!

BUT ...

NOOO!!

!

H-HE ...

... HE SAVED ME...

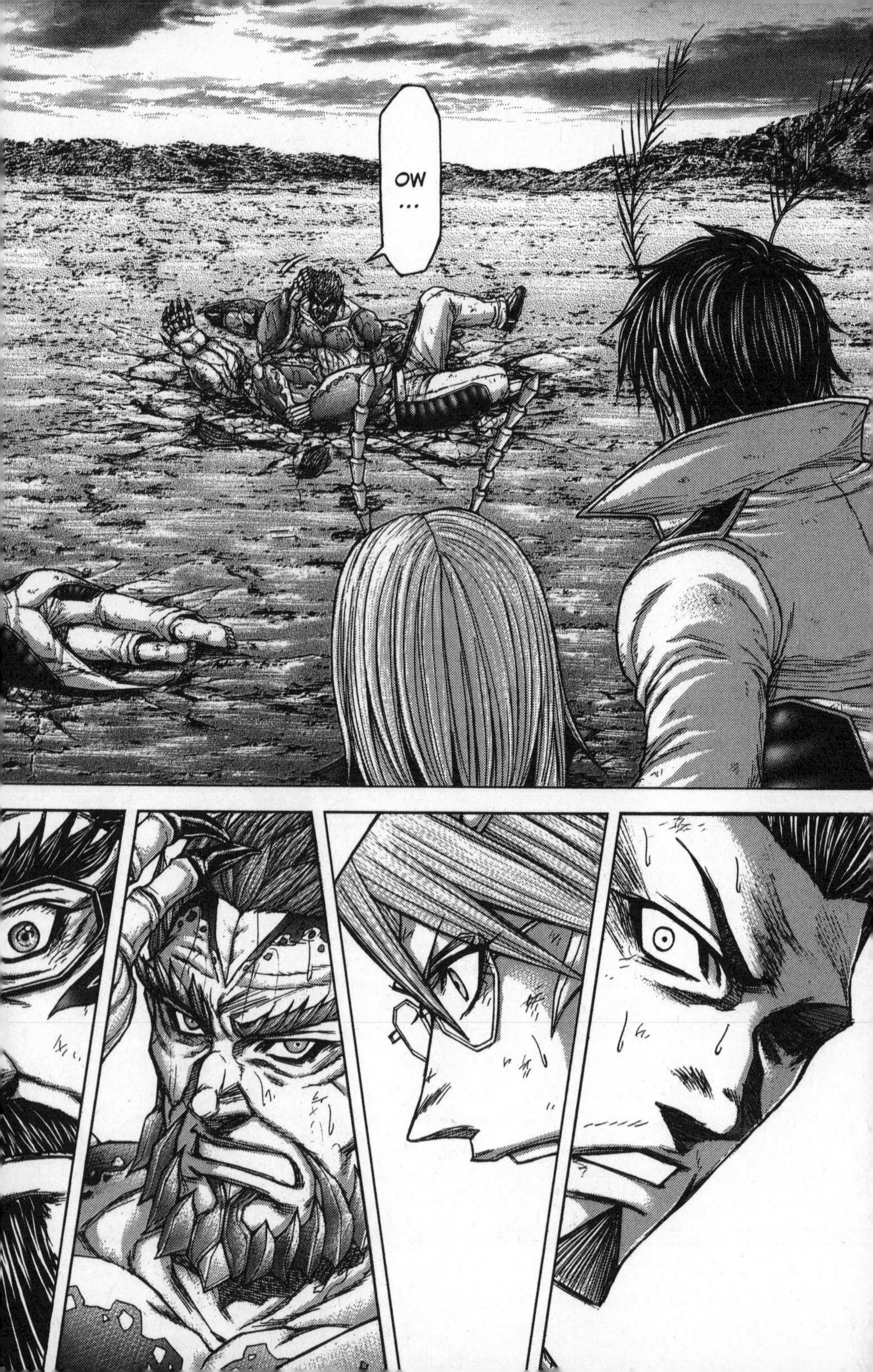
OW
...

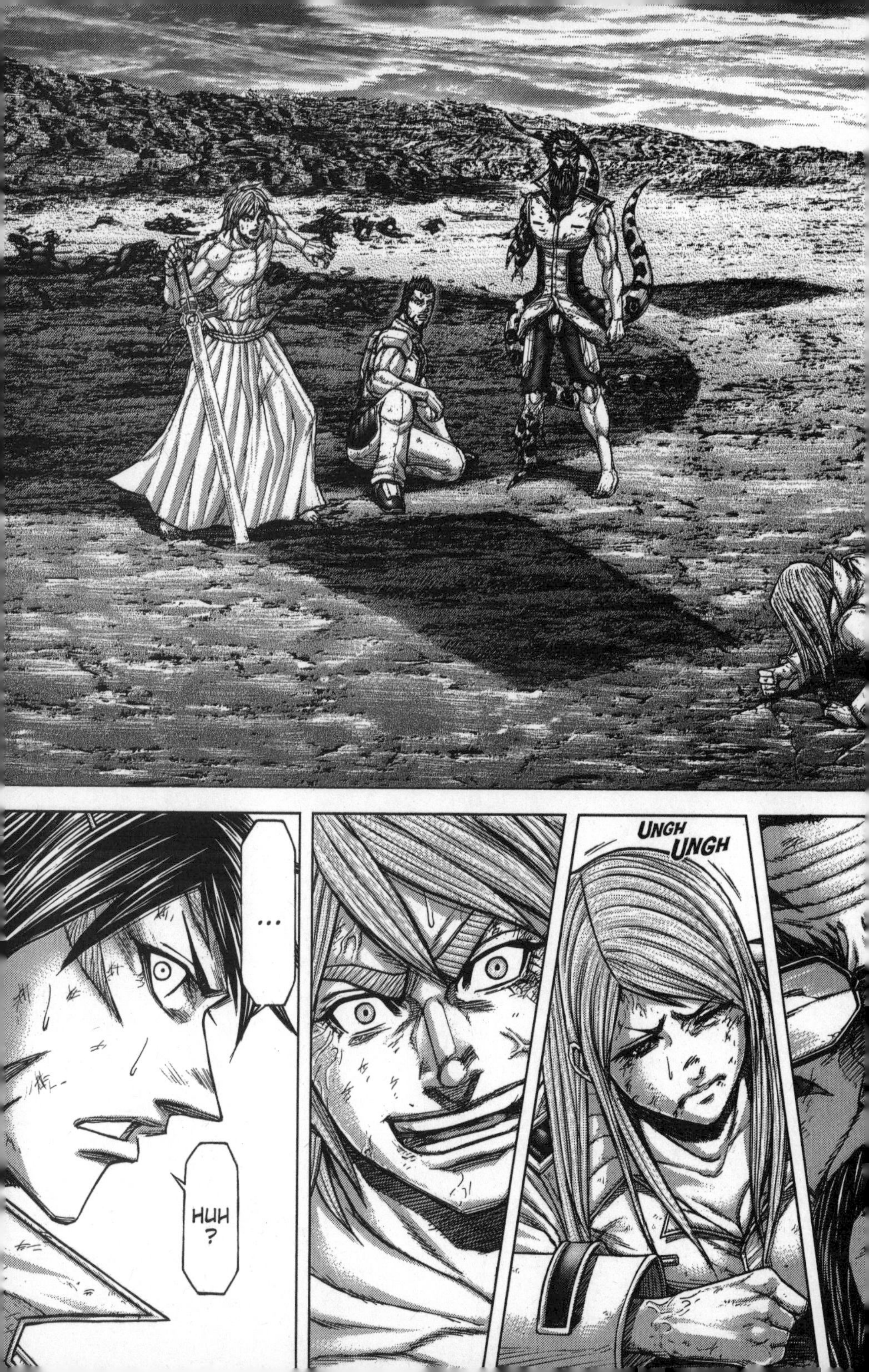
UNGH UNGH
...
HUH?

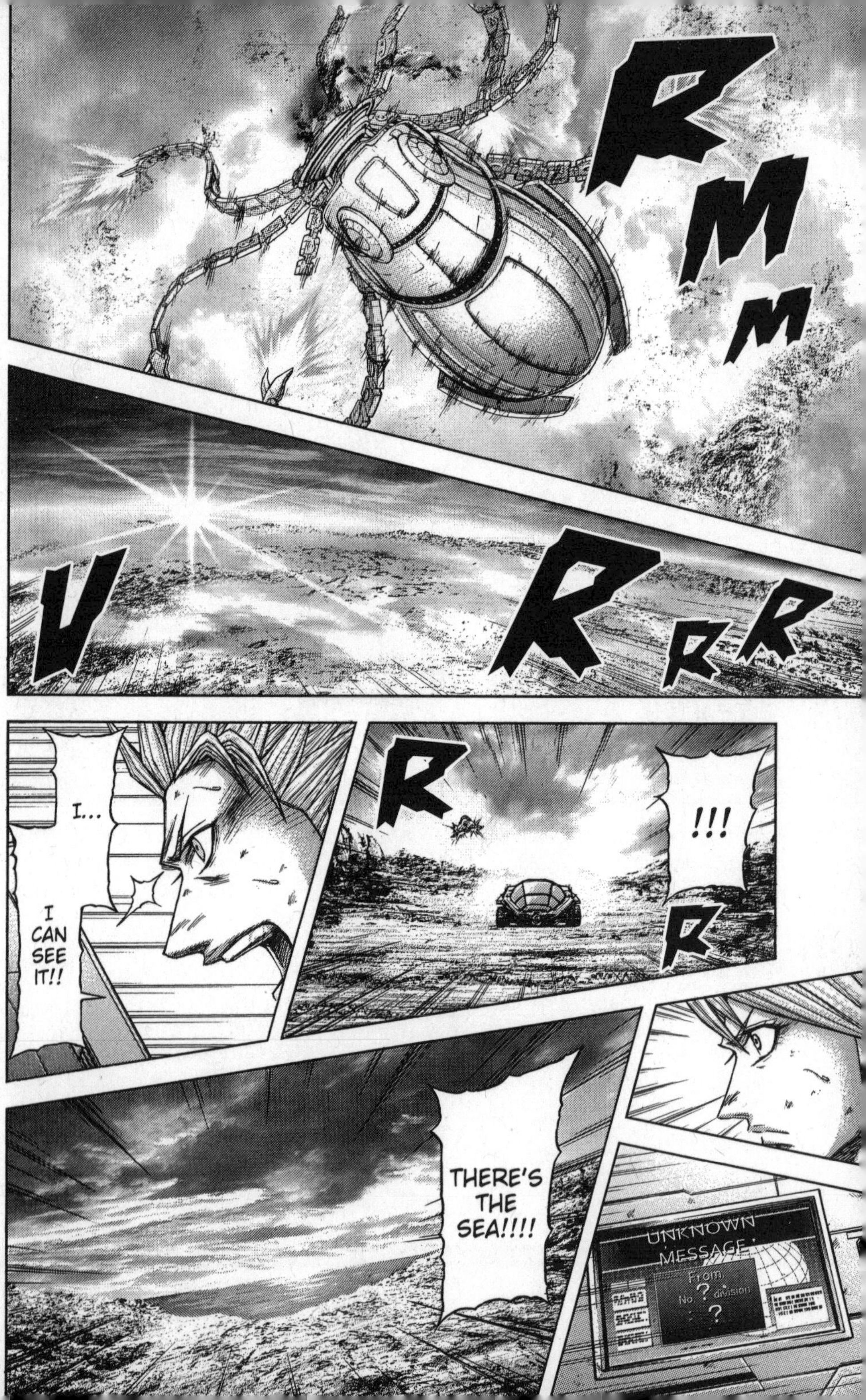

RMM
VRRRR
R
!!!
R
I...
I CAN SEE IT!!
UNKNOWN MESSAGE
From
No ? division
?
THERE'S THE SEA!!!!

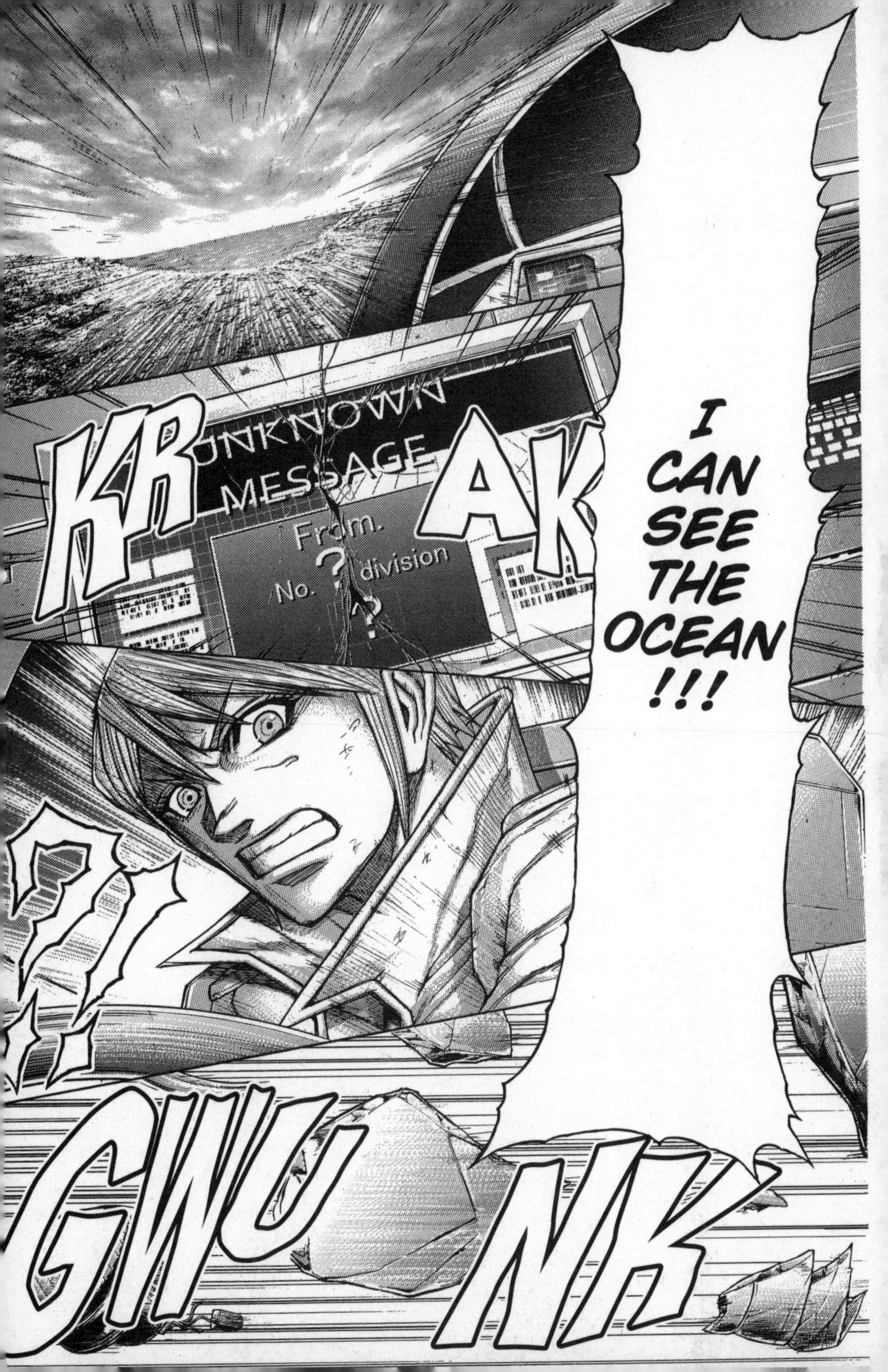

I CAN SEE THE OCEAN!!!
UNKNOWN MESSAGE
From.
No. ? division
?
KRAK
GWUNK

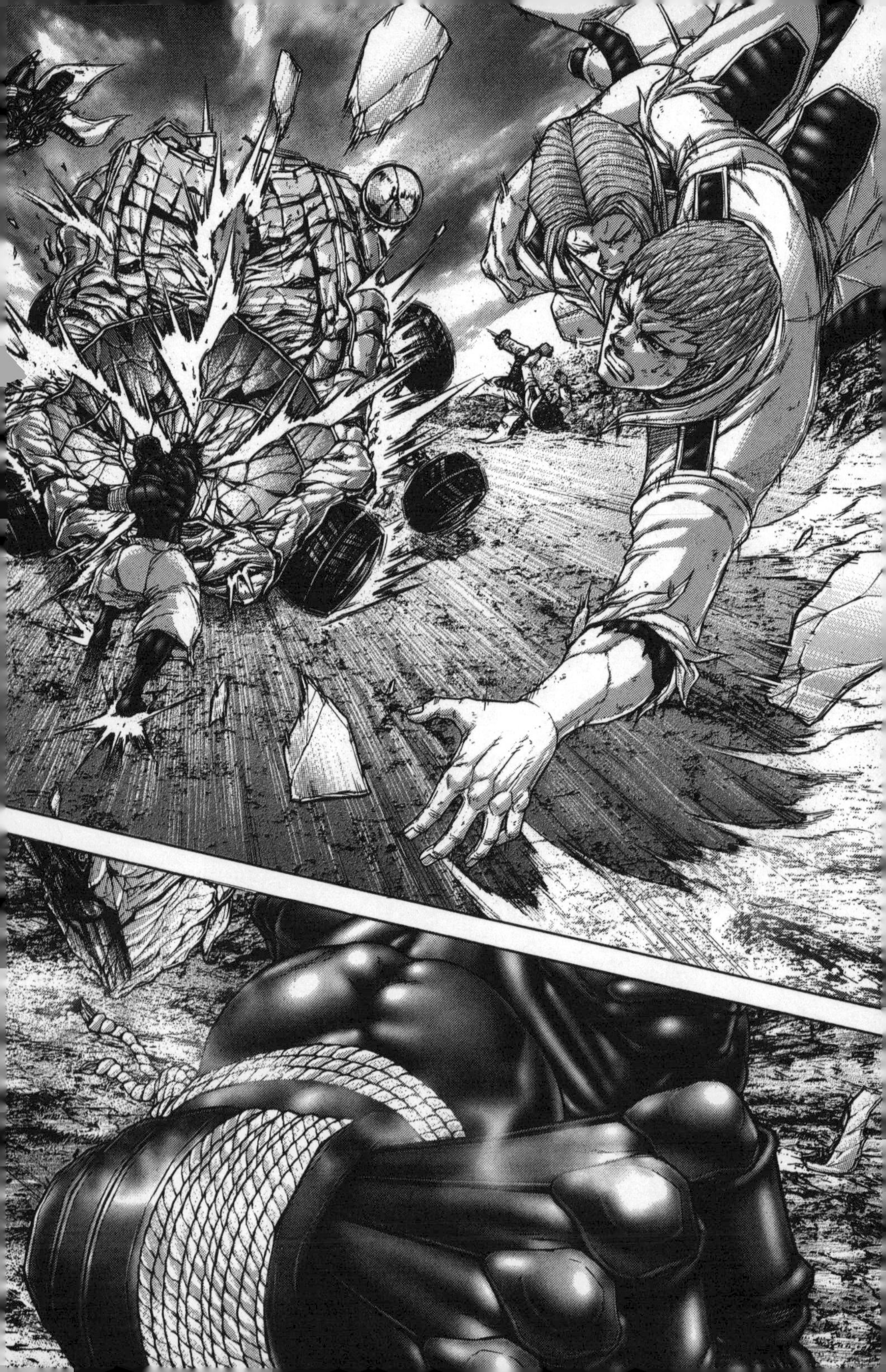

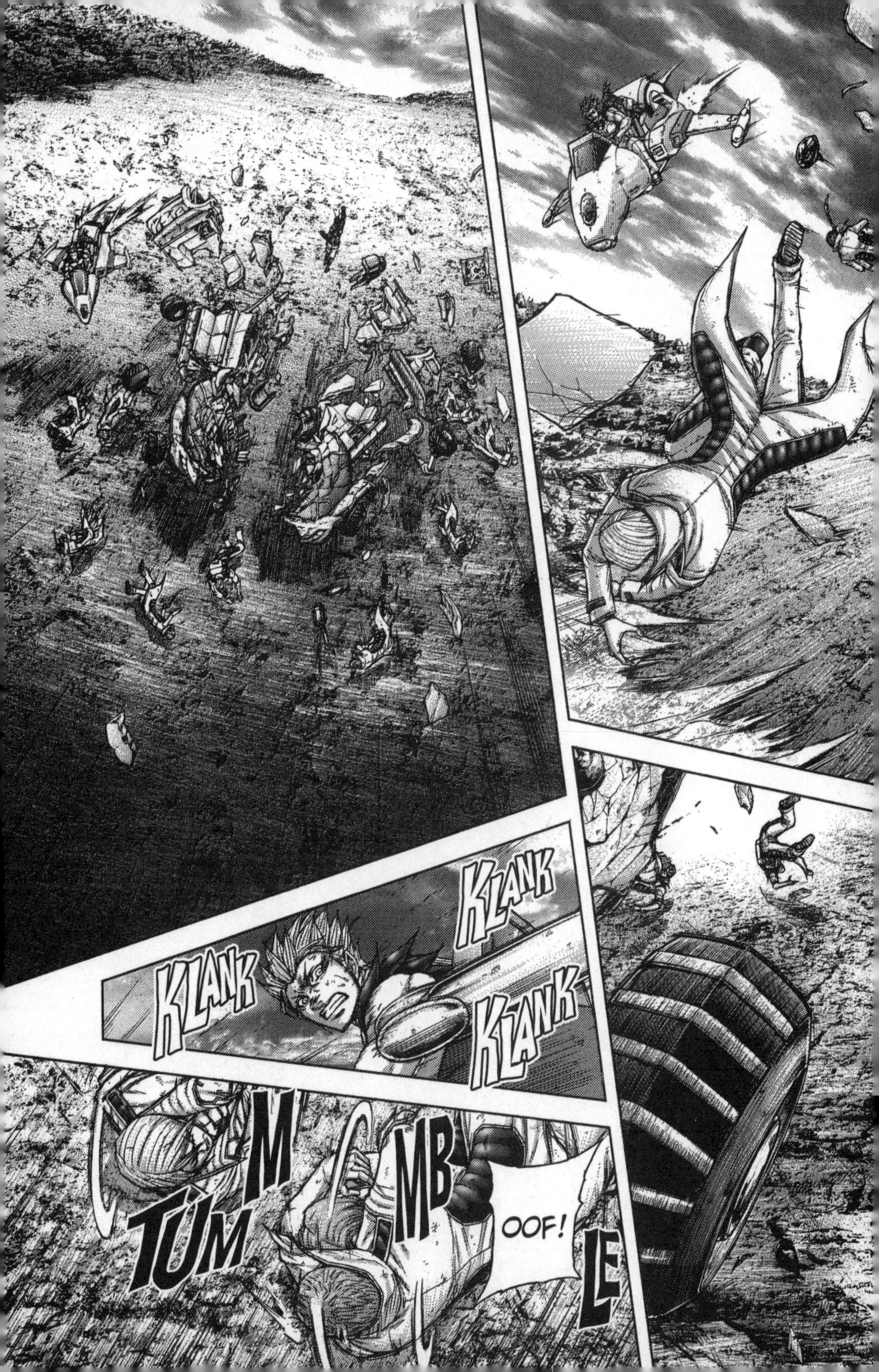
KLANK
KLANK
KLANK
TUMMMBLE
OOF!

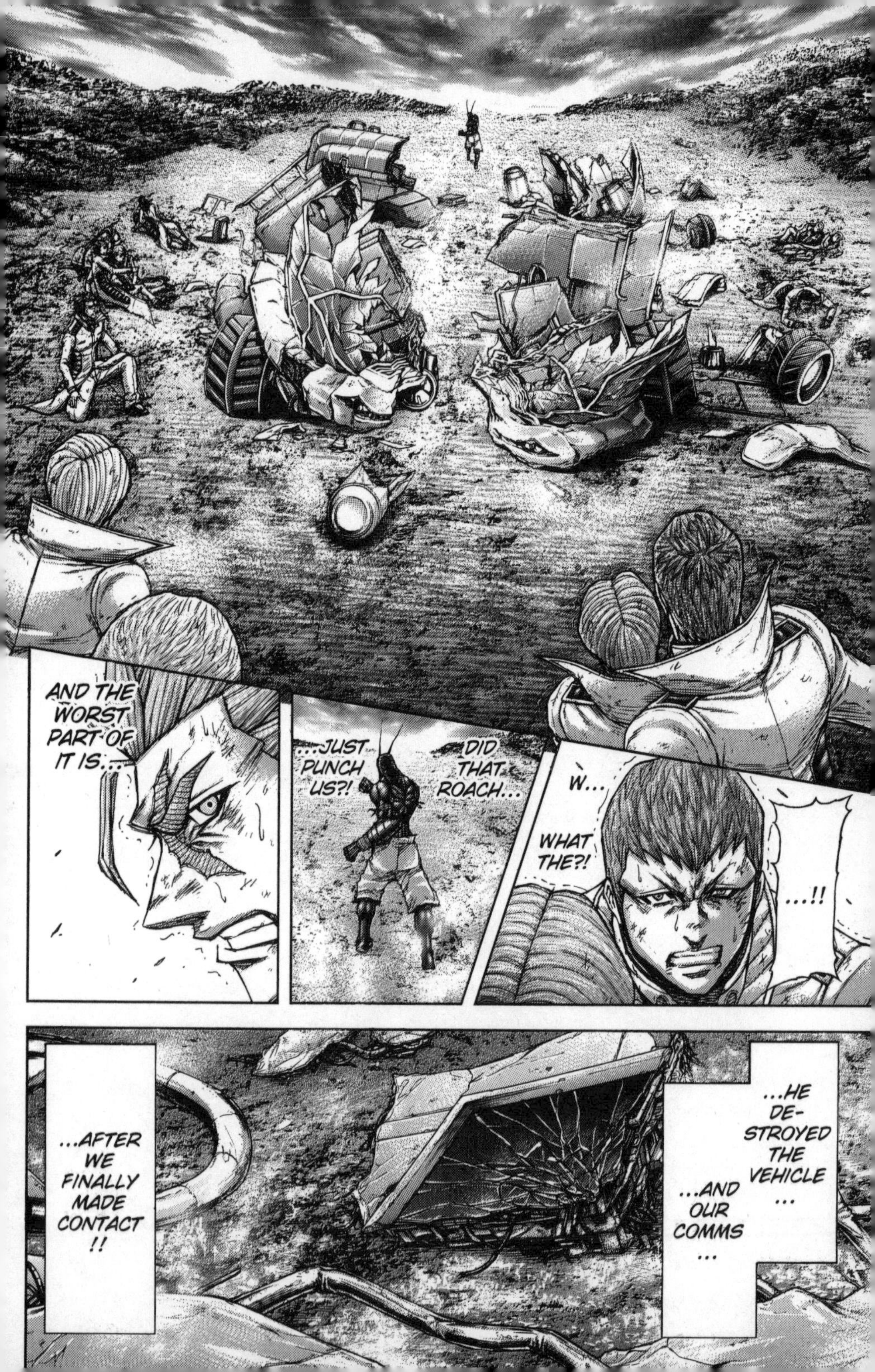

...!!
W... WHAT THE?!
DID THAT ROACH...
...JUST PUNCH US?!
AND THE WORST PART OF IT IS...
...HE DESTROYED THE VEHICLE...
...AND OUR COMMS...
...AFTER WE FINALLY MADE CONTACT!!

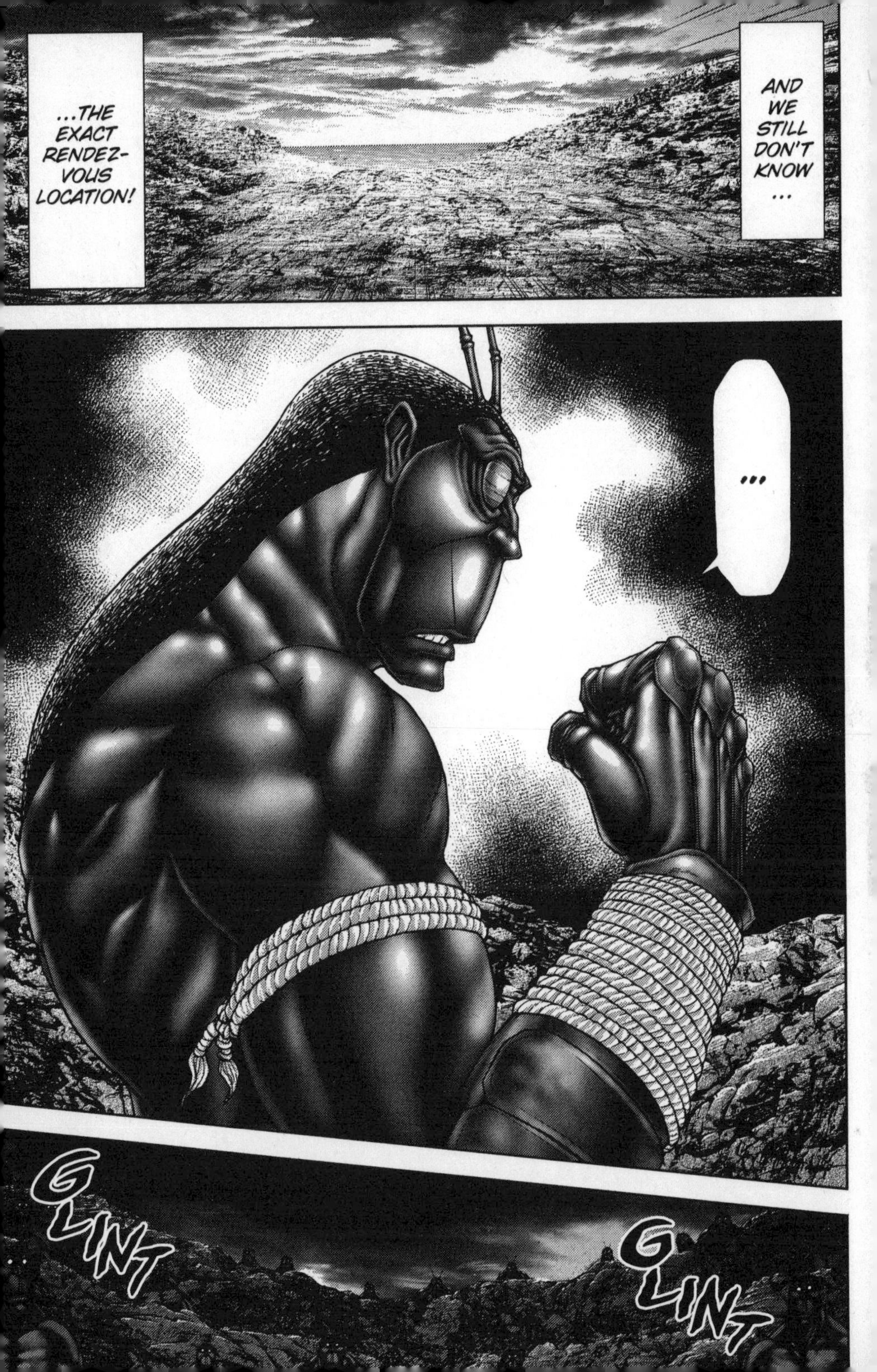
AND WE STILL DON'T KNOW ...
...THE EXACT RENDEZ-VOUS LOCATION!
...
GLINT
GLINT

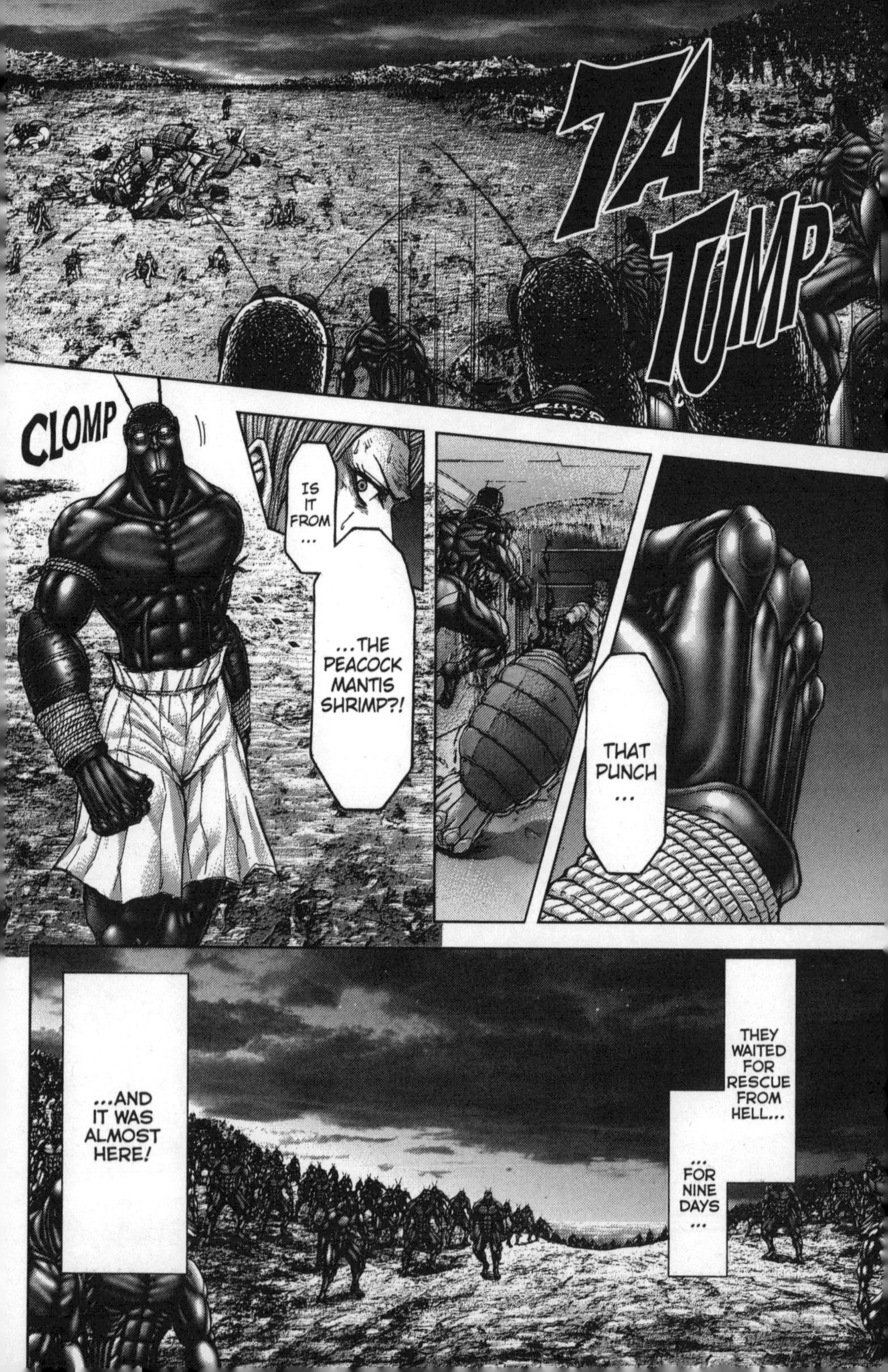
TA TUMP
THAT PUNCH ...
IS IT FROM ...
...THE PEACOCK MANTIS SHRIMP?!
CLOMP
THEY WAITED FOR RESCUE FROM HELL...
...FOR NINE DAYS...
...AND IT WAS ALMOST HERE!

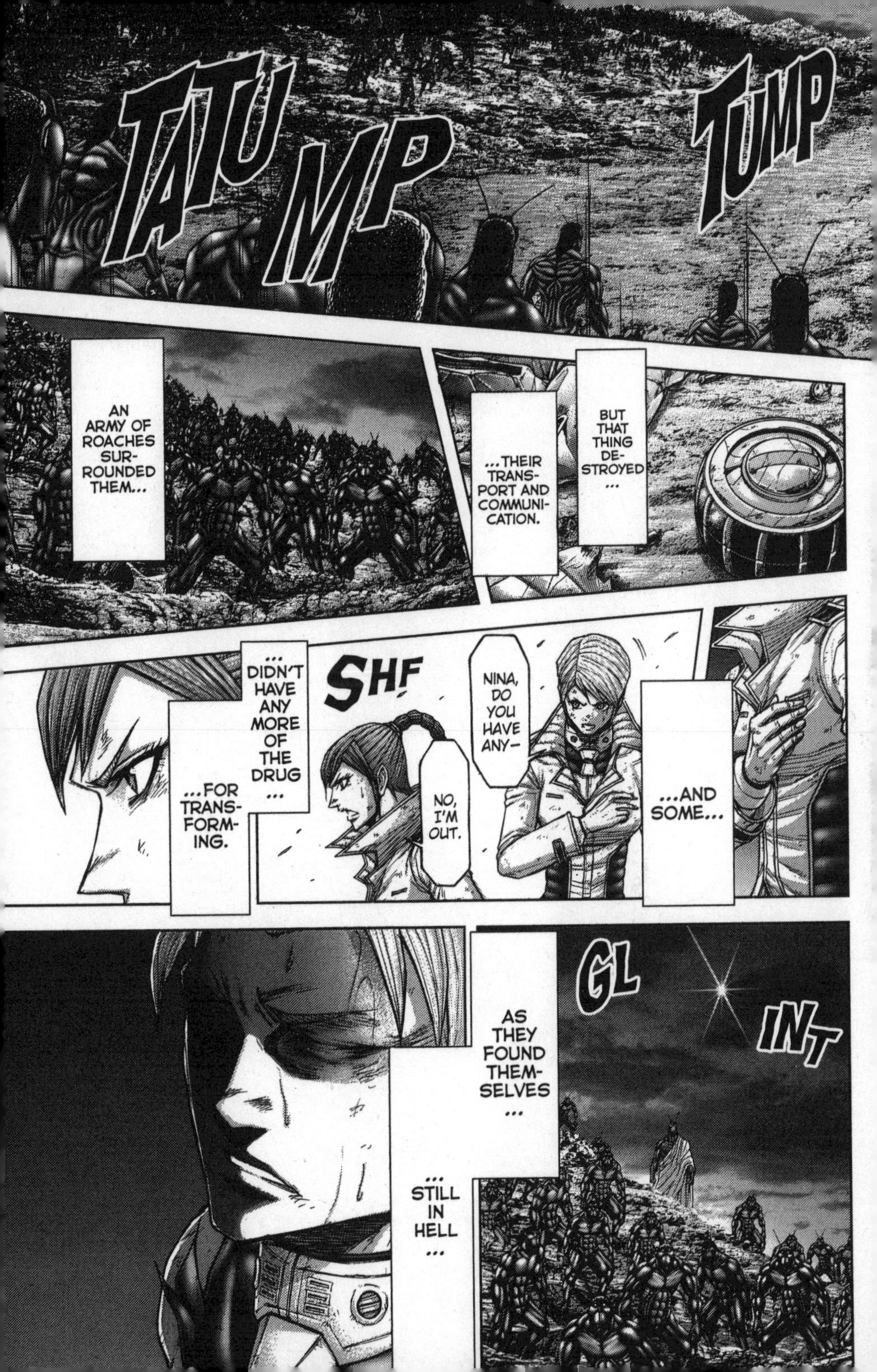
TUMP
TATUMP
BUT THAT THING DESTROYED...
...THEIR TRANSPORT AND COMMUNICATION.
AN ARMY OF ROACHES SURROUNDED THEM...
...AND SOME...
NINA, DO YOU HAVE ANY–
SHF
NO, I'M OUT.
...DIDN'T HAVE ANY MORE OF THE DRUG...
...FOR TRANSFORMING.
GLINT
AS THEY FOUND THEMSELVES...
...STILL IN HELL...

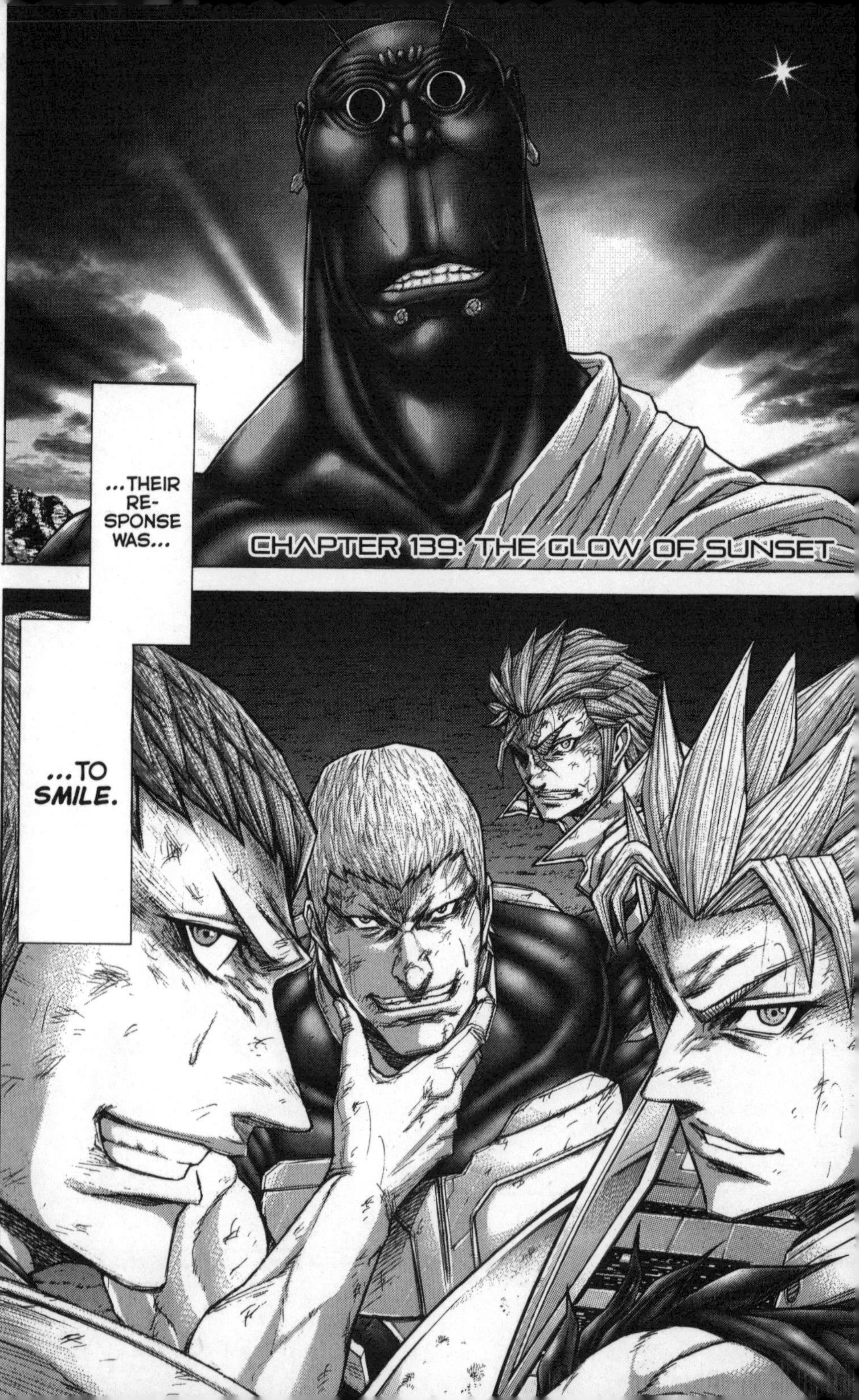
CHAPTER 139: THE GLOW OF SUNSET
...THEIR RE-SPONSE WAS...
...TO SMILE.

TERRA FORMARS

Character

Kai Yanchao ♂

China 38 yrs. 178 cm 81 kg

Operation Base: Ophiocordyceps japonensis

Favorite Food: Boiled egg
Dislikes: Restrooms with hand soap that doesn't match
    the brand on the soap container
Eye Color: Mud
Blood Type: B DOB: July 1 (Cancer)
Hobbies: Moving his stomach all squishy-like

Born the son of a high-ranking official, he grew up in a family with a strong sense of elitism. He is fairly young to be an officer in the military. Other children bullied him, but he was good at his studies and his parents were in positions of authority, so he quickly found success and had all his tormentors demoted. He also did things like have local authorities stop orders to their families' construction companies.

Many feared him, but he got along well with General Bao for some reason and they hung out at ping-pong bars together. They both favor a swift frontal-attack style of play.

Bao Yuilan ♂

China 50 yrs. 183 cm 102 kg

Operation Base: Sea Squirt

Likes: Himself
Favorite Foods: Grilled meat, fermented milk drinks
Dislikes: Restaurants with sticky chili oil bottles
Eye Color: Black Blood Type: AB
DOB: June 6 (Gemini)

He comes from a middle-class home, but he enjoys working hard to improve himself. His aptitude for study and martial arts helped him become successful. He tells everyone they're father and son, but Bao Zhilan on the *Annex* is a sprout that Bao Yuilan created using his ability.

He's married without children. Even if he did have a child, he says he wouldn't be interested in it because it wouldn't be him.

He doesn't get drunk easily and he's a good listener, so when General Kai gets liquored up and rowdy, he drives him home. In ping-pong, he loves a good backspin.

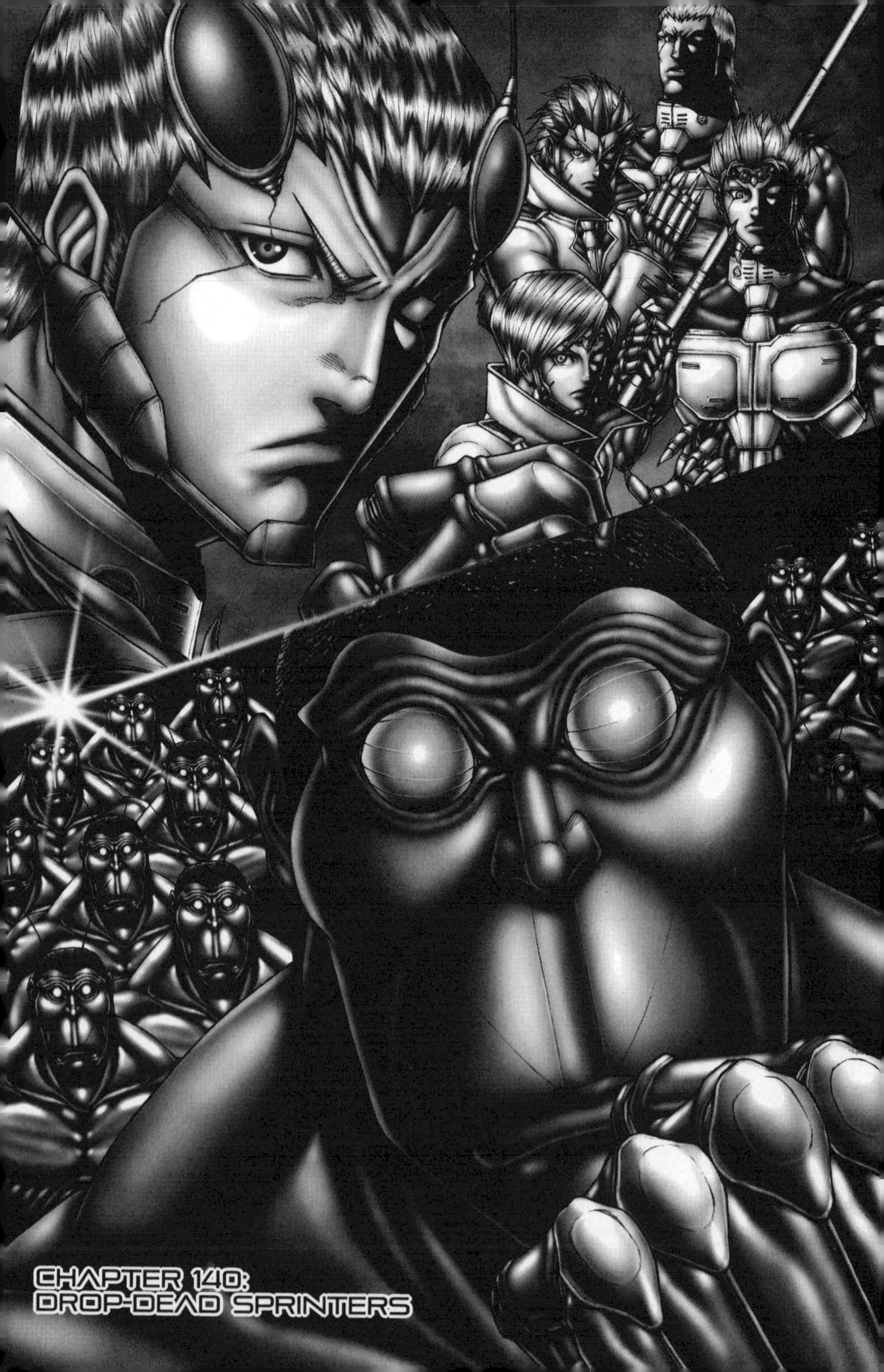
CHAPTER 140:
DROP-DEAD SPRINTERS

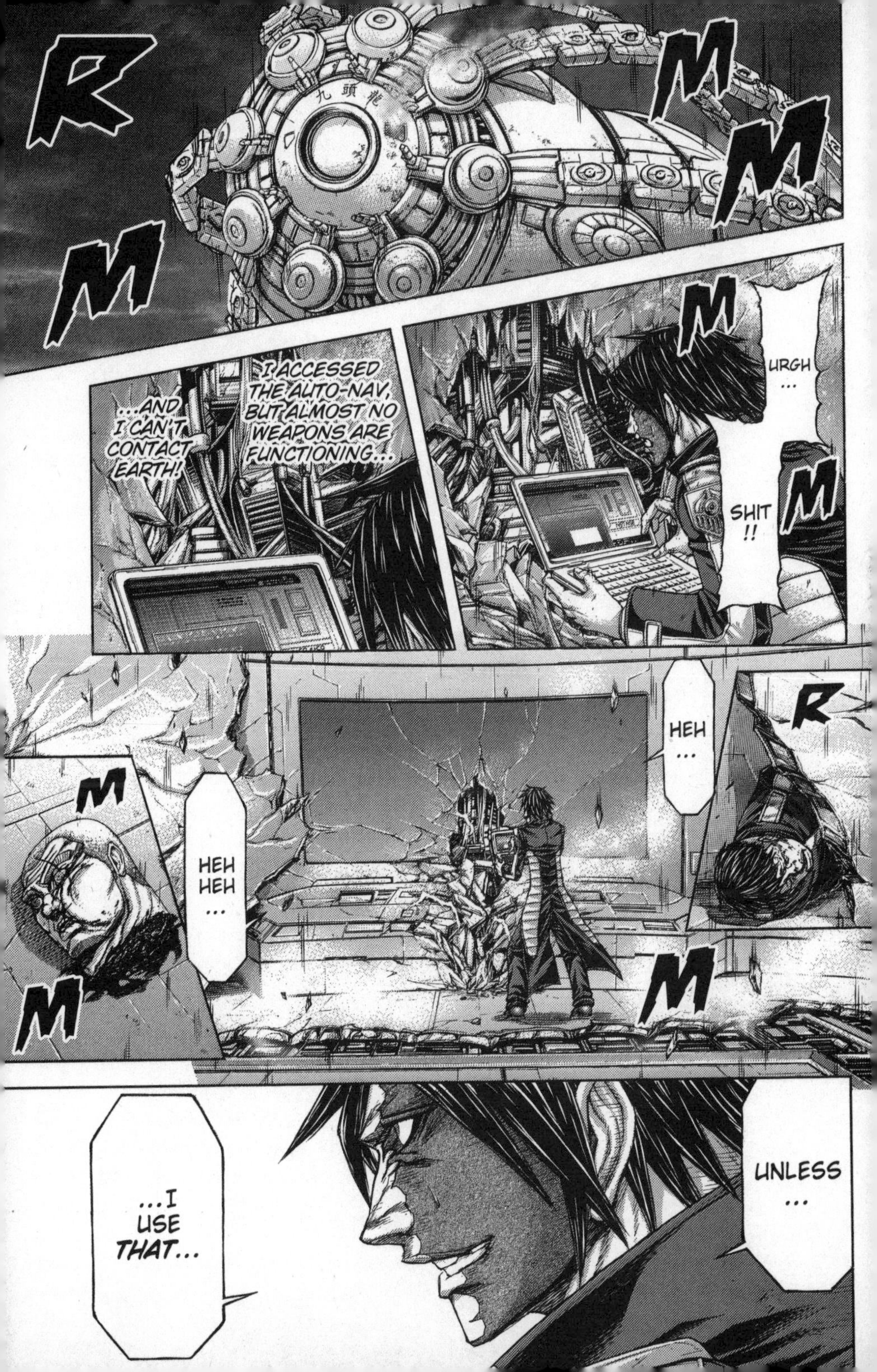
R
M
M
M
M
URGH ...
M
SHIT !!
I ACCESSED THE AUTO-NAV, BUT ALMOST NO WEAPONS ARE FUNCTIONING...
...AND I CAN'T CONTACT EARTH!
R
HEH ...
M
HEH HEH ...
M
M
UNLESS ...
...I USE *THAT*...

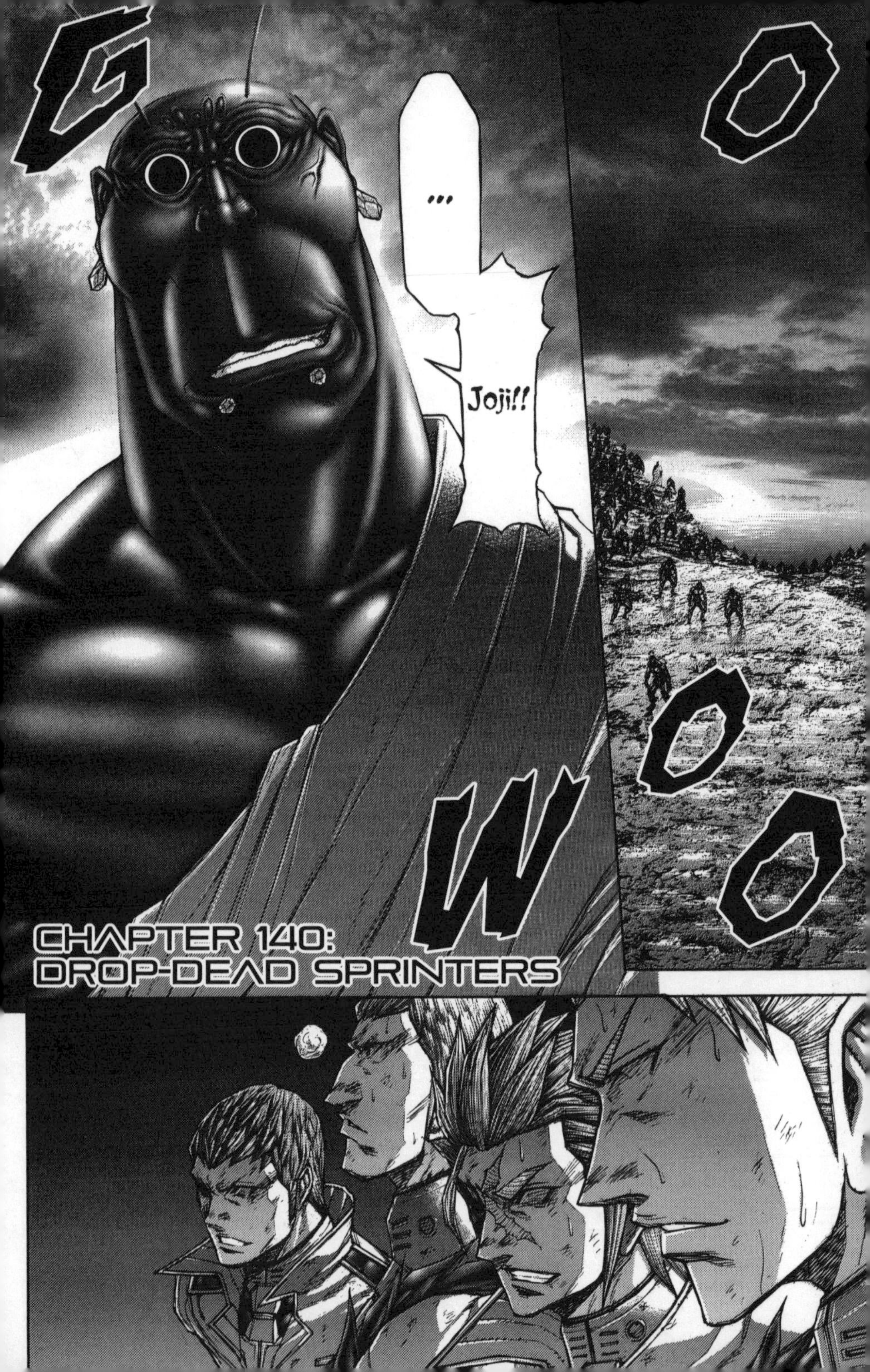
GOWOO
...
Joji!!
CHAPTER 140:
DROP-DEAD SPRINTERS

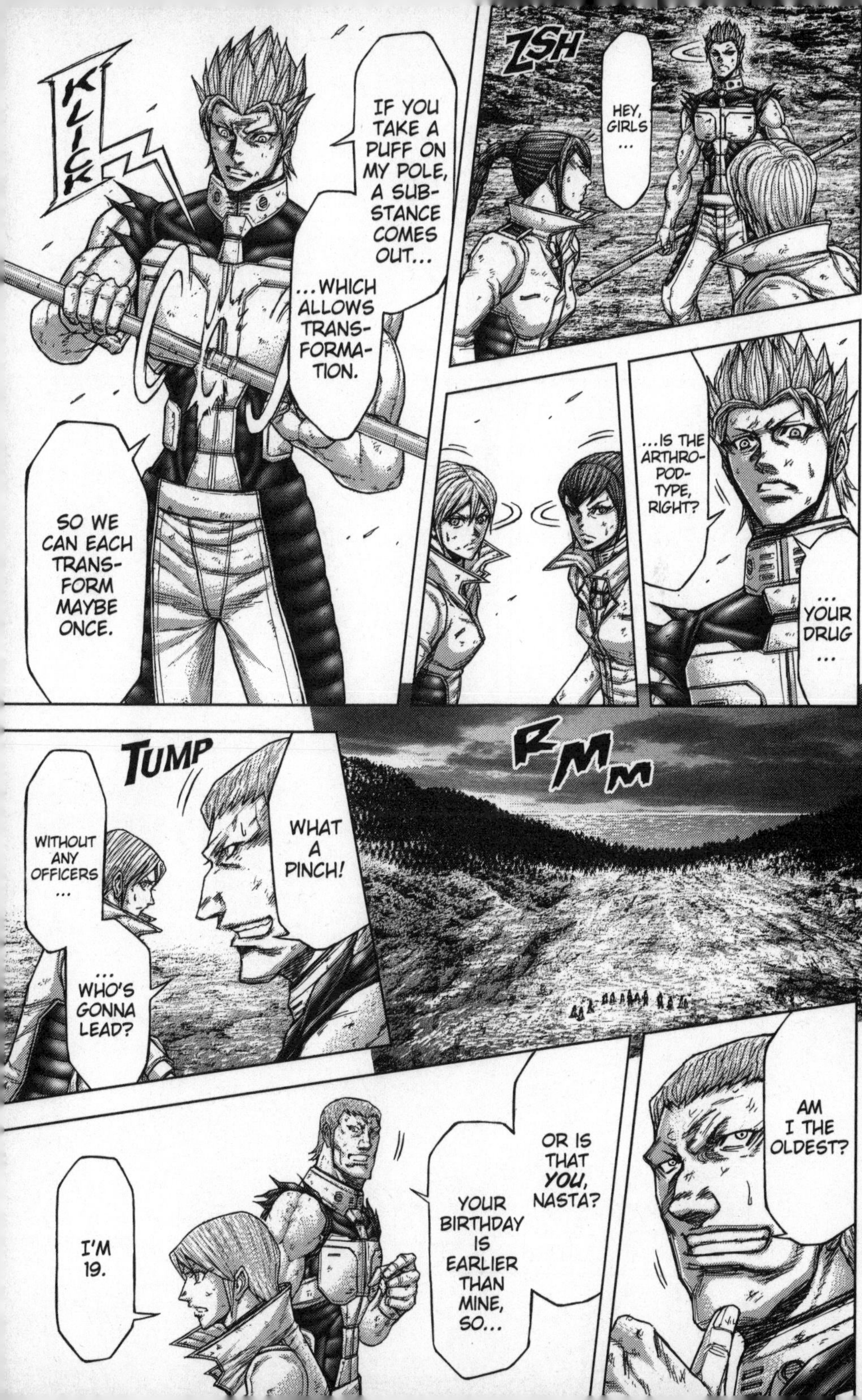
ZSH
HEY, GIRLS...
...YOUR DRUG...
...IS THE ARTHROPOD-TYPE, RIGHT?
KLICK
IF YOU TAKE A PUFF ON MY POLE, A SUBSTANCE COMES OUT...
...WHICH ALLOWS TRANSFORMATION.
SO WE CAN EACH TRANSFORM MAYBE ONCE.
RMM
TUMP
WHAT A PINCH!
WITHOUT ANY OFFICERS...
...WHO'S GONNA LEAD?
AM I THE OLDEST?
OR IS THAT *YOU*, NASTA?
YOUR BIRTHDAY IS EARLIER THAN MINE, SO...
I'M 19.

Nasta: A nickname for Anastasia.

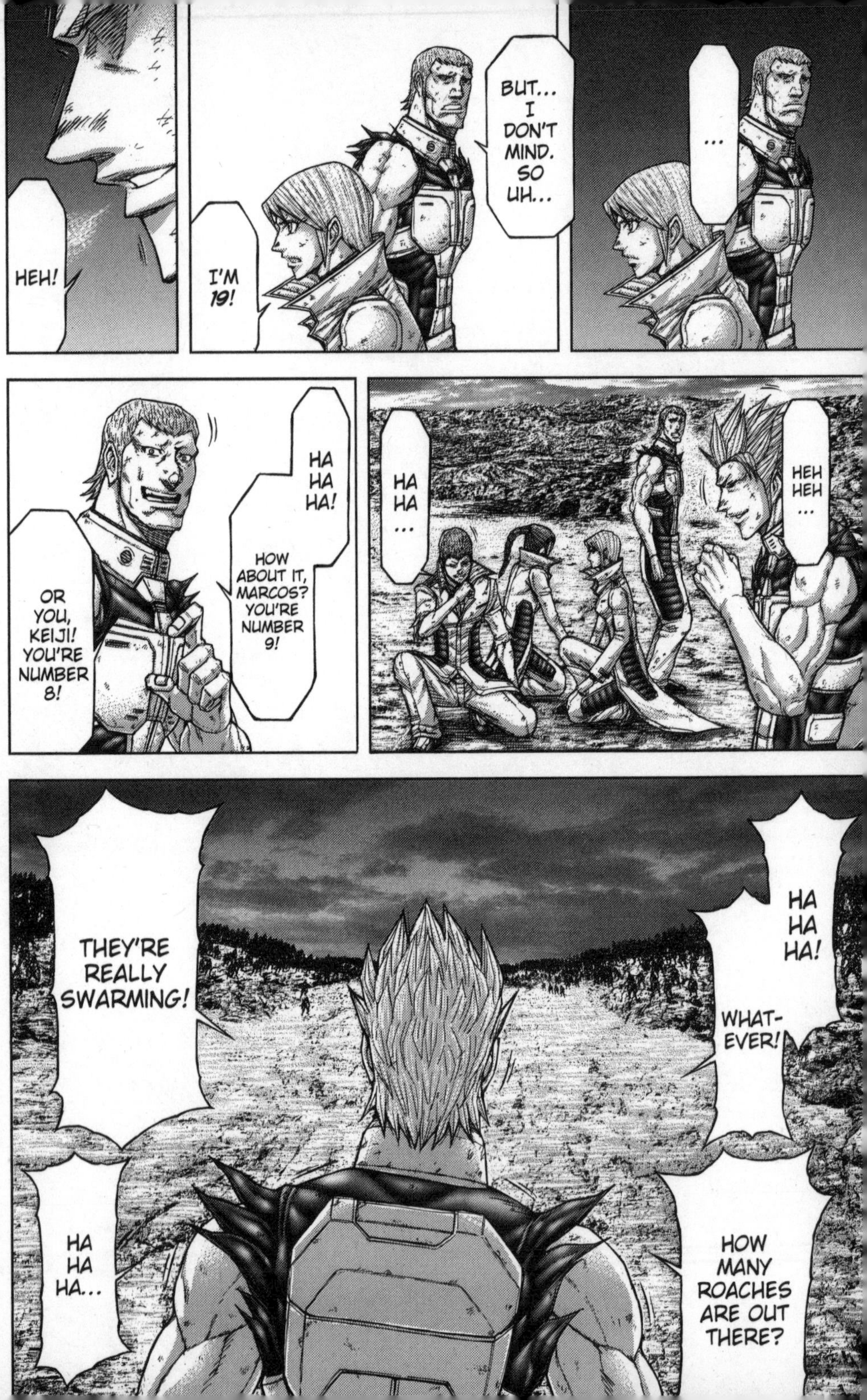
...
BUT... I DON'T MIND. SO UH...
I'M 19!
HEH!
HEH HEH ...
HA HA ...
HA HA HA!
HOW ABOUT IT, MARCOS? YOU'RE NUMBER 9!
OR YOU, KEIJI! YOU'RE NUMBER 8!
HA HA HA!
WHAT-EVER!
THEY'RE REALLY SWARMING!
HOW MANY ROACHES ARE OUT THERE?
HA HA HA...

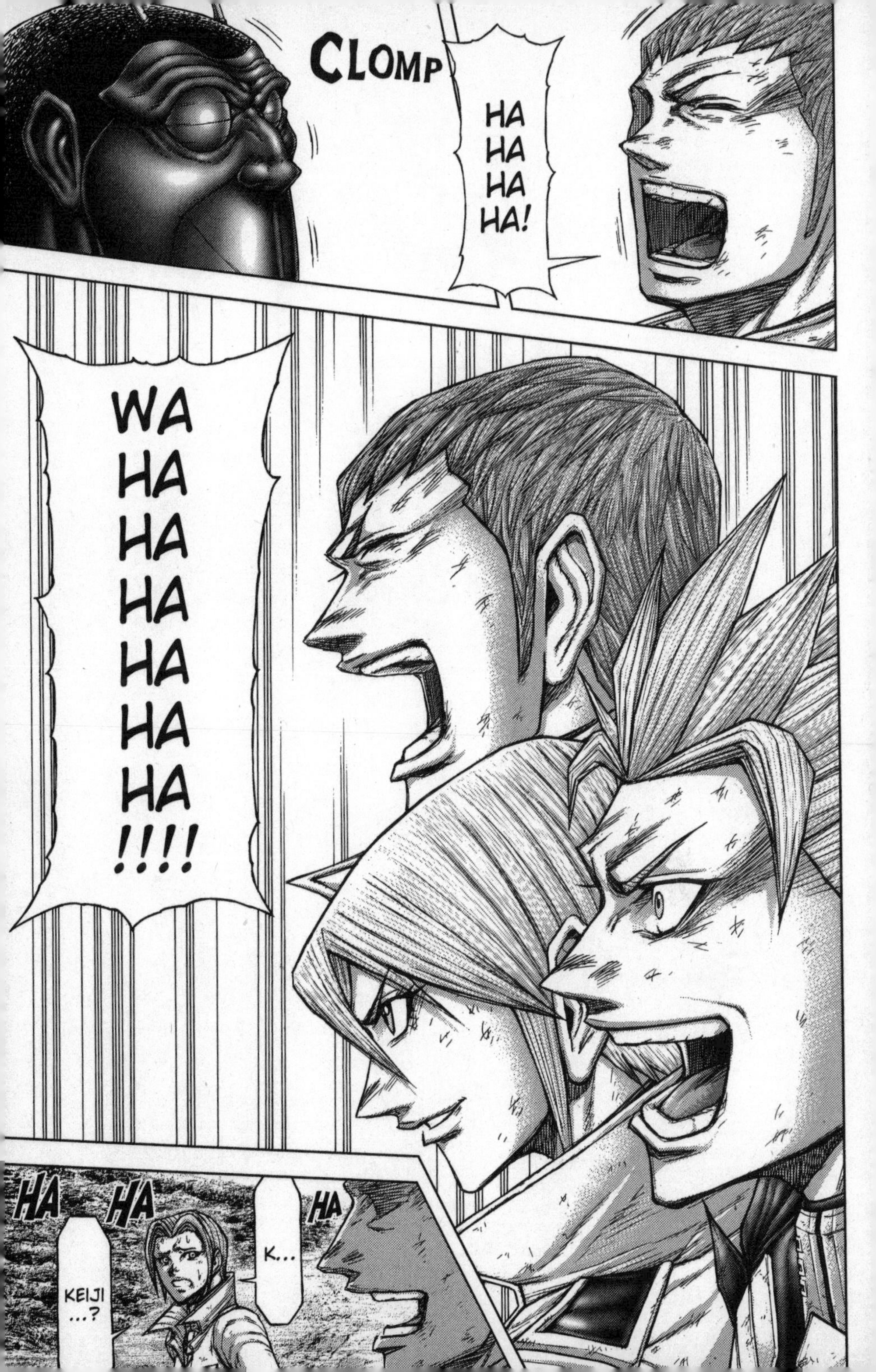
HA HA HA HA!
CLOMP
WA HA HA HA HA HA HA HA!!!!
HA
HA
HA
K...
KEIJI ...?

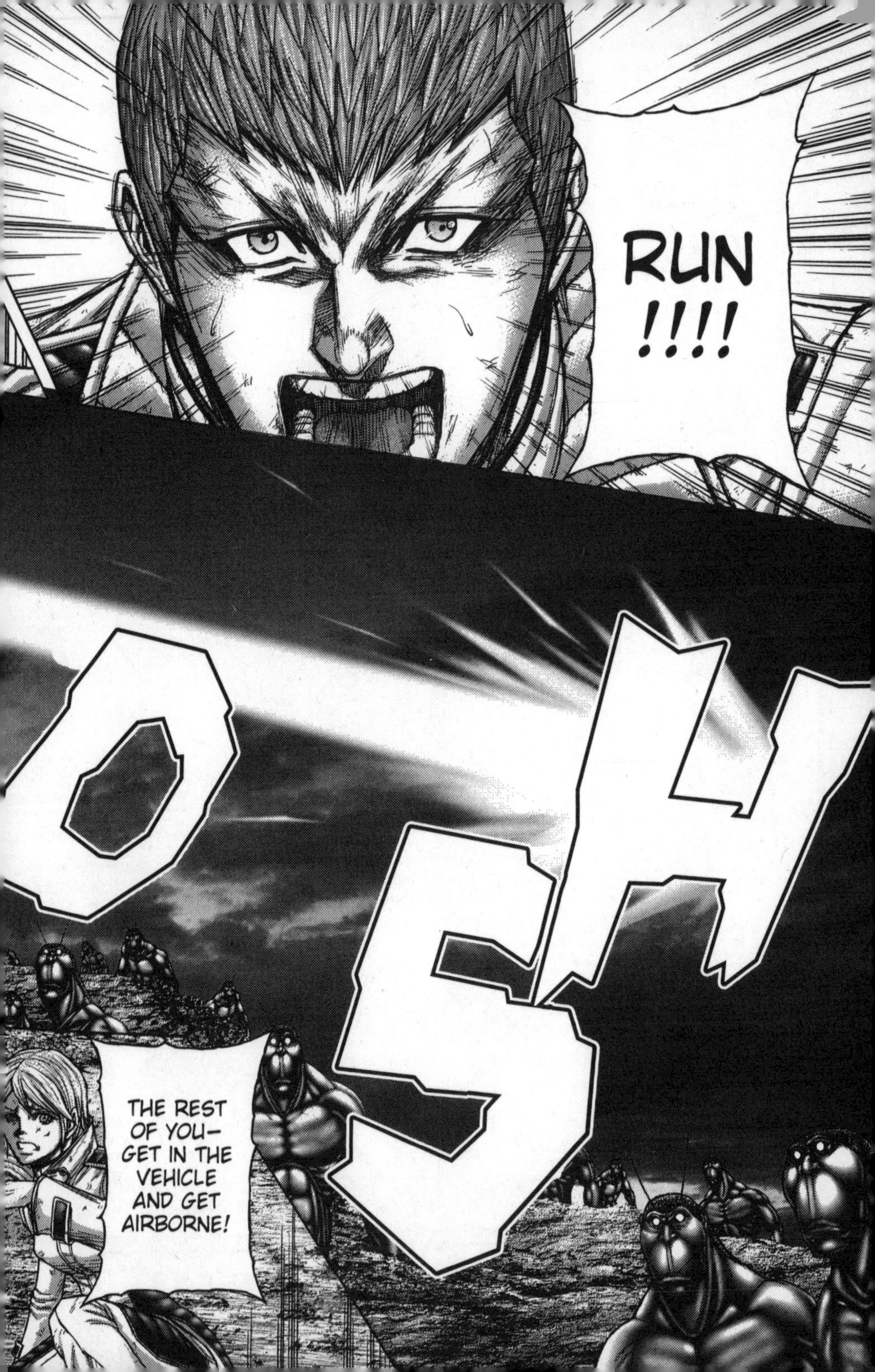
RUN !!!!
OSH
THE REST OF YOU— GET IN THE VEHICLE AND GET AIRBORNE!

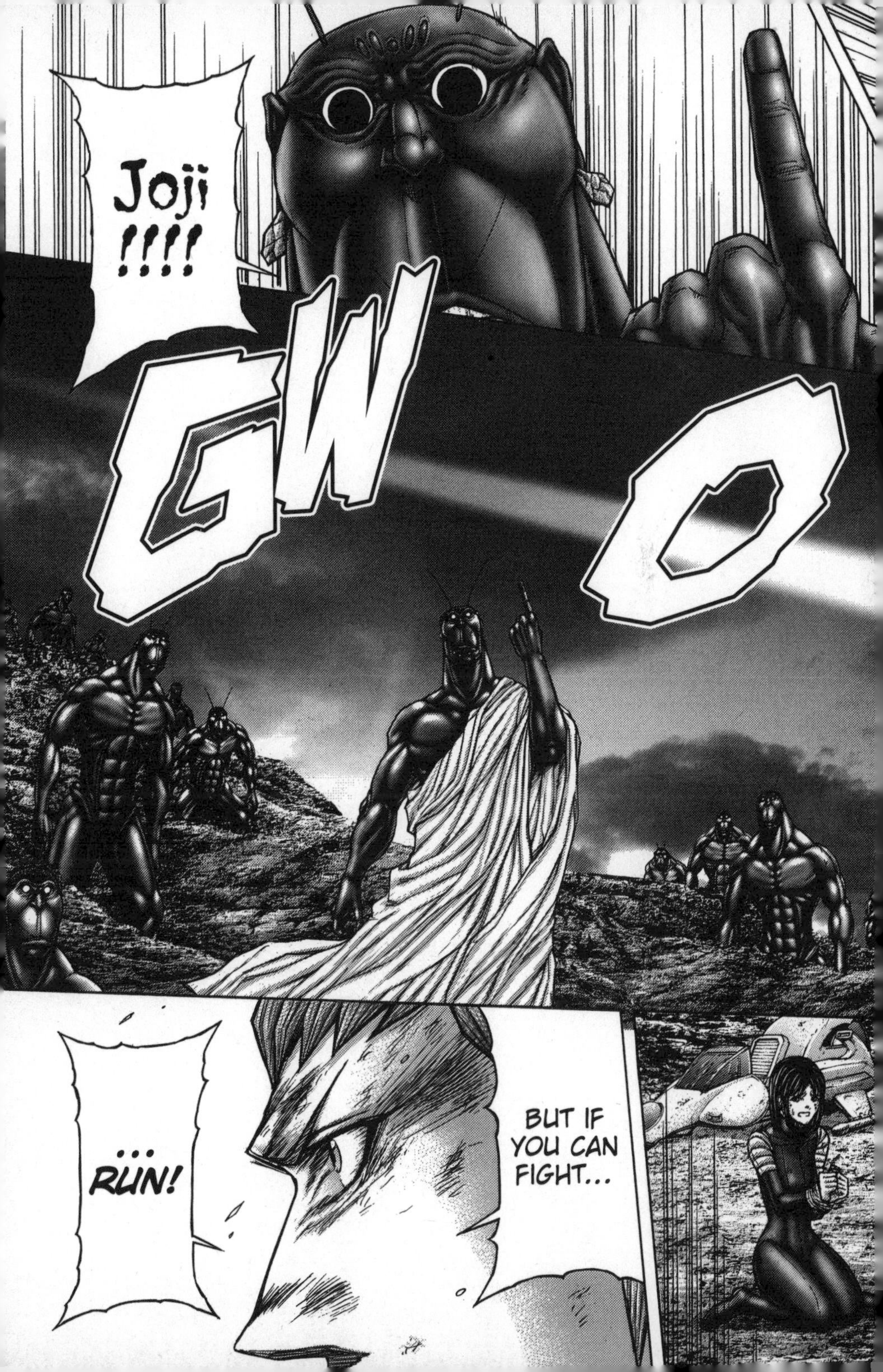
Joji !!!!
GWO
BUT IF YOU CAN FIGHT...
... RÜN!

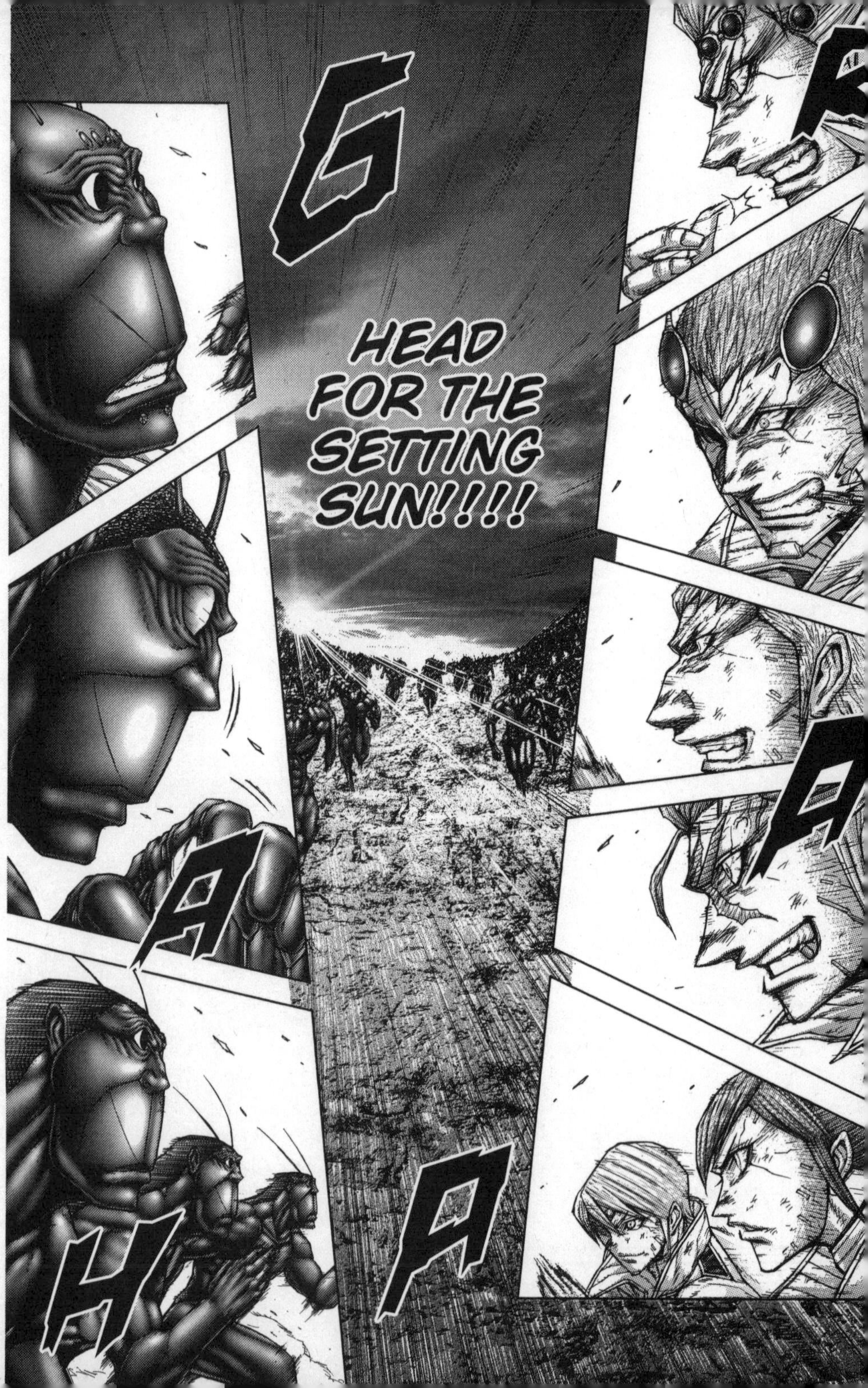
HEAD FOR THE SETTING SUN!!!!

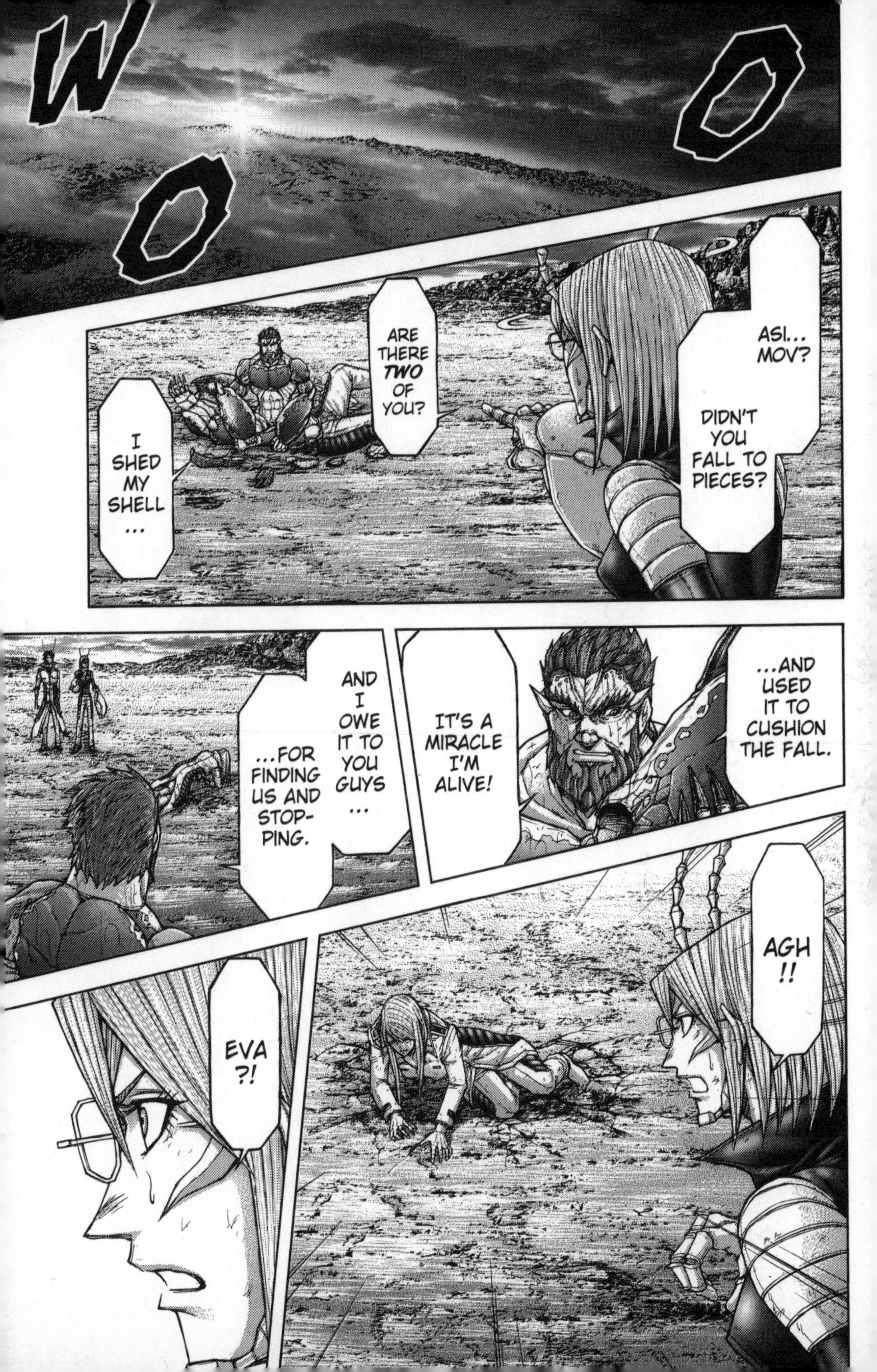
WOO
ASI... MOV?
DIDN'T YOU FALL TO PIECES?
ARE THERE *TWO* OF YOU?
I SHED MY SHELL...
...AND USED IT TO CUSHION THE FALL.
IT'S A MIRACLE I'M ALIVE!
AND I OWE IT TO YOU GUYS...
...FOR FINDING US AND STOP-PING.
AGH!!
EVA?!

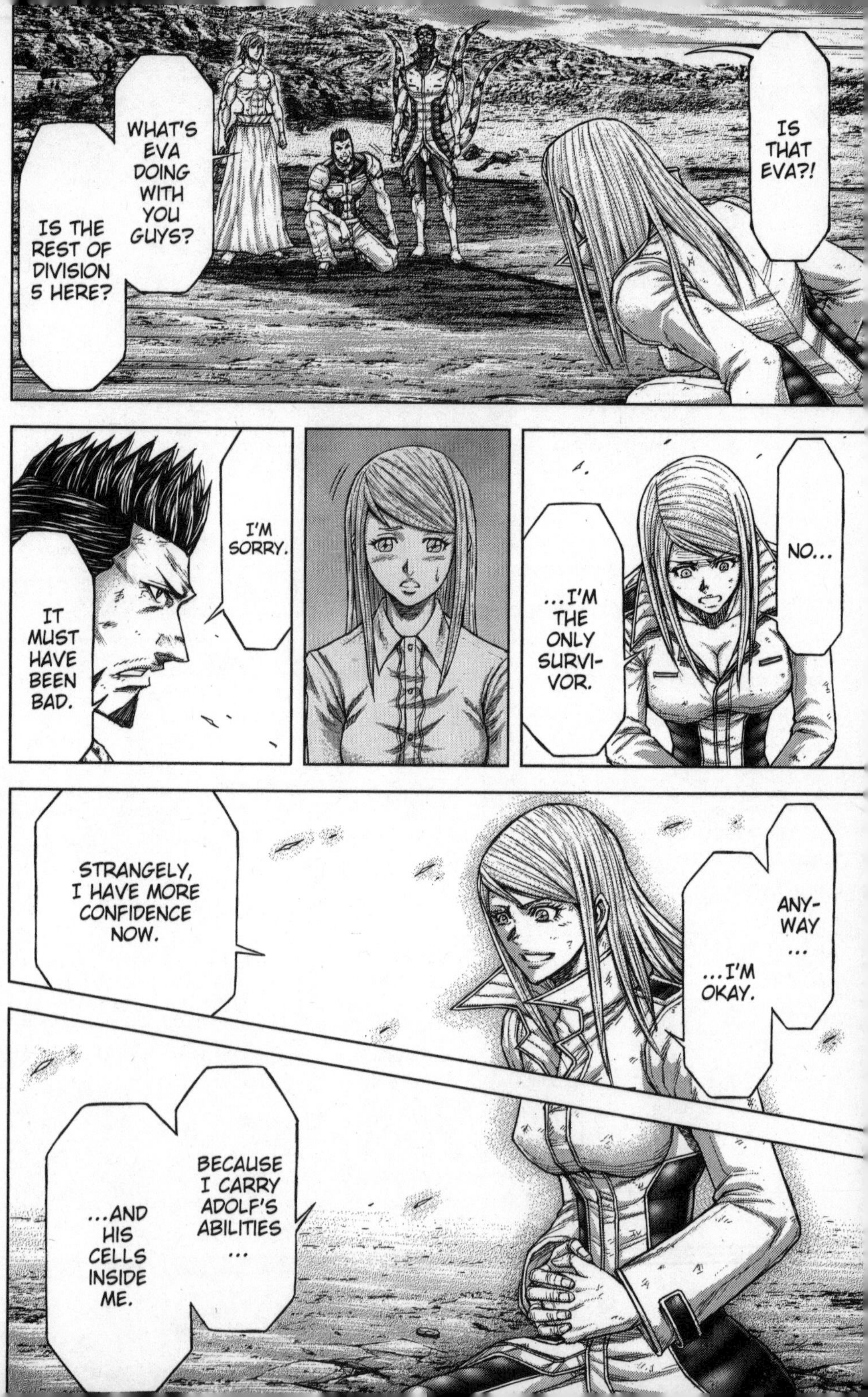
IS THAT EVA?!
WHAT'S EVA DOING WITH YOU GUYS?
IS THE REST OF DIVISION 5 HERE?
NO...
...I'M THE ONLY SURVIVOR.
I'M SORRY.
IT MUST HAVE BEEN BAD.
ANYWAY...
...I'M OKAY.
STRANGELY, I HAVE MORE CONFIDENCE NOW.
BECAUSE I CARRY ADOLF'S ABILITIES...
...AND HIS CELLS INSIDE ME.

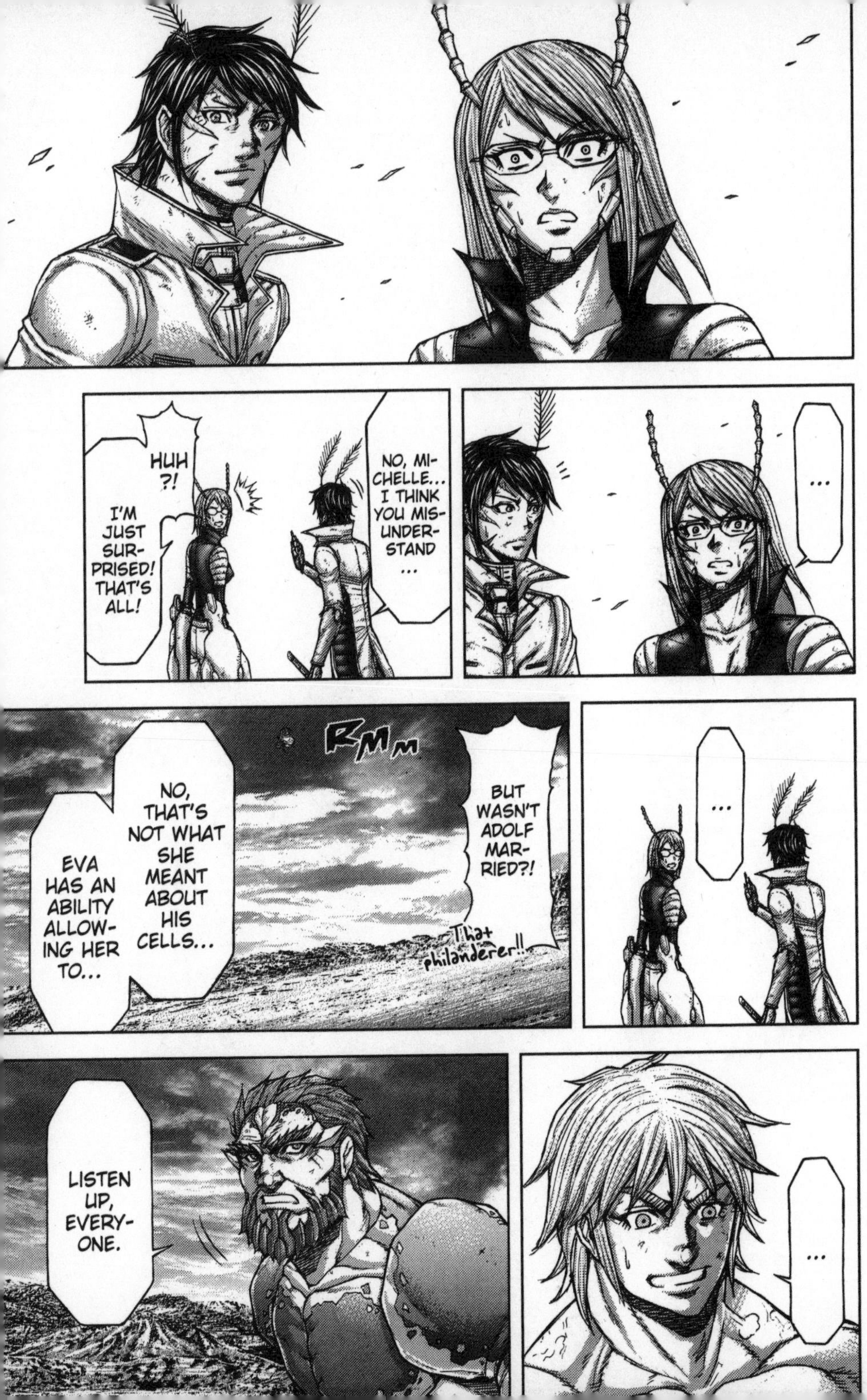
...
NO, MICHELLE... I THINK YOU MISUNDERSTAND...
HUH?!
I'M JUST SURPRISED! THAT'S ALL!
...
BUT WASN'T ADOLF MARRIED?!
RMM
That philanderer!!
NO, THAT'S NOT WHAT SHE MEANT ABOUT HIS CELLS...
EVA HAS AN ABILITY ALLOWING HER TO...
...
LISTEN UP, EVERYONE.

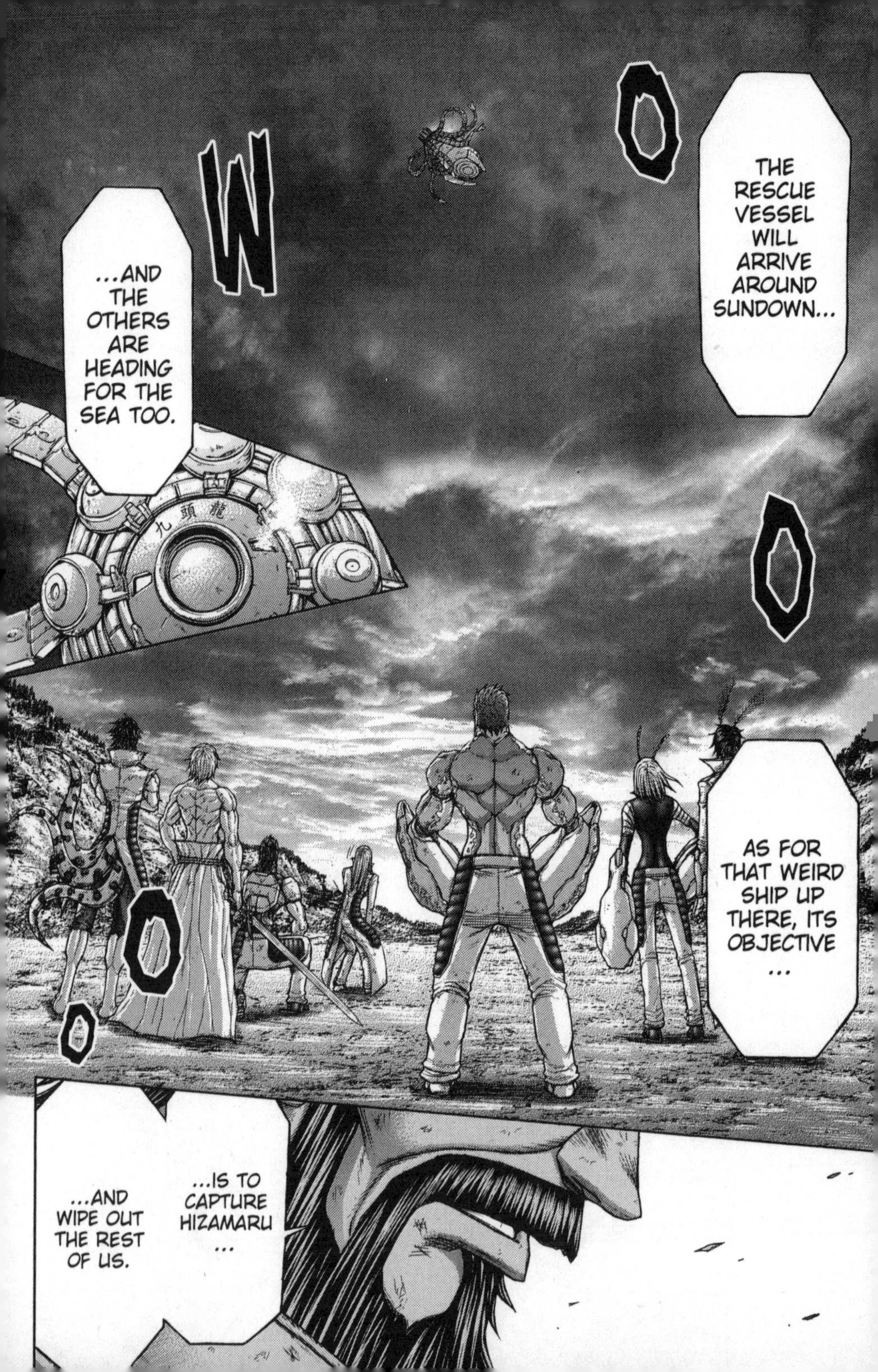
THE RESCUE VESSEL WILL ARRIVE AROUND SUNDOWN...
...AND THE OTHERS ARE HEADING FOR THE SEA TOO.
WOOOOO
AS FOR THAT WEIRD SHIP UP THERE, ITS OBJECTIVE ...
...IS TO CAPTURE HIZAMARU ...
...AND WIPE OUT THE REST OF US.

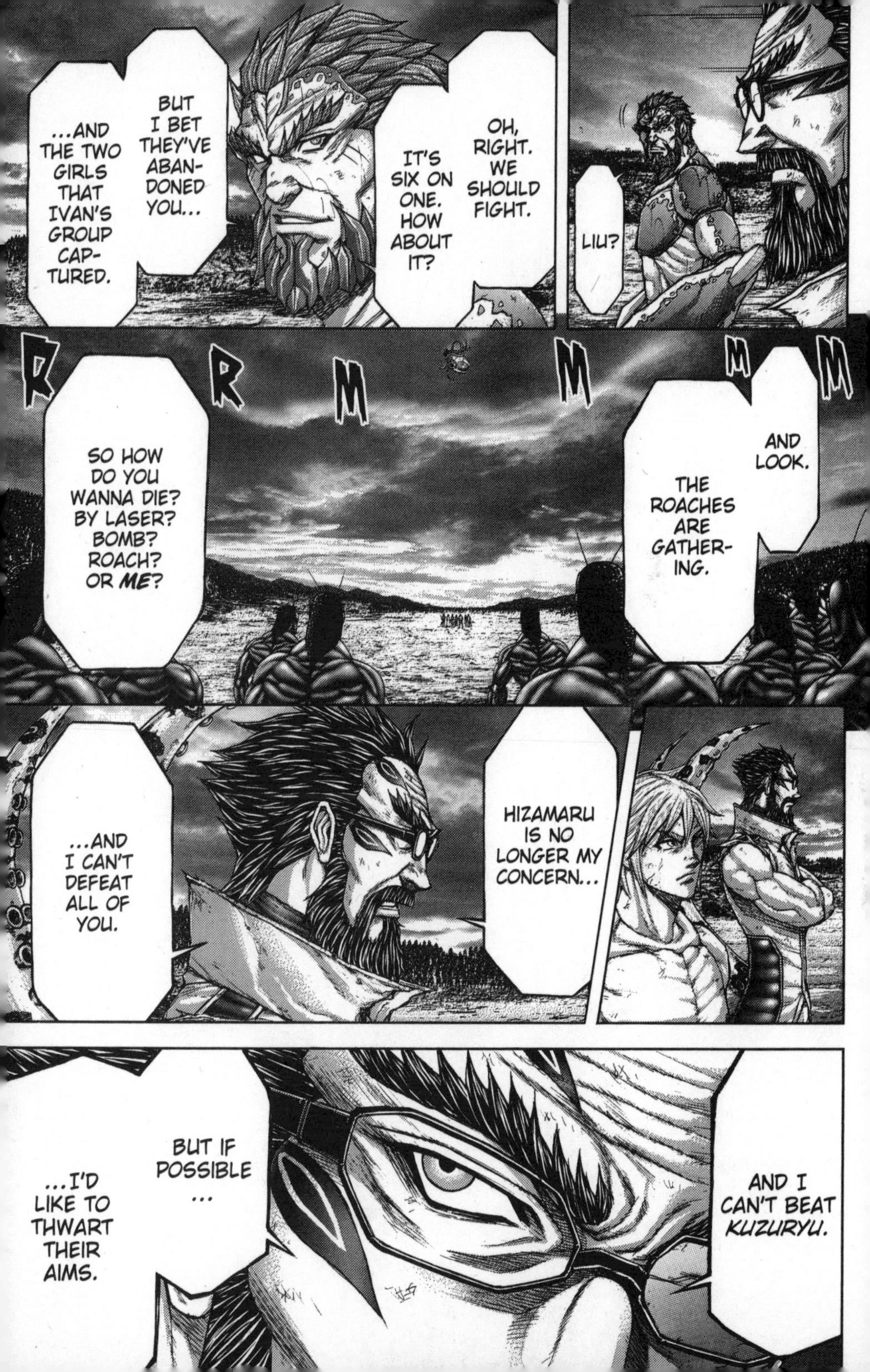
LIU?
OH, RIGHT. WE SHOULD FIGHT.
IT'S SIX ON ONE. HOW ABOUT IT?
BUT I BET THEY'VE ABANDONED YOU...
...AND THE TWO GIRLS THAT IVAN'S GROUP CAPTURED.
RRMMMM
AND LOOK.
THE ROACHES ARE GATHERING.
SO HOW DO YOU WANNA DIE? BY LASER? BOMB? ROACH? OR *ME*?
HIZAMARU IS NO LONGER MY CONCERN...
...AND I CAN'T DEFEAT ALL OF YOU.
AND I CAN'T BEAT *KUZURYU*.
BUT IF POSSIBLE...
...I'D LIKE TO THWART THEIR AIMS.

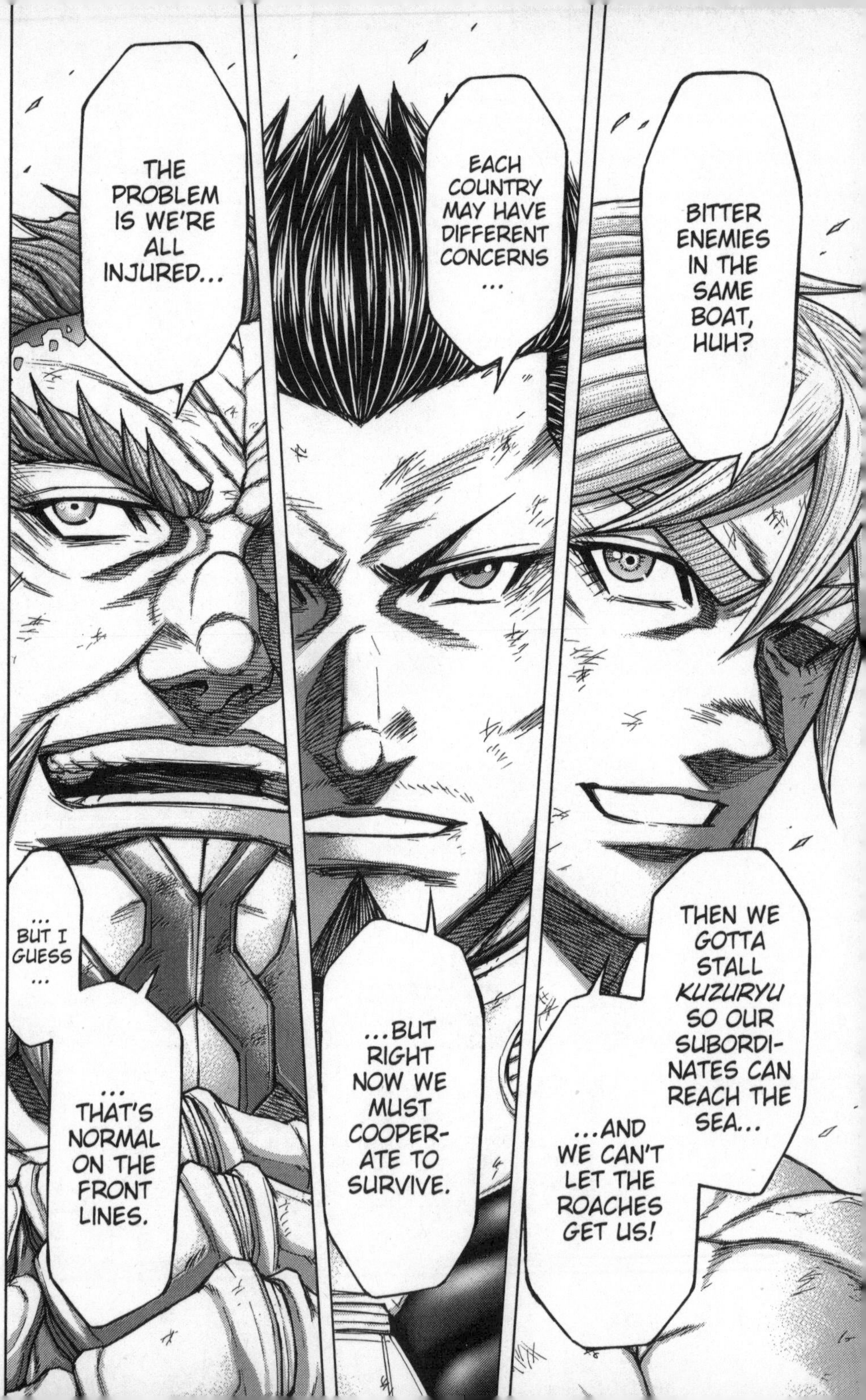
BITTER ENEMIES IN THE SAME BOAT, HUH?
THEN WE GOTTA STALL *KUZURYU* SO OUR SUBORDI-NATES CAN REACH THE SEA...
...AND WE CAN'T LET THE ROACHES GET US!
EACH COUNTRY MAY HAVE DIFFERENT CONCERNS...
...BUT RIGHT NOW WE MUST COOPER-ATE TO SURVIVE.
THE PROBLEM IS WE'RE ALL INJURED...
...BUT I GUESS...
...THAT'S NORMAL ON THE FRONT LINES.

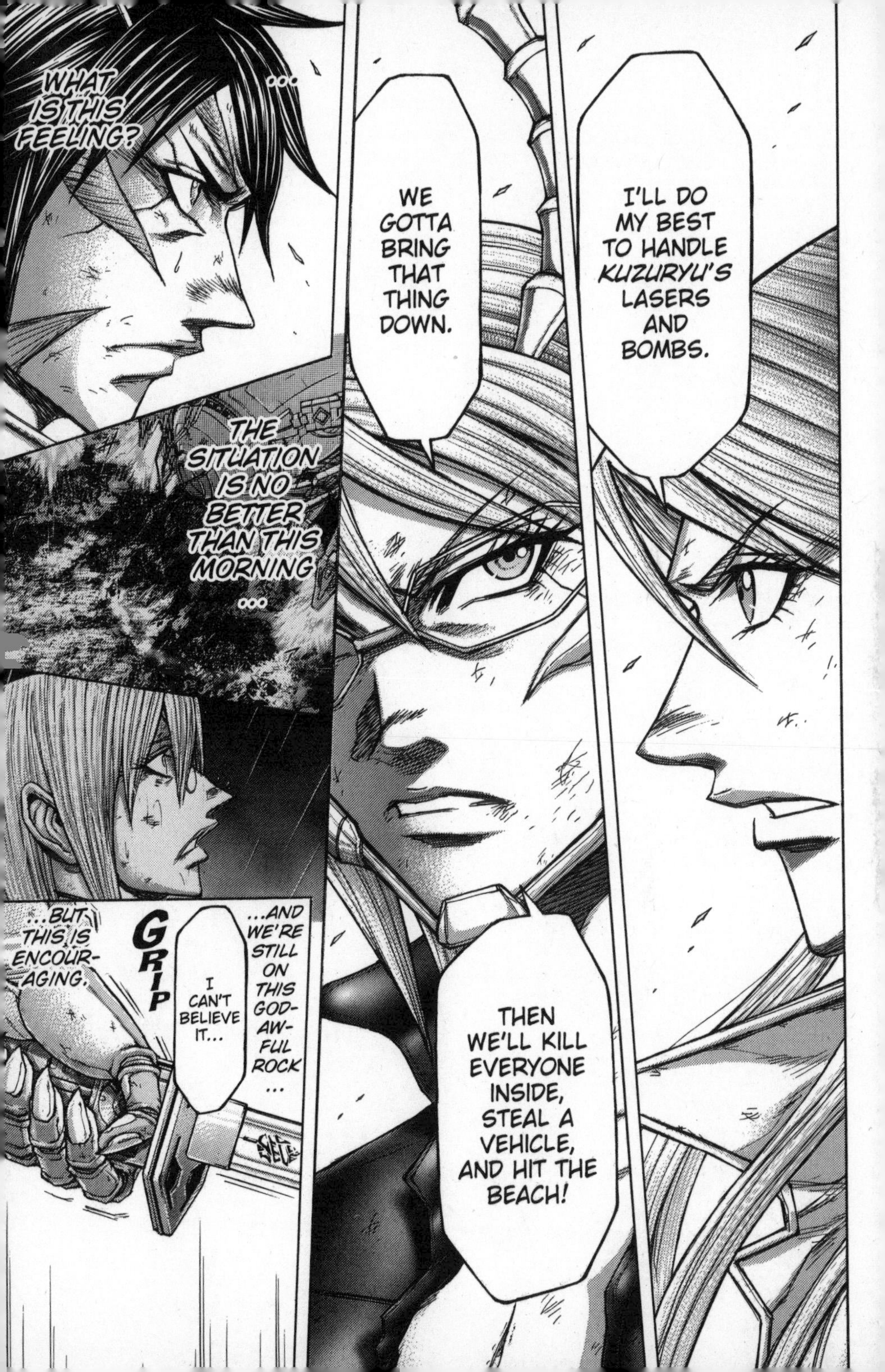
I'LL DO MY BEST TO HANDLE *KUZURYU'S* LASERS AND BOMBS.
WE GOTTA BRING THAT THING DOWN.
THEN WE'LL KILL EVERYONE INSIDE, STEAL A VEHICLE, AND HIT THE BEACH!
...
WHAT IS THIS FEELING?
THE SITUATION IS NO BETTER THAN THIS MORNING...
...AND WE'RE STILL ON THIS GOD-AWFUL ROCK...
I CAN'T BELIEVE IT...
GRIP
...BUT THIS IS ENCOUR-AGING.

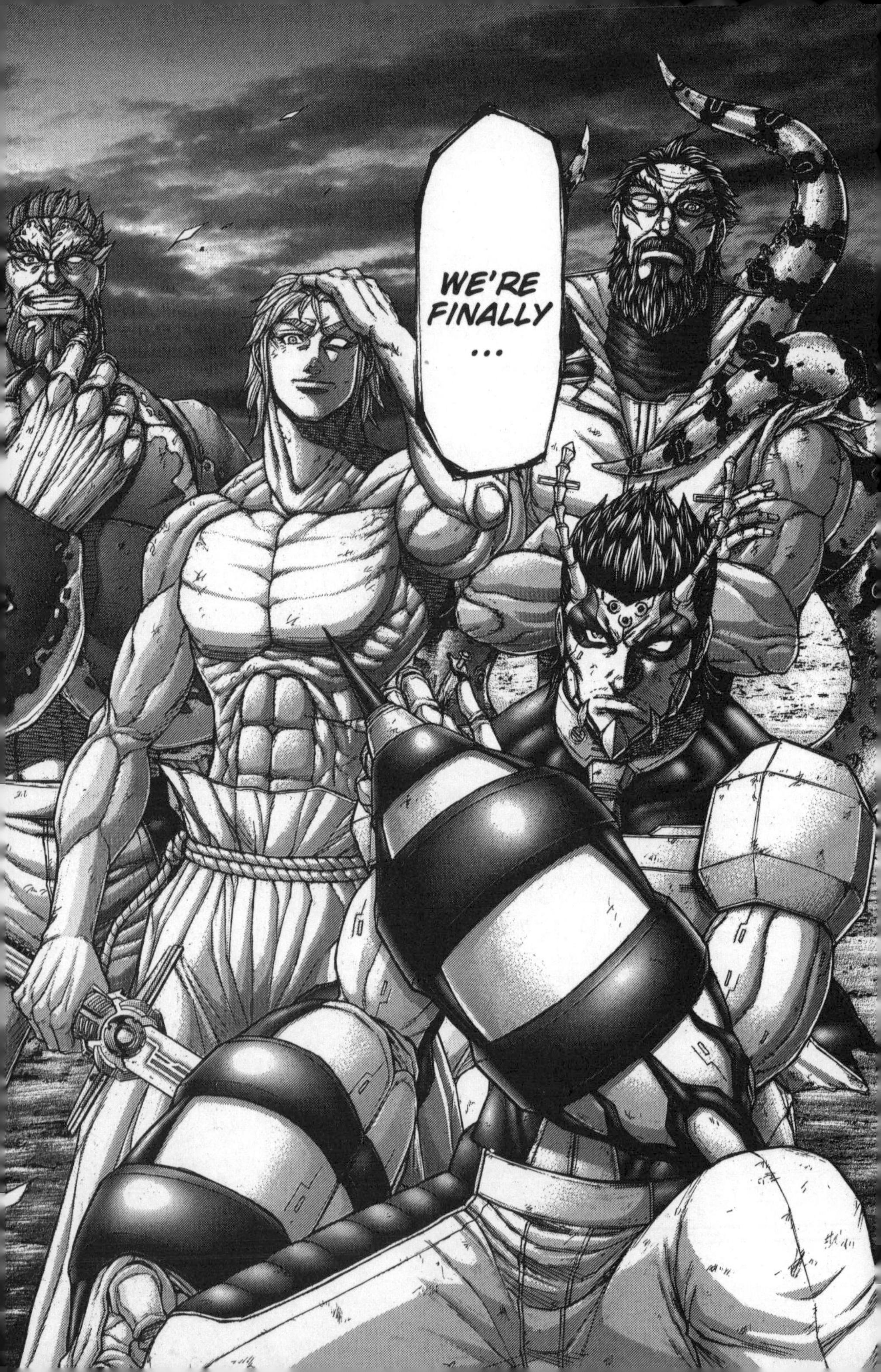
WE'RE FINALLY ...

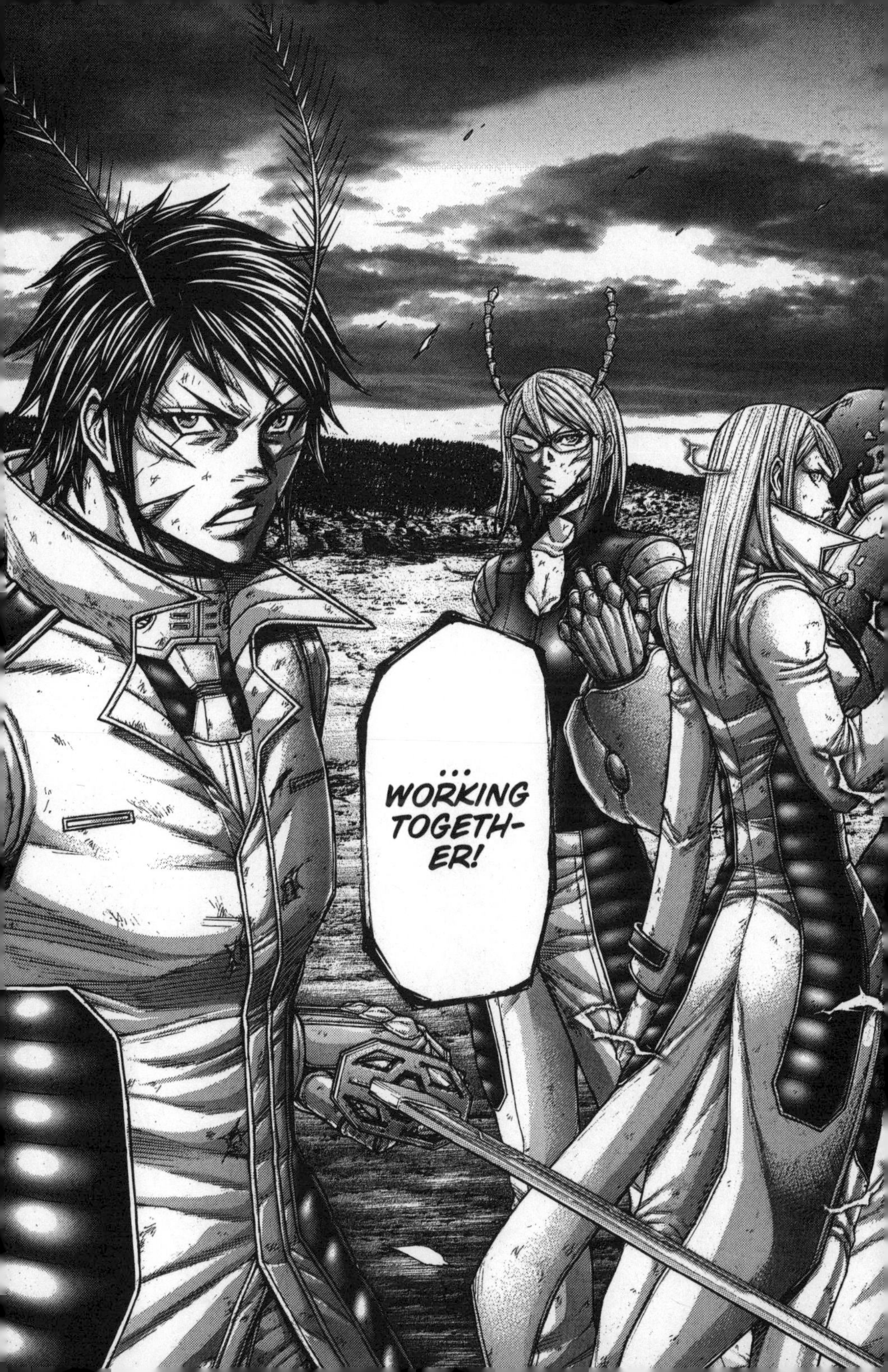
...WORKING TOGETH-ER!

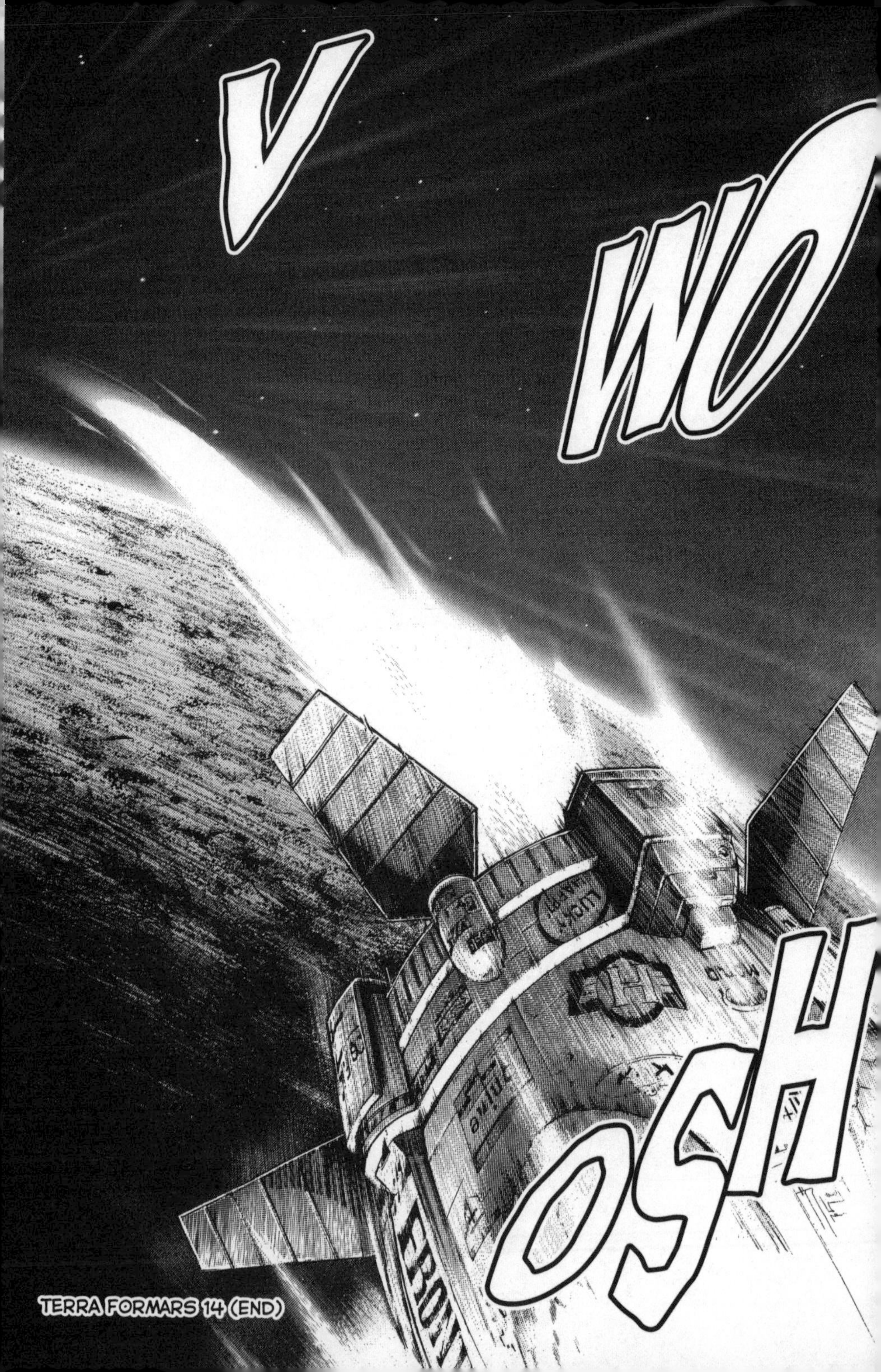
V
WO
OSH
TERRA FORMARS 14 (END)

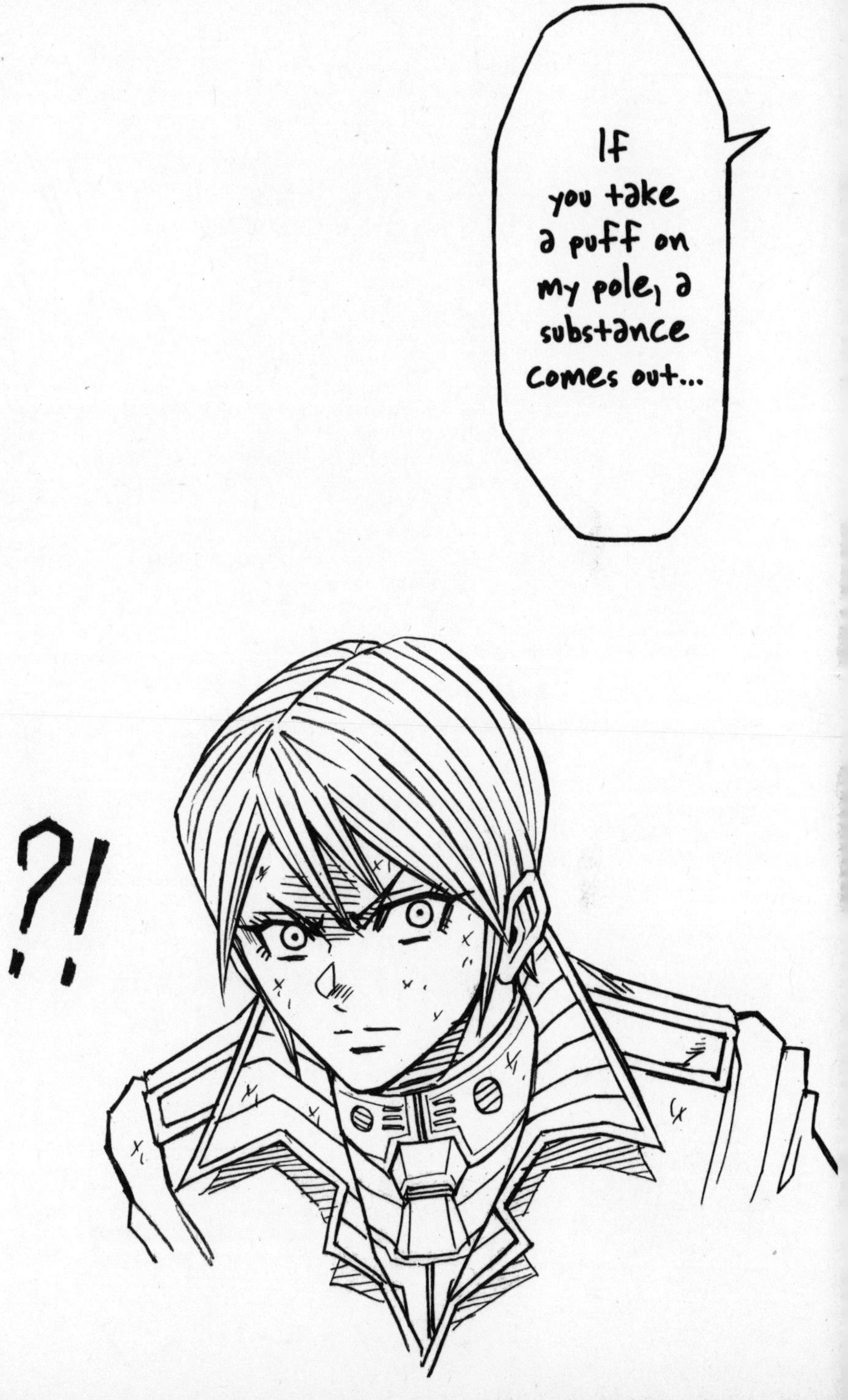
If you take a puff on my pole, a substance comes out...
?!

TERRA FORMARS

Volume 14
VIZ Signature Edition

Story by YU SASUGA
Art by KENICHI TACHIBANA

Translation & English Adaptation/John Werry
Touch-up Art & Lettering/Annaliese Christman
Design/Izumi Evers
Editor/Mike Montesa

Published by VIZ Media, LLC
P.O. Box 77010
San Francisco, CA 94107

10 9 8 7 6 5 4 3 2 1
First printing, September 2016

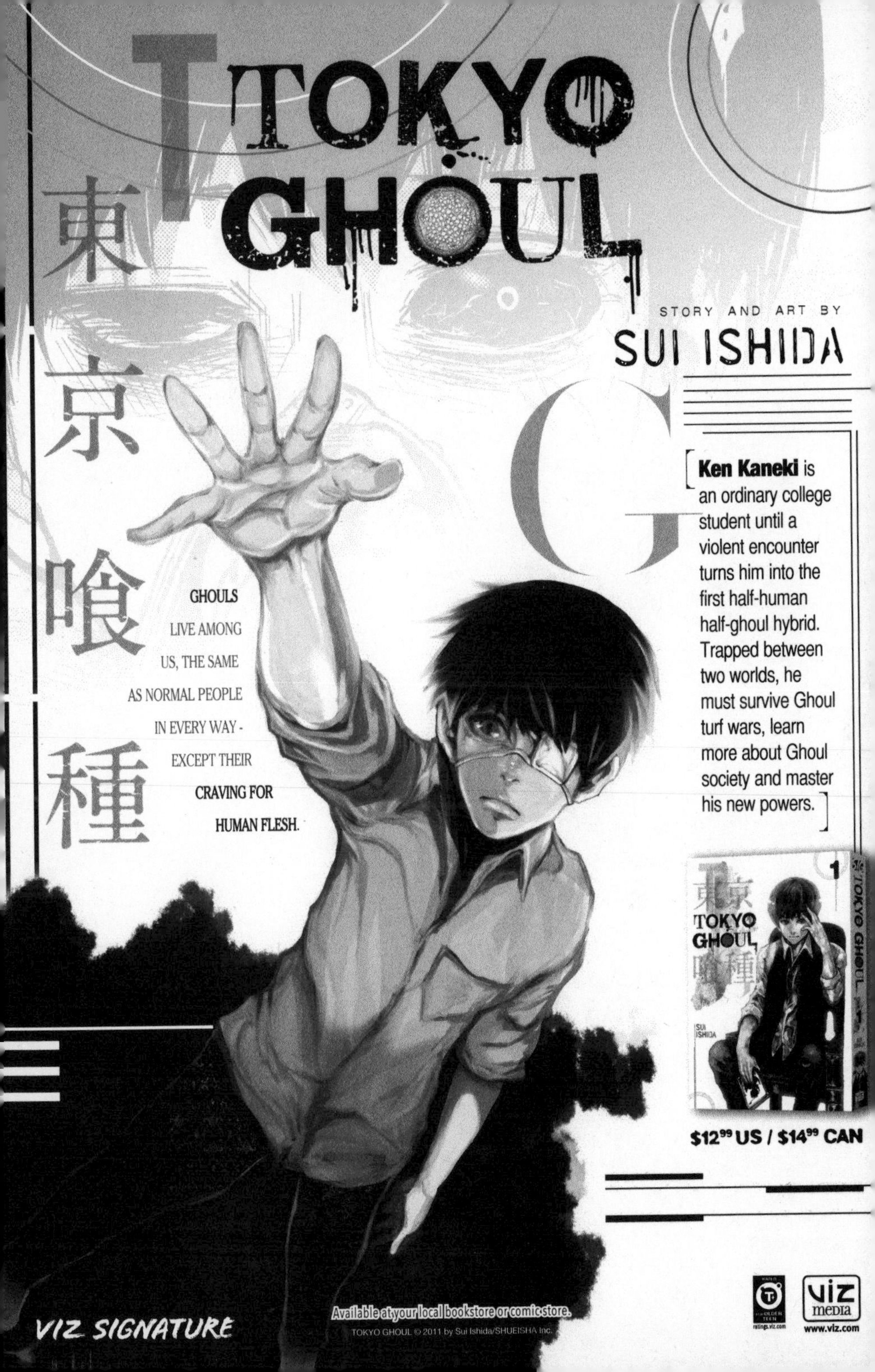
TOKYO GHOUL
東京喰種
STORY AND ART BY
SUI ISHIDA
GHOULS LIVE AMONG US, THE SAME AS NORMAL PEOPLE IN EVERY WAY - EXCEPT THEIR CRAVING FOR HUMAN FLESH.
Ken Kaneki is an ordinary college student until a violent encounter turns him into the first half-human half-ghoul hybrid. Trapped between two worlds, he must survive Ghoul turf wars, learn more about Ghoul society and master his new powers.
$12.99 US / $14.99 CAN
Available at your local bookstore or comic store.
TOKYO GHOUL © 2011 by Sui Ishida/SHUEISHA Inc.
VIZ SIGNATURE
ratings.viz.com
VIZ media
www.viz.com

Hey! You're Reading in the Wrong Direction!

This is the **end** of this graphic novel!

To properly enjoy this VIZ graphic novel, please turn it around and begin reading from **right to left.** Unlike English, Japanese is read right to left, so Japanese comics are read in reverse order from the way English comics are typically read.

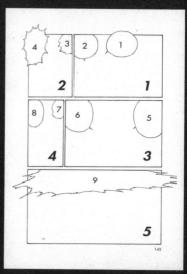

Follow the action this way

This book has been printed in the original Japanese format in order to preserve the orientation of the original artwork. Have fun with it!